Political Brands

To my father John Torres, Jr.,
who taught me early on about the artifice of American politics,
but who loved America despite its flaws

Political Brands

Ciara Torres-Spelliscy

Professor of Law, Stetson University, College of Law, Florida, USA

EE Edward **Elgar**
PUBLISHING

Cheltenham, UK • Northampton, MA, USA

Published by
Edward Elgar Publishing Limited
The Lypiatts
15 Lansdown Road
Cheltenham
Glos GL50 2JA
UK

Edward Elgar Publishing, Inc.
William Pratt House
9 Dewey Court
Northampton
Massachusetts 01060
USA

A catalogue record for this book
is available from the British Library

This book is available electronically in the **Elgar**online
Law subject collection
DOI 10.4337/9781789901825

Printed on elemental chlorine free (ECF)
recycled paper containing 30% Post-Consumer Waste

ISBN 978 1 78990 181 8 (cased)
ISBN 978 1 78990 182 5 (eBook)

Printed and bound in the USA

Contents

Acknowledgments

I would like to thank Stetson University College of Law for the Leroy Highbaugh Sr. Chair, which allowed me the time and resources to write this book; and the Brennan Center for Justice at NYU School of Law for my fellowship and for giving many of the concepts I explore in this book a first home on its influential blog.

I also thank Stetson Law librarians Kristen Moore and Sally Waters and Stetson Law research assistants who have helped me conduct research for years, including Cherilyn Blitch, Joy E. Branham, Courtney Chaipel, Kevin Crews, Michael Davids, Alex Farris, Andrew Graf, Guillermo F. De Guzman Serrano, Max Holzbaur, Christina Jimenez, Ashley Justice, Felicia Kitzmiller, Liz Harbaugh, Adam LaBonte, Christian Moriarty, Clinton Simmons, Meagan Salisbury, Carolina Suazo and Jessica Vander Velde.

Thanks to Joshua A. Douglas, Kitt Hirasaki, Catherine Cooper Lipp and Glynn Torres-Spelliscy, for their editorial feedback. I also wish to thank the following people who took time be interviewed: Kristina Alexander, Jared Bernstein, Atiba Ellis, Lisa Gilbert, Jason Gottlieb, Samuel Issacharoff, Pamela Karlan, Alyssa Katz, Liz Kennedy, Maria Teresa Kumar, Celinda Lake, Ian Millhiser, Burt Neuborne, Jonathan Salant, Ryan Spelliscy, Jennifer Taub, Franita Tolson, Mark Tushnet and Michael Waldman.

I want to thank everyone who talked to me for this book off the record as well. Finally, thank you to my husband, my son and my labradoodle, who all put up with the late nights and travel with good cheer.

Branding itself: an introduction

"Brand is everything, and everything is brand."[1]

What do survivors of a mass shooting in Florida, Russian intelligence officers, Coca-Cola and the president of the United States all have in common? They all try to influence public opinion using branding, even if what is getting branded is the truth, a lie, a myth or a conspiracy.

1.   COMMERCIAL BRANDS

But before we can explore all of that, we need some shared definitions. "Branding" is the process of purposefully repeating a word, concept or logo until it gets stuck in the minds of the public.[2] Commercial branding comes from business entities like partnerships, limited liability companies (LLCs) and corporations. Commercial branding is ubiquitous. Nearly from the moment the average American opens her eyes in the morning to the moment she goes to sleep, branding is everywhere, from the products in her bathroom to the food in her kitchen, the vehicles in her garage, the billboards on her commute, the sign outside her workplace, the product placements on TV and the banner ads online. Brands are so omnipresent in our lives that they sometimes slip into genericide. Linguists Julie Sedivy and Greg Carlson, in their book *Sold on Language*, provide multiple examples of how brands have become shorthand for objects in our daily lives:

> If you stroll across your *linoleum* floor over to your *formica* countertop, check on the stew in the *crock-pot*, pick up the spilled *kitty litter* in the corner with a *kleenex*, pour a bowl of *granola*, and open your freezer to take out a *popsicle* before proposing a game of after-dinner *ping pong*, you are contributing to the genericide of these brand names.[3]

---

[1]   Dan Pallotta, *A Logo Is Not a Brand*, HARV. BUSINESS REV. (June 15, 2011).

[2]   Len Stein, *The Key to Brand Design is "Deliberate Differentiation,"* BRANDINGMAG (Dec. 18, 2017), www.brandingmag.com/2017/12/18/the-key-to-brand-design-is-deliberate-differentiation/ (quoting Debbie Millman) ("'Branding is deliberate differentiation.'").

[3]   JULIE SEDIVY & GREG CARLSON, SOLD ON LANGUAGE: HOW ADVERTISERS TALK TO YOU AND WHAT THIS SAYS ABOUT YOU 47 (2011).

Even as brands seep into our language, they are vulnerable to picking up negative associations and generating revulsion. As Professor Tamara Piety notes in
her book *Brandishing the First Amendment*:

> It is possible to create a brand out of whole cloth. However, because brand value
> is so dependent on imagery built by communication efforts, it is, to some extent,
> always susceptible to sudden shifts in public perceptions. Such shifts may include
> total collapse of all brand value.[4]

Or as David D'Alessandro, president of John Hancock Mutual Life Insurance,
once quipped: "It can take 100 years to build up a good brand and 30 days to
knock it down."[5] In the Twitter age, death of a brand can happen even quicker.

Evidence of the importance of branding to corporations can be seen in
the public relations and advertising budgets of firms.[6] Most of the corporate
money allotted for branding is spent on advertising. As a report in *Fortune*
indicated in 2012, "US companies spend $150 billion annually on advertising
and only $5 billion on public relations."[7] By 2018, advertising in the U.S. hit
the $166 billion mark ($107 billion of it on digital ads).[8] Worldwide spending
on advertising in 2018 was $414 billion ($227 billion of it online).[9]

And some brands exist on a societal level. Think about the ubiquitous "Santa
Claus" brand. When I had my son, my husband and I resolved not to lie to him
about the existence of Santa Claus. I thought this would be easy. How little did
I appreciate the media environment that he would inhabit from age zero to five.
First, there were other caregivers in his life—from grandparents to nursery
school teachers—who told him Santa was real. Then there were ubiquitous
ads on TV, radio and billboards in which Old Saint Nick sold everything from
Coke to M&Ms to Norelco shavers. There was the "mall Santa," with long

---

[4]   TAMARA R. PIETY, BRANDISHING THE FIRST AMENDMENT: COMMERCIAL
EXPRESSION IN AMERICA 33 (2013).

[5]   NAOMI KLEIN, NO LOGO: TAKING AIM AT THE BRAND BULLIES 345 (1999).

[6]   *See* STRATEGIC COMMC'N & PUB. RELATIONS CTR., UNIV. S. CAL. ANNENBERG
SCH. OF COMMC'N & JOURNALISM, GAP VII: SEVENTH COMMUNICATION AND PUBLIC
RELATIONS GENERALLY ACCEPTED PRACTICES STUDY (Q4 2011 DATA) 15 (2012), http://
ascjweb.org/gapstudy/wp-content/uploads/2014/06/GAP-VIII-Presentation-Final-6.12
.2014.pdf.

[7]   Gregory Galant, *Why Public Relations Gets No Respect*, Fortune (Nov. 15,
2012).

[8]   Dana Feldman, *U.S. TV Ad Spend Drops As Digital Ad Spend Climbs To $107B
In 2018*, FORBES (Mar. 28, 2018).

[9]   Rani Molla, *Advertisers will spend $40 billion more on internet ads than on TV
ads this year Thank social, video and mobile.*, RECODE (Mar. 26, 2018), www.recode
.net/2018/3/26/17163852/online-internet-advertisers-outspend-tv-ads-advertisers
-social-video-mobile-40-billion-2018.

lines of children waiting to sit on his lap and tell him their desires. There were men on Christmas pub crawls through Brooklyn dressed in red suits and fake white beards. But the real nail in the coffin for our battle with this branded lie was PBS. My young son saw Santa show up in most of his children's shows, from *Bob the Builder* to *Thomas the Tank Engine*. And for him, that made Santa *real*—at least when he was very young. I could not have been prouder when, as a five-year-old, he said to me and my husband, "Wait, this Santa thing doesn't add up." And we said, "You're right. It doesn't." The spell was broken.

The word "brand" comes from the Old English word "*brond*," meaning "fire,"[10] which in turn came from the Norse word "*brandr*," which meant "burn."[11] Branding's historical roots derive from farmers using a red-hot iron to sear an image, like the initials of the owner or a family crest, into the flesh of livestock. This type of "branding" was a way of telling Farmer Joe's cows from Farmer Steve's cows. The practice of branding cattle goes back thousands of years. According to the Smithsonian, branding dates back to at least 2700 BC, where there is evidence of livestock branding depicted in ancient Egyptian hieroglyphics.[12] By the 1500s, "brand" in English referred "to a mark burned on cattle to show ownership."[13] In the American context, branding cows was important at the slaughterhouse, where payment to the source farms could depend on how many animals bearing a particular "brand" were slaughtered.[14]

Trademarks on hand-crafted goods have a parallel history to agricultural branding. In Europe, during the Middle Ages, craft guilds would stamp craft-works with marks of both the artisan and the guild.[15] The guild mark alerted customers that the creation was up to the guild's high standards.[16] Modern trademarks can serve a similar purpose: think of an ABA™ (American Bar

---

[10] Online Etymology Dictionary, *Branding*, www.etymonline.com/index.php?term=brand ("brand (n.) Old English brand, brond 'fire, flame ...'").

[11] Matt Shadel, *A Brief History of Branding*, Convoy (Jan. 8, 2014), www.weareconvoy.com/2014/01/a-brief-history-of-branding/ ("The modern word Brand is derived from the word 'Brandr', a word from Ancient Norse meaning 'to burn ...'").

[12] Jimmy Stamp, *Decoding the Range: The Secret Language of Cattle Branding*, Smithsonian (Apr. 30, 2013).

[13] Shadel, *supra* note 11.

[14] Jerry McLaughlin, *What is a brand, anyway?*, Forbes (Dec. 21, 2011) ("As the cattle moved across the plains on their way to Chicago slaughter houses, it was easy to determine which ranches they were from because each head of cattle was branded.").

[15] Thomas D. Drescher, *The Transformation and Evolution or Trademarks—from Signals to Symbols to Myth*, 82 Trademark Rep. 301, 314 (1992) ("In the 1300s, master craftsmen in a guild had to choose a mark specific to their work which would be affixed to their products.").

[16] *Id.* at 316 (crafts usually bore a second mark as well, which represented the collective mark of the guild. This mark certified the craft met the regulations and criteria of that guild.).

Association) approved law school. ABA™ accreditation tells the public that that particular school has met the guild's high standards.

The meaning of "branding" has certainly evolved beyond marking livestock with hot irons. According to Mustafa Kurtuldu, "[t]he transition from 'This belongs to me, so leave it ...' to 'This was made by me, so buy it' started to evolve in the 1800's."[17] Commercial branding as Americans know the practice today took off as corporations tried to market what had been previously undistinguishable dry goods, like fungible piles of oats or beans.[18] The "brand" told the customer which corporation was the source of a particular box of oats or can of beans. While it may not have mattered to the average farmwife shopping at a dry goods store on the prairie in the 1800s whether she bought Quaker Oats or Heinz Beans, it mattered a great deal to the Quaker and Heinz corporations, which spent handsomely to advertise the high quality of their oats, beans or whatever else they were selling, so that shoppers around the nation would buy these brands over similar quality, but unadvertised or generic alternatives.[19]

The need for branding is most acute when the market is flooded with nearly indistinguishable and fungible goods. As *Forbes* once explained of Coke:

> In the late 1880s, for example, as the Coca-Cola Company was getting started, there were many soda producers in every market. Before Coca-Cola could get a customer to reach for a Coke, it needed to be sure the customer could distinguish a Coke from all the other fizzy caramel-colored beverages out there ... A Coke is a fizzy caramel-colored soda concocted by those folks in Atlanta.[20]

Coca-Cola was started as patent medicine that was advertised as "an ideal nerve tonic," which contained wine and cocaine. After a local temperance law passed, later formulations of Coke changed to sugar and cocaine. Then finally Coca-Cola went with its modern formula of just sugar and caffeine.[21] In the 1800s, patent medicines were heavily advertised, including strange tinctures which claimed to be miracle cures for exhaustion and headaches. Often the main active ingredient was cocaine, just like the original Coca-Cola.[22] But the corporations making the patent medicines wanted consumers to buy their cocaine, not the other guy's cocaine.

---

[17] Mustafa Kurtuldu, *Brand New: The History of Branding*, DESIGN TODAY (Nov. 29, 2012), www.designtoday.info/brand-new-the-history-of-branding/.

[18] Drescher, *supra* note 15 at 321 (up until the post-Civil War period, many commodities were fungible.).

[19] *Id.* at 323 (Quaker Oats was not started by a Quaker.).

[20] McLaughlin, *supra* note 14.

[21] James Hamblin, *Why We Took Cocaine Out of Soda*, ATLANTIC (Jan. 31, 2013).

[22] Kurtuldu, *supra* note 17.

And this process continues today, as firms try to distinguish their company's cookie-cutter SUV, sedan or pick-up truck from another company's cookie-cutter SUV, sedan or pick-up truck merely with a hood ornament or a name on the bumper. For instance, what love and a hatchback station wagon have to do with each other is a mystery to me, but years of ads have told millions of consumers that "love is what makes a Subaru a Subaru."[23]

Typically, building up positive connotations for a brand is done through advertising using standard puffery.[24] Old standbys for advertisers are the assertion (true or not) that if the customer buys this product, she will be more powerful, rich, intelligent, sexy, envied or successful.[25] But the lies to sell products can get out of hand, as Vance Packard complained in his book *The Waste Makers*: "Millions of consumers are manipulated, razzle-dazzled, indoctrinated, mood-conditioned, and flimflammed."[26]

Jingles to sell products are often "earworms" that get stuck in viewers' heads. They can be so insidious that even if viewers hate the product or the company behind it, the ad copy is stuck in their minds. As Drew Westen notes, "[w]hen even people who don't like your product are humming your jingle, you know you've got them where it counts: in their [neural] networks."[27] Likewise, ad man Nigel Hollis once wrote:

> engaging and memorable ads slip ideas past our defenses and seed memories that influence our behavior. You may not think advertising influences you. But marketers do. And in addition to millions of dollars, they have something else most people don't have: Access to data that proves their point.[28]

---

[23] Diana T. Kurylko, *How Subaru marketing found the 'Love'*, Auto News (Feb. 12, 2018), www.autonews.com/article/20180212/RETAIL03/180219982/how-subaru -marketing-found-the-love.

[24] Raymond Perrier, *Valuation Issues: The Value of a Brand as a Financial Asset*, Corp. Fin. Rev. (March/April 1998).

[25] Deven R. Desai, *From Trademarks to Brands*, 64 Fla. L. Rev. 981, 990–91 (2012) ("Many companies encourage consumers to see a brand as having a personality and to accept the idea that owning a branded good connects the consumer to the brand in some deep, personal way. ... Taken further, a consumer may use a brand to express herself.") (internal citations omitted).

[26] Vance Packard, The Waste Makers 250 (1960 reprinted 1971).

[27] Drew Westen, The Political Brain: The Role of Emotion in Deciding the Fate of the Nation 165 (2007).

[28] Nigel Hollis, *Why Good Advertising Works (Even When You Think It Doesn't)*, Atlantic (Aug. 31, 2011).

As the data crunchers over at Nielsen have found, "[p]ractice (repetition) indeed makes perfect—and can help create durable memories."[29] One of the oddities of advertising brands is that some customers associate repetitive ads with higher-quality products. Objectively, this is somewhat absurd, since a heavily advertised item could be poorly constructed, carcinogenic or addictive. But nonetheless, this is a measurable phenomenon:

> Repetition of an ad may signal to consumers that the brand or product is a good buy, or a quality product. This is sometimes referred to as signaling theory. In 1975, University of Wyoming researchers Anthony McGann and Raymond Marquardt found that ads with high rates of repetition tended to also be rated as high quality in *Consumer Reports*.[30]

And even more disturbingly, the more an ad is repeated, the more viewers will believe it (even if the claim that is being repeated is not true). "Studies suggest that repeated statements are perceived as more truthful than statements made less frequently, 'presumably because repetition imbues the statement with familiarity.' In simple terms: frequency breeds familiarity, and familiarity breed trust."[31]

A well-established brand enables the brand owner to charge a premium over a competing similar generic product or service.[32] Thus, the economic meaning of a "brand" is that value-added quality of a product that convinces a customer

---

[29] David Brandt, *Understanding Memory in Advertising*, Nielsen (Feb. 22, 2017), www.nielsen.com/us/en/insights/journal-of-measurement/volume-1-issue-3/understanding-memory-in-advertising.html; Sean H. K. Kang, *Spaced Repetition Promotes Efficient and Effective Learning: Policy Implications for Instruction*, 3 Behavioral and Brain Sciences 12 (2016) ("Massed repetition eliminates the retrieval process – there is no need to retrieve from memory because the same item was just presented.").

[30] Lisa Magloff, *Repetition as an Advertisement Technique*, Chron (Feb. 1, 2019), https://smallbusiness.chron.com/repetition-advertisement-technique-24437.html.

[31] Jeffry Pilcher, *Say It Again: Messages Are More Effective When Repeated*, Financial Brand (Sept. 23, 2014), https://thefinancialbrand.com/42323/advertising-marketing-messages-effective-frequency/; *see also* Linda Henkel & Mark Mattson, *Reading is believing: the truth effect and source credibility*, 20(4) Conscious Cogn. 1705–21 (Dec. 2011) ("familiarity may create an illusion of truth for statements when people lack source-specifying cues, especially cues regarding the reliability of the source.").

[32] Mark Fenster, *Coolhunting the Law*, 12 Harv. Negot. L. Rev. 157, 161 (2007) ("A successful brand will both command a high premium and control significant market share. In this way, successful brands offer 'brand equity,' an intangible asset with a fuzzily measurable value that can, in some instances, represent a significant portion of a corporation's overall value.") (internal citations omitted); Marc De Swaan Arons, *How Brands Were Born*, Atlantic (Oct. 3, 2011).

to pay more than he would pay for a similar generic product because of a positive association with the source of the product.[33] Thus, a customer might pay 50 percent more for a white J.Crew t-shirt because it is a J.Crew t-shirt, even though objectively it is no different than a no-name white t-shirt.[34]

The largest publicly traded companies are sometimes richer than nations.[35] They are big, global and imposing, but they have two Achilles' heels related to their brands: rejection by their investors and shunning by their customers.[36] If the brand is damaged, the company is likely to suffer.[37] Corporations typically want to add to the value of their brands, not detract from it.[38] The goodwill[39] associated with a brand may well be a company's greatest asset.[40] Indeed, intellectual property litigation is often launched by firms to ensure that no one is using a copyrighted brand logo, trade dress or trademark in a way that

---

[33] *The Lemon Dilemma*, THE ECONOMIST (Oct. 11, 2001), www.economist.com/node/813705 ("[B]rands do help to make the world easier to navigate. A Coke or a Big Mac, say, is almost the same everywhere in the world. The customer knows the quality of a product by its brand.").

[34] *See* Jeremy N. Sheff, *Biasing Brands*, 32 CARDOZO L. REV. 1245, 1260 (2011).

[35] *See* Vincent Trivett, *25 US Mega Corporations: Where They Rank If They Were Countries*, BUSINESS INSIDER (June 27, 2011), www.businessinsider.com/25-corporations-bigger-tan-countries-2011-6.

[36] KLEIN, *supra* note 5, at 334 ("Brand image, the source of so much corporate wealth, is also, it turns out, the corporate Achilles' heel.").

[37] *See* Mario Biagioli, Anupam Chander & Madhavi Sunder, *Brand New World: Distinguishing Oneself in the Global Flow*, 47 U.C. DAVIS L. REV. 455, 465–66 (2013) ("Corporations now invest time and resources into leading the consumers to associate a certain brand with a certain image . . .").

[38] *See* Tim Minahan, *Risk Management Lessons From Toyota*, FORBES (May 10, 2010) ("Your brand is a set of perceptions and images that represent a company or product.").

[39] *See Newark Morning Ledger Co. v. United States*, 507 U.S. 546, 555–56 (1993) ("Although the definition of goodwill has taken different forms over the years, the shorthand description of good-will as 'the expectancy of continued patronage,' *Boe v. Commissioner*, 307 F.2d 339, 343 (9th Cir. 1962), provides a useful label with which to identify the total of all the imponderable qualities that attract customers to the business." (citing *Hous. Chronicle Publ'g Co. v. United States*, 481 F.2d 1240, 1248 n.5 (5th Cir. 1973))).

[40] *See* Jan Lindemann, *Brand Valuation, in* BRANDS AND BRANDING, AN ECONOMIST BOOK 1, 27 (Rita Simmons, *et al.*, eds., 2004) ("If this business were split up, I would give you the land and bricks and mortar, and I would take the brands and trade marks, and I would fare better than you."); Jerre B. Swann & Theodore H. Davis, Jr., *Dilution, An Idea Whose Time Has Gone; Brand Equity as Protectable Property, The New/Old Paradigm*, 1 J. INTELL. PROP. L. 219, 229 (1994) ("As is evident from the merger mania of the 1980's, brands are often more valuable [than] the physical assets of a business.").

would tarnish or harm a brand.[41] As Justice Frankfurter once held: "The protection of trade-marks is the law's recognition of the psychological function
of symbols."[42] And the value of these symbols can reach the billions. *Forbes*
estimated the value of Nike's swoosh at $26 billion;[43] though that pales in
comparison to Apple's "apple with a missing bite" brand, which *Forbes* valued
at $170 billion.[44]

Typically, because they want to be able to charge a premium, most owners
of commercial brands try to steer clear of negative connotations. There are,
of course, a few brands that like to flirt with a more edgy image as a way
to cut through the clutter and enter the public consciousness. Think of Red
Bull's sponsorship of dangerous sporting events and stunts, some of which
have turned deadly.[45] Here, being a "renegade" is part of building the brand.
If branding is in part a battle to grab the audience's attention, then being
"extreme" can actually be helpful in building a brand.

But edgy brands walk a delicate line. If the "extreme" brand or the
"extreme" brand ambassador gets in real trouble socially or legally, then the
company behind the brand can suffer. For instance, before it went bankrupt in
2017,[46] American Apparel had ads with models wearing nothing but socks or
legwarmers, or in other states of undress.[47] The sexualized image seemed to
help sell the brand, which lasted 19 years. American Apparel's founder, Dov
Charney, seemed to revel in the controversy over the sexy ads, which won

---

[41] *See* Lauren Behr, *Trademarks for the Cure: Why Nonprofits Need Their Own Set
of Trademark Rules*, 54 B.C. L. Rev. 243, 256 (2013) ("[The 1996 Federal Trademark
Dilution Act ("FTDA")] established a federal cause of action against use that could
tarnish or devalue a senior user's mark.").

[42] *Mishawaka Rubber & Woolen Mfg. Co. v. S.S. Kresge Co.*, 316 U.S. 203, 205
(1942).

[43] Mike Ozanian, *The Forbes Fab 40: The World's Most Valuable Sports Brands
2015*, Forbes (Oct. 22, 2015), www.forbes.com/sites/mikeozanian/2015/10/22/the
-forbes-fab-40-the-most-valuable-brands-in-sports-2015/#6b79a5df1752.

[44] Kurt Badenhausen, *Apple Heads The World's Most Valuable Brands of 2017 at
$170 Billion*, Forbes (May 23, 2017).

[45] Tom Porter, *Red Bull Under Fire Over Seventh Death at Tyrol Stunt Event*, Int'l
Bus. Times (May 5, 2013).

[46] *Bankrupt Retailer American Apparel Begins Laying Off Thousands of Workers*,
Reuters (Jan. 16, 2017).

[47] *American Apparel Adverts Banned: 'Sexual And Objectifying' Images Show
Models Half Naked*, Huff. Post (Oct. 4, 2013).

the brand earned media[48]—right up until the point his board ousted him after a series of sexual harassment lawsuits were filed against him.[49]

Even spokespersons can hurt brands if they get into enough trouble. For example, when Tiger Woods was suspected of cheating on his wife, many brands that he had endorsed dropped him as a spokesperson.[50] And when Michael Vick got in criminal trouble for dog fighting, brands similarly shunned him.[51] As reported in *Advertising Age*, "[w]hen you hang a brand on one guy, you're taking a huge risk."[52]

Some companies will even rebrand if the old brand has picked up too many negative connotations. In an episode of *The Simpsons*, there is the following colloquy:

> **Kent Brockman from the TV:** In response to the outcry, Lard Lad's parent company, Tianjin Mining and Smelting and Donuts, has issued the following statement: "We are rebranding Lard Lad with an updated statue."
> **Homer:** Ooh, rebranding!
> **Lisa:** That just means admitting failure, Dad.
> **Homer:** Ooh, admitting failure![53]

And indeed, rebranding is typically an admission that the previous brand has failed. An example of this phenomenon is when a mobile payment system called "Isis" decided to rebrand itself as "Softcard" in 2014 because of the possible negative connotation associated with the terrorist group ISIS.[54] The companies involved in the Isis mobile payment project included AT&T, Verizon and T-Mobile, which decided that despite the price of rebranding, it

---

[48] Hannah Marriott, *Dov Charney: the man who put the sleaze factor into American Apparel*, GUARDIAN (June 19, 2014).

[49] Frank Bruni, *A Grope and a Shrug Dov Charney, American Apparel and Sexual Harassment*, N.Y. TIMES (June 30, 2014).

[50] Geoffrey Norman, *Can You Forgive Him?*, 18 WEEKLY STANDARD 26 (2013) ("After the scandal, he [Tiger Woods] lost almost all of his high profile endorsements. … One study estimated shareholder losses from the damage to brands caused by the scandal at between $5 billion and $12 billion.").

[51] Emily B. York, *Phelps Brand Takes a Hit*, 80 ADVERTISING AGE 24, 27 (2009) ("Few brands want a puppy-killing, dogfight-organizing felon. Powerade, Airtran, Hasbro all walked away [from Vick]. So did Nike when the verdict came in.").

[52] Jeremy Mullman, *Reducing Risk of Vick-timization*, 78 ADVERTISING AGE 27 (2007) (quoting Jason Cavnar).

[53] *The Simpsons* Season 28, Episode 1, *Monty Burns' Fleeing Circus*, WIKIQUOTE, https://en.wikiquote.org/wiki/The_Simpsons/Season_28.

[54] *See* Press Release, Michael Abbot, CEO, *ISIS Plans to Rebrand According to CEO*, GREEN SHEET (July 7, 2014).

would be less costly than keeping a tainted brand.[55] Similarly, after the negative addictive and carcinogenic qualities of tobacco became undeniable, Philip Morris (a famous tobacco company) changed its name to Altria in 2003.[56] After a *Mother Jones* exposé of the Corrections Corporation of America, it changed its name to Core Civic.[57] Likewise, Erik Prince's private contractor firm Blackwater has rebranded itself twice after it killed 17 civilians in Iraq in 2007[58]—first to Xe and then to Academi.[59]

But one of the reasons why corporations care enough about their brand to rebrand is branding has power. The most effective branding can get into our heads so deeply that it warps how we see ourselves. As Amanda Hess observed: "now branding has taken over not just work but life itself, seizing control of our appearances, our social relationships, even our approach to civil society."[60] Put another way, "[b]rands allow businesses to reach consumers directly with messages regarding emotion, identity, and self-worth. ..."[61] Branding often plays on our emotions and tries to fill deep psychological needs like wanting to accepted.[62]

Ads—whether they are advertising a product or a candidate—are trying to shape our impression of what's for sale and whether we want *that* in our lives.

---

[55]   Stephen T. Watson, *Isis? ISIS? Similarity Causes Change in Branding*, BUFFALO NEWS (Oct. 6, 2014).

[56]   Elizabeth A. Smith & Ruth E. Malone, *Altria Means Tobacco: Philip Morris's Identity Crisis*, 93(4) AM. J. PUBLIC HEALTH 553–56 (Apr. 2003), www.ncbi.nlm.nih.gov/pmc/articles/PMC1447789/.

[57]   Shane Bauer, *A Stray Email Exposes a Prison Company's Rebranding Efforts. CoreCivic enlists help from a PR firm that boasts an "aggressive media strategy" for countering journalists.*, MOTHER JONES (Jan. 19, 2017), www.motherjones.com/politics/2017/01/corecivic-cca-private-prison-pr-firm-hillenby/.

[58]   Nathan Hodge, *Accused Blackwater Shooters Turning Themselves In*, WIRED (Dec. 8, 2008).

[59]   Nathan Hodge, *Company Once Known as Blackwater Ditches Xe for Yet Another New Name*, WALL ST. J. (Dec. 12, 2011).

[60]   Amanda Hess, *What Happens When People and Companies Are Both Just 'Brands'?*, N.Y. TIMES MAG. (May 1, 2018).

[61]   Deven R. Desai & Spencer Waller, *Brands, Competition, and the Law*, 2010 B.Y.U. L. REV. 1425, 1427 (2010).

[62]   VANCE PACKARD, THE HIDDEN PERSUADERS 47 (1957 REPRINTED 1969) ("'Basically, what you are trying to do,' [Pierre Martineau] advised, 'is create an illogical situation. You want the customer to fall in love with your product and have a profound brand loyalty when actually content may be very similar to hundreds of competing brands.' To create this illogical loyalty, he said, the first task 'is one of creating some differentiation in the mind—some individualization for the product which has a long list of competitors very close to it in content.'").

To get into our brains, being the first to make a first impression matters. As Drew Westen put it:

> We have known for half a century that in advertising, being the first to make a pitch renders an effort at persuasion more effective. The one who gets there first has the widest latitude in shaping [neural] networks while they are most malleable (i.e., when no other dots have been firmly connected.)[63]

One way to get there "first" is to hit customers while they are still children, when their minds still have plasticity. Targeting children is important for advertisers because "[w]e do the overwhelming majority of our learning when we are children. By the time we are seven, most of our mental highways have been constructed." [64] If an advertiser can't get to us as children, it will try to get to us as adults through our emotions,[65] since:

> emotion continues to provide us with new imprints throughout our lives. ... [For instance,] Americans alive today can vividly relive the experience of watching the World Trade Center towers fall. This is because these experiences are so emotionally powerful that they are effectively seared onto our brains.[66]

2. POLITICAL BRANDS

The language of marketing has infected political discourse. Recall when President George W. Bush's Chief of Staff Andrew Card once said, "You don't introduce new products in August," explaining why the administration didn't try to "sell" the second Gulf War to the American public during the summer of 2002.[67] Or as pollster Celinda Lake explained, "whether you're Pepsi or Obama you have to run a campaign to get your brand out."[68]

Political branding comes from the government and from political actors such as candidates, political action committees (PACs), 527s, politically active

---

[63] WESTEN, *supra* note 27, at 346.

[64] CLOTAIRE RAPAILLE, THE CULTURE CODE: AN INGENIOUS WAY TO UNDERSTAND WHY PEOPLE AROUND THE WORLD LIVE AND BUY AS THEY DO 17 (2007).

[65] PACKARD, THE HIDDEN PERSUADERS *supra* note 62, at 219 (quoting Richard Worthington) ("People must be controlled by manipulating their [instincts and emotions] rather than by changing their reasonings. This is a fact of which politicians have always made use when they have persuaded their constituents by appealing to their sentiments, rather than by employing [reasoning], which would never be listened to or at least never prove effective for moving the crowds.").

[66] RAPAILLE, *supra* note 64, at 17.

[67] Elisabeth Bumiller, *Traces of Terror: The Strategy; Bush Aides Set Strategy to Sell Policy on Iraq.*, N.Y. TIMES (Sept. 7, 2002).

[68] Interview with Celinda Lake (Sept. 7, 2018).

non-profits and political parties. When the branding comes from the government, it can be anything from useful public information—like what constitutes a balanced diet based on the best available scientific knowledge, as visualized in the U.S. Department of Agriculture's food pyramid—to actual government propaganda, like lying about what happened at the Gulf of Tonkin.

Branding from the government is propaganda when it feeds the public a particular view that is deeply misleading. Of course, the word "propaganda" carries with it a century of negative connotations.[69] Though interestingly, even the word "propaganda" started with different connotations than what it has now. The word was coined by the Vatican in 1622. The original idea from Pope Gregory XV was to propagate the Christian faith in the New World through "propaganda."[70] Only many centuries later, after the First World War, did the word "propaganda" turn into the ugly manipulative mess that it is today.

Political campaigns are one place where political branding attempts to define candidates, policies, even the state of the nation. Incumbents will try to brand the economy as outstanding and brand themselves as the cause of the nation's success. Challengers will try to brand the country as being on the wrong track and brand themselves as the catalyst for needed change. Another key to success for many vying for high office is the ability to convince disenchanted voters that the candidate can save them. This might explain the election and re-election of Franklin D. Roosevelt, who promised a nation of "forgotten men" going through its worst financial Depression a "New Deal"—one of the all-time great political brands in history.[71]

In candidate campaigns, which often rely on broadcast ads to reach large and dispersed electorates, the first casualty is often the truth. If you think that elections are cerebral affairs decided by logic and facts, I have bad news for you:[72]

> Two-thirds of voters' decisions to support one candidate or another could be accounted for by two simple variables: their partisan feelings and their feelings

---

[69]   Mark Crispin Miller, *Introduction* to Edward Bernays, Propaganda 9 (1928 reprinted 2005) ("Prior to World War One ... propaganda tended not to be the damning term we throw around today ... [Now it means] lies, half-truths, selective history or the other tricks[.]").

[70]   *Id.*

[71]   V.O. Key, Jr., Politics, Parties, & Pressure Groups 187 (1964 5th ed.) ("Poor men, rich men, middle-class men, farmers, workers, all ... could identify themselves with the 'forgotten man,' and they could equally feel themselves deserving of a 'new deal' without insisting on exact definition of the 'new deal' was to be.").

[72]   Packard, The Hidden Persuaders *supra* note 62, at 221 ("Dr. Samuel A. Stouffer, director of the Laboratory of Social Relations, Harvard University... [said] it was a good working rule that people's attitudes are more easily reached through their emotions than through their intellects.").

towards the candidates. Candidates' positions on the issues had only a modest effect on their electoral preferences.[73]

Put another way, depressingly, facts frequently have nothing to do with who is electable. As Joe McGinniss summed up in his book *The Selling of the President*, "Politics, in a sense, has always been a con game."[74]

Often what political ads play on is not the argument that we should support a particular new candidate, but rather that we (the viewer) already support the candidate because the candidate is on our team or in our tribe. As cognitive scientists show, evoking a "team" is a powerful motivator. A recent study showed that "once a group is marked as competitive, Schadenfreude [taking pleasure in the misfortune of others] and Glückschmerz [sorrow felt at the good fortune of others] follow: no learning is required."[75] For some of us, triggering the hatred of another person from another team or love of our team is nearly automatic with the right prompt.

Branding played a crucial role in the 2016 election. As Trump's ex-personal lawyer, Michael Cohen, testified before Congress on February 27, 2019:

> Donald Trump is a man who ran for office to make his brand great, not to make our country great. He had no desire or intention to lead this nation – only to market himself and to build his wealth and power. Mr. Trump would often say, this campaign was going to be the "greatest infomercial in political history." He never expected to win the primary. He never expected to win the general election. The campaign – for him – was always a marketing opportunity.[76]

Branding has surely taken center stage with the Trump Presidency. Trump's repetitive rhetoric can leave the impression that he has a limited vocabulary. But as a master brander, he knows that repetition of catchphrases or an image is the way to hammer a point home. He's not the only one who can deploy this technique. The day after Trump was inaugurated, a Women's March in Washington, D.C. to protest him attracted more attendees than his inauguration. One way the two crowds could be distinguished at a distance was that many in the Trump crowd wore red "Make America Great Again" hats and

---

[73]   WESTEN, *supra* note 27, at 119.

[74]   JOE MCGINNISS, THE SELLING OF THE PRESIDENT 1968 at 26 (1969).

[75]   Mina Cikara, *Intergroup Schadenfreude: motivating participation in collective violence*, 3 CURRENT OPINION IN BEHAVIORAL SCIENCES 12–17 at 14 (2015).

[76]   *Full Transcript: Michael Cohen's Opening Statement to Congress*, N.Y. TIMES (Feb. 27, 2019).

many in the Women's March crowd wore distinctive knitted pink hats.[77] Thus, even the resistance is branded.

Branding techniques do not have to be used for an iniquitous *telos*. For example, branding techniques were used by *Sesame Street* to teach generations of children to read.[78] In 1969:

> John W. Macy, Jr. wrote an investigation of how public broadcasting might better serve American viewers. 'This program [*Sesame Street*] is directed at teaching pre-schoolers letters of the alphabet and numbers by using the commercial advertising techniques of animation, jingles, and so forth,' he wrote.[79]

And there is some discussion of positive uses of branding in this book, like those deployed by survivors of the Parkland massacre. But most of the book is focused on when branding is used to manipulate and abuse the public, often for base political ends.

The results of the 2016 presidential election motivated me to write this book. How, I wondered, could America have elected a brand as president? The other occurrence that motivated me to write this book is a sense that Americans are suffering from "truth decay."[80] To me, electing a brand president and the decay of truth are intertwined, because the more that voters rely on flashy branding to dictate who is electable, the more they are likely to fall for a slick, media-savvy candidate over a competent and truthful one.

I am a campaign finance lawyer by training. And one of the drivers of the high price of political campaigns is the exorbitant cost of advertising. What first got me interested in branding was a statement from Senator Russ Feingold, who warned in 2011 that political spending by companies may cause

---

[77] *Design legend Debbie Millman on branding, illustration and podcasting*, BREED (May 16, 2018), https://breedlondon.com/debbie-millman/.

[78] Joan Ganz Cooney, *The Potential Uses of Television in Preschool Education: a report to the Carnegie Corporation of New York* 10 (1966), www.joanganzcooneycenter .org/wp-content/uploads/2014/01/JGC_1966_report.pdf ("If we accept the premise that commercials are effective teachers, it is important to be aware of their characteristics, the most obvious being frequent repetition, clever visual presentation, brevity and clarity … unfortunately for our children, many teachers may have forgotten what Madison Avenue, with consummate skill, had cribbed from them.").

[79] Erin Blakemore, *Sesame Street's Controversial Early Years*, JSTOR DAILY (Apr. 7, 2017), https://daily.jstor.org/sesame-streets-controversial-early-years/.

[80] Jennifer Kavanagh & Michael D. Rich, *Truth Decay: An Initial Exploration of the Diminishing Role of Facts and Analysis in American Public Life*, RAND CORP. (2018) ("Over the past several decades, the opposite trend has emerged: an erosion of trust in and reliance on objective facts in political debate and civil discourse about public policy.").

the public to view them through a limited partisan lens.[81] As Senator Feingold put it, "We're going to have Republican and Democrat toothpaste."[82] His quote inspired me to look at commercial branding, political advertising and how these two spheres intersect.[83] And that was all before Trump was elected president.

The criminal and congressional investigations into Trump's election in 2016 have provided a treasure trove of information for a researcher like me. In a typical election, political ads that were placed on Facebook for a millisecond could be lost to history. But now some of those ads, because they are suspected to be part of a foreign attack on the integrity of our elections, are part of a permanent and public Congressional record. Like the Congressional investigation into Watergate, which gave the public a rare peek behind the curtain into the 1972 election, the investigations into the 2016 election provide a chance for a deeper dive on how modern elections are transforming.

A final reason that I wanted to write this book is to show the artifice of political branding. Typically, the people using political branding techniques are just trying to manipulate the public. When President Trump calls his Mar-a-Lago golf club in Florida the "Winter White House," that is branding—and not original branding either. President Nixon (1969–74) called his Florida home the "Winter White House" as well.[84] When Special Counsel Robert S. Mueller III's investigation into the 2016 election is called a "witch hunt" by Presidential Advisor Kellyanne Conway, that is branding.[85] Again, it's not original branding. As far back as the 1930s, a search for communists among university pro-

---

[81] The UpTake, *Progressive Toothpaste to Fight Corporate Political Control*, YouTube (June 16, 2011), www.youtube.com/watch?v=isg3sMKwZ1o.

[82] Thomas L. Friedman & Michael Mandelbaum, That Used to Be Us: How America Fell Behind in the World It Invented and We can Come Back 245 (2011) (quoting Senator Feingold).

[83] Ciara Torres-Spelliscy, *Shooting Your Brand in the Foot: What* Citizens United *Invites*, 68 Rutgers U. L. Rev. 1295 (Spring 2016).

[84] Bootie Cosgrove-Mather, *Nixon's Winter White House Razed*, CBS (July 24, 2003), www.cbsnews.com/news/nixons-winter-white-house-razed/ ("Former President Nixon's private sanctuary, known as the Winter White House, was razed. ...").

[85] Pamela Engel & Natasha Bertrand, *Kellyanne Conway just escalated the White House's campaign against Robert Mueller* (July 21, 2017), www.businessinsider .com/kellyanne-conway-robert-mueller-trump-2017-7; John Wagner, *Trump Attacks Mueller Probe for Fourth Straight Morning, Asks if it will "Go on Forever,"* Wash. Post (Nov. 29, 2018); John W. Schoen, *Trump Is Tweeting "Witch Hunt" A Lot More Than He Used To, as Mueller Probe Grinds On and Manafort Goes on Trial,* CNBC (Aug. 1, 2018), www. cnbc.com/2018/08/01/trumps-witch-hunttweets-are-getting -more-frequent-as-mueller-probe.html.

fessors was called a "witch hunt."[86] This phrase also harkens back to the dark days of the Salem witch trials—the original American "witch hunt."[87] When White House Chief Strategist Steve Bannon said, "drain the swamp," about limiting the power of Washington insiders, that was branding. Again, it wasn't original; it went back to President Ronald Reagan, among others.[88] Senator Richard Neuberger also used the phrase "drain the swamp" in a piece in the *New York Times* urging the adoption of public financing for federal elections back in 1956.[89] The original Mother Jones (the woman whom the magazine is named after) also said "drain the swamp" in 1913.[90] Even Speaker of the House Nancy Pelosi in 2006 called for Democrats to "drain the swamp" after years of unified Republican rule under President George W. Bush.[91] But when working for a firm called Cambridge Analytica, Steve Bannon tested the phrase "drain the swamp" years before it was used in the 2016 election campaign by candidate Donald Trump.[92] Clearly, what Mr. Bannon was doing was brand testing, and "drain the swamp" hit the right chord for his target market. My hope is that perhaps when Americans see that "Winter White House," "witch hunt" and "drain the swamp" are all just basic branding trying to sell something, they can be less gullible about falling for messages designed to tug at our emotions

---

[86] *Ickes Assails Acts of 'Witch Hunters'*, N.Y. Times 13 (May 25, 1935) ("Harold L. Ickes, Secretary of the Interior, denounced 'witch hunters …'").

[87] *Salem's 300 Eventful Years*, N.Y. Times p. X18 (Apr. 18, 1926).

[88] Ronald Reagan, *Remarks to the Reagan Administration Executive Forum* (Jan. 20, 1982), www.presidency.ucsb.edu/ws/index.php?pid=42498 ("Speaking of swamps, I want to urge you all not to get bogged down in Potomac fever. … As the old saying goes, 'When you're up to your armpits in alligators, it's sometimes hard to remember that your original intention was to drain the swamp.'").

[89] Richard L. Neuberger, *Who Should Pay for Political Campaigns?*, N.Y. Times (June 3, 1956).

[90] John Kelly, *What's With All Trump's Talk About "Draining the Swamp?"* Slate (Oct. 26, 2016), www.slate.com/blogs/lexicon_valley/2016/10/26/why_do_trump_and _his_supports_keep_talking_about_draining_the_swamp.html ("Etymologist Barry Popik has traced drain the swamp back to the socialist movement of the early 20th century.").

[91] David Espo, *Pelosi Says She Would Drain GOP 'Swamp,'* AP (Oct. 6, 2006), www.washingtonpost.com/wp-dyn/content/article/2006/10/06/AR2006100600056 .html?noredirect=on ("Nancy Pelosi is thinking 100 hours, time enough, she says, to begin to 'drain the swamp' after more than a decade of Republican rule.").

[92] Sue Halpern, *Cambridge Analytica, Facebook, and the Revelations of Open Secrets*, New Yorker (Mar. 21, 2018), www.newyorker.com/news/news-desk/ cambridge-analytica-facebook-and-the-revelations-of-open-secrets ("It was in those early days of 2014, Wylie says, that he and Bannon began testing slogans like "drain the swamp" and "the deep state" and "build the wall," and found a surprising number of Americans who responded strongly to them.").

and obfuscate the truth.[93] President Trump's claim that he is "draining the swamp" is no more credible than thinking your Subaru actually loves you. But the repeated branding can put both Trump and Subaru in a more positive light, such that you may buy Trump's claims just as you might purchase a Subaru station wagon.

Let me close this introduction by noting that "branding" has been called "a process of manufacturing meaning."[94] I don't disagree, but that is precisely why branding's power needs to be interrogated. Manufacturing meaning is a scary power in the wrong hands. During the Third Reich in Germany, propagandist Joseph Goebbels "manufactured meaning" too. It led to genocide and a World War

Here is the structure of this book. Part I, "The Legal Landscape," will look at how the Supreme Court has set the ground rules for political discourse, especially in elections—including whether people can lie in elections, who can fund them, and how much dark money is allowed. This new legal landscape is created by a Supreme Court that has defined corruption incredibly narrowly, to the delight of dishonest politicians everywhere. Part II, "Branding Infecting Politics," will deal with the phenomenon of commercial branding techniques being utilized in political campaigns against the backdrop of America's growing partisan rift. This section will cover elections from Eisenhower to Trump. Part III, "When Branding Gets Pernicious," examines what happens when branding is used to do socially destructive things like damaging the free press, exacerbating racial tensions and undermining the integrity of a presidential election. And finally, Part IV, "Rejecting Toxic Brands," explores how citizens and customers are rejecting certain brands (or in some cases embracing others) because of their perceived political stances. Here, boycotts and other tactics are discussed. In the epilogue, I offer some policy prescriptions to address many of the problems that this book highlights along the way.

---

[93] ROBERT SPERO, DUPING OF THE AMERICAN VOTER 166 (1980) ("The political television commercial ... is a dangerous weapon in the hands of the unscrupulous ...").
[94] Stein, *supra* note 2.

PART I

The legal landscape

Commercial branders often lie to sell soap. Should branders also be able to lie to sell who is standing on a political soapbox? By setting the ground rules for elections, the Supreme Court enables many pathologies in politics, including mendacity and corruption. The results of this can be seen in the ways that dishonest politicians cite to campaign finance cases to try to wriggle out of criminal liability. The results can also be seen in corporate political spending in elections, which was enabled by *Citizens United v. FEC*, and in dark political spending that has reached over $1 billion since 2010.

Instead of allowing for laws that require some truthfulness in political campaigns or that restrain the influence of money in politics, the Supreme Court is deregulating politics into a Wild West where nearly anything goes. The message that the Supreme Court has broadcast is that it will not act as a check on the worst instincts in American politics.

In the cases discussed in this part of the book, the Supreme Court sets the stage for the debased politics where the candidate with the most money tends to win, corrupt politicians duck behind the First Amendment to try to avoid jail time and lying has become such a problem that a national paper of record has to create the "bottomless Pinocchio" to capture the high level of mendacity of the president.

1.   Branding truth

"Truth is not always valued and falsehood is not always punished."[1]

1.   INTRODUCTION

Branding is the process by which an idea is repeated again and again until it is accepted by the target audience. Mass-marketed branding has a target audience of nearly every man, woman and child who consumes.[2] But brand marketing can be microtargeted to a particular demographic, income group or subculture. For example, Dove soap, which targets women with images of empowerment that are ostensibly against lookism, and Ax soap, which targets men with sexist appeals, are both sold by the same company (Unilever), just to different target demos. The same branding techniques can be used in noncommercial spheres. For example, with propaganda, an idea (often an untrue one) is repeated by the government or reiterated by an official to the electorate, until it is accepted as the truth.

With commercial branding, the message is typically a combination of "this product lives up to expectations" and "please buy this product right now." For luxury items, the branding is frequently, "this product is a status symbol" and "when you can afford it, treat yourself to this luxury." There's also the perennial claim that "this product is cool" and "if you buy this product, you'll be cool too." The basic message is to get the public to buy, buy, buy—*but* buy our widget, not the other guy's widget.

With political branding (or government propaganda), the messages can be more varied, since the topics that politics touch can be everything from environmental policy to the price of milk (not that those are completely unrelated either); but at the end of the day, the political brander or government propagandist is also hoping that the public will buy, buy, buy. In the political context, however, the audience is urged to buy our idea, not the other guy's idea.

---

[1]   David Snyder, media attorney at the Florida Bar Reporters Workshop (2018).

[2]   VANCE PACKARD, THE HIDDEN PERSUADERS 217 (1957 reprinted 1969) ("Judge Learned Hand expressed himself as being enormously disturbed by the growth of professional publicists in our society. He called publicity 'a black art' but agreed it has come to stay.").

So how does a well-branded but discredited idea stick around for so long? It works the same way an urban legend does. One of the great human conundrums is why false myths stick around so long. Old wives' tales and urban legends persist in part because they are circulated through networks of trust: a parent, a friend, a peer or a co-worker says the mythic claim and it suddenly takes on an air of truth, especially if it is repeated and reinforced. Take this old wives' tale: "cold water boils faster than hot water." Parents tell this to children in many an American kitchen. Line cooks and chefs tell it to busboys and bar backs. The claim also gets repeated on a myriad of cooking shows on television.[3] The only problem is, it isn't true. Hot water boils faster. But hear something from a trusted source, especially from multiple trusted sources, and the end result is it seems "true." It can be mind-blowing when at long last it is revealed that the physics just doesn't add up for the cold-water-boils-quicker myth.[4] Branders and purveyors of lies tap into the same trusted networks that allow myths and old wives' tales to persist.

Facts have the power to cut through even longstanding myths. For centuries, people believed, as Aristotle had postulated, that heavier objects fall faster than lighter objects. But this myth was shattered by a simple experiment when Galileo dropped two cannon balls of different weights from the Leaning Tower of Pisa. And "when Galileo dropped two balls—a heavy one and a light one—and the world witnessed that both hit the ground at the same time[,] [i]t was the beginning of the end of the Aristotelian, prescientific civilization. . ."[5] Truth still has that power to blast through lies and bluster and act as a myth buster.

This chapter will explore how America is going through a period of truth decay, and that a major catalyst for this decay is the extraordinary level of mendacity issuing from the White House. As explained below, lies started from the very first week of the Trump Administration and, if anything, the pace of dishonesties has accelerated. Two and half years in, the rate of lying from President Trump averaged 15–16 lies a day. Finally, this chapter will explain how the Supreme Court deals with lying. Spoiler alert: it's not reassuring.

---

[3] *'Chef' Thinks That Cold Water Boils Faster Than Hot Water*, HELL'S KITCHEN (May 1, 2018).

[4] Anahad O'Connor, *The Claim: Cold Water Boils More Quickly Than Hot Water*, N.Y. TIMES (Mar. 18, 2008).

[5] ROSSER REEVES, REALITY IN ADVERTISING 151 (1970); *see also id.* at 152 ("scientists began to perform experiments, to see what happened when something was done. It was refreshing, this new philosophy of 'what-when.' Many facts began to appear, suddenly, as fables. Wisdom and experience began to appear, often, as fallacies. Personal opinion began to appear as just that—personal opinion.").

2.   TRUTH TAKES A BEATING

"How can you know what to believe?" asked the blockbuster book, *The Hidden Persuaders*.[6] One answer to this query is: believe the truth. Unfortunately, political actors, governments (foreign and domestic), advertisers and broadcasters, just to name a few, are all trying to influence what the public thinks is true.[7] And, of course, great philosophers have also spent their lives debating the nature of truth and how to discern it.[8] Sidestepping most of these higher-level philosophical debates about the nature of "truth,"[9] there are things that happened—those things are true; and there are things that have never happened—those things are false. For example, there was a war in the 1930s and 1940s called the Second World War; that happened, that is a truth.[10] The idea that Adolph Hitler survived the Second World War is an event that did not happen and is false.[11] There was a genocide of Jewish people during the Second World War; that happened, that is a truth.[12] Denial that there was a Holocaust during the Second World War is a dangerously false claim and therefore a lie.[13] And, of course, there are many things that are much more debatable, or in a grey zone, like whether the color aqua is really blue or green. When discussing truth in this chapter, this word indicates events that actually happened, either in history or more recently.

---

[6]   PACKARD, *supra* note 2, at 257.

[7]   DARRELL M. WEST, AIR WARS TELEVISION ADVERTISING AND SOCIAL MEDIA IN ELECTION CAMPAIGNS 1952–2012 152 (6th Ed. 2016) ("The 1988 presidential campaign was the first to feature ad watches. From time to time, national newspapers printed 'truth boxes' in which ad claims were assessed. ... Viewers often remembered the ad but not the media corrections.").

[8]   DEBBIE MILLMAN, LOOK BOTH WAYS ILLUSTRATED ESSAYS ON THE INTERSECTION OF LIFE AND DESIGN 175–76 (2009) ("The French philosopher Jacques Derrida states that we inhabit 'a world of signs without fault, without truth, and without origin.' One of the central tenets of his philosophy is that 'there is nothing outside the text.'").

[9]   Jennifer Kavanagh & Michael D. Rich, *Truth Decay: An Initial Exploration of the Diminishing Role of Facts and Analysis in American Public Life*, RAND CORP. (2018) ("It is worth noting that although we are calling the phenomenon 'Truth Decay,' we are not talking about "truth" in the philosophical sense and therefore do not offer a specific definition of 'truth'").

[10]   *World War II in Europe*, U.S. HOLOCAUST MEMORIAL MUSEUM, https://encyclopedia.ushmm.org/content/en/article/world-war-ii-in-europe.

[11]   Jefferson Chase & Deutsche Welle, *Hitler's teeth analysis dispels myths of Nazi leader's survival*, USA TODAY (May 21, 2018).

[12]   *About the Holocaust*, YAD VASHEM THE WORLD HOLOCAUST REMEMBRANCE CENTER, www.yadvashem.org/holocaust.html.

[13]   *Holocaust Denial*, SOUTHERN POVERTY LAW CENTER, www.splcenter.org/fighting-hate/extremist-files/ideology/holocaust-denial.

The first thing to realize is that while America is experiencing a period when truth itself is under siege, this could all just be part and parcel of a broader 20-year trend of what researchers at the Rand Corporation have called "truth decay."[14] They define "truth decay" as:

> a set of four related trends: (1) increasing disagreement about facts and analytical interpretations of facts and data, (2) a blurring of the line between opinion and fact, (3) the increasing relative volume, and resulting influence, of opinion and personal experience over fact, (4) declining trust in formerly respected sources of factual information.[15]

The Rand *Truth Decay* report argues that what the United States is currently experiencing is a period when truth is suffering, but that this is not unprecedented. The Rand report notes three other periods in American history which also had indicia of truth decay: the 1880s–90s, 1920s–30s and 1960s–70s.[16] As the authors noted, these periods (the Gilded Age, the Roaring Twenties followed by the Great Depression, and the tumult of the 1960s and 1970s) were marked by economic disruption, which typically made income inequality more severe as a chosen few became wealthy and the have-nots displaced by the new economy struggled to find their footing. During these periods of social and economic uncertainty, lies and demagoguery flourished and truth took a beating.[17]

Just as a product can be branded, "truth" can branded too.[18] Like all branding, the impact is most effective when a brand is repeated again and again from a source of authority. All presidents get a mantle of authority whether they win in a close election or not. Those who win in a landslide get an even

---

[14]   Kavanagh & Rich, *supra* note 9 ("We have adopted the term 'Truth Decay' to describe changes currently affecting the U.S. political debate and civil discourse about public policy.").

[15]   *Id.*

[16]   *Id.* ("A closer look at U.S. history reveals several periods – three in particular – that share many similarities with today along a number of dimensions: the 1880s-1890s, the 1920s-1930s, and the 1960s-1970s").

[17]   *Id.* ("These changes [in the Gilded Age] did not lead to universal gains … because] economic inequality grew sharply during this period, and the gap and polarization between the poorer classes and the rich grew significantly wider"); *id.* ("Economic inequality in the 1920s reached unprecedented levels, which fueled resentment of the elites among lower classes that did not fare as well"); *id.* ("Protests at the time [1960s and 1970s] combined anti-establishment and anti-government sentiments with political and economic unrest.").

[18]   PACKARD, *supra* note 2, at 219 ("Bernays explains … : 'It would be ideal if all of us could make up our minds independently by evaluating all pertinent facts objectively. That however, is not possible.'").

bigger mantle. Nixon was the beneficiary of both. In 1968, more people voted against Nixon (combining votes for Humphrey and Wallace 40 million votes) than voted for him (31.7 million votes).[19] In 1972 Nixon won in a landslide of 46 million votes to McGovern's 28 million. As Robert Spero warned then:

> That [the president's] myths were reinforced by a landslide made them and the mythology all the more dangerous. Huge winning margins tend to bond mythology to the public mind until long after an election is over. Despite ample evidence to the contrary, the public automatically reasons that if so many people voted for the winner, his principles and programs must be just and true.[20]

Like Nixon in 1968, Trump in 2016 lost the popular vote, but he still was cloaked with authority. President Trump has the bully pulpit, not to mention two far-reaching Twitter handles (@realdonaldtrump with 62 million followers and @potus with 26 million followers).[21] And this is in a media environment where roughly 69 percent of Americans consume social media.[22] Most social media users check in at least a once a day.[23] One notable attribute of this era is the embrace by President Trump of all-out, bold-faced lying. Lying about big things; lying about small things; lying about things that are easily disproved; lying about things that are hard to disprove; lying about science; lying about economics; lying about basic math—the list goes on.

"You are entitled to your own opinions, but not your own facts," said Senator Daniel Patrick Moynihan.[24] But this Senator's words of wisdom are ignored as mendacity rains down on America's citizenry from on high, from the Trump White House. Candidate Trump previewed what would happen in the Trump presidency.[25] There was good reason for the *Oxford Dictionary* to

---

[19]   Louis Menand, *Lessons From the Election of 1968*, NEW YORKER (Jan. 8, 2018) ("In close elections, such as those of 1960, 1968, and 1976, the vote is essentially the equivalent of flipping a coin. ... But we interpret the result as though it reflected the national intention, a collective decision by the people to rally behind R., and repudiate D.").

[20]   ROBERT SPERO, DUPING OF THE AMERICAN VOTER 125 (1980).

[21]   Twitter as of June 20, 2019.

[22]   *Social Media Fact Sheet*, PEW (Feb. 5, 2018), www.pewinternet.org/fact-sheet/social-media/ ("in 2005, just 5% of American adults used at least one of these platforms. By 2011 that share had risen to half of all Americans, and today [in 2018] 69% of the public uses some type of social media.").

[23]   *Id.* ("Roughly three-quarters of Facebook users – and around six-in-ten Instagram users – visit these sites at least once a day.").

[24]   Edwin P. Hollander, *Further Ethical Challenges in the Leader-Follower relationship* in ETHICS, THE HEART OF LEADERSHIP, 3RD EDITION 60 (ed. Joanne B. Ciulla 2014).

[25]   Samuel Osborne, *Donald Trump wins: All the lies, mistruths and scare stories he told during the US election campaign*, INDEPENDENT (Nov. 9, 2016).

dub "post-truth" the word of the year in 2016, after the Trump campaign took fact-free campaigning to new heights.[26] Though it's worth noting that President Trump isn't the only president to be notorious for lying. President Nixon (R) and President Clinton (D) were also noted fabulists. Whether it was Nixon's claim that "I'm not a crook" (narrator's voice: he was); or Bill Clinton's claim, "I did not have sexual relations with that woman, Ms. Lewinsky," (narrator's voice: he did),[27] presidents have been known to lie to the American public in significant ways about serious subjects. Or, jumping way back, during the election of 1800, Thomas Jefferson's side accused John Adams of being a hermaphrodite (narrator's voice: he wasn't), while John Adams' side accused Thomas Jefferson of being a Jacobin (narrator's voice: he wasn't).[28]

On the second day in the Trump presidency, Donald Trump claimed erroneously that the crowd at his inauguration was the biggest in history.[29] This was not true. That honor belonged to President Barack Obama's 2009 inaugural,[30] which makes sense as President Obama was the first African American president and Washington, D.C. is a majority Black city.[31] Even the U.S. Park Service put out pictures comparing President Obama's huge inaugural crowd to President Trump's comparatively paltry inaugural crowd.[32] But undaunted, Press Secretary Sean Spicer went to the podium in the White House briefing room and repeated the lie that the crowd at the Trump inauguration was the

---

[26] *Oxford Dictionaries Word of the Year 2016 is...*, OXFORD DICTIONARIES (Nov. 17, 2016), https://www.oxforddictionaries.com/press/news/2016/11/17/WOTY-16.

[27] MILLMAN, *supra* note 8, at 175–176 ("'We really can't know if something is true or not,' maxim of the deconstructionists, or Bill Clinton's infamous equivocation, 'That depends on what the meaning of "is" is.'").

[28] Kerwin Swint, *Adams vs. Jefferson: The Birth of Negative Campaigning in the U.S.*, MENTAL FLOSS (Sept. 9, 2012), http://mentalfloss.com/article/12487/adams-vs -jefferson-birth-negative-campaigning-us; C. James Taylor, *John Adams: Campaigns and Elections*, MILLER CENTER AT UVA (2018), https://millercenter.org/president/ adams/campaigns-and-elections.

[29] *President Trump Remarks at the Central Intelligence Agency*, C-SPAN (Jan. 21, 2017), www.c-span.org/video/?422418-1/president-trump-tells-cia-we-rid-isis&start= 1025.

[30] Joshua Gillin, *Inaugural crowd sizes ranked*, POLITIFACT (Jan. 20, 2017), https:// www.politifact.com/truth-o-meter/article/2017/jan/20/inaugural-crowd-sizes-ranked/ (Obama's 2009 crowd was estimated at 1.8 million people).

[31] *Washington D.C. Quick Facts*, U.S. CENSUS (2017), https://www.census.gov/ quickfacts/fact/table/dc/PST045217#PST045217.

[32] *Side-by-Side Images Show 2009 Inauguration Compared to 2017*, NBC NEWS (Jan. 20, 2017), https://www.nbcnews.com/card/side-side-images-show-2009 -inauguration-compared-2017-n709801;www.nbcnews.com/card/side-side-images -show-2009-inauguration-compared-2017-n709801; *see also* Jon Swaine, *Trump inauguration crowd photos were edited after he intervened*, GUARDIAN (Sept. 6, 2018).

biggest.[33] Now, perhaps one could argue that Spicer did this for an audience of one, the president himself. But Spicer also broadcast this lie to the world—and it sits on the White House's webpage to this day.[34] When a journalist asked Presidential Aide Kellyanne Conway about Spicer's lie, she said Spicer was only providing "alternative facts."[35] Again, that was just in week one, but the rebranding of the truth by the Trump White House had already begun.

President Trump has surrounded himself with individuals who will echo and amplify his misstatements of facts without correcting them. Sean Spicer was all too willing to spread falsehoods. His replacement, Press Secretary Sarah Huckabee Sanders, perpetually told the press corps the functional equivalent that the "sky is green." *Politifact* had Huckabee Sanders' rating as 75 percent "false" and 25 percent "pants on fire."[36] Editorialist Frank Bruni said of Sarah Huckabee Sanders' pressers: "For some 20 minutes every afternoon, down is up, paralysis is progress, enmity is harmony, stupid is smart, villain is victim, disgrace is honor, plutocracy is populism. . ."[37] The war over false narratives that were present in the Trump 2016 campaign continued seamlessly into the Trump presidency. "We have to fight over basic facts these days," *Washington Post* White House reporter Abby Phillip told the audience at the New Establishment Summit.[38] Ms. Phillip reported that the team of fact checkers at her paper are working overtime to just keep up with President Trump's statements, and what's remarkable is that now there is a "segment of the population that is not moved by politicians that deny things that they can see with their own eyes." The *Washington Post* fact checkers reported that in a single day, September 7, 2018, President Trump "publicly made 125 false or misleading statements—in a period of time that totaled only about 120 minutes. It was a new single-day high."[39] On June 10, 2019, the *Washington*

---

[33] *Statement by Press Secretary Sean Spicer*, WHITE HOUSE (Jan. 21, 2017), https://www.whitehouse.gov/briefings-statements/statement-press-secretary-sean-spicer/ ("This was the largest audience to ever witness an inauguration — period — both in person and around the globe.").

[34] *Id.*

[35] Reena Flores, *Kellyanne Conway draws fire after "alternative facts" defense*, CBS NEWS (Jan. 22, 2017), www.cbsnews.com/news/kellyanne-conway-draws-fire-after-alternative-facts-defense/.

[36] *Sarah Huckabee Sanders's file*, POLITIFACT, www.politifact.com/personalities/sarah-huckabee-sanders/.

[37] Frank Bruni, *Sarah Huckabee Sanders Makes the Heart Grow Fonder*, N.Y. TIMES (Nov. 3, 2017).

[38] *Breaking Through "Scandal Fatigue" In the Era of Trump*, VANITY FAIR (Oct. 4, 2017), https://video.vanityfair.com/watch/the-new-establishment-summit-breaking-through-scandal-fatigue-in-the-era-of-trump.

[39] Glenn Kessler, Salvador Rizzo & Meg Kelly, *President Trump has made more than 5,000 false or misleading claims*, WASH. POST (Sept. 13, 2018).

Post reported: "he has been averaging about 16 fishy claims a day. ...".[40] The *Washington Post* decided that President Trump merited an entirely new category for repeated lies which they dubbed the "Bottomless Pinocchio." As the paper explained:

> [t]he president keeps going long after the facts are clear, in what appears to be a deliberate effort to replace the truth with his own, far more favorable, version of it. He is not merely making gaffes or misstating things, he is purposely injecting false information into the national conversation. To accurately reflect this phenomenon, The *Washington Post* Fact Checker is introducing a new category —the Bottomless Pinocchio. That dubious distinction will be awarded to politicians who repeat a false claim so many times that they are, in effect, engaging in campaigns of disinformation.[41]

The paper has given the Bottomless Pinocchio to Trump for his false claims about the U.S. trade deficit, his tax cuts, the border wall, the U.S. economy, NATO, drug trafficking and the Mueller Special Counsel investigations, among many others.[42]

There have been so many lies during the Trump presidency that space limits the ability to list them. The *Washington Post* reports that "As of June 7, [2019] his 869th day in office, the president has made 10,796 false or misleading claims. ...".[43] This tally of lies goes up on a nearly daily basis. But here is a representative sample of some of the biggest whoppers from the mountebank-in-chief. One genre of Trump lies are lies about the state of the economy. This is one of the most puzzling things that he misrepresents, because during the first two years of his presidency, the economy by objective measures was doing reasonably well.[44] But by lying about the economy, he puts other statements about basic facts and mathematics in doubt. Often the president simply does not distinguish between opinion and fact—an indicia

---

[40] Glenn Kessler, Salvador Rizzo & Meg Kelly, *President Trump has made 10,796 false or misleading claims over 869 days*, WASH. POST (June 10, 2019); *see also* Glenn Kessler, *A year of unprecedented deception: Trump averaged 15 false claims a day in 2018*, WASH. POST (Dec. 30, 2018).

[41] Glenn Kessler, *Meet the Bottomless Pinocchio, a new rating for a false claim repeated over and over again*, WASH. POST (Dec. 10, 2018).

[42] Glenn Kessler & Joe Fox, *The false claims that Trump keeps repeating*, WASH. POST (Feb. 19, 2019).

[43] Glenn Kessler, *et al.*, *supra* note 40.

[44] Neil Irwin, *How Good Is the Trump Economy, Really? It depends on whether you look at the level, the direction or the rate of change — three concepts that are often conflated.*, N.Y. TIMES (June 9, 2018) ("The economy looks strongest if you look only at the level of economic activity. . .").

of truth decay.[45] For instance, "[a]lmost 50 times, Trump has claimed that the economy today is the 'greatest' in U.S. history, an absurd statement not backed up by data."[46] As the *Washington Post*'s chief fact checker, Glenn Kessler, further clarified:

> The president can certainly brag about the state of the economy, but he runs into trouble when he repeatedly makes a play for the history books. By just about any important measure, the economy today is not doing as well as it did under Presidents Dwight D. Eisenhower, Lyndon B. Johnson and Bill Clinton — and Ulysses S. Grant.[47]

Relatedly, President Trump lies about the unemployment rate as well: he has falsely claimed that "'[u]nemployment is at historic lows.'" But the *Washington Post* noted that this is "[f]alse. The unemployment rate, currently 3.9 percent, is low but it is not historic."[48]

President Trump also lies about his own standing in the world. When he claimed, "We're respected again as a nation[,]"[49] the fact checkers at the *Washington Post* responded thusly: "False. Polls by Gallup and the Pew Global Attitudes Project show worldwide views of the United States and its president have become more negative since Trump took office."[50] When addressing the U.N. General Assembly in 2018, other world leaders showed how little they respected him. President Trump bragged to the U.N. that his administration "has accomplished more than almost any administration in the history of our country." The response from the assembled group of dignitaries was to break into a gale of laughter. "So true," he said; and when he heard the laughter, he responded, "I didn't expect that reaction."[51]

While he has been under investigation, President Trump has lied about the Special Counsel's Office, the Justice Department and the FBI.[52] One of his classic moves is to call the investigation into Russia and his campaign a "witch

---

[45] Kavanagh & Rich, *supra* note 9 ("Truth Decay [includes] a blurring of the line between opinion and fact in a way that makes it difficult to distinguish between the two …").

[46] Kessler, *et al.*, *supra* note 40.

[47] Glenn Kessler, *Anatomy of a Trump rally: 70 percent of claims are false, misleading or lacking evidence*, WASH. POST (Sept. 12, 2018).

[48] *Id.*

[49] *Id.*

[50] *Id.*

[51] Deirdre Shesgreen & John Fritze, *Trump's boast at the United Nations prompts laughter from world leaders and ridicule on Twitter*, USA TODAY (Sept. 25, 2018).

[52] Natasha Bertrand, *The President Humiliates His Own Department of Justice*, ATLANTIC (Jan. 13, 2019); John Bowden, *McCabe: Trump's "relentless attack" on FBI prompted memoir*, HILL (Feb. 18, 2019).

hunt" or a "hoax."[53] For example, the *New York Times* reports that President Trump has attacked the Russia investigation over 1100 times in two years.[54] These attacks on investigators can do real damage. As the former head of the FBI, James Comey, testified to a House Committee in December of 2018:

> **Comey:** [There have been lies from] the President and his supporters about the nature and quality of the Department of Justice and the FBI. It's shortsighted and anybody who knows those organizations knows it's not true.
> **Nadler:** And what implications might there be under the Justice Department and the rule of law?
> **Comey:** Those kind of lies hurt the ability of the FBI to be believed at a doorway or in a courtroom. That makes all of us less safe. These are honest institutions made up of normal flawed human beings, but people committed to doing things the right way. When they're lied about constantly, it hurts the faith and confidence of the American people in them, and that is bad for all of us. I don't care what your political stripe is."[55]
> **Nadler:** And how does that impact our national security?
> **Comey:** Our national security turns upon the ability of an FBI agent to convince the girlfriend of a jihadi that we will protect her if she cooperates with us. If we're seen as a political group of one kind or another, an untrustworthy group, that trust is eroded and the agent loses the ability to make that case. If a jury doesn't believe an FBI agent when he or she says, "I found this" or "I heard this "in the course of this case, we're less safe because the case can't be made.[56]
> … [W]hen people veer from truth-seeking into trying to find any excuse to bad-mouth an organization that's investigating the President, we've lost our way.[57]

While the *Washington Post* has been keeping track of these false and misleading statements from President Trump, the paper's fact checkers have been very reluctant to call particular statements from him actual "lies." The *New York Times* had already crossed that Rubicon during the 2016 election. After struggling for months about what to do with candidate Trump's repeated deceptions, in September of 2016, it stopped pretending and called out a series of lies as lies.[58]

---

[53]   David Jackson, *As Robert Mueller's Russia probe accelerates, Trump adds to attacks on special counsel*, USA TODAY (Nov. 29, 2018).

[54]   Larry Buchanan & Karen Yourish, *Trump Has Publicly Attacked the Russia Investigation More Than 1,100 Times*, N.Y. TIMES (Feb. 19, 2019).

[55]   James Comey, *Testimony to House Committee on the Judiciary, Joint with the Committee on Government Reform and Oversight* 68 (Dec. 7, 2018).

[56]   *Id.*

[57]   *Id.* at 69.

[58]   Steve LeVine, New York Times *editor on Trump: "We will call out lies,"* QUARTZ (Sept. 20, 2016), https://qz.com/784533/new-york-times-editor-dean-baquet -on-donald-trump-we-will-call-out-lies/ ("'Dean Baquet, the *New York Times*' exec-

One rare exception to the *Washington Post*'s calling a Trump lie a lie came in mid-2018, when President Trump's former lawyer named Michael Cohen pleaded guilty to campaign finance violations in the 2016 presidential election. The backstory of what he was admitting to involved facilitating payments to a porn star with the stage name Stormy Daniels to remain silent during the 2016 election about an affair she allegedly had with Donald Trump years before. Because the payment was to help a federal candidate during a federal election, and because the candidate allegedly directed the payment, it was considered an "in-kind" campaign donation to the Trump campaign. One legal problem about this payment of $130 000 to Stormy Daniels for her silence was that it was too big. The contribution limit at the time was $2700. Another violation of campaign finance law was that the payment wasn't reported properly.[59] Once all of this came to light when Cohen pleaded guilty of violating campaign finance laws in open court in August of 2018, the *Washington Post* put out a rare article calling Trump's denials around the Stormy Daniels payments a bold-faced "lie."[60] As Glenn Kessler wrote: "What we know now: Every answer was false. Trump knew about the payment, he knew Cohen made the payment as part of an effort to kill damaging stories, and he knew Cohen was reimbursed."[61] This confession by Cohen also implicates the possible guilt of the president, who many deem to be an unindicted co-conspirator to Cohen's campaign finance crimes.[62]

Incidentally, Michael Cohen's sentencing memorandum filed by the Southern District of New York on December 7, 2018 explained how Cohen first became Trump's attorney. Cohen lived in a condominium in a Trump-branded building. The condo board was going to rename the building or at least drop the Trump name. Cohen intervened to stop the rebranding of the building. Trump was so appreciative of Cohen's help in this matter that he hired Cohen to work for the Trump Organization as an executive vice president and special counsel.[63] Cohen worked for Trump for a dozen years, right up to the year he

---

utive editor [said] 'But we have decided to be more direct in calling things out when a candidate actually lies.'").

[59]   Ciara Torres-Spelliscy, *Why the U.S. Has the Campaign Finance Laws That Michael Cohen Broke and What Their History Means for Trump*, TIME (Aug. 23, 2018), http://time.com/5376715/campaign-finance-laws-trump/.

[60]   Glenn Kessler, *Not just misleading. Not merely false. A lie*, WASH. POST (Aug. 22, 2018).

[61]   *Id.*

[62]   *Cohen Plea Deal Makes Trump 'Unindicted Co-Conspirator,' Watergate Prosecutor Says*, WBUR (Aug. 22, 2018), www.wbur.org/hereandnow/2018/08/22/cohen-plea-deal-trump-watergate-prosecutor (quoting Nick Akerman).

[63]   USA v. Cohen, 18 C.R. 602 (Government's sentencing memo) at 3 (Dec. 7, 2018), www.documentcloud.org/documents/5453404-USDOJ-Cohen-20181207.html #document/p3.

pleaded guilty. Without Trump's love of his own brand, Cohen would not have been his lawyer.

As the *Washington Post* continues to fact check President Trump, "Trumpian" is becoming a synonym for lying. For instance, the paper used the new word in a sentence: "Trump's tsunami of untruths helped push the count in The Fact Checker's database past 5,000 on the 601st day of his presidency. That's an average of 8.3 *Trumpian* claims a day. . ."[64] And the average only went up the following year to 15 Trumpian lies per day.[65]

It's not just the *Washington Post* that fact checks Trump. This has become standard practice for all sorts of sources—from the Art Institute of Chicago, which notes that a Renoir painting President Trump claims is the genuine article is a really a fake;[66] to *Golf Magazine*, which questions whether he has won any of the golf tournaments he has claimed to win;[67] to Gold Star families, which have had a service member die who were never contacted by the president, when he claimed he had contacted them all.[68]

In the fall of 2018, the *New York Times* caught President Trump in a particularly juicy lie about himself.[69] For decades, Trump had claimed to journalists and in his autographical books that he was a "self-made" man.[70] He claimed that he had received a single $1 million loan from his father, which he repaid and then parlayed into a billion-dollar enterprise.[71] The *New York Times* exposé showed that Trump's father Fred had given his son closer to $60 million and had repeatedly bailed him out when the younger Trump ran a business into the

---

[64] Kessler, *et al.*, *supra* note 40.

[65] Kessler, *supra* note 41.

[66] Lia Eustachewich, *Trump's 'Renoir' painting is a fake: museum*, N.Y. Post (Oct. 20, 2017).

[67] *'He hit the ball on the screws': Sen. Graham details President Trump's improbable 73*, Golf Magazine (Oct. 11, 2017).

[68] Ken Meyer, *CNN Airs Gut-Wrenching Interview with Gold Star Family Who Never Heard from Trump*, Mediaite (Oct. 19, 2017), www.mediaite.com/tv/cnn-airs -gut-wrenching-interview-with-gold-star-family-who-never-received-call-from-trump/

[69] David Barstow, Susanne Craig & Russ Buettner, *Trump Engaged in Suspect Tax Schemes as He Reaped Riches From His Father*, N.Y. Times (Oct. 2, 2018) ("What emerges from this body of evidence is a financial biography of the 45th president fundamentally at odds with the story Mr. Trump has sold in his books, his TV shows and his political life.").

[70] Clotaire Rapaille, The Culture Code: An Ingenious Way to Understand Why People Around the World Live and Buy as They Do 121–22 (2007) ("There is very little 'old money' in America.").

[71] Becca Stanek, *Trump's infamous $1 million loan from his father was apparently just the first of many*, Week (Sept. 23, 2016), https://theweek.com/speedreads/809172/ massive-climate-study-shows-pretty-much-everything-trump-saying-about-climate -change-wrong.

red. In a particularly odd bailout, Fred Trump apparently rescued one of his son's casinos, called the Trump Castle, from ruin by buying $3.35 million in casino chips and then never cashing them back in at the casino.[72] As the authors said:

> The president has long sold himself as a self-made billionaire, but a *Times* investigation found that he received at least $413 million in today's dollars from his father's real estate empire, much of it through tax dodges in the 1990s.[73]

When asked about the myth of President Trump being a "self-made" man, Susanne Craig (one of the authors of the *New York Times* investigation) said flatly, "it's a lie."[74] And notably, it's a lie that he has told most of his adult life, including during his run for president. Ms. Craig told Terry Gross of *NPR*:

> It's interesting ... the lie repeated over and over and passed down into history becomes fact. And I think that we've reset that. I think it's going to take time for this to move into the bloodstream of America. ... [W]e've taken ... a good first stop in resetting exactly the origins of Donald Trump's wealth.[75]

Branding the truth is par for the course for big businesses, many of which spend huge budgets on public relations trying to craft public opinion, so that there are positive views of a particular product, corporation or industry.[76] But when the P.R. tricks are deployed by the Oval Office, what just looked like a little spin from a corporate source looks far more like pernicious propaganda. And it's malignant because it is potentially corrosive to the democratic process

---

[72]   *New York Times publishes investigation. TRANSCRIPT: 10/2/2018, The Rachel Maddow Show*, MSNBC (Oct. 3, 2018), www.msnbc.com/transcripts/rachel-maddow-show/2018-10-03 ("Howard Snyder, walked into Trump's casino in Atlantic City. He went up to the cage where all the cashiers work on the casino floor and he handed them a check for $3.35 million. The cashiers verified that the check was good, and the casino promptly handed over to Howard Snyder a big pile of poker chips. Here you go. Each worth $5,000, $3.3 million worth of poker chips. Howard Snyder took those poker chips, put them in a bag and left.").

[73]   Barstow, *et al.*, *supra* note 69.

[74]   *"I Started With A Million Dollar Loan." Taking Apart Trump's Taxes*, 1A at minutes 6–7 (Oct. 25, 2018), www.npr.org/2018/10/25/660642593/-i-started-with-a-million-dollar-loan-taking-apart-trumps-taxes (quoting Suzanne Craig).

[75]   NPR, *'Times' Journalists Puncture Myth of Trump as Self-Made Billionaire*, FRESH AIR (Oct. 18, 2018), Heard on www.npr.org/2018/10/18/658442355/times-journalists-puncture-myth-of-trump-as-self-made-billionaire (quoting Suzanne Craig).

[76]   V.O. KEY, JR., POLITICS, PARTIES, & PRESSURE GROUPS 93 (1964 5th ed.) ("a widespread attitude among business leaders [was] ... the public be damned. In some formulations they advocated almost a doctrine of divine right.").

itself.[77] As former Federal Bureau of Investigation (FBI) Agent Clint Watts, who worked on cybersecurity, told a magazine recently: "You're seeing some withdrawal from information sources altogether because people don't know what to believe. I worry about that. They've suffered information annihilation, and they're tired. This is what happens in Russia. It leads to political apathy."[78]

3.   THE SUPREME COURT WON'T SAVE US FROM LIARS

What President Trump counts on when he is rebranding the truth to include myth, lies and conspiracy theories is that "the public is enormously gullible at times."[79] Perhaps because of this gullibility, journalist Walter Lippmann argued that freedom of speech should not cover mendacity. As Lippmann wrote in *The Public Philosophy*:

If there is a dividing line between liberty and license, it is where freedom of speech is no longer respected as a procedure of the truth and becomes the unrestricted right to exploit the ignorance, and to incite the passions, of the people. Then freedom is such a hullabaloo of sophistry, propaganda, special pleading, lobbying, and salesmanship that it is difficult to remember why freedom of speech is worth the pain and trouble of defending it. ... It is sophistry to pretend that in a free country a man has some sort inalienable right to deceive his fellow men. There is no more right to deceive than there is a right to swindle, to cheat, or to pick pockets.[80]

But the current Supreme Court (headed by Chief Justice Roberts) has adamantly disagreed with Lippmann's framing of this issue. Much to the chagrin of many a litigant seeking truth, the Supreme Court has protected the right to lie in many circumstances, including in elections. As was previewed in the introduction to this book, facts matter surprisingly little in elections—in part because many voters are voting for emotional, instinctual reasons.[81]

---

[77]   Kavanagh & Rich, *supra* note 9 ("Facts and data have become more important in most other fields, with political and civil discourse being striking exceptions").

[78]   Denise Clifton, *Russia's Campaign to Help Trump Win Was Just the Start And the next attack on US elections, warns former FBI agent Clint Watts, could come from within*, MOTHER JONES (May 23, 2018).

[79]   PACKARD, *supra* note 2, at 216 (quoting *The Public Relations Journal*).

[80]   SPERO, *supra* note 20, at 1 (quoting Walter Lippmann's *The Public Philosophy*).

[81]   DREW WESTEN, THE POLITICAL BRAIN: THE ROLE OF EMOTION IN DECIDING THE FATE OF THE NATION ix (2007) ("the vision of mind that has captured the imagination of philosophers, cognitive scientists, economists, and political scientists since the eighteenth century—a dispassionate mind that makes decision by weighing the evidence and reasoning to the most valid conclusions—bears no relation to how the mind and brain actually work.").

So, isn't lying illegal? Lying is illegal in certain confined circumstances. When an individual is under oath, it is illegal to lie. It is also illegal to lie to federal law enforcement, like the FBI, or to lie in documents that are being filed with the federal government under 18 U.S.C. 1001. Lying about private persons, if the lie is outrageous enough to damage their reputation, can be slander. If the lie about the private person is in writing, that is potentially libel.[82] But when the target of the lie is a public figure, a whole different line of legal precedent applies.[83] Good luck trying to prove that a particular published article about a public figure was committed with the requisite malice to be libelous under controlling U.S. Supreme Court First Amendment doctrine.[84]

Under the law of libel, an injured private citizen can sue for money damages in tort against a person who has spread injurious lies about him or her. *Gertz v. Robert Welch, Inc.* explains, in part, why America has libel laws:

> The legitimate state interest underlying the law of libel is the compensation of individuals for the harm inflicted on them by defamatory falsehood. ... [T]he individual's right to the protection of his own good name 'reflects no more than our basic concept of the essential dignity and worth of every human being.'"[85]

The law of libel provides public figures with fewer protections against personally damaging lies. *Gertz* noted the difference between the rights of private and public figures:

> The communications media are entitled to act on the assumption that public officials and public figures have voluntarily exposed themselves to increased risk of injury from defamatory falsehood concerning them. No such assumption is justified with respect to a private individual. ... He has relinquished no part of his interest in the protection of his own good name, and consequently he has a more compelling call on the courts for redress of injury inflicted by defamatory falsehood. Thus, private

---

[82] New York Times Co. v. Sullivan, 376 U.S. 254, 269 (1964) ("libel can claim no talismanic immunity from constitutional limitations. It must be measured by standards that satisfy the First Amendment.").

[83] *Id.* at 279 ("A rule compelling the critic of official conduct to guarantee the truth of all his factual assertions—and to do so on pain of libel judgments virtually unlimited in amount—leads to a comparable 'self-censorship.' Allowance of the defense of truth, with the burden of proving it on the defendant, does not mean that only false speech will be deterred.").

[84] *Id.* at 279–80 ("The constitutional guarantees require, we think, a federal rule that prohibits a public official from recovering damages for a defamatory falsehood relating to his official conduct unless he proves that the statement was made with 'actual malice'—that is, with knowledge that it was false or with reckless disregard of whether it was false or not.").

[85] Gertz v. Robert Welch, Inc., 418 U.S. 323, 341 (1974).

individuals are not only more vulnerable to injury than public officials and public figures; they are also more deserving of recovery.[86]

For public figures, recovering for libel is nearly impossible unless they can meet the high hurdle of proving actual malice on the part of the person spreading slanderous lies under *New York Times v. Sullivan.* Yet the law of libel can leave some reputations forever in tatters. As Justice Stewart noted, "[t]he destruction that defamatory falsehood can bring is … often beyond the capacity of the law to redeem."[87]

Indeed, the Supreme Court gives Americans wide latitude to lie even when the topic is something serious, like military service. The Supreme Court, in a 2012 case called *U.S. v. Alvarez*, allowed a man to pretend he was a decorated veteran. As Justice Kennedy wrote for the Supreme Court in his *Alvarez* opinion:

> Lying was his habit. Xavier Alvarez … lied when he said that he played hockey for the Detroit Red Wings and that he once married a starlet from Mexico. But when he lied in announcing he held the Congressional Medal of Honor, respondent ventured onto new ground; for that lie violates a federal criminal statute, the Stolen Valor Act of 2005.[88]

The Stolen Valor Act was meant to protect the integrity of the award of military honors.[89] Because someone who is perceived to be a war hero may be lauded with praise, jobs and money, the law is intended to allow only individuals who have actually earned those military honors to claim those plaudits. Thus, the Stolen Valor Act makes lying about getting military honors a crime—or it at least it did until the Supreme Court stepped in.

The Supreme Court considered the Stolen Valor Act to be a content-based restriction on free speech. This type of law is nearly universally held by the federal courts to violate the First Amendment.[90] As the Court explained in *Alvarez*:

> The Government contends the criminal prohibition is a proper means to further its purpose in creating and awarding the Medal [of Honor]. When content-based speech

---

[86]   *Id.* at 345.
[87]   Rosenblatt v. Baer, 383 U.S. 75, 92 (1966) (Stewart, J., concurring).
[88]   U.S. v. Alvarez, 567 U.S. 709, 713 (2012).
[89]   18 U.S.C. §704.
[90]   Rosenberger v. Rector and Visitors of Univ. of Va., 515 U.S. 819, 828–29 (1995):
Discrimination against speech because of its message is presumed to be unconstitu-tional. … When the government targets not subject matter, but particular views taken by speakers on a subject, the violation of the First Amendment is all the more blatant.

regulation is in question, however, exacting scrutiny is required. Statutes suppressing or restricting speech must be judged by the sometimes inconvenient principles of the First Amendment.[91]

Content-based restrictions typically fall on hostile ears at the Supreme Court, as they did in *Alvarez*. As the Court wrote:

> as a general matter, the First Amendment means that government has no power to restrict expression because of its message, its ideas, its subject matter, or its content.' As a result, the Constitution 'demands that content-based restrictions on speech be presumed invalid.'[92]

The rare exceptions of content-based laws that have been upheld typically involve public safety. As the Supreme Court explained:

> content-based restrictions on speech have been permitted, as a general matter, only when confined to the few "'historic and traditional categories [of expression] long familiar to the bar'". Among these categories are advocacy intended, and likely, to incite imminent lawless action; obscenity; defamation; speech integral to criminal conduct; so-called 'fighting words'; child pornography; fraud; true threats; and speech presenting some grave and imminent threat the government has the power to prevent, although a restriction under the last category is most difficult to sustain.[93]

These categories in *Alvarez* track the "low value speech" categories from *Chaplinsky*.[94] Embracing a classic slippery slope argument, the Supreme Court posited in *Alvarez* that if Congress were allowed to criminalize lying about the receipt of the Congressional Medal of Honor, "there could be an endless list of subjects the National Government or the State could single out."[95]

Viewpoint discrimination is thus an egregious form of content discrimination. The government must abstain from regulating speech when the specific motivating ideology or the opinion or perspective of the speaker is the rationale for the restriction.

[91] U.S. v. Alvarez, 567 U.S. 709, 715 (2012).

[92] *Id.* at 715–17(quoting Ashcroft v. American Civil Liberties Union, 535 U.S. 564, 573 (2002)).

[93] *Id.* at 717.

[94] Chaplinsky v. New Hampshire, 315 U.S. 568, 572 (1942) ("These include the lewd and obscene, the profane, the libelous, and the insulting or 'fighting' words -- those which, by their very utterance, inflict injury or tend to incite an immediate breach of the peace. It has been well observed that such utterances are no essential part of any exposition of ideas, and are of such slight social value as a step to truth that any benefit that may be derived from them is clearly outweighed by the social interest in order and morality.").

[95] United States v. Alvarez, 567 U.S. 709, 723 (2012).

Sounding much like Walter Lippmann (above), the lawyers for the government defending the Stolen Valor Act argued that lies should not enjoy First Amendment protections. But the Justices rebuffed this argument: "The Court has never endorsed the categorical rule the Government advances: that false statements receive no First Amendment protection."[96] The Supreme Court found the Stolen Valor statute to be different than others it had previously reviewed, noting: "Our prior decisions have not confronted a measure, like the Stolen Valor Act, that targets falsity and nothing more."[97] And the Court explained: "Even when considering some instances of defamation and fraud, moreover, the Court has been careful to instruct that falsity alone may not suffice to bring the speech outside the First Amendment."[98] The Supreme Court has long held onto the myth that in a market place of ideas, good ideas and true ideas will win out over bad ideas and lies. Referencing George Orwell, the Supreme Court stated: "Our constitutional tradition stands against the idea that we need Oceania's Ministry of Truth."[99] According to the Supreme Court in *Alvarez*, "The only solution to speech that is false is speech that is true[,]"[100] rather than laws against lying.

One of the areas that the Supreme Court acknowledged in *Alvarez* could still be policed for truthfulness was perjury in the courts. But this criminalization of perjury was distinguished from the Stolen Valor Act by the Court as it concluded: "It is not simply because perjured statements are false that they lack First Amendment protection. Perjured testimony 'is at war with justice' because it can cause a court to render a 'judgment not resting on truth.'"[101] *Alvarez* does fit into a long tradition of protecting unpopular speech. As the Supreme Court once explained in the seminal First Amendment case, *New York Times v. Sullivan:* "we consider this case against the background of a profound national commitment to the principle that debate on public issues should be uninhibited, robust, and wide-open. . ."[102]

As the Court in *Alvarez* assumed in a free society, inevitably there will be deceits: "This comports with the common understanding that some false statements are inevitable if there is to be an open and vigorous expression of views in public and private conversation, expression the First Amendment seeks to guarantee."[103] In the end, the Supreme Court ruled that the Stolen

---

[96] *Id.* at 719
[97] *Id.*
[98] *Id.*
[99] *Id.* at 723.
[100] *Id.* at 727.
[101] *Id.* at 720 (internal citations omitted).
[102] New York Times Co. v. Sullivan, 376 U.S. 254, 270 (1964).
[103] United States v. Alvarez, 567 U.S. 709, 718 (2012).

Valor Act violated the First Amendment, thereby siding with the liar Alvarez. As the Court said, it "rejects the notion that false speech should be in a general category that is presumptively unprotected [by the First Amendment]."[104] This result in *Alvarez* is not far off from where the Court ended up in *New York Times v. Sullivan*, which held that "erroneous statement is inevitable in free debate, and that it must be protected if the freedoms of expression are to have the 'breathing space' that they 'need ... to survive ....'"[105]

The Supreme Court has also been tolerant of lying in political campaigns. In 2014, in *Susan B. Anthony List v. Driehaus*, the Supreme Court unanimously allowed a case to go forward which challenged the constitutionality of an Ohio law which made certain false statements illegal in a political campaign. Violation of the Ohio false statement statute was a first-degree misdemeanor. A second conviction under the false statement statute was a fourth-degree felony that carried a mandatory penalty of disfranchisement.

The false statement at issue in the case involved a claim by a political non-profit called the Susan B. Anthony List that candidate Steven Driehaus had voted "to fund abortions with tax dollars" by voting for the Affordable Care Act (ACA). This is patently false, as the ACA specifically restricts the use of federal funds for abortion. Nonetheless—truth be damned—the high court remanded the case so that it could continue.[106] A district court went on to rule in *Susan B. Anthony List v. Ohio Elec. Comm'n* that the Ohio prohibition on lying in political campaigns was unconstitutional because it left the government in the position of deciding what was true or false.[107] On appeal to the Sixth Circuit, citing the *Alvarez* case discussed above, the appellate court agreed the law against lying in Ohio elections should be permanently enjoined.[108] And the

---

[104] *Id.* at 722.

[105] New York Times Co., 376 U.S. at 271–72.

[106] Susan B. Anthony List v. Driehaus, 134 S. Ct. 2334, 2345 (2014) ("And, there is every reason to think that similar speech in the future will result in similar proceedings, notwithstanding SBA's belief in the truth of its allegations."); *see also* Richard L. Hasen, *A Constitutional Right To Lie In Campaigns and Elections?*, 74 Mon. L. Rev. 53 (2013).

[107] Susan B. Anthony List v. Ohio Elections Comm'n, 45 F.Supp.3d 765, 781 (S.D. Ohio 2014).

[108] Susan B. Anthony List v. Driehaus, 814 F.3d 466, 469 (6th Cir. 2016) ("Because the laws are content-based restrictions that burden core protected political speech and are not narrowly tailored to achieve the state's interest in promoting fair elections, we affirm.").

Sixth Circuit noted that other false-statement laws have also been invalidated by courts around the nation:

> Other courts [that have] evaluate[d] similar laws post-*Alvarez* have reached the same conclusion. *See 281 Care Comm. v. Arneson*, 766 F.3d 774, 785 (8th Cir. 2014) ("[N]o amount of narrow tailoring succeeds because [Minnesota's political false-statements law] is not necessary, is simultaneously overbroad and underinclusive, and is not the least restrictive means of achieving any stated goal."), *cert. denied*, —— U.S. ——, 135 S.Ct. 1550, 191 L.Ed.2d 637 (2015); *Commonwealth v. Lucas*, 472 Mass. 387, 34 N.E.3d 1242, 1257 (2015) (striking down Massachusetts' law, which was similar to Ohio's); *see also Rickert v. State Pub. Disclosure Comm'n*, 161 Wash.2d 843, 168 P.3d 826, 829–31 (2007) (striking down Washington's political false-statements law, which required proof of actual malice, but not defamatory nature) ... [109]

Who knows whether the Supreme Court's (and other federal courts') tolerance for lying in politics contributed to the cynicism of many voters who feel politics is a dirty business.[110]

4.   CONCLUSION

It is clear that the Supreme Court won't act as the platonic guardians of truth. Rather, vouchsafing truth is left to the American people. Political scientist Kathleen Hall Jamieson still holds high hopes for American democracy, as she aspires for the nation:

> The size of the United States, the heterogeneity of its population, and the complexity of its role in the international community mean that the kind of deliberative discourse envisioned by Aristotle is beyond our reach. Any whisper of Aristotle or Athens invites the charge of polis envy. But that does not mean we can't aspire to an Athenian ideal characterized by argument and engagement. Just as there are tendencies in candidate speeches, ads and debates that we ought to deplore, there are certain characteristics we ought to consider indispensable to effective democratic discourse. At the core of this model is a belief that democratic deliberation must be practiced if use of it is to become habitual.[111]

Returning to where this chapter started, the problem right now is that the nation is experiencing truth decay. In a democracy, the lack of agreed upon

---

[109] *Id.* at 476.

[110] Denis Muller, *When truth is the first casualty of politics and journalism*, Conversation (Oct. 18, 2016), http://theconversation.com/when-truth-is-the-first-casualty-of-politics-and-journalism-66490.

[111] Kathleen Hall Jamieson, Everything You Think You Know about Politics ... And Why You're Wrong 55 (2000).

truth means that an argument can never be won between partisans. Neither side can be convinced because the argument wasn't about facts in the first place. But recall that truth has taken a beating before and then subsequently returned to central place in policy making and in discourse after the Gilded Age, the Roaring 20s and the 1960s–70s. What restored truth to its rightful place after these three periods? According to Rand's *Truth Decay* report:

> In each previous case, a revival of fact-based and investigative journalism helped reduce the blurring of the line between opinion and fact and championed the primacy of facts over disinformation and opinion. In more than one case, changes in government policy to increase accountability and transparency helped restore trust in government as an information provider, again raising the profile of and emphasis on objective facts.[112]

Americans can restore truth to its rightful place through similar means this time, too. Though Americans need to realize that misinformation could come from abroad given modern communications technology. And unfortunately, truth must contend with lies that are circulated en masse in rapid succession. As Jonathan Swift wrote in 1710, "falsehood flies, and the truth comes limping after it."[113] This was particularly the case in the 2016 American election, when the Russian government unleashed a social media disruption campaign rife with fabrications and falsehoods that were distributed through a network of trust: social media. How does a medium that was used to distribute funny pet videos become a weapon? As reported to the Senate Intelligence Committee:

> Most of the time, social media are not used for politics: they are a place where friends and families connect and reconnect, or where individuals find and share entertainment, popular culture, as well as humorous cat videos. The ubiquity and prominence of social media for everyday life underscores their importance in today's society, and users place high amounts of trust in these platforms.[114]

These potentially benign platforms were weaponized in the 2016 election by the Russian Internet Research Agency, which functioned:

> like a digital marketing agency: develop a brand (both visual and voice), build presences on all channels across the entire social ecosystem, and grow an audience with paid ads as well as partnerships, influencers, and link-sharing. They created media

---

[112] Kavanagh & Rich, *supra* note 9.
[113] Jonathan Swift, *The Examiner* (1710).
[114] Philip N. Howard, *et al.*, *The IRA, Social Media and Political Polarization in the United States, 2012–2018* 39 (2018).

mirages: interlinked information ecosystems designed to immerse and surround targeted audiences.[115]

For more on what the Russians did in the 2016 election, see the chapters "Branding treason" and "Branding racism."

---

[115] Renee DiResta, *et al.*, *The Tactics & Tropes of the Internet Research Agency* 41 (2018).

2.   Branding corruption[1]

"The corruption of the best things gives rise to the worst." David Hume [2]

1.   INTRODUCTION

As this book explores, the process of branding is a skill that involves changing the connotations of words. Thus, branding can reshape nearly any idea, no matter how empirically absurd it might seem at first. Consider Apple™. In 1970, if you heard the sentence, "An apple is a computer," you probably would have thought the speaker was mad. But the continual marketing by Apple Computers has made the sentence, "An Apple is a computer" true. Through brute repetition, nearly any concept can seem plausible if the audience hears it enough times, especially from a source that seems credible or powerful.

One of those powerful sources of branding is the American court system. In law, metaphors abound, and frequently cases are won or lost based on the way the judge conceives of the case, and not necessarily what the facts of the case are.[3] All American courts are bound to respect what the Supreme Court pronounces in matters of Constitutional interpretation. And whether the Justices think of themselves as "branding" the meaning of words, they do it every day that they write a judicial opinion. They are continually branding and rebranding, defining and redefining the meaning of words, whether those words are in regulations, statutes, the Constitution or previous legal opinions.

A prime example of the Supreme Court branding a concept is what the Roberts Supreme Court has done to the meaning of the word "corruption." Before it got its hands on this word, "corruption" had a very broad meaning. But between 2006–19, the Roberts Court branded "corruption" to be a very thin reed of a word. And the more narrowly the Supreme Court defines this

---

[1]   A version of this chapter was first published in Ciara Torres-Spelliscy, *Deregulating Corruption*, 13(2) HARVARD LAW & POLICY REV. 471 (2019).

[2]   DAVID HUME, THE NATURAL HISTORY OF RELIGION 42 (1757).

[3]   DREW WESTEN, THE POLITICAL BRAIN: THE ROLE OF EMOTION IN DECIDING THE FATE OF THE NATION 99 (2007) ("in *Bush v. Gore*, the political and legal decision makers precisely mirrored the general electorate, whose judgments could be predicted with over 80 percent accuracy from their prior emotional prejudices and predispositions, irrespective of the facts.").

word, the more narrowly it will be interpreted by every court in the land, all of which are bound to follow the high court's lead.

The basic branding that the Supreme Court has repeated is: "political corruption only means *quid pro quo* exchanges." This claim has some appeal. It is simplistic and easy to understand. But it also fences out broader ideas of what comprises a corrupt political system.[4] It misses the winks and nods between those politicians in power and those with the financial resources to keep politicians in power through campaign spending. It ignores systemic problems. It deletes data that demonstrates that rich donors get their policy ideas and world views heard by elected officials more than the ignored average citizen.[5] It devalues history, economics and political science. It leaves lawyers arguing about political equality tongue tied because the only acceptable truth to the majority of the Supreme Court is: "political corruption only means *quid pro quo* exchanges."

In a spate of recent decisions, the Supreme Court has constricted the definition of corruption in both campaign finance and criminal cases. The combined impact of these decisions is evident in the difficulty prosecutors have had bringing dishonest politicians to justice. In several high-profile cases, prosecutors had to try a particular politician twice or resentence a politician because of the Supreme Court's increasingly narrow conception of corruption.

In this chapter, "campaign finance reform" refers to the constellation of laws that address money in politics through the following modalities: disclosure of where money in politics came from and where it was spent; contribution limits; source bans (e.g., bans on corporations, unions and foreigners); and public financing. And "criminal anti-corruption laws" refers to honest services fraud and bribery.[6] There are, of course, other criminal anti-corruption laws on the books; they simply will not be discussed here.

Here is how this chapter will proceed. First, this chapter will explore how average Americans conceptualize corruption. Then this chapter will explain the decisions in which the Supreme Court has rebranded the definition of corruption in campaign finance cases and two key criminal cases. This chapter includes a discussion of dissenting opinions, because often dissents are more

---

[4]   V.O. KEY, JR., POLITICS, PARTIES, & PRESSURE GROUPS 363 (1964 5th ed.) ("The common American belief seems to be that politicians are engaged in a dirty business.").

[5]   Ciara Torres-Spelliscy, *Time Suck: How the Fundraising Treadmill Diminishes Effective Governance*, 42 SETON HALL LEGIS. J. 271, 300–01 (2018) ("Martin Gilens argues, based on his empirical studies, '[t]he American government does respond to the public's preferences, but that responsiveness is strongly tilted toward the most affluent citizens.'").

[6]   KEY, *supra* note 4, at 15 ("bribery can occur only in those relations in which private individuals seek to influence the holders of formal authority.").

explicit about the damage the majority engendered. Finally, this chapter will show how this is having a real-world impact on criminal prosecutions of actual corruption.

2.   HOW AVERAGE VOTERS VIEW CORRUPTION

Before delving into how the Supreme Court is smashing the concept of corruption into a fine powder, here is a brief canvass how average citizens view corruption. The United States doesn't ask the entire populace on the U.S. Census what they think of corruption. Instead, what the average American thinks about the corruption is revealed by samples of Americans captured in polls and focus groups.

Polling shows the average American citizen is not in sync with the conservative majority on the Supreme Court on the meaning of political corruption. In the period covered by this chapter from 2006–19, polling revealed deep worries about corruption are top of mind for many citizens. A survey by Gallup found, in response to the question, "Is corruption widespread in the government in this country or not?", 75 percent responded "yes."[7] In a Chapman University survey of American fears, the top fear was revealed as corrupt government officials.[8] A 2018 survey found, "[i]n an open-ended question that asked voters to describe Congress, 'corrupt' is the defining word."[9]

Polls about corruption are often worded differently. In some polls the question is about political dysfunction. For example, the Harvard Kennedy School conducted a poll of young voters in 2018 and asked them to rank responsibility for existing problems in American politics; respondents ranked money in politics as 68 percent responsible.[10] According to Pew:

> Americans of different political persuasions may not agree on much, but one thing they do agree on is that money has a greater – and mostly negative – influence

---

[7]   *75% in U.S. See Widespread Government Corruption*, GALLUP (Sept. 19, 2015), https://news.gallup.com/poll/185759/widespread-government-corruption.aspx.

[8]   *America's Top Fears 2017 Chapman University Survey of American Fears*, WILKINSON COLLEGE (Oct. 11, 2017) ("[Fear of] Corrupt Government Officials [was] 74.5[%.]"), https://blogs.chapman.edu/wilkinson/2017/10/11/americas-top-fears-2017/

[9]   *What Americans Think About Corruption in Congress and the Battle for the Court: Americans Concerned By Influence of Special Interests*, NAVIGATOR RESEARCH (Sept. 18, 2018), https://navigatorresearch.org/what-americans-think-about-corruption-in-congress-and-the-battle-for-the-court/.

[10]   *Survey of Young Americans' Attitudes toward Politics and Public Service 35th Edition*, INSTITUTE OF POLITICS (Mar. 8–25, 2018), http://iop.harvard.edu/sites/default/files/content/Release%202%20Toplines.pdf.

on politics than ever before. Among liberals and conservatives, Republicans and Democrats, large majorities favor limits on campaign spending and say the high cost of campaigning discourages many good candidates from running for president.[11]

A *Washington Post* poll found 60 percent of respondents thought that money in politics was a source of political dysfunction.[12] Additionally, in 2015, a *New York Times*/CBS poll found 84 percent of respondents thought that there was too much money in politics.[13]

Election advocates have worried that the public's justified concerns about the role of money in politics could exacerbate political apathy. One way to measure voter apathy is lackluster voter turnout. According to Pew, the United States has some of the lowest voter turn-out among Western democracies.[14] One commentator even saw political apathy as contagious—the more American voters express their dismay with politics, the more others around them lose faith in the political process as well.[15]

Focus group studies by political scientists also offer a glimpse into the mindset of the American voter. Christopher Robertson, D. Alex Winkelman, Kelly Bergstrand and Darren Modzelewski conducted an experiment where they asked 45 people sitting in a mock grand jury whether they would indict using fact scenarios that were not illegal. The fact scenario was: "a regulated industry sought from a Congressman a deregulatory rider on a major piece of legislation, and the Congressman sought support for his reelection."[16] In the experiment, 73 percent of the mock grand jury were willing to indict. This

---

[11] Drew DeSilver & Patrick van Kessel, *As more money flows into campaigns, Americans worry about its influence*, PEW (Dec. 7, 2015), www.pewresearch.org/fact -tank/2015/12/07/as-more-money-flows-into-campaigns-americans-worry-about-its -influence/.

[12] John Wagner & Scott Clement, *'It's just messed up': Most think political divisions as bad as Vietnam era*, WASH. POST (Oct. 28, 2017) ("At least 6 in 10 Democrats, Republicans and independents say 'money in politics' deserves a lot of blame ...").

[13] *New York Times/CBS News Poll* (May 28–31, 2015), https://assets.documentcloud .org/documents/2091162/poll-may-28-31.pdf ("Thinking about the role of money in American political campaigns today, do you think money has too much influence, too little influence, or is it about right? ... Too much 84%.").

[14] Drew DeSilver, *U.S. Trails Most Developed Countries in Voter Turnout*, PEW (May 21, 2018), www.pewresearch.org/fact-tank/2018/05/21/u-s-voter-turnout-trails -most-developed-countries/ ("The 55.7% VAP turnout in 2016 puts the U.S. ... 26th out of 32 ...").

[15] David DiSalvo, *The Contagious Reason Why Millions Don't Vote*, FORBES (Nov. 14, 2016).

[16] Christopher Robertson, D. Alex Winkelman, Kelly Bergstrand & Darren Modzelewski, *The Appearance and the Reality of Quid Pro Quo Corruption: An Empirical Investigation*, 8(2) J. OF LEGAL ANALYSIS 375–438 (Dec. 1, 2016), https:// academic.oup.com/jla/article/8/2/375/2502553.

could indicate that for the participants in this study, their definitions of bribery and corruption were broader than the legal definitions.

In a different study to test the theory of whether independent spending can never corrupt (as *Citizens United v. FEC* assumed), Rebecca L. Brown and Andrew D. Martin asked study subjects about different levels of political spending. The results exhibited "a statistically significant effect. Respondents had the highest level of faith in democracy when $10,000 was the amount contributed ... and with a contribution of $1 million evoking the lowest average level of faith in democracy."[17] As Brown and Martin concluded:

> The [Supreme] Court has assumed that, in the absence of such corrupt bargains between candidates and donors, money in politics does not adversely affect the electorate. Our study suggests that this is incorrect. ... Simply put, it does not take a bribe to corrode their [the American voters'] faith in the democratic process.[18]

Of course, with 325 million Americans, differences of opinion on corruption likely abound. But the empirical evidence surveyed in polls and political science studies points toward most Americans' caring a great deal about political corruption. And depending on how the question is framed, many Americans see a link between the role of money in politics and corruption in the political system.

3. HOW THE SUPREME COURT HAS CHANGED THE MEANING OF CORRUPTION IN CAMPAIGN FINANCE JURISPRUDENCE

Against this backdrop of public concern about the integrity of American democracy, the Supreme Court has shifted radically, in just a dozen years, in its basic views of money in politics. A key rhetorical move the Roberts Supreme Court has made is redefining what counts as a compelling state interest to justify the constitutionality of campaign finance laws. The Roberts Court has taken a different stance on this area of the law than its predecessor, the Rehnquist Court. Below, this chapter compares and contrasts the Roberts Court's approach to money in politics with the Rehnquist Court's approach.

---

[17]   Rebecca L. Brown & Andrew D. Martin, *Rhetoric and Reality: Testing the Harm of Campaign Spending*, 90 N.Y.U. L. Rev. 1066, 1086 (Oct. 2015).

[18]   *Id.* at 1089–90 (internal citations omitted).

3.1 A Reasonable Take on Campaign Finance Reform from the Rehnquist Court

The Roberts Supreme Court (2005–present) has wreaked havoc on the meaning of the word "corruption"—nearly defining it away to meaninglessness—while simultaneously gutting nearly every campaign finance law it touched. The Supreme Court wasn't always like this. The Roberts Court's approach to political corruption was a drastic change from the Rehnquist Court which preceded it. During the Rehnquist Court (1986–2005),[19] many different campaign finance laws, whose mission is to disincentivize and prevent graft, were upheld, including *Austin v. Michigan Chamber of Commerce*, which upheld a ban on corporate independent expenditures;[20] *McConnell v. FEC*, which upheld nearly every new restriction in the Bipartisan Campaign Reform Act (BCRA), including bans on soft money and corporate electioneering communications;[21] *Nixon v. Shrink Missouri Government PAC*, which upheld Missouri's then-in-effect campaign finance laws;[22] and *FEC v. Beaumont*, which upheld the Tillman Act's ban on direct corporate contributions.[23]

If the Roberts Court conceptualizes corruption as being a personal problem of moral failings, the Rehnquist Court thought of corruption as being a *systemic* problem. The Rehnquist Court had an expansive view of corruption of the political system, which encompassed the special access to lawmakers and attendant influence that large campaign donors often enjoy.[24] As the Rehnquist Court wrote, "Take away Congress' authority to regulate the appearance of undue influence and 'the cynical assumption that large donors call the tune could jeopardize the willingness of voters to take part in democratic governance.'"[25] The Rehnquist Court defined corruption in this far-reaching way: "Corruption is a subversion of the political process. Elected officials are influence[d] to act contrary to their obligations of office by the prospect of financial gain to themselves or infusion of money into their campaigns. ..."[26] The Rehnquist Court continued, opining that enormous political spending could create the appearance of corruption for the American electorate: "there

---

[19] U.S. Supreme Court, *Justices 1789 to Present*, www.supremecourt.gov/about/members_text.aspx.
[20] Austin v. Michigan Chamber of Commerce, 494 U.S. 652 (1990).
[21] McConnell v. Federal Election Commission, 540 U.S. 93 (2003).
[22] Nixon v. Shrink Missouri Government PAC, 528 U.S. 377 (2000).
[23] Federal Election Commission v. Beaumont, 539 US 146 (2003).
[24] Torres-Spelliscy, *Time Suck, supra* note 5.
[25] McConnell, 540 U.S. at 144 (quoting Shrink Missouri, 528 U.S. at 390).
[26] Nixon, 528 U.S. at 389 (citing Federal Election Comm'n v. National Conservative Political Action Committee).

is little reason to doubt that sometimes large contributions will work actual corruption of our political system, and no reason to question the existence of a corresponding suspicion among voters."[27]

The Rehnquist Court made capacious statements about why campaign finance laws were good for a healthy, well-functioning democracy. For example, in *Beaumont* the Court said there is a:

> public interest in 'restrict[ing] the influence of political war chests funneled through the corporate form.' ... '[S]ubstantial aggregations of wealth amassed by the special advantages which go with the corporate form of organization should not be converted into political "war chests" which could be used to incur political debts from legislators.'[28]

The Court referred to this as "war-chest corruption."[29]

These rulings from the Rehnquist Court upholding campaign finance laws were decided by a closely divided Court, which left them vulnerable to reversal.[30] If Justices Rehnquist and O'Connor were persuadable on the issue of regulating money in politics, their replacements Justices Roberts and Alito were dogmatically hostile to campaign finance reform.[31] Consequently, as soon as their replacements donned their robes, they joined three other conservative members of the Court to dismantle campaign finance laws and the precedent that had protected them.

3.2   Hostility to Campaign Finance Reforms by the Roberts Court

By contrast with its predecessor, the Roberts Court strangely equates spending money with voting[32] and then equates the ability to raise money with fame.[33] At oral arguments, Justice Alito has shown absurd tolerance for letting more money into politics. For instance, in oral argument in *McCutcheon* (a case that challenged the $123 000 limit on giving to candidates and political parties), in response to the Solicitor General saying, "Justice Alito, ... circumvention

---

27   *Id*. at 395.

28   Beaumont, 539 U.S. at 154 (internal citation omitted).

29   *Id*. at 155.

30   Derigan Silver & Dan V. Kozlowski, *Preserving the Law's Coherence:* Citizens United v. FEC *and Stare Decisis*, 21 Comm. L. & Pol'y 39 (2016).

31   Ciara Torres-Spelliscy, *The Democracy We Left Behind in Greece and McCutcheon*, 89 N.Y.U. L. Rev. Online 112, 116–17 (2014).

32   McCutcheon v. Federal Election Com'n, 572 U.S. 185, 191 (2014).

33   Davis v. Federal Election Com'n, 554 U.S. 724, 742 (2008) ("Different candidates have different strengths. Some are wealthy; others have wealthy supporters who are willing to make large contributions. Some are celebrities ...").

is not the only problem. The delivery of the solicitation and receipt of these very large checks is a problem, a direct corruption problem ...."[34] Justice Alito responded sarcastically:

> I just don't understand that. You mean, at the time when the person sends the money to this hypothetical joint fundraising committee, there is a corruption problem immediately, even though what if they just took the money and they burned it? That would be a corruption problem there?[35]

Back in the real world, campaign money is not lit aflame. It is spent on campaign salaries, political consultants, web designers, yard signs, door hangers, pins, bumper stickers, office space, rally spaces, bunting, balloons, caterers, as well as print, broadcast and internet political ads—in other words, on branding. Justice Alito's hypothetical seems willfully blind to how political campaigns actually work.

The Roberts Court sees campaign finance reform as negatively impacting American democracy, from acting as incumbency protection plans[36] (which the data does not support, but that fact is of little consequence to this Court),[37] to silencing First Amendment speakers,[38] to discriminating against the rich.[39] While equality is prized in other parts of the election law, like in the one person, one vote jurisprudence[40]—or in even *Bush v. Gore*, which demands equality in counting votes[41]—equality is anathema to the Roberts Court in the area of campaign finance, as the Court made clear in its most recent campaign finance case *McCutcheon*:

> No matter how desirable it may seem, it is not an acceptable governmental objective to 'level the playing field,' or to 'level electoral opportunities,' or to 'equaliz[e] the

---

[34] Oral Argument Tr. of *McCutcheon v. Federal Election Commission* at 50–51 (General Verrilli), www.supremecourt.gov/oral_arguments/argument_transcripts/2013/12-536_2k81.pdf.

[35] Oral Argument Tr. of *McCutcheon v. Federal Election Commission* at 51 (Alito J.), www.supremecourt.gov/oral_arguments/argument_transcripts/2013/12-536_2k81.pdf.

[36] Randall v. Sorrell, 548 U.S. 230, 248 (2006).

[37] Ciara Torres-Spelliscy, Kahlil Williams & Thomas Stratmann, *Electoral Competition and Low Contribution Limits* (Brennan Center 2009).

[38] Citizens United v. Federal Election Com'n, 558 U.S. 310, 326 (2010); McCutcheon, 572 U.S. at 229 ("We must decline to draw, and then redraw, constitutional lines based on the particular media or technology used ...").

[39] Davis, 128 S.Ct. at 2764.

[40] Reynolds v. Sims, 377 U.S. 533 (1964); Baker v. Carr, 369 U.S. 186 (1962).

[41] Bush v. Gore, 531 U.S. 98 (2000).

financial resources of candidates.' The First Amendment prohibits such legislative attempts to 'fine-tun[e]' the electoral process, no matter how well intentioned.[42]

The only exceptions to this hostility to campaign finance laws between 2006–19 came in *Bluman*, which summarily upheld the ban on foreigners' spending in elections; and in *Williams-Yulee v. Florida Bar*, which upheld a ban on the personal solicitation of campaign funds by judicial candidates.[43]

The Roberts Court's conservative majority has a different ideological view about money in politics than previous iterations of the Supreme Court; and it certainly holds a contrasting view from the liberal minority on the bench. If other Supreme Courts in the past thought of money as threatening democratic integrity, for the conservative majority of the Roberts Court, money is at least benign or even a laudatory addition to the democratic process. The conservative majority on the Roberts Court has reduced the justification for campaign finance reform to merely *quid pro quo* corruption. And it has even restricted what counts as a *quid pro quo*. The 180-degree turn from the Rehnquist Court to the Roberts Court on the matter of campaign finance was nearly immediate. The Supreme Court went from upholding nearly all campaign finance laws it reviewed under Chief Justice Rehnquist's leadership to striking down nearly all campaign finance laws it reviewed on Chief Justice Roberts' watch.

The first chance for the Roberts Court to expose its new hostility to campaign finance arrived in the *Randall* case. But the *Randall* case would be the last campaign finance case in the Roberts Court written by a liberal Justice—in this case, Justice Breyer. Arguably, Justice Breyer wrote the opinion carefully to do as little harm to existing campaign finance jurisprudence as possible while striking down Vermont's law, which contained expenditure limits and the lowest contribution limits in the nation.[44]

The change in tone around the meaning of corruption isn't in Justice Breyer's opinion for the Court, but rather in Justice Kennedy's concurrence. In his *Randall* concurrence in 2006, Justice Kennedy began to plant the seeds of doubt about the conception of political corruption that would be reaped in future cases. As Justice Kennedy wrote: "There is simply no way to calculate just how much money a person would need to receive before he would be corrupt or perceived to be corrupt (and such a calculation would undoubtedly vary by person)."[45] This type of language was dismissive of corruption as a real problem and sentiments like this would move to center stage in later cases.

---

[42] McCutcheon, 572 U.S. at 207 (internal citation omitted).

[43] Bluman v. Federal Election Com'n, 565 U.S. 1104 (2012); Williams-Yulee v. Florida Bar, 575 U.S. _ (2015).

[44] Randall v. Sorrell, 548 U.S. 230 (2006).

[45] *Id.* at 273 (Kennedy, J. concurring in the judgment).

Meanwhile, Justice Breyer would never be given the pen again in a campaign finance case. But the Roberts Court's rebranding of corruption had begun.

One year later, *Davis v. FEC*, with Justice Alito writing for the Court, struck down the Millionaire's Amendment—a mechanism to help candidates facing a self-financed rich opponent raise enough money to keep competitive by raising the contribution limit for the non-self-financed candidate.[46] Justice Alito found the law's allowance to raise more money against a self-financed candidate was unconstitutional, writing: "The burden imposed by [the Millionaire's Amendment] on the expenditure of personal funds is not justified by any governmental interest in eliminating corruption or the perception of corruption."[47] Justice Alito thereby rejected the government's asserted interest in leveling the playing field between wealthy and non-wealthy candidates:

> 'Congress enacted [the Millionaire's Amendment],' the Government writes, 'to reduce *the natural advantage* that wealthy individuals possess in campaigns for federal office ... [P]reventing corruption or the appearance of corruption are the only legitimate and compelling government interests thus far identified for restricting campaign finances ...[48]

The dissent by Justice Stevens in *Davis* took issue with narrowing the justification for campaign finance to merely preventing corruption and its appearance. As Justice Stevens explained: "The Court is simply wrong when it suggests that the 'governmental interest in eliminating corruption or the perception of corruption,' is the sole governmental interest sufficient to support campaign finance regulations ..."[49] Moreover, Justice Stevens continued:

> ... we [Justices of the Supreme Court] have long recognized the strength of an independent governmental interest in reducing both the influence of wealth on the outcomes of elections, and the appearance that wealth alone dictates those results. In case after case, we have held that statutes designed to protect against the undue influence of aggregations of wealth on the political process—where such statutes are responsive to the identified evil—do not contravene the First Amendment.[50]

---

46   Davis v. Federal Election Com'n, 554 U.S. 724 (2008).
47   *Id.* at 740–41.
48   *Id.* at 741 (internal references removed) (emphasis in the original).
49   *Id.* at 754–56 (Stevens, J. dissenting).
50   *Id.* at 754–56 (2008) (Stevens, J. dissenting) (citing *Austin v. Michigan Chamber of Commerce*, 494 U.S. 652, 660 (1990) (upholding statute designed to combat "the corrosive and distorting effects of immense aggregations of wealth that are accumulated with the help of the corporate form ...").

Justice Stevens thus based his critique on the conservative majority's cherry-picking supportive precedents, while ignoring cases that contradicted them.

In *Wisconsin Right to Life (WRTL) II*, the Court continued the process of dismantling BCRA that it had started in *Davis*.[51] This time, the Court considered a different part of the law that allowed for the regulation of "electioneering communications" or what are sometimes referred to as "sham issue ads."[52] In BCRA, "electioneering communications" are defined as broadcast ads that mention a federal candidate right before a federal election, which cost at least $10 000 and reach at least 50 000 constituents.[53] In *Wisconsin Right to Life (WRTL) II*, the Supreme Court in 2007 found that certain political ads from a nonprofit corporation could not be constitutionally regulated, even though they fit the statutory definition of regulatable campaign ads. Writing for the majority of the Court, Chief Justice Roberts stated: "None of the interests that might justify regulating WRTL's ads are sufficiently compelling. ... Issue ads like WRTL's are not equivalent to contributions, and the corruption interest cannot justify regulating them."[54] Additionally, the Roberts Court seemed almost petulant in claiming that *McConnell* from just four years prior had gone too far in its conception of what could corrupt the political system:

> *McConnell* arguably applied this interest [in preventing corporate expenditures] ... to ads that were the 'functional equivalent' of express advocacy. But to justify regulation of WRTL's ads, this interest must be stretched yet another step to ads that are *not* the functional equivalent of express advocacy. *Enough is enough.*[55]

In his dissent in *WRTL II*, Justice Souter, writing for the liberal minority, argued that a more expansive view of political corruption was more appropriate than the narrow conception embraced by the majority. Justice Souter lamented that just a few years earlier, the Supreme Court had embraced a broader definition of political corruption:

> Neither Congress's decisions nor our own have understood the corrupting influence of money in politics as being limited to outright bribery or discrete *quid pro quo;*

---

[51]   Federal Election Commission v. Wisconsin Right to Life, Inc., 551 U.S. 449 (2007) ("WRTL II").

[52]   *Primer on Issue Ads Issue Advocacy: Electioneering Issue Advocacy vs. Genuine Issue Advocacy*, PUBLIC CITIZEN (undated), www.citizen.org/article/primer-issue-ads (last visited October 8, 2018).

[53]   Ciara Torres-Spelliscy, *Transparent Elections after* Citizens United, BRENNAN CENTER (Mar. 1, 2011).

[54]   WRTL II, 551 U.S. at 452 (internal citations omitted).

[55]   *Id.* at 478–79 (emphasis added).

campaign finance reform has instead consistently focused on the more pervasive distortion of electoral institutions by concentrated wealth, on the special access and guaranteed favor that sap the representative integrity of American government and defy public confidence in its institutions.[56]

But alas, the *WRTL II* majority thereby ignored a century of precedents.

The Court really accelerated its deregulatory pace in 2010 in *Citizens United*, a case that was argued twice.[57] *Citizens United* concluded five to four that corporations (and, by logical extension, unions) had a First Amendment right to spend an unlimited amount on political ads in any American election. To reach this result, the Court invalidated parts of two federal statutes (BCRA and Taft-Hartley) and all state laws that had previously banned expenditures by corporations. In *Citizens United*, Justice Kennedy, writing for the majority, relied on *Buckley* in narrowing the definition of corruption, thereby skipping and invalidating intervening case law that held to the contrary:

> The practices *Buckley* noted would be covered by bribery laws, if a *quid pro quo* arrangement were proved. The Court, in consequence, has noted that restrictions on direct contributions are preventative, because few if any contributions to candidates will involve *quid pro quo* arrangements. The *Buckley* Court … did not extend this rationale to independent expenditures, and the Court does not do so here.[58]

He concluded for the Court in *Citizens United*: "Limits on independent expenditures [by corporations] … have a chilling effect extending well beyond the Government's interest in preventing *quid pro quo* corruption. The anticorruption interest is not sufficient to displace the speech here in question."[59]

If Justice Kennedy tipped his hand in his *Randall* concurrence about how he really was not all that concerned about political corruption, his failure of the imagination about how politics really works was also evident in the *Citizens United* majority when he wrote that: "we now conclude that independent expenditures, including those made by corporations, do not give rise to corruption or the appearance of corruption."[60] According to Justice Kennedy's strange world view: "The appearance of influence or access, furthermore, will not cause the electorate to lose faith in our democracy."[61] He thereby turned an empirical question into a statement of law.

---

[56]   *Id.* at 522.
[57]   Citizens United v. Federal Election Com'n, 558 U.S. 310 (2010) (Argued Mar. 24, 2009—Reargued Sept. 9, 2009).
[58]   *Id.* at 356–57 (internal citations omitted).
[59]   *Id.* at 357.
[60]   *Id.* (internal citations omitted).
[61]   *Id.* at 359–60.

Justice Stevens' view of how politics can and should operate could not have been more different than Justice Kennedy's descriptive and normative views. Justice Stevens, in his dissent in *Citizens United*, argued that the laws at issue in the case "target a class of communications [from corporations] that is especially likely to corrupt the political process ..."[62] For Justice Stevens, there were multiple reasons that justified regulating money in politics, including "Congress' legitimate interest in preventing the money that is spent on elections from exerting an 'undue influence on an officeholder's judgment,'" and from creating "'the appearance of such influence'" beyond the sphere of quid pro quo relationships."[63]

As Justice Stevens explained, corruption exists on a spectrum; it is not a single act:

> Corruption can take many forms. Bribery may be the paradigm case. But the difference between selling a vote and selling access is a matter of degree, not kind. And selling access is not qualitatively different from giving special preference to those who spent money on one's behalf. Corruption operates along a spectrum ... [Congress' legislative history for BCRA included] *a record that stands as a remarkable testament to the energy and ingenuity with which corporations, unions, lobbyists, and politicians may go about scratching each other's backs ...*[64]

He added:

> Unlike the [conservative] majority's myopic focus on quid pro quo scenarios ... this broader understanding of corruption has deep roots in the Nation's history. 'During debates on the earliest [campaign finance] reform acts, the terms "corruption" and "undue influence" were used nearly interchangeably.'[65]

For Justice Stevens, his conservative colleagues on the bench sorely underestimated the damage that can be done to the faith of average voters in a political process rife with undue influence by large political spenders. As Justice Stevens explained:

> Our undue influence cases have allowed the American people to cast a wider net through legislative experiments designed to ensure, to some minimal extent, that officeholders will decide issues ... on the merits or the desires of their constitu-

---

[62]   *Id.* at 419 (Stevens, J. dissenting in part).

[63]   *Id.* at 447–48 (Stevens, J. dissenting in part) (internal citations omitted).

[64]   *Id.* at 447–48 (Stevens, J. dissenting in part) (internal citations omitted) (emphasis added).

[65]   *Id.* at 451 (Stevens, J. dissenting in part) (citing Pasquale, *Reclaiming Egalitarianism in the Political Theory of Campaign Finance Reform*, 2008 U. ILL. L. REV. 599, 601).

encies, and not according to the wishes of those who have made large financial contributions—or expenditures—valued by the officeholder.[66]

Justice Stevens noted the corrupting effect corporate-sponsored political ads could have on the American political process. According to him, corporate independent expenditures had become:

> essentially interchangeable with direct contributions in their capacity to generate quid pro quo arrangements. In an age in which money and television ads are the coin of the campaign realm, it is hardly surprising that corporations deployed these ads to curry favor with, and to gain influence over, public officials.[67]

And in a dissent filled with poignant zingers he added: "A democracy cannot function effectively when its constituent members believe *laws are being bought and sold.*"[68]

Building on the hostility to campaign finance reform in *Randall, Davis, WRTL II* and *Citizens United*, the Roberts Court then set its sights on Arizona when it granted cert. in *Bennett*.[69] Arizona's public financing system allowed for extra rescue funds to a candidate who was running "clean," using only public financing moneys, if that candidate's opponent spent over certain thresholds or if independent spending against the clean candidate went over certain thresholds. This Arizona system was intended to prevent publicly financed candidates from becoming sitting ducks who could be roundly out-spent without any ability to fight back.

When Arizona's public financing system was challenged as violating the First Amendment, lawyers for the State justified the law by fitting it into the Roberts Court's crabbed vision of preventing *quid pro quo* corruption. The Court nonetheless rejected this framing of the law. Chief Justice Roberts, writing for the majority in *Bennett*, stated: "when confronted with a choice between fighting corruption and equalizing speech, the drafters of the matching funds provision chose the latter."[70]

---

[66]   *Id.* at 449–50 (Stevens, J. dissenting in part) (internal quotation marks and citation omitted).

[67]   *Id.* at 454–55 (Stevens, J. dissenting in part).

[68]   *Id.* at 452–53 (Stevens, J. dissenting in part) (emphasis added).

[69]   Arizona Free Enterprise Club's Freedom Club PAC v. Bennett, 564 U.S. 721 (2011).

[70]   Bennett, 564 U.S. at 749 (internal citations omitted).

Chief Justice Roberts admonished the *Bennett* dissenters that democracy is not a game:

> 'Leveling the playing field' can sound like a good thing. But in a democracy, campaigning for office is not a game. It is a critically important form of speech. The First Amendment embodies our choice as a Nation that, when it comes to such speech, the guiding principle is freedom—the 'unfettered interchange of ideas'—not whatever the State may view as fair.[71]

The dissent by Justice Kagan shot right back at him:

> Arizonans deserve better. Like citizens across this country, Arizonans deserve a government that represents and serves them all. And no less, Arizonans deserve the chance to reform their electoral system so as to attain that most American of goals. Truly, democracy is not a game. I respectfully dissent.[72]

Justice Kagan's dissent in *Bennett* was more realistic about American political history, noting that "[c]ampaign finance reform over the last century has focused on one key question: how to prevent massive pools of private money from corrupting our political system."[73] In so doing, Justice Kagan echoed the sentiments of the majority in cases decided by the Rehnquist Court.

As Justice Kagan's dissent in *Bennett* recognized, the Arizona public financing system was enacted by the people of Arizona in response to actual political corruption in the AzScam scandal, not some imagined or hypothetical problem. AzScam was a corruption scandal involving cash bribes, wherein seven Arizona legislators were arrested and one-tenth of the Arizona legislature resigned from office.[74] As Justice Kagan noted:

> Arizona had every reason to try to develop effective anti-corruption measures ... the State suffered 'the worst public corruption scandal in its history.' In ... 'AzScam,' nearly 10% of the State's legislators were caught accepting campaign contributions or bribes in exchange for supporting a piece of legislation ... [Then the citizens of Arizona] adopted the public funding ...[75]

Thus, to Justice Kagan, the State was constitutionally justified in crafting a public financing system to prevent another AzScam-scale fiasco.

---

[71] *Id.* at 750.

[72] *Id.* at 785 (Kagan, J. dissenting).

[73] *Id.* at 757 (Kagan, J. dissenting).

[74] Alyssa Newcomb, *Caught on Tape: Massive Arizona Sting Forced Reforms*, ABC News (Oct. 25, 2010), https://abcnews.go.com/Blotter/caught-tape-massive-arizona-sting-forced-reforms/story?id=11949443.

[75] Bennett, 564 U.S. at 761 (Kagan, J. dissenting).

Moreover, Justice Kagan felt that the *Bennett* conservative majority was holding Arizona to a new double standard. As she said: "This Court ... has never said that a law restricting speech (or any other constitutional right) demands two compelling interests. One is enough. And this statute has one: preventing corruption."[76] For Justice Kagan, the Arizona public financing system was, as the State's attorneys had argued, intended to lawfully prevent political corruption: "When private contributions fuel the political system, candidates may make corrupt bargains to gain the money needed to win election. And voters ... may lose faith that their representatives will serve the public's interest."[77]

Continuing the trend of deregulation, in 2012, the Supreme Court summarily reversed the Montana Supreme Court without even granting oral argument in *American Tradition Partnership*. Montana had tried to keep its century-old corporate expenditure ban in place despite *Citizens United*. The U.S. Supreme Court would have none of it and invalidated the ban.[78] In a dissent from the summary reversal written by Justice Breyer for the liberal minority, he argued: "Montana's experience, like considerable experience elsewhere since the Court's decision in Citizens United, casts grave doubt on the Court's supposition that independent expenditures do not corrupt ..."[79]

The most recent case to deregulate campaign finance law was *McCutcheon* in 2014.[80] Mr. McCutcheon challenged the aggregate biennial limits of $123 000 under the Federal Election Campaign Act. He wished to donate $1776 to a number of federal candidates. But because of the aggregate limit, he could not give $1776 to every candidate whom he wanted to support. Chief Justice Roberts opens *McCutcheon* thusly:

> There is no right more basic in our democracy than the right to participate in elect-ing our political leaders. Citizens can exercise that right in a variety of ways: They can run for office themselves, vote, urge others to vote for a particular candidate, volunteer to work on a campaign, and contribute to a candidate's campaign. This case is about the last of those options. The right to participate in democracy through political contributions is protected by the First Amendment ... Congress may not regulate contributions simply to reduce the amount of money in politics ...[81]

Here one can see a stark example of the contrasting world views between the conservative and liberal wings of the Supreme Court. For Chief Justice

---

[76] *Id.* at 783 (Kagan, J. dissenting).
[77] *Id.* at 776–77 (Kagan, J. dissenting) (internal citations omitted).
[78] American Tradition Partnership, Inc. v. Bullock, 567 U.S. 516, 517 (2012).
[79] *Id.* at 517.
[80] McCutcheon v. Federal Election Com'n, 572 U.S. 185, 191 (2014).
[81] McCutcheon, 572 U.S. at 191 (internal citation omitted).

Roberts, money is as beneficial to democracy as voting. For the dissent in *McCutcheon*, money is a potential menace. The Chief Justice in *McCutcheon* seems particularly tone deaf about the common-sense meaning of political corruption, writing:

> government regulation may not target the general gratitude a candidate may feel toward those who support him or his allies, or the political access such support may afford. 'Ingratiation and access ... are not corruption.' They embody a central feature of democracy ...[82]

Thus, to the Chief Justice, the dependence of Congress or the President on large political donors is only natural.

In *McCutcheon*, Chief Justice Roberts continued to insist that only *quid pro quo* corruption counted as an acceptable reason to enact campaign finance reform. He stated campaign finance regulations must target:

> 'quid pro quo' corruption or its appearance. That Latin phrase captures the notion of a direct exchange of an official act for money. 'The hallmark of corruption is the financial quid pro quo: dollars for political favors.' Campaign finance restrictions that pursue other objectives, we have explained, impermissibly inject the Government 'into the debate over who should govern.' And those who govern should be the last people to help decide who should govern.[83]

The Chief Justice also narrowed what *quid pro quo* meant in the following way: "[s]pending large sums of money in connection with elections, but not in connection with an effort to control the exercise of an officeholder's official duties, does not give rise to such *quid pro quo* corruption."[84]

McCutcheon was notable because it was the first time that the Supreme Court has specifically overruled a holding from *Buckley*. *Buckley* upheld aggregate limits. *McCutcheon* ruled the same aggregate limits were unconstitutional. This is different than previous cases like *Randall* and *Citizens United*, which purported to be faithful to *Buckley*.[85]

Justice Breyer, in his dissent in *McCutcheon*, calls out the limited vision of corruption by the plurality:

> The plurality's first claim—that large aggregate contributions do not 'give rise' to 'corruption'—is plausible only because the plurality defines 'corruption' too

---

[82] *Id.* at 192 (internal citation omitted).
[83] *Id.* (internal citation omitted) (emphasis in the original).
[84] *Id.* at 208.
[85] *Id.* at 227.

narrowly ... In the plurality's view, a federal statute could not prevent an individual from writing a million dollar check to a political party ...[86]

Justice Breyer also notes the larger context of the First Amendment's place in America's democratic tradition: "the anticorruption interest that drives Congress to regulate campaign contributions is a far broader, more important interest ... in maintaining the integrity of our public governmental institutions."[87]

Justice Breyer explains the importance of preventing the appearance of corruption in a democratic system where political apathy is a real risk. As he says:

> a cynical public can lose interest in political participation altogether. ... Democracy ... cannot work unless 'the people have faith in those who govern.' ... we can and should understand campaign finance laws as resting upon a broader and more significant constitutional rationale than the plurality's limited definition of 'corruption' suggests.[88]

To sum up the rhetorical moves by the Roberts Court in the area of campaign finance jurisprudence, over the vigorous objections of liberal Justices and despite precedents to the contrary, the conservative majority on the Roberts Court has compressed the justification for campaign finance reform to merely *quid pro quo* corruption. And it has even constricted what counts as a *quid pro quo*.

4.   EVER-SHRINKING ANTI-CORRUPTION CRIMINAL LAW

Just as the Rehnquist Court embraced a more capacious view of what counted as political corruption, it also recognized that political contributions could be an element in a crime. In *McComick,* a case about money going to a state legislator in West Virginia, the Court ultimately exonerated Mr. McComick, but before it did so the Court noted:

> This is not to say that it is impossible for an elected official to commit extortion in the course of financing an election campaign. Political contributions are of course vulnerable if induced by the use of force, violence, or fear.[89]

---

[86]   *Id.* at 235 (Breyer, J. dissenting).
[87]   *Id.* at 235–36 (Breyer, J. dissenting) (internal citations omitted).
[88]   *Id.* at 238–39 (Breyer, J. dissenting).
[89]   McCormick v. U.S., 500 U.S. 257, 273 (1991) ("The receipt of such contributions is also vulnerable under the [Hobbs] Act as having been taken under color of

The Roberts Supreme Court hasn't just been narrowing the definition of corruption in the area of campaign finance law; it has simultaneously been tightening the definition of corruption in criminal law too. It redefined what counts as "honest services fraud" in *Skilling* in 2010, which arose out of the massive corporate fraud at Enron. Mr. Skilling was an executive at Enron when the fraud happened and originally received a sentence of 24 years for his crimes.[90] Skilling argued that his conviction for honest services fraud was erroneous. Justice Ginsburg, writing for the Court, agreed with him and concluded:

> In proscribing fraudulent deprivations of 'the intangible right of honest services,' § 1346, Congress intended at least to reach schemes to defraud involving bribes and kickbacks. ... Because Skilling's alleged misconduct entailed no bribe or kickback, it does not fall within § 1346's proscription.[91]

After Skilling won in the Supreme Court, he was resentenced to 14 years.[92]

Honest services fraud has been used by federal prosecutors to go after corrupt politicians and, as in Skilling's case, corporate fiduciaries who owe a duty of loyalty to shareholders. Thus, when the Supreme Court compressed the definition of honest services fraud, it opened new defenses for accused faithless corporate fiduciaries, as well as accused corrupt politicians. And as noted below, politicians have had convictions vacated based on *Skilling*.

The Supreme Court has not only narrowed the definition of honest services, it has also narrowed the understanding of what counts as an official act. In 2016, in a case called *McDonnell,* the Court unanimously rejected the Governor of Virginia's conviction for bribery. Governor McDonnell accepted $175 000 in gifts and loans, including payment for his daughter's wedding, from businessman Jonnie Williams. The case turned on what counts as an "official act" for the purposes of anti-bribery laws.[93] The prosecution in the case argued that when the Governor set up meetings on behalf of Williams, the

---

official right, but only if the payments are made in return for an explicit promise or undertaking by the official to perform or not to perform an official act.").

[90]   Skilling v. U.S., 561 U.S. 358, 375 (2010).

[91]   *Id.* at 368.

[92]   Press Release, U.S. Dept. of Justice, *Former Enron CEO Jeffrey Skilling Resentenced to 168 Months for Fraud, Conspiracy Charges* (June 21, 2013).

[93]   McDonnell v. U.S., 136 S.Ct. 2355, 2365 (2016) ("the federal bribery statute, 18 U.S.C. § 201 ... makes it a crime for 'a public official or person selected to be a public official, directly or indirectly, corruptly' to demand, seek, receive, accept, or agree 'to receive or accept anything of value' in return for being 'influenced in the performance of any official act.' § 201(b)(2). An 'official act' is defined as 'any decision or action on any question, matter, cause, suit, proceeding or controversy, which may at any time be pending, or which may by law be brought before any public official, in such official's official capacity, or in such official's place of trust or profit.' § 201(a)(3).").

quid pro quo was complete. But the Supreme Court decided that merely setting up meetings (with nothing more done) would not constitute an "official act." As the Supreme Court wrote:

[A]n official act ... must involve a formal exercise of governmental power that is similar in nature to a lawsuit before a court, a determination before an agency, or a hearing before a committee. It must also be something specific and focused that is 'pending' or 'may by law be brought' before a public official.[94]

And thus, the Court vacated Governor McDonnell's conviction.

Chief Justice Roberts rejected the prosecutors' theory of the case in *McDonnell*, writing:

the Government's expansive interpretation of 'official act' would raise significant constitutional concerns. [The law] prohibits quid pro quo corruption ... In the Government's view, nearly anything a public official accepts—from a campaign contribution to lunch—counts as a quid; and nearly anything a public official does—from arranging a meeting to inviting a guest to an event—counts as a quo.[95]

Thus, Chief Justice Roberts wrote of the worry of criminalizing normal politics:

conscientious public officials arrange meetings for constituents, contact other officials on their behalf, and include them in events all the time. The basic compact underlying representative government assumes that public officials will hear from their constituents and act appropriately on their concerns. ... The Government's position could cast a pall of potential prosecution over these relationships. ... Officials might wonder whether they could respond to even the most commonplace requests for assistance, and citizens with legitimate concerns might shrink from participating in democratic discourse.[96]

Not unlike the Supreme Court's position in campaign finance cases, the Court in *McDonnell* sees no problem with a Governor who is deeply in debt receiving money from a businessman who wants the State to do things for him in return. In the Court's estimation, Williams was just like any other poor constituent

---

[94]   *Id.* at 2371–72.
[95]   *Id.* at 2372.
[96]   *Id.*

who hadn't paid for the Governor's daughter's wedding. Chief Justice Roberts, writing for a unanimous Court, concluded:

> this case is distasteful; it may be worse than that. But our concern is not with tawdry tales of Ferraris, Rolexes, and ball gowns. It is instead with the broader legal implications of the Government's boundless interpretation of the federal bribery statute.[97]

Many Court watchers were left wondering, post-*McDonnell*, exactly what would count as criminal corruption.

5. WHAT DOES A CROOKED POLITICIAN HEAR FROM THE SUPREME COURT?

What the Supreme Court has done to rebrand and deregulate corruption has not fallen on deaf ears. In particular, those facing criminal prosecutions for political corruption have been eager to make arguments in court that, just like Governor McDonnell, they should be free men. Some have also argued that campaign finance cases like *McCutcheon* and *Citizens United* indicate that their "crimes" were not "crimes" at all.

Political corruption is an entirely bipartisan phenomenon. Ex-Governor McDonnell from Virginia was a Republican. But one of the most infamous Governors in prison is the Democratic ex-Governor of Illinois, Rod Blagojevich. In January 2009, Blagojevich was impeached by the Illinois legislature.[98] Then he went through a series of federal trials for corruption. One of the charges he faced was for trying to sell the U.S. Senate seat vacated by President-elect Obama. In 2011, he was convicted on 17 charges and sent to prison for 14 years.[99]

In 2013, Blagojevich launched an appeal, arguing that his convictions should be vacated. At points, he cited *Citizens United* in support of his argument: "Blagojevich's decision to ask [a particular individual] to help fundraise … did not make it a crime. See Citizens United. …"[100] The Seventh Circuit agreed with some of Blagojevich's legal arguments, including that exchanging a public appointment for a public appointment was different than exchanging an official act for a private gain. This resulted in his being eligible for resen-

---

[97] *Id.* at 2375.

[98] *Impeached Illinois Gov. Rod Blagojevich has been Removed from Office*, CHI. TRIB. (Jan. 30, 2009).

[99] Tal Kopan, *Who is Rod Blagojevich and what was he convicted of?*, CNN (May 31, 2018), www.cnn.com/2018/05/31/politics/who-is-rod-blagojevich-conviction/index.html.

[100] USA v. Blagojevich, 2013 WL 3914027 at *58 (7th Cir. 2013) (Brief for Defendant-Appellant) (internal citation omitted).

tencing.[101] He was resentenced in 2016, but the judge decided to keep his term in prison exactly the same.[102] Blagojevich appealed back to the Seventh Circuit, arguing that the judge should have reduced his prison sentence, citing *McDonnell*. The Seventh Circuit disagreed.[103]

In 2017, Blagojevich urged the Supreme Court to review his case. In his cert. petition, Blagojevich's lawyers cited to *McDonnell* and *McCutcheon*:

> the location of the line between lawful campaign solicitation and felony extortion is a question of undeniable practical importance to candidates throughout the country. *See, e.g., McDonnell.* ... The present uncertainty also implicates constitutional concerns of the highest order. Seeking and making campaign donations implicates fundamental First Amendment rights. *See, e.g., McCutcheon* ...[104]

In April 2018, the Supreme Court refused to hear Blagojevich's appeal, which left him in prison.[105]

New York is neck and neck with Illinois when it comes to dysfunctional State government.[106] Two consecutive New York Senate Majority Leaders have been criminally charged, as has a Speaker of the Assembly.[107] These prosecutions were spearheaded by U.S. Attorney Preet Bharara, who made prosecuting political corruption a priority. Joseph Bruno was the Majority Leader in the New York Senate for 14 years, until 2008. In December 2009, Bruno was convicted of two counts of honest services mail fraud for his failure to disclose conflicts of interest while serving as a Senator.[108] Bruno appealed his conviction to the Second Circuit, citing *Skilling*. The Second Circuit agreed with his argument, stating: "In light of Skilling, we vacated Bruno's convic-

---

[101] USA v. Blagojevich, 794 F.3d 729, 734 (7th Cir. 2015) ("We conclude ... a proposal to trade one public act for another, a form of logrolling, is fundamentally unlike the swap of an official act for a private payment.").

[102] *Blagojevich faces 8 years more in prison after judge sticks to 14-year term*, CHI. TRIB. (Aug. 9, 2016).

[103] USA v. Blagojevich, 854 F.3d 918, 921 (7th Cir. 2017) ("According to Blagojevich, McDonnell calls the reasoning of our first decision into question. Not so.").

[104] Blagojevich v. USA, 2017 WL 8794297 at 26–27 (Nov. 2, 2017) (Pet. for Cert.).

[105] SCOTUS Blog, *Blagojevich v. United States*, www.scotusblog.com/case-files/cases/blagojevich-v-united-states (Cert. denied Apr. 16, 2018).

[106] Michael Cooper, *So How Bad Is Albany? Well, Notorious*, N.Y. TIMES (July 22, 2004).

[107] Grace Segers, *Percoco Verdict Proves Corruption Won't Go Unpunished, After All*, CITY & STATE N.Y. (Mar. 13, 2018), www.cityandstateny.com/articles/politics/new-york-state/percoco-found-guilty-corruption-charges.html ("Silver and Skelos had their charges vacated in 2017, based on ... McDonnell v. United States.).

[108] *See* 18 U.S.C. §§ 1341, 1346.

tions."[109] Then Bruno faced a second trial, but this time the jury acquitted him on all charges.[110]

After Bruno, Dean Skelos was the on-again-off-again Majority Leader between 2008 and 2015. (Because of turmoil in a split chamber, there were actually disputes about who held the gavel.) He was indicted in 2015. Following a jury trial in 2016, Skelos and his son, Adam, were convicted of Hobbs Act conspiracy, Hobbs Act extortion, honest services wire fraud, conspiracy and federal program bribery. They appealed their convictions.[111] The Second Circuit agreed, applying *McDonnell* to the case, that the jury instructions on what constituted an "official act" was too expansive and vacated the convictions.[112] The pair were retried. Dean Skelos argued in 2018 that his indictment should be dismissed because the grand jury had not been instructed properly under *McDonnell*.[113] The judge overseeing his case denied this request.[114] On July 17, 2018, Skelos and his son were convicted for a second time.[115]

Meanwhile, Sheldon "Shelly" Silver served as Speaker of the New York Assembly for 21 years. After Silver was convicted of honest services fraud and other crimes in 2015, he appealed.[116] The Second Circuit ruled in his favor in 2017, finding that the jury instruction on what counted as an "official act" was too broad.[117] The Second Circuit concluded: "we hold that the District Court's instructions on honest services fraud and extortion do not comport with McDonnell ... we VACATE ... conviction on all counts ..."[118] The Second Circuit's opinion was appealed to the Supreme Court, which refused to hear the *Silver* case.[119] Federal prosecutors decided to retry Silver. In May of 2018,

---

[109] U.S. v. Bruno, 531 Fed.Appx. 47, 48 (2d Cir. 2013) (denying double jeopardy bars second criminal trial for Bruno).

[110] USA v. Bruno, Criminal Docket for Case 1:09-cr-00029-GLS-1 ("Jury Verdict as to Joseph L. Bruno (1) Not Guilty") (May 16, 2014).

[111] United States v. Skelos, 707 Fed.Appx. 733, 733–36 (2d Cir. 2017).

[112] *Id*. at 736.

[113] United States v. Skelos, 2018 WL 2849712, at *2 (S.D.N.Y. 2018).

[114] *Id*. at *1.

[115] James T. Madore, *Dean Skelos, son convicted of corruption*, NEWS DAY (July 17, 2018).

[116] United States v. Silver, 184 F.Supp.3d 33, 37 (S.D.N.Y. 2016).

[117] Matt Zapotosky, *The Bob McDonnell Effect*, WASH. POST (July 3, 2017).

[118] United States v. Silver, 864 F.3d 102, 105–06 (2d Cir. 2017) (internal citations omitted); Alan Feuer, *Why Are Corruption Cases Crumbling? Some Blame the Supreme Court*, N.Y. TIMES (Nov. 17, 2017).

[119] Silver v. U.S., 138 S.Ct. 738 (2018) (cert. denied).

Silver was convicted a second time.[120] Once again, Silver has appealed;[121] so this saga is not over yet.

Next door in New Jersey, a high-profile political corruption prosecution fell apart in 2018.[122] In 2015, U.S. Senator Robert Menendez was charged with bribery for his relationship with a donor to a Super PAC that supported the Senator.[123] In 2017, a corruption trial of Senator Menendez ended with a hung jury.[124] After the hung jury, Senator Menendez moved for acquittal. In January 2018, the trial judge agreed to acquit on seven charges, but refused on 11 others.[125] Interestingly he did not accept Senator Menendez's arguments about the application of *McDonnell*, since "a rational juror could find that Defendants entered into a quid pro quo agreement."[126]

The trial court judge also refused to acquit Senator Menendez based on his reading of *Citizens United*. As the judge stated:

> the Government alleges that Defendants engaged in a quid pro quo bribery scheme, not that either defendant violated campaign finance regulations ... the charges in this case concern bribery, not political speech ... nothing in Citizens United or related cases implies a First Amendment bar to bribery prosecutions.[127]

And the trial judge in Senator Menendez's case noted, "a donation to an independent Super PAC can constitute 'anything of value'" under bribery law.[128] Nonetheless a few months later, in 2018, the DOJ decided not to pursue the case and dropped all charges against Senator Menendez.[129]

---

[120] USA v. Silver, Docket No. 1:15-cr-00093 (S.D.N.Y. May 11, 2018) (Jury verdict of guilty on all counts).

[121] *Id.* (Aug. 13, 2018) (Notice of Appeal filed).

[122] Feuer, *supra* note 118 ("[a jury] declared that they were deadlocked in the high-profile corruption trial [ ] of Robert Menendez, a Democratic senator from New Jersey ...").

[123] United States v. Menendez, 137 F.Supp.3d 688, 691 (D.N.J. 2015) ("On April 1, 2015, Defendants Robert Menendez. ... [was] indicted ... on charges of bribery and related crimes.").

[124] Joseph Ax, *Corruption trial of Senator Menendez ends in mistrial*, REUTERS (Nov. 16, 2017), www.reuters.com/article/us-new-jersey-menendez/corruption-trial-of -senator-menendez-ends-in-mistrial-idUSKBN1DG2NP.

[125] United States v. Menendez, 291 F.Supp.3d 606, 640 (D.N.J. 2018) ("Defendants' Rule 29 motion is granted in part, and denied in part.").

[126] *Id.* at 616 (citing McDonnell).

[127] *Id.* at 621.

[128] *Id.* at 622.

[129] Laura Jarrett, Dan Berman & Sarah Jorgensen, *Justice Dept. won't retry Sen. Bob Menendez*, CNN (Jan. 31, 2018), www.cnn.com/2018/01/31/politics/menendez -charges-dismiss/index.html.

To sum up, in the wake of *McDonnell*, *Skilling*, *Citizens United* and *McCutcheon*'s deregulation of corruption, ex-Governor Blagojevich was resentenced, Majority Leader Bruno was retried and exonerated by a jury, Majority Leader Skelos was retried, Assembly Speaker Silver was retried and U.S. Senator Menendez had a hung jury followed by the dismissal of all charges. As this complicated story shows, upon retrial, Skelos and Silver were both convicted for a second time. But these examples show the extra lengths to which federal prosecutors must go in order to bring corrupt politicians to justice in the fraught legal environment created by the Supreme Court.

6. CONCLUSION

With respect to the argument that the Supreme Court is just avoiding criminalizing politics, this chapter provides evidence that they are going too far in the other direction: allowing potential criminals freedom.[130] Politicians who have been charged with serious allegations of political corruption are using the Supreme Court's rebranding of corruption, including its lax interpretations of what counts as corruption from both campaign finance and criminal cases, to their legal advantage.

Given this legal background, is it surprising to have accusations of corruption reaching the president's Cabinet and even the Oval Office?[131] Not really. This is the path that the Supreme Court began charting for the nation in 2006. That any individual gave in to temptation left open by the Supreme Court to be corrupt is, of course, the fault of each person. But the Supreme Court opened the door wide for corruption to dance in, high-kicking, like a line of Rockettes. And here's a sobering thought: The Supreme Court may not be done rebranding corruption.

---

[130] Ciara Torres-Spelliscy, *The Supreme Court Throws Kryptonite at Democracy's Supermen*, HUFF. POST (June 30, 2016), www.huffingtonpost.com/ciara-torresspelliscy/scotus-throws-kryptonite-_b_10758060.html.

[131] Tom Scheck, *Ethics Be Damned: More than half of Trump's 20-person Cabinet has engaged in questionable or unethical conduct*, APM (Feb. 16, 2018), www.marketplace.org/2018/02/16/world/ethics-be-damned-more-half-trumps-20-person-cabinet-has-engaged-questionable-or.

3. Branding corporations

1. INTRODUCTION

The Supreme Court's stances on truth and corruption shape the legal landscape for American politics. Another key legal ingredient to add to this mix is how the Supreme Court deals with corporate money in politics. An offshoot of this is the dark money problem, though dark money is not actually the Supreme Court's fault.

Citizens United v. FEC from 2010 gives corporate managers a power they may not actually want to wield: the ability to spend corporate resources on politics.[1] Because politics is a risky business and politicizing business is risky,[2] managers who spend corporate resources on elections may negatively impact their company's own brands.[3] The public can see from disclosures at select publicly traded firms that managers are using corporate resources (and not just their own funds) in politics. And the public can, and does, judge them for it. Indeed, former Senator Russ Feingold has warned: "We're going to have Republican and Democrat toothpaste."[4] But after 2017, the world for brands is even more fraught when an unexpected angry tweet from President Trump can send a company's stock into temporary freefall.[5]

---

[1]   *See* Citizens United v. FEC, 558 U.S. 310, 365–66 (2010); Lucian A. Bebchuk & Zvika Neeman, *Investor Protection and Interest Group Politics*, 23 Rev. of Fin. Studies 3 at 1089 (2010) ("corporate insiders may be able to use some of the resources of the publicly traded companies under their control to influence politicians").

[2]   *See* Nate Silver, The Signal and the Noise: Why So Many Predictions Fail but Some Don't 411 (2012) ("In politics, a domain in which the truth enjoys no privileged status, it's anybody's guess.").

[3]   *See* Michael Hadani & Douglas A. Schuler, *In Search of El Dorado: The Elusive Financial Returns on Corporate Political Investments*, 34 Strategic Mgmt. J. 165, 165–66 (2013) ("We find that firms' political investments are significantly and negatively related to market valuation[.]").

[4]   Thomas L. Friedman & Michael Mandelbaum, That Used to Be Us: How America Fell Behind in the World It Invented and We can Come Back 245 (2011) (quoting Senator Feingold).

[5]   Chris Jackson & Clifford Young, *Brand Risk in the New Age of Populism: Four Key Tactics for Surviving Hyper-Partisan Consumers*, Ipsos 1 (2017) ("since the election of Donald Trump, it is clear that avoiding politics is not always in a brand's control.

Scandal can hurt a corporate brand.[6] And getting in the middle of a political fight can be a scandal in and of itself for a corporation. As Professor Robert W. Emerson argues, businesses jumping into the middle of politics is about as smart as dropping a lit match while standing in a pool of gasoline and the result is likely the same: getting burned badly.[7] As he puts it:

> to take such potentially off-putting *noncommercial* stands on matters of ideology, theology, or sheer personal philosophy appears ... plainly pigheaded. They are picking a needless fight, a bad-for-business action with the reaction, intended or not, being to convert a purely commercial [trade]mark into a brand with strong, perhaps incendiary, political overtones.[8]

In short, a businessperson could be shooting his or her brand in the proverbial foot by getting involved in politics. The old adage that business and politics don't mix is borne out by the history of corporations getting boycotted for perceived and actual political stances.[9]

In the digital age, politically active corporations in the United States are facing a perfect storm that makes corporate political expenditures and taking public stances on political issues particularly perilous. Ingredients of this perfect storm include the increasingly politically polarized American public and technological advances that place data about the political affiliations of brands in the palms of consumers' and shareholders' hands, which facilitates boycotts and divestment. Chris Jackson and Clifford Young urge that in this environment of political polarization:

> Smart brands should undertake a top-to-bottom evaluation of potential political risks ... [including] [p]olitical statements from company leaders; association with divisive political figures; actions or statements associated with protests; carrying products associated with divisive political figures; or contributing funds towards political issues.[10]

... how does a brand 'manage' when the leader of the free world blasts them in his 5 a.m. tweet?").

[6]   Michael J. Freno, *Trademark Valuation: Preserving Brand Equity*, 97 TRADEMARK REP. 1055, 1056 (2007) ("whereas scandal can increase public recognition for a trademark (theoretically strengthening the mark from a legal perspective and even making a mark 'famous'), scandal can simultaneously hurt the brand.").

[7]   *See* Robert W. Emerson & Jason R. Parnell, *Franchise Hostages: Fast Food, God, and Politics*, 29 J.L. & POL. 353, 357 (2014).

[8]   *Id.*

[9]   *See id.* at 359–67 (discussing the repercussions following the issuance of politically-charged statements by Chik-Fil-A and Papa John's respective directors).

[10]   Jackson & Young, *supra* note 5, at 9.

Companies should be wary of getting in the middle of political fights precisely because it places the value of their brand at risk. The worth of a brand to a large company is often millions of dollars, and in a few cases multiple billions of dollars.[11]

This chapter will explain what the Supreme Court has allowed and disallowed in the area of corporate money in politics. It will then provide data on how corporations are taking advantage of their post-2010 right to spend in elections. It will go on to explore how corporate political activities could run into difficulties with customers and investors—corporate America's two Achilles' heels related to their brands.

2.   THE SUPREME COURT'S RULINGS ON CORPORATE MONEY IN POLITICS

There are two key operative rulings from the Supreme Court on corporate money in politics: *Citizens United v. FEC* from 2010 and *FEC v. Beaumont* from 2003. As discussed in Chapter 2, *Citizens United* allows corporations (both nonprofit and for profit, both publicly traded and privately held) to spend an unlimited amount on political ads, so long as the spending is independent.[12] As the Supreme Court found in *Citizens United*:

> [The] prohibition on corporate independent expenditures is ... a ban on speech. ... Speech is an essential mechanism of democracy, for it is the means to hold officials accountable to the people. ... The right of citizens to inquire, to hear, to speak, and to use information to reach consensus is a precondition to enlightened self-government and a necessary means to protect it.[13]

---

[11]   Justin Anderson, *Measuring the Financial Value of Brand Equity*, J. Bus. Admin. Online 1 (Spring 2011) ("[B]rand equity is defined as the financial value that a firm derives from customer response to the marketing of a brand."); Deven R. Desai, *From Trademarks to Brands*, 64 Fla. L. Rev. 981, 1018–19 (2012) ("well before modern assessments of brand value developed, companies asserted that brands were worth millions of dollars ... [F]rom the late 1980s onwards, 'intangible assets—usually in the form of brand names—represent[ed] the larger share' of a company's overall value." (third alteration in original) (footnote omitted)); Ivana Kottasova, *The Value of a Brand: Apple and Google Top $100 Billion*, CNN (Oct. 10, 2014), www.cnn.com/2014/10/09/business/most-valuable-brands/.

[12]   Citizens United, 558 U.S. at 370; Ronald Dworkin, *The Decision That Threatens Democracy*, N.Y. Rev. Books (May 13, 2010).

[13]   Citizens United, 558 U.S. at 339.

Right after *Citizens United*, a D.C. Circuit case called *SpeechNow* allowed
for the creation of federal Super PACs.[14] The D.C. Circuit found in light of
Citizens United that "the government has no anti-corruption interest in limiting contributions to an independent expenditure group."[15] A Super PAC is
different than other federal PACs because it can take in contributions from
unlimited sources in unlimited amounts, so long as its funders are not foreign
nationals and the spending is done independently. Post-*Citizens United*, many
publicly-traded companies have exercised their new rights under *Citizens
United* and *SpeechNow* by giving large donations to Super PACs; in many
cases, corporate donations are as large as $1 million. However, it should be
noted that both *Citizens United* and *SpeechNow* upheld the disclosure of the
sources of money in politics as being perfectly constitutional. As the D.C.
Circuit said in *SpeechNow*:

> [T]he public has an interest in knowing who is speaking about a candidate and who
> is funding that speech, no matter whether the contributions were made towards
> administrative expenses or independent expenditures. Further, requiring disclosure
> of such information deters and helps expose violations of other campaign finance
> restrictions, such as those barring contributions from foreign corporations or indi-
> viduals. These are sufficiently important governmental interests to justify requiring
> *SpeechNow* to ... report to the FEC ...[16]

Meanwhile, corporations (both nonprofit and for profit, both publicly traded
and privately held) are still banned from making direct donations to federal
candidates under the 1907 Tillman Act.[17] This law was most recently upheld
by the Supreme Court in *FEC v. Beaumont*.[18] As the Supreme Court in
Beaumont explained:

> the [Tillman Act's corporate treasury spending] ban has always done further duty
> in protecting 'the individuals who have paid money into a corporation or union
> for purposes other than the support of candidates from having that money used to
> support political candidates to whom they may be opposed.'[19]

---

[14]   SpeechNow.org v. FEC, 599 F.3d 686, 695 (D.C. Cir. 2010), *cert. denied
sub nom* Keating v. FEC, __ S. Ct. __, 2010 WL 4272775 (Nov. 1, 2010) (holding
that federal PACs which only make independent expenditures may accept unlimited
contributions).
[15]   *Id.*
[16]   SpeechNow.org, 599 F.3d at 698.
[17]   Tillman Act of 1907, Pub. L. No. 59-36, 34 Stat. 86.
[18]   *FEC v. Beaumont*, 539 U.S. 146 (2003) (direct contribution ban from nonprofit
corporation is consistent with the First Amendment).
[19]   *Id. at* 154; *id.* at 159–60 ("[C]oncern about the corrupting potential underlying
the corporate ban may indeed be implicated by advocacy corporations.").

To sidestep the Tillman Act restrictions, many corporations have corporate PACs which are funded by individuals associated with the corporation, such as employees and executives.[20] A corporate PAC cannot use corporate treasury funds, but corporate PACs can be an important source of funding for federal candidates. *Beaumont* is still good law even after *Citizens United*.[21]

So under *Citizens United* (and its offshoot, *SpeechNow*) and *Beaumont*, corporations can buy as many corporate-funded ads as they desire in any American election and can give an unlimited amount of corporate donations to a federal Super PAC, but a corporation cannot give money directly to federal candidates. An additional complication to all of the above is that each of the 50 states has its own election laws regulating state level and local elections, including laws governing corporate money in politics. In some states, like Virginia, there are no restrictions on corporate spending in state elections; whereas in others, like Massachusetts, corporations are wholly banned from making political contributions to candidates for state office.[22]

3.   PUBLICLY TRADED CORPORATIONS' SPENDING IN POLITICS

One way that a company can earn a reputation for being a Republican or Democratic company is if its corporate PAC or corporate leaders fund the Republican or Democratic Party or partisan candidates. Past experience shows that directors at public firms were already in the habit of spending their own money on politics.[23] For example, one study noted that over 83 percent of Fortune 500 CEOs and board members make personal campaign contribu-

---

[20]   *Id.* at 163 ("The PAC option allows corporate political participation without the temptation to use corporate funds for political influence, quite possibly at odds with the sentiments of some shareholders …").

[21]   U.S. v. Danielczyk, 683 F.3d 611, 614 (4th Cir. 2012) (*Beaumont* is still good law), *cert. denied,* No. 12-579, 2013 WL 656067 (Feb. 25, 2013). *Accord* Minn. Citizens Concerned for Life, Inc. v. Swanson, 692 F.3d 864, 867–69 (8th Cir. 2012); Preston v. Leake, 660 F.3d 726, 729 (4th Cir. 2011); Ill. Liberty PAC v. Madigan,---F. Supp. 2d---, 2012 WL 4764152 at **1-3 (N.D. Ill. Oct. 5, 2012), *aff'd,* No. 12-3305, 2012 WL 5259036 (7th Cir. Oct. 24, 2012); *see also* Iowa Right to Life Comm., Inc. v. Tooker, 795 F. Supp. 2d 852, 869 (S.D. Iowa 2011), *certified question answered,* Iowa Right To Life Comm., Inc. v. Tooker, 808 N.W.2d 417 (Iowa 2011) ("pursuant to *Beaumont,* Iowa can generally ban all direct corporate contributions.").

[22]   1A Auto, Inc. v. Director of the Office of Campaign & Political Finance (Mass. Supreme Ct. Sept. 6, 2018) (upholding Massachusetts' corporate contribution ban), *cert. denied* 88 U.S. ____ (2019) (U.S. May 20, 2019) (No. 18-733).

[23]   Adam Bonica, Avenues of Influence: On the Political Expenditures of Corporations and Their Directors and Executives 15 (2013), www.princeton .edu/csdp/events/Bonica11072013/SSRN-id2313232.pdf ("Of the sample of direc-

tions.[24] Specifically, over 90 percent of directors make contributions, which is much higher than the contribution rates for other politically active professionals, such as lawyers who contribute at a rate of 45–50 percent.[25]

When *Citizens United* was first decided, there was an open question about whether publicly traded corporations would exercise their new First Amendment rights. Nearly a decade later, a data set has emerged. According to the Center for Responsive Politics which runs the webpage *Open Secrets*, in 2010 Alliance Resource Partners, L.P. (ticker ARLPT) gave $2 425 000 to American Crossroads (R); American Financial Group (ticker AFG) gave $400 000 to American Crossroads (R); MGM Resorts (ticker MGM) gave $300 000 to Patriot Majority (D); Clean Energy Fuels Corp (ticker CLNE) gave $175 000 to Patriot Majority (D); and Ultra Petroleum (UPL) gave $50 000 to the Club for Growth Action(R), for $3 350 000 total from publicly traded companies to Super PACs in 2010.

Then in 2012, Chevron (ticker CVX) gave $2.5 million to the Congressional Leadership Fund (R);[26] Clayton Williams Energy (ticker CWEI) gave $1 million to American Crossroads (R);[27] Chesapeake Energy (ticker CHK) gave $125 000 to Make Us Great Again (R);[28] Scotts Miracle-Gro (ticker SMG) gave $200 000 to Restore our Future (R);[29] CONSOL Energy (ticker CNX) gave $150 000 to Restore our Future (R);[30] and Hallador Energy (ticker HNRG) gave $100 000 to Restore our Future (R).[31] This totaled $4 250 000 from publicly traded companies to Super PACs in 2012.

The story was much the same in the 2014 midterm. In 2014, Alliance Resource Partners, L.P. (ticker ARLPT) gave $1.5 million to American Crossroads (R) and Hallador Energy (ticker HNRG) gave the group over

---

tors and CEOs of Fortune 500 companies, at least 83 percent have made political contributions.").

[24] *Id.*

[25] *Id.* at 32–33 ("[T]he remarkably high participation rate of over 90 percent of directors ... sets them apart from those employed in other high paying professions. ... [E]stimates of contribution rates ... place medical doctors at around 15 to 20 percent and lawyers, who are known for their involvement in politics, at around 45 to 50 percent.").

[26] *Congressional Leadership Fund: Top Donors, 2012 Cycle*, OpenSecrets.org, www.opensecrets.org/outsidespending/contrib.php?cmte=C00504530&cycle=2012.

[27] *American Crossroads: Top Donors, 2012 Cycle*, OpenSecrets.org, www.opensecrets.org/outsidespending/contrib.php?cmte=C00487363&cycle=2012.

[28] *Make Us Great Again: Top Donors, 2012 Cycle*, OpenSecrets.org, www.opensecrets.org/outsidespending/contrib.php?cmte=C00499731&cycle=2012.

[29] *Restore Our Future: Donors*, OpenSecrets.org, www.opensecrets.org/outsidespending/contrib_all.php?cycle=2012&type=A&cmte=C00490045&page=4.

[30] *Id.*

[31] *Id.*

$200 000;[32] meanwhile, KapStone Paper and Packaging Corp. (ticker KS) gave $1 250 000 and BB&T (ticker BBT) gave $156 925 to Freedom Partners Action Fund;[33] Chevron (ticker CVX) and Alliance Resource Partners, L.P. (ticker ARLPT) gave $1 million each to Congressional Leadership Fund (R); while Apollo Education Group Inc. (ticker APOL) and Swisher (ticker SWSH) gave a more modest $50 000 each.[34] This totaled $5 206 925 from publicly traded companies to Super PACs in 2014.

In the 2016 election, corporate spending from publicly traded companies continued to rise. In 2016 Chevron (ticker CVX) gave $2 million to the Senate Leadership Fund[35] and $1.3 million to the Congressional Leadership Fund (R);[36] Next Era Energy (ticker NEE) gave to $1 million Right to Rise (Jeb Bush)[37] and $100 000 to Conservative Solutions (Rubio);[38] Devon Energy (ticker DVN) gave $750 000 to the Senate Leadership Fund (R)[39] and $500 000 to the Congressional Leadership Fund (R);[40] The GEO Group (ticker GEO) gave $200 000 to the Senate Leadership Fund (R), $100 000 to Right to Rise (Jeb Bush),[41] $100 000 to Conservative Solutions (Rubio)[42] and $225 000 to Rebuilding America Now (Trump);[43] Alliance Holdings GP (ticker AHGP) gave $475 000 to the Congressional Leadership Fund (R);[44] Duke Energy (ticker DUK) gave $150 000 to the Senate Leadership Fund (R);[45] Masimo

---

[32] *American Crossroads: Top Donors, 2014 Cycle*, OPENSECRETS.ORG, WWW .opensecrets.org/outsidespending/contrib.php?cmte=C00487363&cycle=2014.

[33] *Freedom Partners Action Fund: Top Donors, 2014 Cycle*, OPENSECRETS.ORG, www.opensecrets.org/outsidespending/contrib.php?cmte=C00564765&cycle=2014.

[34] *Congressional Leadership Fund: Top Donors, 2014 Cycle*, OPENSECRETS.ORG, www.opensecrets.org/outsidespending/contrib.php?cmte=C00504530&cycle=2014.

[35] *Senate Leadership Fund Donors*, 2016 Cycle, OPENSECRETS.ORG, WWW .opensecrets.org/pacs/pacgave2.php?cycle=2016&cmte=C00571703.

[36] *Congressional Leadership Fund: Top Donors, 2016 Cycle*, OPENSECRETS.ORG, www.opensecrets.org/pacs/pacgave2.php?sort=A&cmte=C00504530&cycle=2016& Page=1.

[37] *Right to Rise Donors, 2016 Cycle*, OPENSECRETS.ORG, www.opensecrets.org/ pacs/pacgave2.php?cycle=2016&cmte=C00571372.

[38] *Conservative Solutions Donors, 2016 Cycle*, OPENSECRETS.ORG, WWW .opensecrets.org/pacs/pacgave2.php?sort=A&cmte=C00541292&cycle=2016&Page= 2.

[39] *Senate Leadership Fund Donors, 2016 Cycle*, *supra* note 35.

[40] *Congressional Leadership Fund Donors, 2016 Cycle*, *supra* note 36.

[41] *Right to Rise: Top Donors, 2016 Cycle*, *supra* note 37.

[42] *Conservative Solutions Donors, 2016 Cycle*, *supra* note 38

[43] *Rebuilding America Now Donors, 2016 Cycle*, OPENSECRETS.ORG, WWW .opensecrets.org/pacs/pacgave2.php?cmte=C00618876&cycle=2016.

[44] *Congressional Leadership Fund: 2016 Cycle*, *supra* note 36.

[45] *Senate Leadership Fund Donors, 2016 Cycle*, *supra* note 35.

Corporation (ticker MASI) gave $100 000 to the Senate Majority PAC (D);[46] Brown & Brown Inc (ticker BRO) gave $100 000 to Right to Rise (Jeb Bush);[47] Alico Inc (ticker ALCO) gave $100 000 to Right to Rise (Jeb Bush);[48] and Altria Client Services LLC, a subsidiary of Altria Group Inc. (ticker MO), gave $175 000 to the Congressional Leadership Fund (R).[49] This totaled $6 975 000 from publicly traded companies to Super PACs in 2016.

The 2018 midterm appears to have been a watershed moment in terms of corporate political spending by publicly traded companies. It was way up, in terms of both number of firms and aggregate spending. It was also skewed heavily Republican. In 2018 Chevron (ticker CVX) gave $1.75 million to the Congressional Leadership Fund (R)[50] and $1.9 million to the Senate Leadership Fund (R);[51] Valero Services, a subsidiary of Valero Energy Corporation (ticker VLO), gave $1.5 million to the Congressional Leadership Fund (R)[52] and $250 000 to the Senate Leadership Fund (R);[53] RAI Services Company, which operates as a subsidiary of Reynolds American Inc. (ticker RAI), gave $850 000 to the Congressional Leadership Fund (R)[54] and $450 000 to the Senate Leadership Fund (R);[55] Occidental Petroleum (ticker OXY) gave $750 000 to the Congressional Leadership Fund (R)[56] and $400 000 to the Senate Leadership Fund (R);[57] Marathon Petroleum (ticker MPC) gave $530 000 to the Congressional Leadership Fund (R)[58] and $1.53 million to the Senate Leadership Fund (R);[59] Scotts Miracle-Gro (ticker SMG) gave $350 000 to the Congressional Leadership Fund (R)[60] and $50 000 to America First Action (R);[61] Altria Client Services, a limited liability company that

---

[46] *Senate Majority PAC Donors, 2016 Cycle*, OPENSECRETS.ORG, www.opensecrets .org/pacs/pacgave2.php?sort=A&cmte=C00484642&cycle=2016&Page=2.

[47] *Right to Rise: Top Donors, 2016 Cycle, supra* note 37.

[48] *Id.*

[49] *Congressional Leadership Fund: 2016 Cycle, supra* note 36.

[50] *Congressional Leadership Fund: Donors, 2018 Cycle*, OPENSECRETS.ORG, www .opensecrets.org/outsidespending/contrib.php?cmte=C00504530&cycle=2018.

[51] *Senate Leadership Fund Donors, 2018 Cycle,* OPENSECRETS.ORG, www .opensecrets.org/outsidespending/contrib.php?cmte=C00571703&cycle=2018.

[52] *Congressional Leadership Fund: 2018 Cycle, supra* note 50.

[53] *Senate Leadership Fund Donors, 2018 Cycle, supra* note 51.

[54] *Congressional Leadership Fund: 2018 Cycle, supra* note 50.

[55] *Senate Leadership Fund Donors, 2018 Cycle, supra* note 51.

[56] *Congressional Leadership Fund: 2018 Cycle, supra* note 50.

[57] *Senate Leadership Fund Donors, 2018 Cycle, supra* note 51.

[58] *Congressional Leadership Fund: 2018 Cycle, supra* note 50.

[59] *Senate Leadership Fund Donors, 2018 Cycle, supra* note 51.

[60] *Congressional Leadership Fund: 2018 Cycle, supra* note 50.

[61] *America First Action Donors, 2018 Cycle*, OPENSECRETS.ORG, www.opensecrets .org/outsidespending/contrib.php?cmte=C00637512&cycle=2018.

services Altria (ticker MO), gave $332 930 to the Congressional Leadership Fund (R)[62] and $325 000 to the Senate Leadership Fund (R);[63] ConocoPhillips (ticker COP) gave $250 000 to the Congressional Leadership Fund (R)[64] and $1 million to the Senate Leadership Fund (R);[65] Ai Altep Holdings, an affiliate of EP Energy Corp (ticker EPE), gave $1 million to the Senate Leadership Fund (R);[66] Alliance Coal, LLC, which operates as a subsidiary of Alliance Resource Partners LP (ticker ARLP), gave $1 million to the Senate Leadership Fund (R);[67] Next Era Energy (ticker NEE) gave $1 million to the Senate Leadership Fund (R);[68] Devon Energy Production Company, L.P., which operates as a subsidiary of Devon Energy Corporation (ticker DVN), gave $600 000 to the Senate Leadership Fund (R);[69] Peabody Investments, a subsidiary of Peabody Energy (ticker BTU), gave $500 000 to the Senate Leadership Fund (R);[70] Boeing Co (ticker BA) gave $250 000 to the Senate Leadership Fund (R);[71] MGM Resorts International (ticker MGM) gave $250 000 to the Senate Leadership Fund (R);[72] and Continental Resources (ticker CLR) gave $550 000 to America First Action (R).[73] Former Florida Governor Rick Scott, who successfully challenged Bill Nelson for his Senate seat, was a particularly common beneficiary of this corporate largesse in 2018. Heritage Insurance (ticker HRTG) gave $200 000 to New Republican PAC (Scott);[74] GEO Group (ticker GEO) gave $175 000 to New Republican PAC (Scott);[75] Select Medical Holdings Corp (SEM) gave $150 000 to New Republican PAC (Scott);[76] Alico Inc (ALCO) gave $100 000 to New Republican PAC (Scott);[77] Copart Inc (ticker CPRT) gave $100 000 to New Republican PAC (Scott);[78] and Sunseeker Resorts, an affiliate of Allegiant Travel Company (ticker ALGT),

---

[62] *Congressional Leadership Fund: 2018 Cycle, supra* note 50.
[63] *Senate Leadership Fund Donors, 2018 Cycle, supra* note 51.
[64] *Congressional Leadership Fund: 2018 Cycle, supra* note 50.
[65] *Senate Leadership Fund Donors, 2018 Cycle, supra* note 51.
[66] *Id.*
[67] *Id.*
[68] *Id.*
[69] *Id.*
[70] *Id.*
[71] *Id.*
[72] *Id.*
[73] *America First Action Donors, 2018 Cycle, supra* note 61.
[74] *New Republican PAC Donors, 2018 Cycle*, OPENSECRETS.ORG, www.opensecrets.org/outsidespending/contrib.php?cmte=C00544544&cycle=2018.
[75] *Id.*
[76] *Id.*
[77] *Id.*
[78] *Id.*

gave $100 000 to New Republican PAC (Scott).[79] This totaled $18 192 930 from publicly traded companies to Super PACs in 2018.

This disclosed corporate political spending from publicly traded companies listed above likely understates the true scope of such spending because corporate money can be spent in the "dark"—in other words, hidden by using opaque intermediaries.[80] In fact, between 2010–19, over $1 billion spent in federal elections was from an untraceable, dark source.[81] Over $111 million of this dark money was routed through the U.S. Chamber of Commerce, an opaque business trade association.[82] Dark money has long been criticized by election reform advocates like Liz Kennedy, who said, "[I]f an educated customer is the best consumer, then we should also want educated citizens to make the best voters."[83]

Another interesting thing about the data above is that, despite all of the corporate money going the Republicans' way in 2018, the House still flipped to the Democrats—and many of the Democratic candidates who won ran while refusing to take any corporate PAC money:

Sixty percent of all flipped House seats switching from one party to another were flipped by champions of campaign finance reform, and more than half (51.2 percent) of House seats that flipped were won by first-time candidates. In total, 15 states had

---

[79]   *Id.*

[80]   Karin Kamp, *Clip: What You Need to Know About Dark Money*, MOYERS & Co. (Mar. 21, 2014), http://billmoyers.com/2014/03/21/what-you-need-to-know-about -dark-money/.

[81]   Ciara Torres-Spelliscy, Opinion, *Court Ruling Drowned Politics in Dark Money: The Front Burner*, ORLANDO SENTINEL (Mar. 13, 2015), www.orlando sentinel.com/ opinion/os-ed-citizens-united-front-burner-con-20150312-story.html; Anna Massoglia, *State of Money in Politics: Billion-dollar 'dark money' spending is just the tip of the iceberg*, OPEN SECRETS (Feb. 21, 2019), https://www.opensecrets.org/news/2019/02/ somp3-billion-dollar-dark-money-tip-of-the-iceberg/.

[82]   *US Chamber of Commerce: Outside Spending Summary 2012*, OPENSECRETS.ORG, www.opensecrets.org/outsidespending/detail.php?cycle=2012&cmte=C90013145 (showing 2012 spending at $32 255 439); *US Chamber of Commerce: Outside Spending Summary 2014*, OPENSECRETS.ORG, www.opensecrets.org/outsidespending/ detail.php?cycle=2014&cmte=C90013145 (showing 2014 spending at $35 464 243); *US Chamber of Commerce: Outside Spending Summary 2016*, OPENSECRETS.ORG, www.opensecrets.org/orgs/summary.php?id=D000019798&cycle=2016 (showing 2016 spending at $29 099 947); *US Chamber of Commerce: Outside Spending Summary 2018*, OPENSECRETS.ORG, WWW.OPENSECRETS.ORG/ORGS/SUMMARY.PHP?ID= D000019798&CYCLE=2018 (showing 2016 spending at $11 908 413), *see also* Dave Levinthal, *Trade Groups to Top Corporations: Resist Political Disclosure*, CTR. FOR PUB. INTEGRITY (Jan. 27, 2016), www.publicintegrity.org/2016/01/27/19185/trade -groups-top-corporations-resist-political-disclosure.

[83]   Interview with Liz Kennedy (May 7, 2018).

at least one House seat flip by candidates who campaigned on refusing contributions from corporate PACs."[84]

Additionally—with the exception of MGM Resorts, which gave $300 000 to Patriot Majority (D); Clean Energy Fuels Corp, which gave $175 000 to Patriot Majority (D); and Masimo Corporation, which gave $100 000 to the Democratic Senate Majority PAC—*all* of the other corporate donations to Super PACs listed above from 2010–18 were for the benefit of Republicans. If, as Michael Jordan once said, "Republicans buy sneakers too,"[85] perhaps it would behoove these corporate donors to remember that Democrats also pump gas, go on vacation and mow their lawns. Why? Because as researchers Costas Panagopoulos *et al.* found, when consumers learned about the corporate political spending for companies behind popular brands, they said that they would change their consumption to match their own partisan views.[86]

4.   ACTIVIST CONSUMERS

For the management consultants at McKinsey, there is no such thing as bad attention. As they wrote in a recent report about navigating negative stories about a product on social media:

> Despite the grueling news stories about reputational damage spinning out of control – often dramatized as 'social media shit storms' – none of the companies we looked at in our research actually suffered any significant or sustained impact on sales or stock price – provided they reacted swiftly and constructively to arising criticism. In fact, some companies managed to turn even negative attention into positive buzz ...[87]

---

[84]   Manuela Ekowo, *Running without corporate PAC backing is a winning strategy*, ReThink Media (Jan. 17, 2019), https://rethinkmedia.org/resource/running-without-corporate-pac-backing-winning-strategy?authkey=98449583425da507a9 2a2d586803afcab40993d6b983f647a6820a7376c090df.

[85]   Naomi Klein, No Logo: Taking Aim at Brand Bullies 186 (1999).

[86]   Costas Panagopoulos *et al.*, *Risky Business: Does Corporate Political Giving Affect Consumer Behavior?* (Oct. 26, 2016) (unpublished), rubenson.org/wp-content/uploads/2016/10/Panagopoulos-etal.pdf ("It appears that few people have much background knowledge about the political sympathies of leading national chains, but when told which corporations are the largest or most lopsided contributors to a political party, respondents express their partisanship through their consumption choices.").

[87]   Frank Mattern *et al.*, *Turning Buzz into Gold How Pioneers Create Value from Social Media*, McKinsey & Co 10 (2012), www.mckinsey.com/~/media/mckinsey/dotcom/client_service/bto/pdf/turning_buzz_into_gold.ashx.

But not every company can turn a brand crisis into a brand opportunity, because the hyper-branded America of the early twenty-first century is also a hyper-partisan America.[88] Partisan rifts are real and growing.[89] The consequence of four in ten internet users following brands on social media is that commercial brands can influence what their followers think. But it's a two-way street—the public can push back against behavior they dislike from a brand online too:[90]

> The rapid expansion of social media has provided a platform for any consumer to express their opinions and find like-minded people. As a consequence, social media has become the ground-zero for most brand crisis. Especially as consumers have become polarized, they have sorted themselves into online communities of likeminded people. These communities allow for the politicization of brands to 'go viral' and spread from consumer to consumer rapidly.[91]

As a result, brands today are increasingly vulnerable to subversion and coop-tation on social media. Post-*Citizens United*, there are perils for a commercial brand being perceived as overtly partisan. Chris Jackson and Clifford Young found "no matter which way a company moves politically, there are quite likely going to be customers who object."[92]

Customers may not just be polarized into Republican and Democratic camps; they may also be divided on myriad wedge issues like marriage

---

[88] Carroll Doherty, *7 Things to Know About Polarization in America*, Pew (June 12, 2014), www.pewresearch.org/fact-tank/2014/06/12/7-things-to-know-about -polarization-in-america/ ("The share of Americans who express consistently conserva-tive or consistently liberal opinions has doubled over the past two decades, from 10% to 21%. As a result, the amount of ideological overlap between the two parties has dimin-ished." (emphasis omitted)).

[89] *Id.* ("Partisan antipathy has risen. The share of Republicans who have very unfa-vorable opinions of the Democratic Party has jumped from 17% to 43% in the last 20 years. Similarly, the share of Democrats with very negative opinions of the Republican Party also has more than doubled, from 16% to 38%." (emphasis omitted)); Eli Pariser, The Filter Bubble: How the New Personalized Web Is Changing What We Read and How WE Think What the Internet is Hiding From You 88 (2011) ("[P]artisans of one political stripe tend not to consume the media of another.").

[90] Brad Smith, *31 Advertising Statistics to Know in 2018*, Word Stream (July 19, 2018), www.wordstream.com/blog/ws/2018/07/19/advertising-statistics ("4 in 10 inter-net users say they follow their favorite brands on social media. ... Beyond that, 1 in 4 internet users also follow brands from which they're considering making a purchase—meaning that even if they aren't customers yet, the content you share with your follow-ers could be the determining factor in whether they convert.").

[91] *Brand Risk in the New Age of Populism: Four Key Tactics for Surviving Hyper-Partisan Consumers*, Ipsos 9 (June 7, 2017), www.ipsos.com/sites/default/files/ 2017-06/IpsosPA_POV_PoliticsAndBrands.pdf.

[92] *Id.*

equality, reproductive health and the environment. Customers are increasingly interested in social issues. As YouGov found:

> Between November 2016 and February 2017 ... 31% of US adults increased their level of support for a specific cause. The issues that gained the most backing during this time period were immigration (51%), women's rights (43%), diversity and inclusion (41%), education (40%), and the environment (38%).[93]

Thus, taking a stand on these wedge issues can cause as much tumult for corporate brands as giving money to Republicans or Democrats.

But remaining neutral may be tougher for commercial brands. In 2018, SAP found "[m]ore than half (54 percent) of American consumers consider themselves to be socially conscious shoppers ..."[94] Marketing company Sprout likewise revealed in 2018 that "[t]wo-thirds of consumers (66%) say it's important for brands to take public stands on social and political issues ..."[95] Others have also found that "consumers are ... increasingly organizing their behavior around their political identity. With consumers demanding a certain political behavior, the ability to stay on the sidelines is disappearing."[96] And to make these choices extra complicated for corporate leaders, another survey found about half of Americans want corporations to remain politically neutral, while the other half want them to take political stands.[97]

In contrast to a time when brand owners could speak in a monologue,[98] today brands operate in an environment where millions of end users can talk back to them in negative and positive ways simultaneously.[99] Consider the example

---

[93] Yael Bame, *Two-thirds of US adults support boycotting brands over politics*, YouGov (Mar. 8, 2017) https://today.yougov.com/news/2017/03/08/two-thirds-US-adults-support-boycotting-brands/.

[94] *Americans Prefer to Buy from Socially Conscious Companies This Holiday Shopping Season, SAP Study Finds*, SAP (Dec. 4, 2018), https://news.sap.com/2018/12/socially-conscious-companies-holiday-shopping-season-sap-study/

[95] *#BRANDSGETREAL Championing Change in the Age of Social Media*, Sprout Social (2018), https://sproutsocial.com/insights/data/championing-change-in-the-age-of-social-media/.

[96] Jackson & Young, *supra* note 5, at 4.

[97] *CEOs: We Have a Reputation Problem*, Harris Poll (Mar. 20, 2017), www.theharrispoll.com/business/CEO-Reputation-Problem.html ("The additional Harris Poll research, which was conducted among more than 2,000 U.S. adults February 27 – March 1, shows that Americans are divided when it comes to companies mixing business and politics. Half (51%) of consumers expect companies to have a clear position on visible political matters ...").

[98] Klein, *supra* note 85, at 343.

[99] *See, e.g.*, Jon Krawczynski & Anne M. Peterson, *NBA's Quick Action Helps Rescue Clippers' Brand*, Yahoo! Sports (May 4, 2014), http://sports.yahoo.com/

of Super Bowl ads that get "pre-released" online before the big game.[100] End users can opt in to see the ads and help create buzz by sharing them with professional and friend networks, giving the ads a wider audience than they would reach on Super Bowl Sunday alone.[101] But this is a risky approach if the ad is poorly conceived.[102] The pre-release could be a flop.[103] Customers could share the ad blanketed with criticism and loathing, undermining the firm's most expensive ad buy of the year.[104]

There are many ways for consumers to clap back at what they see as anti-social behavior on the part of commercial brands. One classic tactic is to try to pressure advertisers to abandon a TV show that violates a social norm. Take *Fox News* as an example. When *Fox News* personality Tucker Carlson said that immigration was making America "poorer and dirtier," some viewers urged advertisers to drop support for the show. Groups like Sleeping Giants have kept pressure on advertisers to stop supporting what they deem objectionable content on air and online.[105] Part of the goal of Sleeping Giants is "making 'bigotry and sexism less profitable' over all."[106] With Sleeping Giants' pressure, "the campaign has persuaded at least 17 major advertisers to bail [from Carlson's show], including Jaguar Land Rover, Pacific Life Insurance and IHOP. ..."[107] This particular effort at an advertiser boycott didn't impact

---

news/nbas-quick-action-helps-rescue-175437862--nba.html (observing that Clippers' owner Donald Sterling's comments created a Twitter furor).

[100] The first "viral" pre-release was Volkswagen's 2011 "The Force" ad, which was viewed 11 million times in the week before the Super Bowl. *See* Saba Hamedy & Meg James, *Why Are Super Bowl Ads Posted Online Early?*, L.A. TIMES (Feb. 1, 2015).

[101] *Id.* (In 2014, pre-released ads were watched 2.5 times more than ads aired during the game.)

[102] David Griner, Opinion, *Five Myths About Super Bowl Ads*, WASH. POST (Jan. 30, 2015) (describing how GoDaddy's preview generated enough feedback to cause the company to create a new ad for the Super Bowl).

[103] Arin Greenwood, *GoDaddy Pulls 2015 Super Bowl Ad After Slew of Negative Feedback from Animal Advocates*, HUFF. POST (Jan. 27, 2015), www.huffingtonpost .com/2015/01/28/godaddy-2015-super-bowl-ad_n_6557548.html (noting that over 35,000 users "signed an online petition calling for GoDaddy to" cancel the ad).

[104] The hashtag #NoDaddy trended on Twitter as users shared the ad. *Id.*

[105] Sapna Maheshwari, *Revealed: The People Behind an Anti-Breitbart Twitter Account*, N.Y. TIMES (July 20, 2018) ("after the 2016 election, an anonymously run Twitter account emerged with a plan to choke off advertising dollars to *Breitbart News* ...").

[106] *Id.*

[107] Jack Shafer, *Stop the Stupid Tucker Carlson Boycott. Advertisers should be independent of journalists, and not just the other way around.*, POLITICO (Dec. 19, 2018), www.politico.com/magazine/story/2018/12/19/stop-the-stupid-tucker-carlson-boycott -223387.

Carlson, who simply doubled down on his claims about why immigration is evil, in his view.[108]

Another tactic to get a brand to change its behavior is to urge the public to boycott it directly. Facebook has been subject to many efforts over the years to gets users to delete their accounts. These calls often happen on Twitter using the hashtag #deletefacebook. This happened again when a Facebook executive, Joel Kaplan, showed up to support the elevation of Judge Brett Kavanaugh to the Supreme Court despite accusations that he was guilty of sexual assault. Here, "the executive broke one of the cardinal rules of business branding. 'If you're a strong brand, never get involved with the Holy Trinity: sex, religion, and politics. ... '"[109]

It can also be difficult for a brand to know what will set off a protest. The bourbon makers at Jim Beam may have been shocked when:

> the hashtag #BoycottJimBeam emerged after the actress Mila Kunis, a spokes-woman for the liquor company since 2014, said on 'Conan' that she has been donating to Planned Parenthood under Vice President Mike Pence's name in a form of 'peaceful protest.'[110]

A brand may also get a bad reputation through "guilt by association." Because so many online ads are placed by algorithm, an ad for a benign product could end up on the banner ad of content that is racist, sexist or otherwise offensive.[111] As Paul Heibert warns, "Nearly half of US adults who have encountered online content that they consider racist, sexist, or hateful report viewing the brand advertising next to it more negatively as a result."[112] This problem

---

[108] *As advertisers flee, Tucker Carlson doubles down on claim that immigration makes the United States "poorer and dirtier,"* MEDIA MATTERS (Dec. 17, 2018), www .mediamatters.org/video/2018/12/17/advertisers-flee-tucker-carlson-doubles-down -claim-immigration-makes-united-states-poorer-and/222335.

[109] JP Mangalindan, *Why a Facebook executive's appearance at the Kavanaugh hearing was a big mistake,* YAHOO FINANCE (Oct. 7, 2018), https://finance.yahoo.com/ news/facebook-execs-appearance-kavanaugh-hearing-big-mistake-123027873.html ?soc_src=social-sh&soc_trk=tw (quoting Russell Quinan).

[110] Sapna Maheshwari, *Pizza Is Partisan, and Advertisers Are Still Adjusting,* N.Y. TIMES (Nov. 19, 2017).

[111] Paul Farhi, *The mysterious group that wants to kill Breitbart's ad revenue, one tweet at a time,* CHIC. TRIB. (Sept. 22, 2017) ("Sleeping Giants' basic approach is to raise awareness among *Breitbart's* advertisers that they are, in fact, *Breitbart* advertisers.").

[112] Paul Heibert, *Brands beware: Ads adjacent to offensive online content can hurt,* YOUGOV (Apr. 11, 2017), https://today.yougov.com/news/2017/04/11/brands-beware -ads-adjacent-to-offensive-content/.

has been highlighted again and again by Sleeping Giants. As the *New York Times* reported, Sleeping Giants:

> urged people to collect screenshots of ads on *Breitbart* and then question brands about their support of the site. Sleeping Giants correctly guessed that many companies did not know where their digital ads were running, and advertisers were caught off guard as the account circulated images of blue-chip brands in proximity to headlines like 'Birth Control Makes Women Unattractive and Crazy.'[113]

The *Chicago Tribune* reported that *Breitbart* may have lost as many as 2000 digital advertisers from these name and shame efforts.[114]

5.   ENGAGED SHAREHOLDERS

Corporate political activism has given some shareholders heartburn and consequently conflicts over the propriety of the corporate role in politics have spilled over into the annual corporate proxies at many publicly traded firms. Shareholder actions asking for more socially responsible behavior by companies have taken off in the past two decades with socially responsible investing (SRI).[115] SRI has matured to the point where returns on socially responsible investments are equal to or greater than other investments,[116] as major institutional investors have adopted the approach.[117] In 2018, "[s]ustainable, responsible and impact investing (SRI) assets have expanded to $12.0 trillion in the United States …"[118] And many firms are apparently responding

---

[113]   Maheshwari, *supra* note 105.

[114]   Farhi, *supra* note 111 ("Sleeping Giants' database lists nearly 2,000 companies that have declared Breitbart off limits since November – an astonishing figure, though one hard to confirm because some ad buys recur.").

[115]   *See* Jacob Park & Sonia Kowal, *Socially Responsible Investing 3.0: Understanding Finance and Environmental, Social, and Governance Issues in Emerging Markets*, 18 Geo. Pub. Pol'y Rev. 17, 18 (2013).

[116]   Sarah Pickering, *Our House: Crowdfunding Affordable Homes with Tax Credit Investment Partnerships*, 33 Rev. Banking & Fin. L. 937, 975 (2014) ("[T]here is evidence that certain forms of SRI may outperform traditional investments in periods of financial crisis.").

[117]   Li-Wen Lin, *Corporate Social and Environmental Disclosure in Emerging Securities Markets*, 35 N.C.J. Int'l L. & Com. Reg. 1, 6–7 (2009) ("Large institutional investors … (e.g. CalPERS, the largest public pension fund in the United States), have adopted responsible investment principles.").

[118]   Press Release, *US SIF Foundation Releases 2018 Biennial Report on US Sustainable, Responsible and Impact Investing Trends*, US SIF (Oct. 31, 2018), www.ussif.org/blog_home.asp?Display=118.

to pressure from SRI investors by including reporting about corporate social responsibility.[119]

Since *Citizens United*, socially responsible investors have played a key role in shaping corporate behavior about political spending by placing shareholder proposals about corporate political spending transparency on corporate proxies.[120] In 2018, Lisa Woll, US SIF Foundation CEO, said: "Money managers and institutions are utilizing ESG criteria and shareholder engagement to address a plethora of issues including climate change, diversity, human rights, weapons and political spending …"[121]

As the US SIF reported, "Disclosure and management of corporate political spending and lobbying were also top concerns. Shareholders filed 295 proposals on this subject from 2016 through 2018."[122] According to Si2, "Investor support for board oversight and disclosure of election spending—both directly from companies and indirectly through nonprofit intermediaries such as trade associations—reached an all-time high of just over 33 per cent in 2016."[123] Twelve public firms had a majority of their shareholders vote in favor of political transparency between 2011–16.[124] One driver of high votes in favor of disclosure of corporate political spending could be the largest proxy advisor ISS's pro-disclosure stance.[125] Moreover, in 2015, the California Public Employees' Retirement System (CalPERS), one of the world's largest investors, also updated its *Global Principles of Accountable Corporate Governance*

---

[119] Michael R. Siebecker, *Trust & Transparency: Promoting Efficient Corporate Disclosure Through Fiduciary-Based Discourse*, 87 Wash. U. L. Rev. 115, 127 (2009) ("In 2008, 86% of companies in the S&P 100 Index included information about social and environmental business practices on their websites.").

[120] Tracey M. Roberts, *Innovations in Governance: A Functional Typology of Private Governance Institutions*, 22 Duke Envtl. L. & Pol'y F. 67, 79 (2011).

[121] *US SIF Foundation Releases 2018 Biennial Report on US Sustainable, Responsible and Impact Investing Trends*, *supra* note 118.

[122] *Report on US Sustainable, Responsible and Impact Investing Trends 2018*, US SIF 6 (Oct. 2018), www.ussif.org/files/Trends/Trends%202018%20executive%20summary%20FINAL.pdf.

[123] Heidi Welsh & Robin Young, *How Leading U.S. Corporations Govern and Spend on State Lobbying*, SUSTAINABLE INVESTMENTS INSTITUTE (Mar. 1, 2017), https://papers.ssrn.com/sol3/papers.cfm?abstract_id=2940518.

[124] Email with Heidi Welsh, Executive Director, Sustainable Investments Institute (Jan. 26, 2019).

[125] INT'L S'HOLDER SERVS., INC., 2012 U.S. PROXY VOTING SUMMARY GUIDELINES 64 (2012), www.issgovernance.com/files/2012USSummaryGuidelines1312012.pdf.

to include a section on political contributions by companies. CalPERS urges the boards of companies it invests in to:

> disclose on an annual basis the amounts and recipients of monetary and non-monetary contributions made by the company during the prior fiscal year. If any expenditure earmarked or used for political or charitable activities were provided to or through a third-party to influence elections of candidates or ballot measures or governmental action, then those expenditures should be included in the report.[126]

Building on these SRI efforts, on October 1, 2018 a diverse group of academics and investors petitioned the Securities and Exchange Commission asking for a new rulemaking on environmental, social and governance (ESG) disclosures. The petition was authored by Professors Cynthia A. Williams and Jill E. Fisch, and was signed by investors and associated organizations representing more than $5 trillion in assets under management, including CalPERS, the New York State Comptroller, the Illinois State Treasurer, the Connecticut State Treasurer and the Oregon State Treasurer. The petition "calls for the Commission to initiate notice and comment rulemaking to develop a comprehensive framework requiring issuers to disclose identified environmental, social, and governance (ESG) aspects of each public-reporting company's operations."[127] If adopted, this would make it easier for retail and institutional investors to compare ESG disclosures apples to apples across publicly traded firms. Depending on the wording of such a new disclosure rule, dark money from publicly traded corporations could be put to an end.

6.   THE POLITICAL MINEFIELD FOR COMMERCIAL BRANDS

Data shows that partisans may be attracted to different commercial brands. Some of this is completely illogical. But in other cases, the brands themselves have made points of being "right wing" or "lefty." Engagement Labs' Brad Fay found "some brands are more polarizing than others. ... Brands such as Allstate Insurance, Capital One, Panera, JetBlue, KitchenAid and the NBA were 'blue brands.' Audi, American Express, GE, Hobby Lobby, Kroger and

---

[126] *Global Governance Principles*, California Public Employees' Retirement System 27–28 (Mar. 16, 2015), www.calpers.ca.gov/docs/forms-publications/global-principles-corporate-governance.pdf.

[127] SEC petition No. 4-730 (Oct. 1, 2018), www.sec.gov/rules/petitions/2018/petn4-730.pdf. Nota bene: the author is a signatory.

State Farm were 'red brands.'"[128] In 2017, The Harris Poll similarly found that some brands attract Democrats and other brands Republicans:

> The top 10 brands, in order, according to Democrats, are: Amazon.com; 3M Company; Wegmans; Tesla Motors; Apple; The Coca-Cola Company; Costco; Under Armour; Publix Super Markets; and UPS. The top 10 brands, in order, according to Republicans, are: Chick-fil-A; Amazon.com; Johnson & Johnson; Publix Super Markets; UPS; USAA; Hobby Lobby; Google; Lowe's; 3M Company.[129]

Only Publix and Amazon crossed the partisan divide to appeal to both Republicans and Democrats.

Hobby Lobby has been aggressive at pushing the message that it is a conservative Christian brand, including by litigating the right not to pay for its employees' birth control up to the Supreme Court.[130] Another brand that has pushed its Christian agenda is Chick-fil-A, which got lots of press when CEO Dan Cathy waded into the marriage equality debate against gay marriage.[131] Cathy later recanted.[132] Nonetheless, Chick-fil-A has also financially supported anti-gay groups with millions of dollars.[133] And polling shows that customers pick up on these partisan/ideological cues. According to The Harris Poll:

> As companies wrestle with how to approach a divided U.S. political climate ... [research shows that] Americans view the reputations of some companies as aligned with their individual values. Republicans hold the reputations of Chick-fil-A and

---

[128]   Greg Sterling, *Do brand politics impact consumer purchases? It's complicated,* MARKETING LAND (Dec. 4, 2018), https://marketingland.com/do-brand-politics-impact-consumer-purchases-its-complicated-252772?utm_campaign=Press%20Coverage&utm_content=80813993&utm_medium=social&utm_source=twitter&hss_channel=tw-408609766.

[129]   *2017 Harris Poll RQ® Summary Report,* HARRIS POLL 12 (Feb. 2017), www.theharrispoll.com/reputation-quotient.

[130]   Burwell v. Hobby Lobby, 573 U.S. ___ (2014).

[131]   Leanna Garfield, *Pro-LGBTQ-rights consumers vow to boycott Chick-fil-A after it announces it's opening in Toronto – here's why the fast-food chain is so controversial,* BUSINESS INSIDER (July 27, 2018), www.businessinsider.com/chick-fil-a-lgbt-twitter-jack-dorsey-apology-marriage-equality-2018-6 ("In 2012, Chick-fil-A CEO Dan Cathy ignited a backlash after he said the company was 'guilty as charged' for backing 'the biblical definition of the family unit.'").

[132]   Clare O'Connor, *Chick-fil-A CEO Cathy: Gay Marriage Still Wrong, But I'll Shut Up About It and Sell Chicken,* FORBES (Mar. 19, 2014) ("Dan Cathy – a self-described evangelical Christian – says he made a mistake.").

[133]   Garfield, *supra* note 131 ("The company has donated millions of dollars to anti-LGBT+ organizations.").

Hobby Lobby - companies that have vocally shared their conservative beliefs - significantly more favorably than Democrats do.[134]

Other studies have found that "[i]n the land of 'two Americas,' it turns out Republicans and Democrats don't even like the same foods"[135]—and they may not even be shopping at the same grocery stores. One article posited that the increase of Whole Foods stores in the suburbs (which tend to cater to more wealthy college-educated women) could predict a 2018 blue wave in congressional races.[136] The blue wave happened; whether it had anything to do with Whole Foods is debatable.

Commercial brands can also get dragooned into political fights without their consent. For example, when Texas Senator Wendy Davis filibustered an anti-abortion bill in the Texas legislature for 11 straight hours without so much as a bathroom break, she was wearing distinctive pink tennis shoes made by a brand called Mizuno. To express their support for Davis' filibuster and her stance in favor of reproductive rights, many customers started commenting in product reviews of her shoes on Amazon. One Amazon customer gushed, "OMG, what I can do with these shoes is amazing! They fully support my right to control my body! It's like I have a say about my future. Who would have thought that a pair of shoes could represent self-determination?"[137] Another noted:

> Whether running a marathon, hiking the Pacific Crest Trail, or launching a filibuster to exercise the democratic process, the right footwear will empower you to focus on what is important, and not on whether your feet are hurting. Wearing her pink Mizuno's, a Texas lawmaker with the steely resolve of a branding iron single-handedly stopped an effort to drastically curtail abortion in the Lone Star

---

[134] *Corporate Reputation Politically Polarized as Companies Wrestle with Taking a Stand for Their Values*, HARRIS POLL (Feb. 9, 2017), www.theharrispoll.com/business/Corporate-Reputation-Politically-Polarized.html.

[135] Chris Wilson, *Do You Eat Like a Republican or a Democrat?*, TIME (July 18, 2016), http://time.com/4400706/republican-democrat-foods/.

[136] Maria Recio, *Will Whole Foods locations explain a blue wave?*, AMERICAN-STATESMAN (Oct. 30, 2018), www.statesman.com/news/20181030/will-whole-foods-locations-explain-blue-wave ("For some Republican congressional incumbents, proximity to a Whole Foods grocery store might be unwelcome.").

[137] Nulani, *Walk Tall!*, AMAZON: MIZUNO WOMEN'S WAVE RIDER 16 RUNNING SHOE CUSTOMER REVIEWS (June 28, 2013), www.amazon.com/Mizuno-Womens-Wave-Rider-Running/product-reviews/B008KFY53K/ref=cm_cr_getr_d_paging_btm_59?ie=UTF8&showViewpoints=1&sortBy=bySubmissionDateDescending&tag=thehuffingtop-20&filterByStar=positive&pageNumber=59.

State … Ms. Davis proved what we feminists have been saying for 40+ years, "I am woman, and I am strong."[138]

When the press reports revealed that the CEO of Mizuno was actually a Republican donor, the significance of that fact was also debated among the Amazon comments. One commenter argued that the campaign finance donations were insignificant: "overall, not a lot of [Mizuno] money is going to any political party. When you look at the big picture-these aren't very political people … You can buy without feeling bad!"[139] Another disagreed and found the CEO's political donations to Republicans were disqualifying:

> I was going to buy these to 'stand with Wendy' but when I found out Mizuno's donation history to the Republican Party (you know, the guys who made her stand there all night to stick up for women), I took the same amount of money and donated it to Wendy.[140]

Yet another pointed out the irony of Davis wearing shoes made by a company that supported Republicans: "it was nice to see Senator Wendy Davis defeat the misogynists with their own shoes."[141]

---

[138]   Jill Clardy, *When The Going Gets Tough, The Tough Strap On Their Mizuno's*, AMAZON: MIZUNO WOMEN'S WAVE RIDER 16 RUNNING SHOE CUSTOMER REVIEWS (June 28, 2013), www.amazon.com/Mizuno-Womens-Wave-Rider-Running/ product-reviews/B008KFY53K/ref=cm_cr_getr_d_paging_btm_54?ie=UTF8& showViewpoints=1&sortBy=bySubmissionDateDescending&tag=thehuffingtop-20& filterByStar=positive&pageNumber=54.

[139]   Lindsay M. Coleman, *YOU CAN BUY WITHOUT FEELING BAD*, AMAZON: MIZUNO WOMEN'S WAVE RIDER 16 RUNNING SHOE CUSTOMER REVIEWS (June 30, 2013), www.amazon.com/Mizuno-Womens-Wave-Rider-Running/product-reviews/ B008KFY53K/ref=cm_cr_getr_d_paging_btm_49?ie=UTF8&showViewpoints=1& sortBy=bySubmissionDateDescending&tag=thehuffingtop-20&filterByStar=positive &pageNumber=49.

[140]   MMF, *Next time I need to stick up for women, I'll choose footwear from a company that doesn't support the Republican Party*, AMAZON: MIZUNO WOMEN'S WAVE RIDER 16 RUNNING SHOE CUSTOMER REVIEWS (July 1, 2013), www.amazon .com/Mizuno-Womens-Wave-Rider-Running/product-reviews/B008KFY53K/ ref=cm_cr_getr_d_paging_btm_6?ie=UTF8&showViewpoints=1&sortBy= bySubmissionDateDescending&tag=thehuffingtop-20&filterByStar=critical& pageNumber=6.

[141]   Morrenin Jovan Byars, *Unfortunately, looks like the shoe maker donated to the pro-uterus confiscation radicals*, AMAZON: MIZUNO WOMEN'S WAVE RIDER 16 RUNNING SHOE CUSTOMER REVIEWS (July 1, 2013), www.amazon.com/Mizuno-Womens -Wave-Rider-Running/product-reviews/B008KFY53K/ref=cm_cr_getr_d_paging _btm_6?ie=UTF8&showViewpoints=1&sortBy=bySubmissionDateDescending&tag= thehuffingtop-20&filterByStar=critical&pageNumber=6.

Branding expert Debbie Millman has argued that "[b]randing has become … about belonging to a tribe, to a religion, to a family. Our ability to brand our beliefs gives us that sense of belonging."[142] This tribal aspect can be seen among the women who bought Davis's shoes as they recognize each other in public. One woman noted that "[i]t's also kind of cool when I use the gym at work and I see other women wearing the same ones and we give each other a nod, kind of like we're both on Wendy's team."[143] Another customer noted, "I get lots of compliments when in public wearing the shoes. Many people recognize the 'Wendy' shoes."[144] Another reported, "I really bought the shoes to make a political statement. … I get a lot of 'Go Girl' when I wear them."[145] And beyond the tribal aspect, one reviewer called the shoes iconic:

> A woman in Texas can never tell what the day might hold. She may need to run in out of the rain, or jump over a fire ant pile, or stand and explain to a bunch of old white men why they have no business telling women what they need to do with their own bodies. These colorful lightweight shoes are just what the doctor ordered. … They are now the iconic shoe of the pro[-]choice movement here in Texas.[146]

Not surprisingly, some Amazon shoppers were dismayed by the politicization of a pair of pink running shoes. One complained, "Wow, politicizing running

---

[142] Len Stein, *The Key to Brand Design Is "Deliberate Differentiation"*, BRANDING MAG (Dec. 18, 2017), www.brandingmag.com/2017/12/18/the-key-to-brand-design-is-deliberate-differentiation/.

[143] Laura Matis, *Great Shoe!*, AMAZON: MIZUNO WOMEN'S WAVE RIDER 16 RUNNING SHOE CUSTOMER REVIEWS (Dec. 21, 2013), www.amazon.com/Mizuno-Womens-Wave-Rider-Running/product-reviews/B008KFY53K/ref=cm_cr_getr_d_paging_btm_28?ie=UTF8&showViewpoints=1&sortBy=bySubmissionDateDescending&tag=thehuffingtop-20&filterByStar=positive&pageNumber=28.

[144] Carm, *Mizuno shoes*, AMAZON: MIZUNO WOMEN'S WAVE RIDER 16 RUNNING SHOE CUSTOMER REVIEWS (Sept. 5, 2013), www.amazon.com/Mizuno-Womens-Wave-Rider-Running/product-reviews/B008KFY53K/ref=cm_cr_getr_d_paging_btm_38?ie=UTF8&showViewpoints=1&sortBy=bySubmissionDateDescending&tag=thehuffingtop-20&filterByStar=positive&pageNumber=38.

[145] DWest, *My "Wendy Davis" shoes*, AMAZON: MIZUNO WOMEN'S WAVE RIDER 16 RUNNING SHOE CUSTOMER REVIEWS (Oct. 24, 2013), www.amazon.com/Mizuno-Womens-Wave-Rider-Running/product-reviews/B008KFY53K/ref=cm_cr_getr_d_paging_btm_33?ie=UTF8&showViewpoints=1&sortBy=bySubmissionDateDescending&tag=thehuffingtop-20&filterByStar=positive&pageNumber=33.

[146] kimberly piccolo, *Perfect!*, AMAZON: MIZUNO WOMEN'S WAVE RIDER 16 RUNNING SHOE CUSTOMER REVIEWS (July 24, 2013), www.amazon.com/Mizuno-Womens-Wave-Rider-Running/product-reviews/B008KFY53K/ref=cm_cr_getr_d_paging_btm_42?ie=UTF8&showViewpoints=1&sortBy=bySubmissionDateDescending&tag=thehuffingtop-20&filterByStar=positive&pageNumber=42.

shoes? Really? Yuck."[147] And another concluded, "Seriously? You HAD to bring politics into shoes? Geez! As if we don't already have enough divisions among us!"[148]

Davis won the day. She filibustered until the end of the Texas legislative session. But the Governor called a special session where the same regressive legislation became law.[149] Davis ran for Governor of Texas in 2014 and lost. But when the Texas law that she had filibustered was challenged, the Supreme Court found it unconstitutionally burdened the ability of Texas women to access abortions—the very same reason that she articulated in her 11-hour filibuster.[150]

Brands occasionally feel pressured to take political stances. Some of these stances are nonpartisan, like urging citizens to vote. As *Vogue* reported, "Ahead of the midterm elections, designers like Tory Burch and Prabal Gurung made *Vote* merch that gave all proceeds to the Rock the Vote organization."[151] Several companies pushed:

> [the] Time To Vote … campaign launched by CEOs of companies that include SouthWest Airlines, Lyft, Farmers Insurance, and others, to persuade people to get out and vote. The cool thing? These brands offered paid time off to their employees to take the day off and go vote.[152]

---

[147] C. Pennell, *Reply: These shoes (and a woman's body) have a way of shutting the whole thing down*, AMAZON: MIZUNO WOMEN'S WAVE RIDER 16 RUNNING SHOE CUSTOMER REVIEWS (2013), www.amazon.com/Mizuno-Womens-Wave -Rider-Running/product-reviews/B008KFY53K/ref=cm_cr_getr_d_paging _btm_65?ie=UTF8&showViewpoints=1&sortBy=bySubmissionDateDescending&tag =thehuffingtop-20&filterByStar=positive&pageNumber=65.

[148] F. Mitchell, *Reply: These shoes (and a woman's body) have a way of shutting the whole thing down*, AMAZON: MIZUNO WOMEN'S WAVE RIDER 16 RUNNING SHOE CUSTOMER REVIEWS (2013), www.amazon.com/Mizuno-Womens-Wave -Rider-Running/product-reviews/B008KFY53K/ref=cm_cr_getr_d_paging _btm_65?ie=UTF8&showViewpoints=1&sortBy=bySubmissionDateDescending&tag =thehuffingtop-20&filterByStar=positive&pageNumber=65.

[149] David Yaffe-Bellany, *Five years after Wendy Davis filibuster, Texas abortion providers struggle to reopen clinics*, TEXAS TRIBUNE (June 25, 2018), www .texastribune.org/2018/06/25/five-years-after-wendy-davis-filibuster-abortion-clinics/.

[150] *Whole Woman's Health v. Hellerstedt*, 579 U.S. ___ (2016).

[151] Brooke Bobb, *From Runway Protests to a #MeToo Blackout, Here Are 12 Ways Fashion Tried to Change the World in 2018*, VOGUE (Dec. 19, 2018).

[152] Lauren Bordelon, *How did political brands fare over the US midterms?*, SOCIAL ELEMENT (Nov. 22, 2018), https://thesocialelement.agency/how-did-political-brands -fare-over-the-us-midterms/.

Polling later showed that brands that participated in the Time To Vote initiative saw a 16 percent bump in positive sentiment from the public.[153]

And some stances by commercial brands are much more overtly one sided and decidedly anti-Trump. For example, "Airbnb daringly challenge[d] Donald Trump's travel ban. ..."[154] And fashion designer Jeremy Scott:

> wore a DIY T-shirt with the words Tell your senators no on Kavanaugh splashed across the front. Just below, he added the phone number to a Washington, D.C., office fielding calls from people voicing their opinions about President Trump's nomination of the accused sexual abuser Brett Kavanaugh to the U.S. Supreme Court.[155]

Along similar lines:

> In response to the December 2017 announcement that President Trump's administration would reduce the size of two national monuments in Utah ... Chris Leba created a ... collection inspired by Grand Staircase-Escalante and Bears Ears parks ... with 100 percent of the profits going to the Ute tribe PAC and SUWA, the Southern Utah Wilderness Alliance.[156]

And perhaps most stridently, "[t]he outdoor clothing brand Patagonia recently launched a campaign titled 'The President Stole Your Land', attacking US government policy. ... This is laying the foundations of an entirely new type of politically motivated brand: activist brands."[157]

As a result, some commercial brands can move to the vanguard of social change:

> Some don't just reflect our ideas of the world but also push for change before the majority has seen the change coming. [Commercial] [b]rands aren't simply passive barometers, they are also change agents, contributing to the flood that turns the tide of social acceptabilities; from equality and environmentalism to even our sense of identity.[158]

---

[153] *Id.*

[154] Tom Morgan, *Never Mind the Politics, Here's the Brand*, A NEW TYPE OF IMPRINT (Apr. 2018), www.anewtypeofimprint.com/news-2/2018/9/14/never-mind-the-politics-heres-the-brand.

[155] Bobb, *supra* note 151.

[156] *Id.*

[157] Morgan, *supra* note 154.

[158] *Id.*

7.   CODA: THE ROGUE CANDIDATE AND CORPORATE BRANDS

Finally, one risk that corporate brands run when they support a politician is that the politician will get into an embarrassing scandal that will tarnish the image of the brand. This happened in the 2018 U.S. Senate race in Mississippi. A White candidate named Cindy Hyde-Smith who was running against an African American candidate said of a cattle rancher, "If he invited me to a public hanging, I'd be on the front row."[159] Pictures of Hyde-Smith in a confederate outfit that she posted to her Facebook page with the words "Mississippi history at its best!" also surfaced during the 2018 election.[160] These problematic comments led corporate PACs that had supported her to ask for their political donations back, including the corporate PACs of Google, Facebook, Walmart, AT&T, Major League Baseball, Leidos, Union Pacific, Boston Scientific, Pfizer,[161] Amgen, Ernst & Young[162] and Aetna.[163] But some corporate PACs didn't comment on whether they would ask for their donations back, including Amazon's.[164] After the election, however, Hyde-Smith's campaign had not returned the money. A few corporate PACs got their money back by cancelling their checks.[165] All in all, Senator Hyde-Smith has "apparently not returned over $50,000 in political action committee donations, despite

---

[159] Chris Cillizza, *Just when you thought Cindy Hyde-Smith couldn't make her "public hanging" comment any worse* ..., CNN (Nov. 12, 2018), www.cnn.com/2018/11/12/politics/cindy-hyde-smith-public-hanging-comment/index.html (quoting Hyde-Smith).

[160] Dan Mangan, *Republican Sen. Cindy Hyde-Smith wore Confederate rebel hat in Facebook photo—"Mississippi history at its best!"*, CNBC (Nov. 24, 2018), www.cnbc.com/2018/11/20/mississippi-republican-sen-cindy-hyde-smith-wore-confederate-cap-for-facebook-post.html.

[161] Taylor Telford, *Google joins list of companies seeking refund of campaign donation to Sen. Cindy Hyde-Smith after 'public hanging' comment*, WASH. POST (Nov. 27, 2018).

[162] Judd Legum, *Google asks Cindy-Hyde Smith to refund its contribution*, POPULAR INFO (Nov. 26, 2018), https://popular.info/p/google-asks-cindy-hyde-smith-to-refund ("Union Pacific, Boston Scientific, Walmart, Leidos, AT&T, Pfizer, Amgen, Ernst & Young — have asked Cindy Hyde-Smith to refund their donations. Major League Baseball also asked Hyde-Smith to refund its $5000 donation. ... A spokesperson for Google ... confirms that it has requested a refund from Cindy Hyde-Smith.").

[163] Fredreka Schouten, *Some companies are still waiting for Cindy Hyde-Smith to refund donations*, CNN (Dec. 28, 2018), www.cnn.com/2018/12/27/politics/cindy-hyde-smith-campaign-refunds/index.html.

[164] Telford, *supra* note 161 ("Amazon.com did not respond to multiple requests for comment about its plans to seek a refund of its $2,500 donation.").

[165] Schouten, *supra* note 163.

refund requests from the companies that made them."[166] This means that for forever and a day, the brands that tried to distance themselves from her will be listed as contributors to this racially controversial campaign. What commercial brands may learn the hard way is when supporting a political candidate, they will be in for a penny, in for a pound.

---

[166] Josh Israel, *Sen. Cindy Hyde-Smith ignored requests for refunds after she embraced voter suppression and public lynchings*, THINK PROGRESS (Dec. 31, 2018), https://thinkprogress.org/misssissippi-senator-hyde-smith-kept-corporate-pac-money -after-racism-76562359c137/.

PART II

Branding infecting politics

The tricks of commercial branding—recognizable catchphrases, logos, jingles and brute repetition—were all put to work as TV came into its own in the 1950s with Eisenhower's campaign. He had a catchy tune from Irving Berlin called "I like Ike" and short TV spots from Rosser Reeves of the Ted Bates agency, many of which ended with the tagline, "Now is the time for all good Americans to come to the aid of their country." In a word, Ike was willing to be "merchandized," while his opponent Adlai Stevenson refused. Presidential politics would never be the same. The power of broadcast ads could shape how a nation perceived a candidate.

But of course, liberal and conservative voters may be attracted to different ideas that fit and confirm their world view. And just as powerful as broadcast ads are to politics, so too is the power to narrowcast messages that appeal to a small but pivotal slice of the electorate. The following chapters deal with the psychology of liberals and conservatives, as well as how presidential campaigns, from 1952 through 2016, used media to influence the electorate and brand their candidates.

4. Branding partisanship

"We now have a Commander in Chief who may, with little to no warning, use his social media following to force a brand into the political limelight. ... This singling out of companies propels consumers to reevaluate the brand through a partisan lens and can break existing brand loyalties."[1]

1. INTRODUCTION

The 2016 election was notable for its partisan rancor. One element that made this rancor worse than usual was the amplification of the normal baseline vitriol by Russian operatives, who sought to deepen divisions among Americans.[2] But the Russians could not have been so effective without real divisions in America. Another reason the 2016 election was particularly partisan is the Trump campaign's routinization of rage. And technology was used to harness those emotional divisions and spread them into the social media feeds of millions of Americans. As *Forbes* reported about the Trump 2016 campaign a few weeks after the election, "If the campaign's overarching sentiment was fear and anger, the deciding factor at the end was data ..."[3]

Lest anyone glorify the past as some nonpartisan utopia, partisanship has fractured Americans since George Washington was president. Political parties that many founding fathers were wary of formed anyway and caused deep divisions. As historian Rosemaie Zagarri notes, early partisans were as unreasonable as partisans today, viewing "party politics as a Manichean battle between good and evil."[4] Indeed, she describes how "[p]arty sentiment politicized everyday life. Independence Day, for example, became a partisan

---

[1] Chris Jackson & Clifford Young, *Brand Risk in the New Age of Populism: Four Key Tactics for Surviving Hyper-Partisan Consumers*, Ipsos 4 (2017).

[2] David McCabe & Sara Fischer, *How Russians use social media to divide Americans*, Axios (Sept. 28, 2017), www.axios.com/how-russians-use-social-media-to -divide-americans-1513305823-1664ea55-c345-487b-b1b1-d3e028243f88.html.

[3] Steven Bertoni, *Exclusive Interview: How Jared Kushner Won Trump The White House*, Forbes (Nov. 22, 2016).

[4] Rosemarie Zagarri, *Women and Party Conflict in the Early Republic* in Beyond the Founders: New Approaches to the Political History of the Early American Republic 112 (eds. Jefferey L. Pasley, Andrew W. Robertson and David Waldsteicher 2004) (referring to 1801).

holiday. Federalists and Democratic-Republicans throughout the country held their own separate celebrations, parades, picnics, and orations."[5] That's right: early partisans used to be so angry at each other that they held separate Fourth of July celebrations.

Is America any less partisan today? Nope, and it may be worse. The data wizards over at Pew have been tracking partisanship for decades. In 2017, the first year of the Trump presidency, Pew found partisan divide among Americans to be the most severe that it has measured in 24 years. Its report showed: "Currently, 44% of Democrats and Democratic leaners have a very unfavorable opinion of the GOP, based on yearly averages of Pew Research Center surveys; 45% of Republicans and Republican leaners view the Democratic Party very unfavorably."[6] In 2016, Pew found 45 percent of Republicans viewed the Democratic Party as a threat to the nation's wellbeing and 41 percent of Democrats felt the same way about the GOP.[7] Even "[d]ata from dating apps indicates the extent to which ideology and partisanship are important factors for Americans. They are among the most important just behind race …"[8] And many partisans want their children to keep marriages within one party.[9]

Drew Westen once said Democrats and Republicans "seem like two species, living in parallel universes, unable to speak the same language. We hear the same evidence and come to diametrically opposed conclusions. …"[10] Why are modern partisans (liberals and conservatives) so far apart ideologically? Cognitive scientists have bad news for anyone trying to breach the partisan divide.[11] Based on decades of research, many scientists conclude that the

---

[5]   *Id.* at 111.

[6]   *The Partisan Divide on Political Values Grows Even Wider. Sharp shifts among Democrats on aid to needy, race, immigration*, PEW (Oct. 5, 2017), www.people-press .org/2017/10/05/the-partisan-divide-on-political-values-grows-even-wider/.

[7]   *Partisanship and Political Animosity in 2016. Highly negative views of the opposing party – and its members*, PEW (June 22, 2016), www.people-press.org/2016/ 06/22/partisanship-and-political-animosity-in-2016/.

[8]   Jackson & Young, *supra* note 1, at 8.

[9]   *Partisan voters in U.S. increasingly prefer their children to marry within the party, study finds*, WOMEN IN THE WORLD (Feb. 2, 2017), https://womenintheworld .com/2017/02/02/partisan-voters-in-u-s-increasingly-prefer-their-children-marry -within-the-party-study-finds/ ("[In 2016] — 60 percent of Democrats said they would prefer their child to marry a Democrat in the 2016 poll, while 63 percent of Republicans prefer their child to marry a Republican.").

[10]   DREW WESTEN, THE POLITICAL BRAIN: THE ROLE OF EMOTION IN DECIDING THE FATE OF THE NATION 90 (2007).

[11]   Dana R. Carney, John T. Jost, Samuel D. Gosling & Jeff Potter, *The Secret Lives of Liberals and Conservatives: Personality Profiles, Interaction Styles, and the Things They Leave Behind*, 29 INTERNAT'L SOC. OF POL. PSYCH. 815–16 (2008) ("[There is]

differences between liberals and conservatives are "more than 'skin deep.'"[12] In short, part of why conservatives and liberals find agreement on key issues so vexingly elusive is there is growing evidence that their respective brains are not processing information identically.

Add to that biology the social fact that many American have sorted themselves into communities of likeminded individuals. As Will Wilkinson has found: "liberals (low conscientiousness, high openness to experience) and conservatives (high conscientiousness, low openness) have distinctive personalities, and there's reason to believe we've been sorting ourselves into communities of psychologically/ideologically similar people."[13] And there is a huge confirmation bias problem for both liberals and conservatives who surround themselves with members of their own group.[14]

One of the reasons why each group can talk past the other is both sides are likely to assume, wrongly, that the rest of the nation thinks just like they do. As Dr. John Hibbing explains:

> What's interesting about both groups [conservatives and liberals] is that there is a very powerful illusion that we have that the rest of the world sees the world the way that we see the world. And if [others] come to a different conclusion, it must be because they're being deliberately obtuse ... as opposed to the idea that people are actually ... seeing the world the same way, but their reactions to the world might actually be very different.[15]

This is known as a false consensus. And the more a person encounters only likeminded people, the more the false consensus is reinforced. Of course, "encountering" could mean in person, but it could also mean an encounter on

---

consensus over more than seven decades ... that the two personality dimensions that should be most related to political orientation are Openness to Experience—consistently theorized to be higher among liberals—and Conscientiousness—sometimes theorized to be higher among conservatives.").

12   *Id.* at 834.

13   David Roberts, *Donald Trump and the rise of tribal epistemology*, Vox (May 19, 2017), www.vox.com/policy-and-politics/2017/3/22/14762030/donald-trump-tribal -epistemology (quoting Wilkinson).

14   Jennifer Kavanagh & Michael D. Rich, *Truth Decay: An Initial Exploration of the Diminishing Role of Facts and Analysis in American Public Life*, RAND CORPORATION (2018).

15   Shankar Vedantam, *Nature, Nurture and Your Politics*, NPR (Oct. 8, 2018), www.npr.org/templates/transcript/transcript.php?storyId=654127241.

social media, where the person "encountered" lives across the country, but thinks exactly alike.[16] As journalist Ian Millhiser notes colorfully:

> what changed is if I wanted to form a political community that consisted entirely of left-leaning constitutional lawyers of Jewish descent, I could find my tribe online. And I don't care what your tribe is. Say that you want to find a community of black transgender history PhD students. Even at that level of granularity and similarity, you can find that tribe. The reason that I think that matters is people get into politics in part because they are looking for an identity group that validates them. Today, people can find that sense of social belonging with people who are much more similar to them than used to be the case. And I worry that this leads to a politics where people are less accustomed to dealing with people who are unlike them – and that they can potentially become less tolerant of these differences as a result.[17]

Here is how this discussion of partisanship will proceed. First, this chapter will discuss the findings of cognitive scientists which note some heritability for partisan preferences and evidence that liberals and conservatives simply perceive the world differently from one another. Second, this chapter will explore how that "nature" is reinforced by "nurture." Then this chapter will touch on how partisans define themselves and how they frequently misperceive the members of the opposing party. But even as the two major political parties pull away from one another, they struggle to reach large swaths of Americans, as roughly 40 percent remain registered as independents or unregistered with any political party.[18]

2.   NATURE

For decades, cognitive scientists have observed that one of the big differences between self-identified liberals and self-identified conservatives is how each group perceives and deals with threats.[19] As a general rule, conservatives perceive more threats in the world and want policies to deal with those dangers.

---

[16]   Ryan Grenoble, *Christopher Wylie Warns Senators: Cambridge Analytica, Steve Bannon Wan 'Culture War,'* Huff. Post (May 16, 2018), www.huffingtonpost.com/entry/christopher-wylie-cambridge-senate-testimony_us_5afc59b0e4b0779345d51218 ("'We're seeing a resegregation of society that's catalyzed by algorithms,' Wylie said. Sites like Facebook reward informational echo chambers where partisan views are reinforced instead of challenged. 'Instead of a common fabric,' he said, 'we're tearing that fabric apart.'").

[17]   Interview with Ian Millhiser (July 19, 2018).

[18]   Jeffrey M. Jones, *Americans' Identification as Independents Back Up in 2017,* Gallup (Jan. 8, 2018), https://news.gallup.com/poll/225056/americans-identification-independents-back-2017.aspx.

[19]   Carney, *et al., supra* note 11, at 814 ("Building on earlier traditions of research on authoritarianism and uncertainty avoidance, numerous studies have shown that lib-

And as a general rule, liberals perceive far fewer threats in the world and are consequently far more open to new experiences and tolerant of strangers. Generalizing, of course, for a conservative, a stranger is a possible threat. For a liberal, a stranger is a possible friend.[20] Psychologists have even found differences in how much liberals and conservative smile.[21] Liberals apparently smile more.

Perhaps because conservatives perceive a chaotic world, they seem to crave order:[22]

> For instance, conservatives show greater neurocognitive sensitivity to changes in habitual patterns ... tend to more rigidly organize their living and working spaces, and express preferences for simple and easily interpretable pieces of art, whereas liberals display more integrative complexity and tolerance of ambiguity.[23]

In some studies, researchers have been able to map these personality traits to support for particular politicians. For instance, in 1968, a study found:

> supporters of liberal and left-wing candidates in the 1968 Presidential primaries (e.g., E. McCarthy, N. Rockefeller, and R. F. Kennedy) scored disproportionately at the 'life-loving' end of the scale, whereas supporters of conservative and right-wing candidates (e.g., R. Nixon, R. Reagan, and G. Wallace) scored disproportionately at the 'mechanistic' end of the scale.[24]

---

erals tend to score higher than conservatives on individual difference measures of openness, cognitive flexibility, and integrative complexity ...").

[20] *Id.* at 813 ("People who 'resonate' with left-wing ideologies believe that people are basically good and that the goal of society should be to foster human creativity and experience. Those who 'resonate' with right-wing ideologies, by contrast, believe that people are inherently flawed and that the function of society is to set rules and limits to prevent irresponsible behavior.").

[21] *Id.* at 829 ("Liberals were more expressive, smiled more, and were more engaged in conversation with confederates ... [conservatives] did reflect the kind of withdrawn, reserved, inhibited, and even rigid interaction style that many theorists have associated with conservatism over the years.").

[22] *Id.* at 814 ("conservatives tend to possess stronger personal needs for order, structure, closure, and decisiveness in comparison with liberals. ... With regard political conservatism as an ideological belief system that is significantly (but not completely) related to motivational concerns having to do with the psychological management of uncertainty and fear.").

[23] Luigi Castelli & Luciana Carraro, *The Automatic Conservative: Ideology-Based Attentional Asymmetries in the Processing of Valenced Information*, PsycEXTRA Dataset (2011); *see also* Carney, *et al.*, *supra* note 11, at 834 ("Liberals did appear to be more open, tolerant, creative, curious, expressive, enthusiastic, and drawn to novelty and diversity, in comparison with conservatives, who appeared to be more conventional, orderly, organized, neat, clean, withdrawn, reserved, and rigid.").

[24] *Id.* at 812–13.

Plenty of Republican and Democratic policy preferences flow from the same basic juncture of how threatening a given danger is perceived to be. As Dr. John Hibbing said:

> one of the favorite things for conservatives to say about liberals is that they just don't get it - meaning that ... they don't appreciate that it's a dangerous world ... But it's not that they don't get it because they're being obtuse or they're not informed. They read about events in the world, and they just don't respond to them in the same way.[25]

Meanwhile, "[t]he liberal world view is mostly the opposite. Liberals take a more optimistic view of the world as being somewhat more benign. For them, government is a vehicle through which the citizens of a democracy can solve problems and improve the well-being and happiness of most people."[26]

For Republicans, support of easy access to guns, military spending and support for police makes sense if the underlying motivation is feeling psychologically unsafe.[27] As Dr. Hibbing said:

> immigration, defense, police, law and order ... are ... at the core of political differences ... [Conservatives] would want a set of policies put forward by our government that helped to reduce those threats ... I'm going to do it by allowing people to be well-armed. I'm going to do it by spending a lot on defense. I'm going to empower police. I'm going to have the death penalty. ... [T]o a threat-sensitive mindset, [those] are steps that ... make sense. They just can't really understand why anybody would be opposed to those kinds of things because this would help us to be a safer place.[28]

And for more open-minded Democrats, who don't perceive threats as so omnipresent or severe, reasonable gun control, less military spending and more libertarian laws fit their world view.

---

[25]   Vedantam, *supra* note 15.

[26]   Nigel Barber, *Why Liberal Hearts Bleed and Conservatives Don't. Why politicians have trouble listening to each other*, PSYCHOLOGY TODAY (Oct. 8, 2012).

[27]   Vedantam, *supra* note 15.

[28]   *Id.* (quoting Hibbing); DEBBIE MILLMAN, LOOK BOTH WAYS. ILLUSTRATED ESSAYS ON THE INTERSECTION OF LIFE AND DESIGN 157 (2009) ("In the book Safe ... Paola Antonelli writes, 'Safety is an instinctive need that has guided human choices through history.'").

How hardwired are these different (liberal and conservative) world views? The data is complicated and experts disagree.[29] One twin study suggests there is a genetic component at work. As Dr. Hibbing reported:

> we did indeed find that the political views were quite heritable ... our results suggested that maybe 30 or 40 percent of our political views come from genetics ... that obviously leaves, you know, 50, 60, 70 percent that comes from the environment.[30]

One indication that some of these differences may be hardwired is some of the underlying personality traits that cognitive scientists say indicate the liberal/conservative divide are present in children. For instance, they could find these traits in nursery school: "preschool children who later identified themselves as liberal were perceived by their teachers as: self-reliant, energetic, emotionally expressive, gregarious, and impulsive. By contrast, those children who later identified as conservative were seen as: rigid, inhibited, indecisive, fearful, and overcontrolled."[31] Other data suggests not only that partisanship is partially inherited; it is possible that the intensity of partisanship is also inherited. Peter K. Hatemi *et al.* found: "With regard to political party affiliation, people appear to be influenced by a biological propensity to be intense or apathetic regardless of how they were raised or which party they were raised to support."[32] It's also important to acknowledge that partisanship is not entirely genetically pre-determined. Peter K. Hatemi *et al.* note clearly, "It is critical to avoid oversimplification in the understanding of genetic sources of variation. There is no gene 'for' being a Republican or Democrat ... or any other complex trait."[33]

---

[29] Carney, *et al.*, *supra* note 11, at 808 ("as Tomkins (1963) argued long ago, ideological differences between the left and right are partially rooted in basic personality dispositions. That is, ideology both reflects and reinforces individual differences in fundamental psychological needs, motives, and orientations toward the world.").

[30] Vedantam, *supra* note 15 (quoting Hibbing); *see also* Carney, *et al.*, *supra* note 11, at 815 ("[There is] growing evidence that there is a heritable component of political attitudes (Alford, Funk, and Hibbing, 2005)—appear to substantiate the convictions of Adorno *et al.*, Tomkins, Wilson, and many others that basic personality dimensions underlie ideological differences between the left and right.").

[31] Carney, *et al.*, *supra* note 11, at 815.

[32] Peter K. Hatemi, John R. Alford, John R. Hibbing, Nicholas G. Martin & Lindon J. Eaves, *Is There a 'Party' in Your Genes?*, 62 POL. RESEARCH Q. 598 (2008); *id.* at 597 ("[t]he data suggest, however, that the source of partisan intensity is quite distinct and influenced in part by genetic differences comparable to, but different from, those that have long been regarded as constitutive of differences in personality.").

[33] *Id.* at 598.

3.   NURTURE

If the cognitive scientists are correct that the personality traits that tend to sort individuals into left and right-leaning political parties is at least 30 percent heritable (e.g, nature), that leaves approximately 70 percent for nurture. So how does our socialization lead to partisanship? Drew Westen, in his book *The Political Brain*, observes that "in most stable Western democracies, ... political affiliation tends to be handed from generation to generation like a family heirloom."[34] Political scientists agree that parents have an enormous influence on shaping their children's political leanings. They have concluded that "[p]arents socialize their children to become Republicans or Democrats, and this socialization has a lasting, though not immutable, impact on their affiliation well into adulthood ..."[35]

As Dana R. Carney *et al.* explain, "Sources of threat and/or uncertainty in the social world (e.g., death, dissent, immigration, complexity, ambiguity, social change, and anarchy) were seen as prompting conservative ideological responses, including conventionalism, ethnocentrism, authoritarianism, militarism, moral rigidity, and religious dogmatism."[36] The threat of doom and gloom can trigger more conservative responses even among non-conservatives. As Drew Westen notes, "[m]ore than 250 experiments in over a dozen countries have demonstrated that reminding people of their mortality—activating networks about the fear of death—tends to tilt our brains to the right."[37]

Aside from genetics and rearing, there is what the individual experiences in life. Psychologists who study partisanship have found, "political orientation is affected by situational variables; there is a good deal of evidence suggesting that environmental factors such as threat can and do produce ideological shifts."[38]

And then there is the "Big Sort" in the United States—the process of choosing where to live after a stage of education (high school, college or graduate school) is completed. Many Americans "sort" to a place with politically like-minded individuals.[39] And again, this allows many individuals to inhabit information bubbles that reinforce partisan proclivities.[40] Political parties that need voters will often try to pitch their platforms to match the prejudices of their

---

[34]   WESTEN, *supra* note 10, at 27.
[35]   Hatemi, *et al.*, *supra* note 32, at 597.
[36]   Carney, *et al.*, *supra* note 11, at 814.
[37]   WESTEN, *supra* note 10, at 264.
[38]   Carney, *et al.*, *supra* note 11, at 834–35 (internal citations omitted).
[39]   *Id.* at 835 ("political segregation has been growing rapidly in the United States, with an increasing number of people moving to areas with like-minded residents.").
[40]   Roberts, *supra* note 13.

base.[41] As Jennifer Kavanagh and Michael Rich argue, "People have always been partial to their own experience and beliefs over disconfirming facts, and political parties have always used carefully crafted narratives to support specific policy positions."[42] And being "well-educated" won't necessarily allow people to sidestep the lure of self-affirming partisan thinking. As Drew Westen points out, the cleverer the partisan, the more elaborate the excuses she will come up with to justify a cherished belief. He finds, "the more sophisticated people are politically ... the more able they are to develop complex rationalizations for dismissing what they don't want to believe."[43] He notes, even more darkly, "While the philosopher Martin Heidegger was sympathizing with the Nazis, many Germans of far lesser intellectual means were not. Indeed, the most dangerous kind of psychopath is a smart one."[44]

Further, how we are socialized fosters implicit biases against outgroups that each person picks up along the way. As Mahzarin R. Banaji, Max H. Bazerman and Dolly Chugh describe:

> Most of us believe that we are ethical and unbiased. We imagine we're good decision makers .... But more than two decades of research confirms that, in reality, most of us fall woefully short of our inflated self-perception. We're deluded by what Yale psychologist David Armor calls the illusion of objectivity, the notion that we're free of the very biases we're so quick to recognize in others.[45]

As Eli Pariser wrote in his book *The Filter Bubble*, filtering away facts that would challenge a cherished belief happens each time individuals use a search engine to look for information—not because of the searcher, but because of the search engine's algorithms: "since December 2009 ... you get the result that Google's algorithm suggests is best for you in particular—and someone else may see something entirely different. In other words, there is no standard Google anymore."[46]

Media is also likely to give audiences a distorted view of what the opposing party is really like.[47] So ironically, the more a person consumes political

---

[41] WESTEN, *supra* note 10 at 12 ("Political persuasion is about networks and narratives.") (italics in the original).

[42] Kavanagh & Rich, *supra* note 14.

[43] WESTEN, *supra* note 10, at 100.

[44] *Id.* at 133.

[45] Mahzarin R. Banaji, Max H. Bazerman & Dolly Chugh, *How (Un)ethical Are You?*, HARV. BUS. REV. 3 (Dec. 2003).

[46] ELI PARISER, THE FILTER BUBBLE 2 (2011).

[47] Douglas Ahler & Gaurav Sood, *The Parties in our Heads: Misperceptions About Party Composition and Their Consequences*, 80(3) J. OF POLITICS, 964, 965 (Apr. 27, 2018), http://dx.doi.org/10.1086/697253 ("The most common interpersonal channel

news, the more distorted view she may have of her ideological opposites.[48] As Douglas Ahler and Gaurav Sood find, "The most voracious news consumers … are thus most liable to hold skewed perceptions about party composition."[49] And tribal living patterns may make perceptions more rigid. If you really live in a partisan bubble, you may never run into your political opposite in real life. "Because of partisan homophily, partisans are less likely to have personal information about the out-party, rendering impersonal information – e.g., media portrayals of the parties – more meaningful."[50]

Outside of the purely partisan context, other studies have focused on the psychology of in-group and out-group dynamics and found "[p]eople who identify strongly with their social groups experience intergroup Schadenfreude – pleasure in response to threatening out-group members' misfortunes."[51] This study also found, "Schadenfreude [taking pleasure in the pain of others] and Glückschmerz [pain in response to others' good fortune] are natural responses in zero-sum contexts; if 'they' are unhappy, 'we' are pleased."[52] One disturbing finding in this study was "that a target can invoke these malicious emotional responses in the absence of any personal history or direct contact with the perceiver, merely because of their group membership and its associated stereotypes."[53] Troublingly, this research seems to indicate that an individual does not even have to meet a person from another "out" group to hate her. Other research finds that certain biases like racial antipathy cut across the partisan divide.[54]

Plenty of politicians have tried to exploit these Us/Them divisions. For instance, "one of [Presidential candidate George] Wallace's favorite themes

---

[that allows societal-level knowledge to reach us] for politics continues to be the mass media").

[48] *Id.* ("perceptions about party composition became less accurate as interest in political news increases").

[49] *Id.*

[50] *Id.*

[51] Mina Cikara, *Intergroup Schadenfreude: motivating participation in collective violence*, 3 Current Opinion in Behavioral Sciences 12–17 at 12 (2015).

[52] *Id.* at 14.

[53] *Id.*

[54] Mark P. Zanna, Leanne S. Son Hing, Greg A. Chung-Yan & Leah K. Hamilton, *A Two-Dimensional Model That Employs Explicit and Implicit Attitudes to Characterize Prejudice*, 94 J. of Personality and Soc. Psych. 971 (2008) ("The nature of prejudice varies from person to person; wideranging responses might characterize an individual's racial attitudes. Conservatives might act in a biased manner (i.e., treating outgroups differently from ingroups) but rationalize their response as fair. Liberals who value egalitarianism might demonstrate unintentional bias.").

[was] Us vs Them. Wallace always attempted to pinpoint the 'enemies' and to set up a dichotomy for his audiences."[55] And moreover:

> The Us vs. Them strategy is evident in nearly all of Wallace's rhetoric on crime in the streets. By distinguishing between the good guys and the bad guys, Wallace forced his audiences to make a choice. They could opt for the bad guys: the federal government, the anarchists, the national parties. Or they could side with the good guys: Wallace and his supporters.[56]

At this point in American history, some combination of genetics, familial reinforcement and the filter bubble has resulted in political parties that are themselves more homogeneous. And consequently, being "Republican" or "Democrat" has become, as Lilliana Mason argues, a "mega-identity."[57] According to Dr. Mason, "'A single vote can now indicate a person's partisan preference *as well as* his or her religion, race, ethnicity, gender, neighborhood and favorite grocery store.'"[58] Perhaps this is caused by people losing faith in other entities that provided structure before. "With less confidence in formal institutions, people have turned to social groups and ideology as the organizing forces for their identity. Paradoxically, while formal political parties have declined in stature, the power of partisan identification (party ID) has exploded."[59]

4.   BRANDING THEM

One way to define a personal identity is to define it in opposition to another identity. This is clearly another way individuals decide which side—Democrat or Republican—fits their self-perceptions. Basically, one way to pick a side is to declare, "Well, I'm certainly not that." This is sometimes dubbed "negative

---

[55]   Marianne Worthington, *The Campaign Rhetoric of George Wallace in the 1968 Presidential Election*, Ucumberlands, www.ucumberlands.edu/downloads/academics/history/vol4/MarianneWorthington92.html.

[56]   *Id.*

[57]   Perry Bacon Jr., *Democrats Are Wrong About Republicans. Republicans Are Wrong About Democrats*, Five Thirty Eight (June 26, 2018), https://fivethirtyeight.com/features/democrats-are-wrong-about-republicans-republicans-are-wrong-about-democrats/.

[58]   Yascha Mounk, *The Rise of McPolitics Democrats and Republicans belong to increasingly homogeneous parties. Can we survive the loss of local politics?*, New Yorker (July 2, 2018).

[59]   *Brand Risk in the New Age of Populism: Four Key Tactics for Surviving Hyper-Partisan Consumers*, Ipsos 8 (June 7, 2017), www.ipsos.com/sites/default/files/2017-06/IpsosPA_POV_PoliticsAndBrands.pdf.

partisanship."[60] And a Pew Research Center poll "found that about 40 percent of both Democrats and Republicans belong to their party because they oppose the other party's values, rather than because they are particularly aligned with their own party."[61]

Scholars Douglas Ahler and Gaurav Sood asked the pollsters at YouGov to ask American adults to estimate the make-up of the subgroups in Republican and Democrat parties. Then the scholars double checked the estimates against the actual make-up of the Republican and Democratic parties.[62] Surprise, surprise: the estimates were way off.[63] One thing this could show is that generally Americans polled were extraordinarily bad at math.[64] But the other potential problem is one of the reasons that Americans may think it is impossible to communicate with a person from the opposite political party is because they hold wildly out-of-whack stereotypes of who makes up each party.[65] Ahler and Sood asked participants:

> what percentage of Democrats are black, or lesbian, gay or bisexual? What percentage of Republicans earn more than $250,000 a year, or are age 65 or older? What they found was that Americans overall are fairly misinformed about who is in each major party — and that members of each party are even more misinformed about who is in the *other* party.[66]

In reality, the typical voter in both the Republican and Democratic parties is White, straight, middle class and Christian.[67] But when you ask Republicans

---

[60]　*See* Alan I. Abramowitz & Steven Webster, *The rise of negative partisanship and the nationalization of U.S. elections in the 21st century*, 41 ELECTORAL STUDIES 12–22 (Mar. 2016).

[61]　Bacon, *supra* note 57.

[62]　Ahler & Sood, *supra* note 47, at 965 ("reliance on representatives leads to 'distorted distributions' of beliefs and group composition, in which people 'overweight representative types'").

[63]　*Id.* ("People make large systematic errors when thinking about the parties' composition, considerably overestimating the extent to which partisans belong to party-stereotypical groups").

[64]　*Id.* at 978 ("Even in cases where party-stereotypical groups comprise just a sliver of the population … people think that members of these groups constitute upward of 40% of the party they 'fit'").

[65]　*Id.* ("Across five studies, we find that people hold erroneous beliefs about the composition of the two major parties").

[66]　Bacon, *supra* note 57.

[67]　*Id.* at 965 ("Majorities of supporters of both parties are white, middle-class, and heterosexual, and both parties' modal supporters are middle-aged, non-evangelical Christians").

the make-up of the Democratic Party, the guesses are way off.[68] One way to look at it is that this study shows Americans typically overestimate the size of a group that they find threatening. For instance, "Blacks made up about a quarter of the Democratic Party, but Republicans estimated the share at 46 percent. Republicans thought 38 percent of Democrats were gay, lesbian or bisexual, while the actual number was about 6 percent."[69] And Democrats weren't any better at guessing about the GOP. "Democrats estimated that 44 percent of Republicans make more than $250,000 a year. The actual share was 2 percent."[70] In short, "the parties in our heads," as Ahler and Sood write, "are not the parties in real life."[71] Many Americans may simply misread how liberal Democrats and conservative Republicans are.[72] This is a problem if these stereotypes feed resentment.[73] But these misperceptions may also generate votes for "our team."[74] Hence, political parties themselves likely have an incentive to drive divisions in the hopes of harvesting more votes for Team R or Team D.

5. MICROTARGETING PARTISANS

Political scientists and cognitive researchers are not the only ones to pick up the fact that political biases are deeply rooted in psychology. Political actors are willing to brand messages to appeal to these deep psychological differences. If commercial marketers play on our hopes and dreams, often political branders are playing on our deepest fears. Furthermore, to the extent customers are living in their own tribal worlds, marketers will try to reach customers in their respective bubbles.[75] This means mass marketers increasingly need to micro-

---

[68]   *Id.* at 966 ("Republicans' perceptions of Democratic composition exhibit significantly more bias than do Democrats'").

[69]   *Id.* at 968.

[70]   Bacon, *supra* note 57; Ahler and Sood, *supra* note 47, at 965 ("Americans believe that 32% of Democrats are gay, lesbian, or bisexual (only 6.3% are in reality), and that 38% of Republicans earn over $250,000 per year (just 2.2% do in reality.)").

[71]   Bacon, *supra* note 57.

[72]   *Id.* at 973 ("respondents with the most skewed estimates of Democratic composition tended to see Democrats as 13 points more likely to take liberal positions. Similarly, respondents who most overestimated Republicans' tendency to be rich, evangelical, etc., tended to see the mass-level GOP as 13 points more likely to take conservative positions.").

[73]   Ahler & Sood, *supra* note 47, at 972 ("Believing that opposing partisans hold more extreme policy preferences, and feeling more socially distant from them, are both liable to cause citizens to become less receptive to out-party communications and less likely to consider voting for that party.").

[74]   *Id.* at 972.

[75]   *See* NATHAN ABSE, INTERACTIVE ADVERT. BUREAU, BIG DATA DELIVERS ON CAMPAIGN PROMISE: MICROTARGETED POLITICAL ADVERTISING IN ELECTION 2012,

target sub-demographic groups.[76] This behavior is also seen among political campaigns that narrowcast to smaller slices of the electorate.[77] Indeed, these phenomena are intertwined as political campaigns use consumer data to profile potential voters.[78] Now as a consequence, "political dossiers may be the largest unregulated assemblage of personal data in contemporary American life."[79] Campaigns have long used predictive analytics to decide where to deploy resources. As early as 1980, the Reagan campaign used computers to try to figure out where to focus their quest for electoral votes. Their computer model predicted that Carter would be weak in the South and that freed up Reagan to divert money from California and Texas to Louisiana and Kentucky.[80]

Orwell is used repeatedly to describe the Trump era, but Orwell wasn't the only one predicting democratic dystopias. In 1955 Isaac Asimov wrote a short story called "Franchise," in which the winner of the 2008 election was determined by a computer.[81] As Ira Rubinstein observed, "the last two presidential campaigns [2004 and 2008] resemble Asimov's vision of predictive statistical

---

at 3–5 (2012), www.iab.com/wp-content/uploads/2015/07/Innovations_In_Web _Marketing_ and_Advertising_delivery.pdf.

[76] *See id.* at 10 ("Online advertising played a role in the 2004 and 2008 election cycles. But now, in 2012, online political advertising buys have grown enormously and for the first time microtargeting has become a crucial, go-to tool for both major presidential candidates and every outside group …").

[77] *See* Thomas Fitzgerald, *Profiling is Key to '06 Turnout: Campaigns Are Mining Consumer Data for Votes*, PHILA. INQUIRER (Oct. 29, 2006), http://articles.philly.com/ 2006-10-29/news/25417727_1_campaign-manager-swing-voter-voter-vault.

[78] *See* DANIEL KREISS, TAKING OUR COUNTRY BACK: THE CRAFTING OF NETWORKED POLITICS FROM HOWARD DEAN TO BARACK OBAMA 134 (2012) ("[E]-mail staffers [in the Obama campaign] continually segmented their supporter lists on the basis of personal information and closely tracked the effectiveness of appeals by monitoring click throughs."); Allison Brennan, *Microtargeting: How Campaigns Know You Better Than You Know Yourself*, CNN (Nov. 5, 2012), www.cnn.com/2012/11/05/politics/voters -microtargeting; *MicroTargeting for Political Campaigns*, TARGETPOINT CONSULTING (June 11, 2010), www. targetpointconsulting.com/microtargeting-for-political -campaigns/; LILLIE CONEY, PETER G. NEUMANN AND JON PINCUS, ELEC. PRIVACY INFO. CTR., E-DECEPTIVE CAMPAIGN PRACTICES REPORT 2010: INTERNET TECHNOLOGY AND DEMOCRACY 2.0, at 9 (2010), http://epic.org/privacy/voting/E_Deceptive_Report _10_2010.pdf ("[Voter p]rofiles are used to develop expectations regarding the behavior of individuals based on their activities, preferences for a wide range of products and services, … religious beliefs, … type of work, neighborhood, … level of education, … military service membership, foreclosure status of a primary home, employment status, as well as emotional or mental state regarding the economy.").

[79] Ira Rubinstein, *Voter Privacy in the Age of Big Data*, 2014 WIS. L. REV. 861 (2014).

[80] David Burnham, *Reagan's Campaign Adds Strategy Role to Use of Computer*, N.Y. TIMES (Apr. 23, 1984).

[81] Isaac Asimov, *Franchise*, IF: WORLDS OF SCIENCE FICTION (Aug. 1955).

analysis, harnessed to big data, playing a central role in determining electoral outcomes."[82] Why? Because campaigns used data-driven, computer-powered microtargeting to reach voters. As the *Washington Post* summed up:

> Microtargeting, as its name implies, is a way to identify small but crucial groups of voters who might be won over to a given side, and which messages would do the trick. It's a bit scary because ... microtargeters know who you are and try to push your personal hot button so that you'll choose their candidate.[83]

The types of questions that a microtargeter wants to know are: "Do you have children? Do you shop in high-end stores or hunt for bargains on eBay? Do you support the Sierra Club or Club for Growth?"[84] As Peter Swire points out, when candidates:

> know exactly what each voter cares about ... it creates a huge temptation to exaggerate or lie. Insularity is a side effect of superficiality and distortion because voter microtargeting makes it increasingly difficult to have a public argument when there is no 'basis for a common conversation about ... political decision[s].'[85]

For most of the second half of the twentieth century, broadcasting messages to the electorate was the most efficient way to communicate with vast numbers of voters. Broadcasting has some drawbacks, as media markets may capture heterogeneous populations of voters. Therefore, coded dog whistles to a base were used instead of explicitly saying words that would appeal only to one side of the political spectrum (and turn off the other side).[86] Broadcasting political ads could have had a moderating effect on messaging because in theory, the whole nation was watching. Instead of broadcasting, now more electioneering is microtargeted to hit a subset of voters.[87] As Ira Rubinstein wrote, microtargeting voters "represents a partial retreat from huge media buys for undifferentiated mass audiences ('broadcasting') in favor of tailoring messages to

---

[82]   Rubinstein, *supra* note 79, at 863.

[83]   Steven Levy, *The Technologist: In Every Voter, A Microtarget*, WASH. POST, April 23, 2008, at D01.

[84]   Brennan, *supra* note 78.

[85]   Rubinstein, *supra* note 79, at 909.

[86]   *See* generally IAN HANEY-LÓPEZ, DOG WHISTLE POLITICS: HOW CODED RACIAL APPEALS HAVE REINVENTED RACISM AND WRECKED THE MIDDLE CLASS (2013).

[87]   Philip N. Howard, *et al.*, *The IRA, Social Media and Political Polarization in the United States, 2012–2018* 39 (2018), https://comprop.oii.ox.ac.uk/wp-content/uploads/sites/93/2018/12/IRA-Report.pdf ("this effective impression management—and fine-grained control over who receives which messages—is what makes social media platforms so attractive to advertisers, but also to political and foreign operatives.").

the 'needs, wants, expectations, beliefs, preferences, and interests' of a target audience as determined by data analysis ('narrowcasting.')"[88]

Targeting certain voters with certain messages goes way back,[89] to as early as 1840:

> A Whig-committee campaign memo in 1840 advised that it was the duty of a party subcommittee to 'keep a constant watch on the doubtful voters, and have them talked to by those in whom they have the most confidence, and also to place in their hands such documents as will enlighten and influence them.'[90]

The beauty of microtargeting is potentially "candidates can surgically locate the one sympathetic supporter in an otherwise unsympathetic neighborhood."[91] The old way of microtargeting voters was to use direct mail. Some campaigns run both broadcast and narrowcast campaigns simultaneously. This dual approach allows a campaign to run contradictory messaging at the same time, just to different audiences. This is particularly key in presidential races where a few hundred votes in a particular state can mean the difference in who wins the White House. As a piece called "The Persuadable Voter" noted:

> microtargeting, swing voters in swing states can be told that the issues he or she cares about are the issues that are a priority to the candidate. ... [T]elevision advertising by both candidates in the 2004 presidential election contained almost no references to the issues of gay marriage or abortion, while these were more prominently featured in direct-mail communication. Emphasizing potentially controversial issues through microtargeting, rather that [sic] the general media, allows for a 'ground war' fought on wedge issues to be run simultaneously with less controversial issues in the traditional 'air war.'[92]

Microtargeting a few hundred key voters in a close election could swing a district, a state or even the Electoral College.[93] This arguably happened in 2004:

> Nationally, 8% of African Americans voted for [George W.] Bush, but in Ohio he received 16% of the African American vote. The Bush campaign also focused on

---

[88]   Rubinstein, *supra* note 79, at 882.

[89]   D. Sunshine Hillygus & Todd G. Shields, The Persuadable Voter: Wedge Issues in Presidential Campaigns 155 (2008).

[90]   *Id.*

[91]   *Id.* at 157.

[92]   *Id.* at 47.

[93]   Lawrence R. Jacobs & Robert Y. Shapiro, *Polling Politics, Media, and Election Campaigns*, 69 Public Opinion Q. 635, 639 (2005) ("The use of polls to microtarget individual voters for personalized mobilization efforts reflects a new grassroots strategic orientation and a significant shift away from an emphasis on media buys and television-based outreach."); Auren Hoffman, *It Takes Tech to Elect a President,*

New Mexico, a state Bush lost in 2000 by 366 votes, and microtargeted Hispanics. Result: The white vote for Bush fell 2% in 2004, but his Hispanic vote increased 12%—enough to put him over the top in the state.[94]

And the Bush campaign also microtargeted for religion: "the Republican Party use[d] ... voter microtargeting to mobilize evangelical voters in particular. ..."[95] Democrats quickly followed suit in the following elections with their own microtargeting.[96]

As technology has evolved, the ability to microtarget voters electronically with specific messages has increased. For example, voters can be microtargeted with banner ads on their computers that have tailored message selected especially for them. As David Mark describes in his book *Going Dirty*:

> Banner ads on the Internet may prove to be the fastest growing forum for launching microtargeted campaign attacks because so much information can be gathered on individual Web viewers based on the sites they have visited and data they must often submit to gain access. Banner ads ... combine the targeting power of both television ads and direct mail. Ads can be tailored to geographic location based on ZIP codes or other pieces of information gathered on a website. On news sites, banner ads can be made to show up only above stories about specific topics, such as health care or tax cuts.[97]

Moreover, as the technology evolves, campaigns are eager to deploy the next new tool to scoop up voters:

> The capacity for micro-targeting is expanding by the minute, as search engines like Google provide advertisers with information that allows them to place targeted ads on the Web pages of users depending on the words they have searched and sites they have visited. For example, in 2006, *Yahoo!* began using complex models to analyze what their 500-plus million users look for when they search, the pages they read, and

---

BLOOMBERG (Aug. 25, 2008) ("In 2004, ... [Karl] Rove, invested in better ways to reach voters in heavily Democratic areas.").

[94] Hoffman, *supra* note 93.

[95] Tim Taylor, *All Things to All People the Republican Party's Use of Religious Messages in Direct Mail During the 2004 Presidential Election*, 13 GEO. PUB. POL'Y REV. 25, 29 (2008) (Internal citation omitted).

[96] Greg R. Murray & Anthony Scime, *Microtargeting and Electorate Segmentation: Data Mining the American National Election Studies*, 9 J. OF POLITICAL MARKETING 143, 147 (AUG. 2010) ("Democratic campaign operatives, following their Republican counterparts, intend to allocate substantial resources to creating and mining databases of existing and potential supporters.") (Internal citations omitted).

[97] DAVID MARK, GOING DIRTY: THE ART OF NEGATIVE CAMPAIGNING 232–233 (2009).

the ads they click. *Yahoo!* users then receive custom-designed advertisements that directly address their interests.[98]

Emails are another way political campaigns target voters. The Obama campaigns in 2008 and 2012 were notorious for how much email they sent supporters and would-be supporters:

> For example, in 2008, barackobama.com saw an unprecedented level of online activity, with reports indicating that 3 million donors made a total of 6.5 million online donations (adding up to more than $500 million); 13 million voters shared their e-mail addresses and the campaign sent more than more than 1 billion e-mails with about 7,000 different messages ...[99]

The 1 billion emails appeared to be effective, as Obama was in the Oval Office for eight years.

Another way of targeting voters personally is through their mobile devices. Typically, that's a smartphone, but it could also be other portable technology, including smart watches, so long as it has the capacity to deliver a text message. Campaigns that can't get voters to answer a phone are happy to spam a phone number with political text messages.[100]

Politicians have long been criticized for talking out of both sides of their mouths; microtargeting allows them to take opposing positions simultaneously. "[A]n essential strategy of microtargeting [is] turning out the base with fiery rhetoric while persuading swing voters with moderate argument."[101] And depending on the subtleties of the issue, microtargeting could allow a candidate to take even more than two positions on a single issue, to multiple different voters:

> Microtargeting allows candidates to surgically deliver different messages to different constituencies, thus expanding the arsenal of potential wedge issues that can be used in the campaign. With direct mail, email, telephone calls, text messaging, Web advertising, and the like, candidates can narrowcast issue messages to some voters even if others in their coalition might disagree or consider the issue less important. Microtargeting enables candidates to use double-edged issues.[102]

Microtargeting also allows for a certain plausible deniability for campaigns, since some voters may not have seen a targeted ad with a particularly offensive

---

[98]   WESTEN, *supra* note 10, at 216.
[99]   Rubinstein, *supra* note 79, at 875.
[100] MARK, *supra* note 97, at 232–33.
[101] Taylor, *supra* note 95, at 40.
[102] HILLYGUS & SHIELDS, *supra* note 89, at 151.

take on an issue that only a few voters witnessed, which can lessen alienation of voters. Ira Rubinstein argued the consequence of microtargeting is that:

> Campaign messages ... have little to do with the priorities of the American public. Of course, political candidates have always said what they think people want to hear, not what they should hear. But voter microtargeting makes politics not only superficial but also distorted and insular. Distortion occurs when candidates precisely calibrate which message will appeal to certain individuals, create multiple versions of the same message, and deliver them to individuals meeting the predetermined criteria, via e-mail, online ads, cable TV, or social media.[103]

This type of multi-messaging has the potential to upend politics.[104] The logical end game is likely pitches to audiences of one, 325 million times over.

Microtargeting is also effective at finding unicorn voters—those who are registered with one party, but agree with the opposite party on a wedge issue:[105]

> In the 2004 presidential race, Democrats sought to identify 'the libertarian white male in Cobb County, Georgia, who would swing their way if approached appropriately,' while Republicans sought 'the socially conservative African American on the South Side of Chicago who might vote for a Republican.'[106]

As the *Washington Post* noted:

> Careful analysis can yield counterintuitive opportunities to win votes. In 2004, Republican microtargeting in New Mexico found a strain of education-obsessed Hispanic moms who responded positively to mailings and phone calls touting George W. Bush's No Child Left Behind law. Democratic microtargeters discovered what they called Christian Conservative Environmentalists. Find such people (by data-mining the information), craft a message that resonates with their particular bugaboos, contact them directly, and you may get votes that otherwise would never have found their way into your tally.[107]

And as Marc Rotenberg of the Electronic Privacy Information Center declared in the 2008 election, "'campaigns can go beyond directing a mailing to the Hispanic or Jewish community, and instead can figure out what John Smith at 286 Main Street is thinking.'"[108]

---

[103] Rubinstein, *supra* note 79, at 909.
[104] Hillygus & Shields, *supra* note 89, at 15.
[105] Taylor, *supra* note 95, at 29.
[106] Rubinstein, *supra* note 79, at 882–83.
[107] Levy, *supra* note 83.
[108] *Id.*

At its worst, microtargeting voters is a type of gross manipulation. Steven Levy reported in the *Washington Post* how the Romney campaign in 2012 targeted voters it categorized as "strivers":

> [Microtargeting] … identified another group, one not quite sold on Romney but susceptible to a pitch on his economic policies. These were people who didn't make as much money as the country-clubbers but displayed consumer habits similar to those of the snob set—drove sport-utility vehicles, went to the theater, bought natural foods … 'they identified with the politics of those they are emulating.' Calls to those strivers with messages about Romney's tax policies got results. … The Romney camp has sorted out individuals whose striving makes them vulnerable to a pitch that, at least with their current financial status, is at odds with their economic interests. Would they have been as susceptible if the caller informed them why they were the ones receiving the call? *According to our data, you're living beyond your means. Wouldn't you like to vote that way, too?*[109]

So what is the dataset that political actors use to microtarget voters? Each vendor has its own secret recipe. But the basic ingredients are the same:

> Both major parties collect conventional information from publicly available records on registered voters such as party registration, voting history, and driver's licenses. But the parties and strategists increasingly are enhancing these records with in-depth consumer data gathered from varied sources such as supermarkets, magazine subscriptions, charitable contributions, online book vendors, drugstores, automobile dealerships, and issue surveys.[110]

Americans who spend their days online for work or pleasure are inadvertently leaving a trail of data, which data-miners are all too happy to hoover up like a vacuum cleaner and sell to political operatives. CNN reported in the 2012 election:

> Jim Walsh of DSPolitical said the company has so far aggregated more than 600 million cookies -- or tags on Internet user IP addresses that track movements online -- and has worked to match them against lists of some 250 million voters in the United States. This all is aimed at helping them determine how someone might vote and then reaching them wherever they go online.[111]

Both political parties microtarget voters. "[B]y the mid-nineties, the Republican National Committee (RNC) began working to create an integrated national

---

[109] *Id.* (emphasis added).
[110] Murray & Scime, *supra* note 96, at 146 (internal citations omitted).
[111] Brennan, *supra* note 78.

voter file."[112] By 2004, Republicans had the Voter Vault and Democrats had DataMart.[113]

There's a small cottage industry for microtargeting voters:

> Aristotle, Camelot, and Catalist [all] collect individual voter records, merge them with other public and commercial data, and provide them for a fee to campaigns. For instance, Catalist claims to maintain a database of over 265 million persons (more than 180 million registered voters and 85 million unregistered adults). The data include ... contact information ... commercial and census data. The company Aristotle claims that in addition to the wealth of demographics Aristotle already provides for high level micro-targeting, you can now identify your voters based on their interests and hobbies.[114]

Additionally, political strategy firms like:

> Democratic DSPolitical and Republican CampaignGrid are gathering or buying ... detailed information about how often a potential voter has cast a ballot in addition to data on what they read, where they shop and other consumer behavior tracked for decades off line.[115]

And there are data operations that essentially cater to the super-wealthy. The Mercers (father Robert and daughter Rebekah) had (the now defunct) Cambridge Analytica and the Koch Bothers (David and Charles) had i360.[116]

Polling that is used to microtarget voters may encourage a candidate to take an idiosyncratic position to appeal to voters, at least in appeals to select voters:

> Instead of polling driving candidates to converge on the midpoint of public opinion (as the median voter model would predict), polls and other sources of information are being used to selectively mobilize support from targeted subgroups of voters. Polls are being used to narrow rather than widen the appeal of candidates.[117]

And, not surprisingly, the same tactics that target voters can also be used for political fundraising: "Campaigns use donor lists extensively to identify poten-

---

[112] Rubinstein, *supra* note 79, at 876.

[113] *Id.*

[114] Burkhard C. Schipper & Hee Yeul Woo, *Political Awareness, Microtargeting of Voters, and Negative Electoral Campaigning*, 17 n. 7 (May 2, 2017), https://ssrn.com/abstract=2039122; Rubinstein, *supra* note 79, at 876–77.

[115] Brennan, *supra* note 78.

[116] Kenneth P. Vogel & Jeremy W. Peters, *Alabama Victory Provides Blueprint for New Bannon Alliance*, N.Y. Times (Sept. 28, 2017) ("the Mercers steered candidates and groups they funded to a data firm in which they are major investors, Cambridge Analytica, which competes with the Koch-backed data firm i360.").

[117] Jacobs & Shapiro, *supra* note 93, at 639 (internal citation omitted).

tial contributors and use complicated algorithms to identify non-donors who look like donors but have not yet contributed."[118]

In 2008 and 2012 the Obama campaign used microtargeting to get more people registered to vote. Their goal was to get more Democrats and people sympathetic to Obama registered.[119] As Sasha Issenberg wrote:

> The breakthrough was that registration no longer had to be approached passively. … New techniques made it possible to intelligently profile nonvoters: commercial data warehouses sold lists of all voting-age adults, and comparing those lists with registration rolls revealed eligible candidates, each attached to a home address to which an application could be mailed.[120]

Microtargeting was also used aggressively by the Trump campaign in 2016. As the Trump campaign's Brad Parscale told PBS:

> When you decide you're going to run for president of the United States, now you have hard-matched data with consumer data, matched with voter history, matched with very comprehensive polling data from all over the country. When you do that, you put that into a machine and then you start to learn. What you start to learn is how people react in areas, people, and individualize what they call hard ID'd. Hard ID's are then matched with phone numbers, email addresses and everything. By the time all those pieces are put together, then you can actually pull out an audience. You can say I want to find everybody in this portion of Ohio that believes that the wall needs to be built, that thinks that possibly trade reform needs to happen, and so we want to show them a job on trade and immigration. Then you take that; you export it out into Excel file—very simple. You import it into Facebook with PI in it, which is personal information that's matchable data—you know, addresses, phone numbers, whatever you have—and Facebook has been in the job of scraping that all from you, and then it just matches them. Then you have a little button on your computer that says that audience, and you can use that for all your ads.[121]

---

[118]   Hans J.G. Hassell & J. Quin Monson, *Campaign Targets and Messages in Direct Mail Fundraising*, 36 POLITICAL BEHAVIOR 359, 360 (June 2014).

[119]   Sasha Issenberg, *How Obama's Team Used Big Data to Rally Voters*, MIT TECHNOLOGY REVIEW (Dec. 19, 2012), www.technologyreview.com/s/509026/how-obamas-team-used-big-data-to-rally-voters/ ("Applying microtargeting models identified which nonregistrants were most likely to be Democrats and which ones Republicans.").

[120]   *Id.*

[121]   James Jacoby, *The Facebook Dilemma: Brad Parscale*, PBS (Aug. 8, 2018), www.pbs.org/wgbh/frontline/interview/brad-parscale/.

In the same interview, Parscale also explained how Facebook allowed the Trump campaign to expand its audience by using the "Lookalike Audience" feature:

> if you have one audience, let's say 300,000 people, you can click a button, and it will find people who look like those 300,000 people … you could say, 'Hey, I really need a 600,000-person audience. I only know 300,000.' Upload 300,000, see how well it [Facebook] can find people, and then the testing would allow us to see if that was accurate or not. … Facebook Lookalike Audiences are pretty amazing. I mean, it's why the platform's great. Now, that's probably one advantage over a mailer, because U.S. Postal Service doesn't tell you that. The TV channels will do that some, the addressable TV and some of them. But the Lookalike Audience is probably one of the most powerful features of Facebook.[122]

Later, the Trump campaign would be accused of using psychographic data as well to target voters.

Finally, microtargeting by definition typically means that certain voters are ignored because they are considered unworthy of a campaign's time: "Voter microtargeting thereby makes possible a political strategy that not only departs from the democratic ideal but also exacerbates inequities in the American political system, which routinely ignores voters who have been 'excluded or marginalized from the political process.'"[123]

6.   CONCLUSION

As will be explored later in this book, the partisan bubbles that many Americans have sorted themselves into place many in an information echo chamber where little from the opposite side of the political spectrum is likely to penetrate.[124] This has also made many Americans easier to manipulate, even if the person doing the manipulating is sitting in another country, or isn't even another human being at all.

---

[122] *Id.*

[123] Rubinstein, *supra* note 79, at 908.

[124] For more on branding and politics see Ciara Torres-Spelliscy, *Shooting Your Brand in the Foot: What Citizens United Invites*, 68 RUTGERS U. L. REV. 1295 (Spring 2016).

5. Branding candidates on TV

"A leadership responsible only to an uninformed or partially informed electorate can bring nothing but disaster to our world." Edward R. Murrow[1]

1. INTRODUCTION

Political advertising often treats political candidates as one more product to be sold. Back in the 1950s, a historian commented: "An American presidential campaign is one of the most awesome spectacles known to man; the fate of the nation may hinge on the outcome of what seems to be a donnybrook among demagogues and Madison Avenue types."[2] Little has changed in half a century. Describing branding Hillary Clinton in 2016, marketing strategist Peter Sealey told the *Washington Post*: "'It's exactly the same as selling an iPhone ...'"[3]

So what makes a presidential candidate electable? Surely it's not raw intellect. Plenty of incredibly bright men and women have failed. The exceptionally erudite Adlai Stevenson was a twice-failed Democratic nominee for president.[4] He is credited with having the following exchange with a voter who said, "'Every thinking person will be voting for you.' Adlai Stevenson replied: 'Madam, that is not enough. I need a majority.'"[5] And ever since the dawn of the television age, getting to that Electoral College majority has typically required a slick television campaign. Or as Joe McGinniss pontificated, "Television seems particularly useful to the politician who can be charming but lacks ideas."[6]

Self-branding for politicians is simple: repeat, repeat, repeat an idea about yourself until it gets stuck in the minds of the public. Politicians will also try to brand their opponents with negative connotations through the same technique.

---

[1] ROBERT SPERO, DUPING OF THE AMERICAN VOTER 1 (1980) (quoting Murrow).

[2] V.O. KEY, JR., POLITICS, PARTIES, AND PRESSURE GROUPS 501 (4th ed. 1958).

[3] Philip Rucker & Anne Gearan, *The making of Hillary 5.0: Marketing wizards help re-imagine Clinton brand*, WASH. POST (Feb. 21, 2015) (quoting Peter Sealey).

[4] *Adlai Ewing Stevenson: An Urbane, Witty, Articulate Politician and Diplomat, Obituary*, N.Y. TIMES (July 15, 1965).

[5] DREW WESTEN, THE POLITICAL BRAIN: THE ROLE OF EMOTION IN DECIDING THE FATE OF THE NATION 25 (2007).

[6] JOE MCGINNISS, THE SELLING OF THE PRESIDENT 1968 at 29 (1969).

Candidates must brand themselves as "being presidential." Back in the 1950s, political scientist Eugene Burdick thought of the president as a "father figure." Though Burdick worried, "Is it healthy in a democracy that citizens desire a leader who will protect them? ... Are Americans ... looking for a heroic leader of the totalitarian type?"[7]

The reason that politicians can brand themselves or political opponents so easily is most politicians are not well known. For all their power over the lives of average Americans, most voters cannot pick an elected politician out of a police line-up. A poll from 2017 showed just 37 percent of Americans could name their member of Congress.[8] A survey by Johns Hopkins found even fewer (20 percent) could name a state legislator.[9] Lacking fame, most politicians are a *tabula rasa* that can be written on by friend and foe alike. And so the branding war is on.

The question when Jimmy Carter ran for president was "Jimmy who?" The ad wizards at Coca-Cola gave the reassuring answer that Carter was an honest peanut farmer—a welcome change from Richard "I'm not a crook" Nixon. But politicians have a tough audience to win over, because "'[l]ike farmers, voters are never happy.'"[10]

This chapter will run through the highlights of the advertising tactics of the major presidential candidates from 1952–88. A recurring leitmotif is that the candidate with the better advertising shop typically wins.

2.   EISENHOWER '52 AND '56

Since televisions became ubiquitous in American households, elections have involved selling the candidate as a brand on TV.[11] In 1948, Governor of New York Thomas Dewey, the Republican who ran against Harry Truman, tried the new technology by rolling out a few television ads. One of his impressions of the new medium remains true today: advertising on television is expensive.[12]

---

[7]   VANCE PACKARD, THE HIDDEN PERSUADERS 186 (1957 reprinted 1969) (quoting Burdick).

[8]   *Just 37% of Americans can name their Representative*, HAVEN INSIGHTS (May 31, 2017), www.haveninsights.com/just-37-percent-name-representative/.

[9]   Press Release, *JHU Survey: Americans Don't Know Much About State Government*, JOHNS HOPKINS (Dec. 11, 2018), https://releases.jhu.edu/2018/12/11/jhu-survey-americans-dont-know-much-about-state-government/.

[10]   Richard Stengel & Eric Pooley, *Inside the high-tech machine that set Clinton and Dole polls apart*, CNN (Nov. 6, 1996), www.cnn.com/ALLPOLITICS/1996/elections/time.special/pollster/index.shtml (quoting pollster Fred Steeper).

[11]   KEY, *supra* note 2, at 514.

[12]   Michael Beschloss, *Eisenhower, an Unlikely Pioneer of TV Ads*, N.Y. TIMES (Oct. 30, 2015) ("Dewey ... realized that making use of [TV] in 1952 would be expen-

As one author put it, "Tom Dewey did not buy the idea of lowering himself to the commercial environment of a toothpaste ad. ... Certainly a man of Dewey's prominence did not need to be commercialized to beat the hick Truman."[13] Pollsters predicted a win for Dewey. But the 1948 election resulted in the famous picture of a victorious Truman holding a newspaper that had been printed too soon with the erroneous headline, "Dewey Defeats Truman!"

Dewey advised candidate Dwight D. Eisenhower in 1952 that if he was going to embrace the new medium of television, then "'[d]on't forget, let's get a hell of a lot of money!'"[14] The Republican Party raised the money and got Eisenhower into the living room of nearly every American with a TV.[15] Historian Michael Beschloss noted that the "result was the beginning of the world we know today, where presidential candidates compete to raise billions of dollars that will be spent largely on commercials."[16] Campaign finance laws were relatively lax at the time and the only meaningful restriction was the a ban on federal candidates taking money directly from the treasuries of corporations and unions. But in the 1950s, corporate and union political action committees (PACs) sprang up to avoid this ban.

By the time of Eisenhower's candidacy, frequently the same ad men pushing soap and toothpaste also pushed political candidates like Ike too. As Vance Packard wrote in *The Hidden Persuaders*:

> many of the nation's leading public-relations experts have been indoctrinating themselves in the lore of psychiatry and the social sciences in order to increase their skill at 'engineering' our consent ... this ... approach is showing up nationally in the professional politicians' intensive use of symbol manipulation and reiteration on the voter, who more and more is treated like Pavlov's conditioned dog.[17]

Not unlike the branding of products, candidates are packaged and marketed, some more subtly than others. If you want to see branding at work in politics, look at the men in make-up.[18] With a few rare exceptions like Shirley Chishom, Margaret Chase Smith and Hillary Clinton, most presidential candidates throughout American history have been men. Yet part of the packaging of male

---

sive. Before then, money had not been so decisive in presidential politics ... there were only so many campaign signs, bumper stickers and buttons you could buy.").

[13]   SPERO, *supra* note 1, at 33.

[14]   Beschloss, *supra* note 12 (quoting Dewey).

[15]   *Elections from 1924 to 1964*, VIRGINIA HISTORY, www.virginiahistory.org/ collections-and-resources/virginia-history-explorer/getting-message-out-presidential -campaign-1.

[16]   *Id.*

[17]   PACKARD, *supra* note 7, at 4.

[18]   The author is referring to politicians, not to drag queens.

candidates includes make-up, oftentimes to make them look healthier than they actually are.

By 1952, General Eisenhower had been Supreme Commander of NATO, a five-star general in the U.S. Army and the president of Columbia University, yet the ad men working on his campaign deemed Ike to be a weak speaker. The solution to his poor ability to pontificate was to script him into short soundbites. Thus, to brand and sell the man who had helped win the Second World War, the ad men decided to make 40 short 20-second-long TV commercials where Ike appeared to answer questions from average Americans.[19] In these TV spots, Eisenhower did not wear his glasses and wore make-up—presumably to look a bit more matte.[20] He won his 1952 election. He continued to wear make-up for TV appearances as president[21] and even took acting lessons to improve his TV image.[22]

A few years later during his re-election campaign, make-up was even more necessary to help "sell" Ike to the American people.[23] He had had a heart attack in 1955 and there were concerns that during his recovery, he did not look healthy enough.[24] The pancake make-up was reportedly much more liberally applied to Eisenhower—not just to touch up his look, but to mask his illness.[25] One TV columnist criticized the president's look the day he announced he would run for re-election: "both the lighting and make-up—if, indeed, the President permitted the pancake touch-up … seemed to be aimed at making Gen. Eisenhower look pale."[26] Putting make-up on a sick man and

---

[19] John E. Hollitz, *Eisenhower and the Admen: the Television Spot Campaign of 1952*, 66(1) WISC. MAG. OF HISTORY 25 (Aut. 1982), www.jstor.org/stable/4635688 ?seq=1#page_scan_tab_contents.

[20] Beschloss, *supra* note 12 ("When the cameras rolled, Eisenhower, wearing makeup, his eyeglasses removed, read from cue cards with huge letters.").

[21] Merlo J. Pusey, *Eisenhower the President* 26 (1956) ("As a measure of his devotion to his task, he even submitted to make-up for his television performances[.]").

[22] *Television and the 1956 campaign*, CQ (Sept. 6, 1955), https://library.cqpress .com/cqresearcher/document.php?id=cqresrre1955090600 ("President Eisenhower relies on the actor-director, Robert Montgomery, to coach him for television appearances[.]").

[23] PACKARD, *supra* note 7, at 191 ("The President [Eisenhower] stated that he was going to rely on … television—which had brought a new kind of persuader-consultant into the party councils: the TV adviser and make-up consultant.").

[24] Cody White, *"Heart Attack Strikes Ike," President Eisenhower's 1955 Medical Emergency in Colorado*, NAT'L ARCHIVES BLOG (Sept. 22, 2016), https://text-message .blogs.archives.gov/2016/09/22/heart-attack-strikes-ike-president-eisenhowers-1955 -medical-emergency-in-colorado/.

[25] PACKARD, *supra* note 7, at 192 ("[Robert Montgomery] was on hand to advise the President on lighting, make-up, and delivery.").

[26] *Id.* at 108 (quoting TV columnist Harriet Van Horne).

pretending he is up for the most demanding job in the world is a typical way to sell a product—essentially, showing the purchasing public more sizzle and less steak.[27]

Another trick Eisenhower used in 1952 was the televised "fake impromptu news conference," which was full of campaign staffers. Thus, the event appeared to be spontaneous, when it was really all but scripted.[28] Ike looked more natural in these fake pressers than the canned speeches of his opponent, Adlai Stevenson, even when Stevenson had some of the most skilled speech-writers around.[29]

When Eisenhower did these things (the acting lessons, the soundbites and the make-up), television was new. Democrat Adlai Stevenson, like Dewey, thought television was below the stature of the office he was seeking. Stevenson was a long-form candidate in a country that was losing its attention span. His speech before the Democratic National Convention in 1952 included this soaring rhetoric:

> Here, on the prairies of Illinois and the Middle West, we can see a long way in all directions. We look to east, to west, to north and south. Our commerce, our ideas, come and go in all directions. Here there are no barriers, no defenses, to ideas and aspirations. We want none; we want no shackles on the mind or the spirit, no rigid patterns of thought, no iron conformity. We want only the faith and conviction that triumph in free and fair contest. That, my friends, is the American story, written by the Democratic Party, here on the prairies of Illinois, in the heartland of the nation.[30]

In stark contrast to Stevenson's lofty speeches,[31] in 1952 the Democrats' lackluster self-defeating slogan was, "You never had it so good."[32] They ran a TV ad with a woman singing, "I love the Gov," and another which told voters not to worry about how to pronounce Adlai's first name and just vote for

---

[27]   *Id.* ("The idea is to sell the sizzle rather than the meat.").

[28]   Craig M. Allen, *TV and the Presidential Campaign: Insights into the Evolution of Political Television* 21 (1987) ("Eisenhower conducted a special television 'news conference,' substituting questions from reporters with those developed by his campaign staff and asked by handpicked volunteers.").

[29]   John Kenneth Galbraith, *Adlai Stevenson of Illinois*, N.Y. Times (Mar. 7, 1976) ("John Bartlow Martin ... became one of Stevenson's best speechwriters. ... [N]o one ... could make a point more succinctly, support it more sharply with evidence and then, of all things, stop.").

[30]   Richard Henry, *Eleanor Roosevelt and Adlai Stevenson* 35 (2010).

[31]   *Id.* at 36 ("win or lose, can campaign not as a crusade to exterminate the opposing party, ... but as a great opportunity to educate and elevate a people.").

[32]   *Elections from 1924 to 1964, supra* note 15.

him.[33] This didn't sell as well as Eisenhower's ads, which pushed the theme, "Peace, progress and prosperity,"[34] and other ads had the infectious tune, "I like Ike."[35] The slogan avoided the multiple syllable name of the candidate, Eis-en-how-er. With "I like Ike," his media team had "packag[ed] the World War II General in one of the slickest, most memorable political advertising campaigns in U.S. history."[36]

Besides having a catchier slogan, the Republicans in 1952 also did the equivalent of running the table on political television ads. In October 1952, "Democrats bought only $77,000 of airtime, compared to $1.5 million for the Republicans."[37] And the Democrats unwisely decided to use their TV time on speeches that ran in the 10:30 pm time slot when many voters had work the next morning.[38] The Democrats also thought that the merchandizing of Ike would make voters reject him. According to Beschloss, "Stevenson himself declared that Eisenhower's commercials were destined to backfire, adding: 'This isn't a soap opera. This isn't Ivory Soap versus Palmolive.'"[39] Stevenson, despite his intellect, could not have been more wrong. Diplomat Harlan Cleveland told Rosser Reeves, the creator of Eisenhower's 1952 television campaign, "You're sabotaging Democracy. You're trying to take a complex presidential personality, trim it down to a few slogans, reduce it to fifteen seconds, and use your rat-ta-tat-tat technique."[40] The ad men behind Ike were unrepentant. To them, the whole point was "'merchandising Eisenhower's frankness, honesty and integrity.'"[41]

Democrats in 1956 had learned the powerful role TV had played in electing Ike in 1952. They wanted to match the Republicans, but they couldn't raise enough money for a comparable media campaign. Moreover, the Democrats also struggled to get top ad agencies to take their accounts—the agencies did

---

[33] *1952 Eisenhower VS. Stevenson*, Museum of the Moving Image (2016), www.livingroomcandidate.org/commercials/1952.

[34] *Elections from 1924 to 1964, supra* note 15.

[35] Claire Suddath, *A Brief History of Campaign Songs*, Time (undated), https://content.time.com/time/specials/packages/article/0,28804,1840981_1840998_1840902,00.html ("Irving Berlin — the man who gave us ...*God Bless America* ... — penned this memorable number for the wartime hero-turned 1952 Presidential candidate.").

[36] *Id.*

[37] Dennis W. Johnson, *Democracy for Hire: A History of American Political Consulting* 69 (2016).

[38] *Id.* at 70 ("To save money, the thirty-minute speeches were set for 10:30 to 11:00 p.m. on Tuesday and Thursday nights ...").

[39] Beschloss, *supra* note 12.

[40] Spero, *supra* note 1, at 32 (quoting Harlan Cleveland).

[41] *Id.* at 35 (quoting Ben Duffy president of Batten, Barton, Durstine & Osborn).

not want to alienate their commercial clients, who were mostly Republicans.[42] Finally, in January of 1956, the Democrats landed a contract with a small advertising firm, although they were still behind the eight ball because Republicans had already purchased key blocks of ad time for the Fall of 1956.[43] Stevenson was the candidate again for a rematch with the incumbent Eisenhower. Five of Eisenhower's ads in 1956 featured women with direct appeals to women voters, including one African American woman.[44] Ike won re-election in 1956 handily.

3.   KENNEDY '60

John F. Kennedy had two key attributes that led him to be an ideal television candidate: he was good-looking and rich.[45] The good-looking part made him telegenic.[46] The rich part enabled him to spread his message via TV screen.[47] His opponent, Richard Nixon, largely shunned TV for most of the 1960 campaign. This left Kennedy with more room to maneuver into the minds of American voters.

In the first Kennedy/Nixon debate, artifice may have played an outsized role in how the candidates were received by the public. Nixon underestimated the power that the television camera would have on the public's perceptions. Nixon "was underwhelmed by the event at any rate. 'Television is not as effective as it was in 1952,' he had told a journalist. 'The novelty has worn off.'"[48] Before the first debate on September 26, 1960, "[a]t the studio, the challenger [Kennedy] was the first one asked whether he would appreciate the services of a makeup artist. He refused. The champion [Nixon], taking the bluff, refused in turn."[49] Then Kennedy had his own team do his make-up. "The result was that Kennedy looked and sounded good on television, while Nixon looked pale

---

[42]   Allen, *supra* note 28, at 17 ("in late 1955, six major advertising agencies refused requests to handle the account of the Democratic National Committee for fear of offending their Republican clients.").

[43]   *Id.*

[44]   *1956 Eisenhower VS. Stevenson*, MUSEUM OF THE MOVING IMAGE (2016), www .livingroomcandidate.org/commercials/1956.

[45]   Don Gonyea, *How JFK Fathered the Modern Presidential Campaign*, NPR (Nov. 16, 2013), www.npr.org/2013/11/16/245550528/jfk-wrote-the-book-on-modern -presidential-campaigns.

[46]   *Id.* ("Dallek says JFK was visionary in recognizing TV's potential ...").

[47]   *Id.*

[48]   RICK PERLSTEIN, NIXONLAND: THE RISE OF A PRESIDENT AND THE FRACTURING OF AMERICA 52 (2008).

[49]   *Id.*

and tired …"[50] An estimated 70 million Americans or roughly two-thirds of the electorate watched the debate.[51] According to Kennedy's Presidential Library, "[s]tudies would later show that of the four million voters who made up their minds as a result of the debates, three million voted for Kennedy."[52]

Physical looks really shouldn't be a qualification for president, but they surely played a role in 1960. As Rick Perlstein wrote in *Nixonland*:

> When Walter Cronkite asked his embarrassing question about all the people who couldn't put their finger on why they disliked him, Nixon answered … that it might be his appearance. 'Oh, I get letters from … [people] who support me,' he said. 'And they say, "Why do you wear that heavy beard when you are on television?"' 'Actually, … I can shave and within thirty seconds before I go on television and I still have a beard, unless we put some powder on, as we have done today.'[53]

But Joe McGinniss had a slightly different diagnosis. He described the Nixon/Kennedy debate thusly: "Television would be blamed but for all the wrong reasons. They would say it was makeup and lighting, but Nixon's problem went deeper than that … America took its Richard Nixon straight and did not like the taste."[54]

If Eisenhower had the catchy "I like Ike" ditty, Kennedy also had a better campaign song than Nixon. Nixon's campaign song was "Click with Dick."[55] By contrast to Nixon's puzzling song, Kennedy's song "High Hopes" was sung by Frank Sinatra in a snappy tempo.[56]

Arguably, Nixon was running a 1950 campaign in 1960. Nixon promised to go to all 50 states and he did. But it also could have cost him the election because he didn't spend enough time in swing states.[57] Instead of using

---

[50]   *How the Kennedy-Nixon debate changed the world of politics*, NATIONAL CONSTITUTION CENTER (Sept. 26, 2017), https://constitutioncenter.org/blog/the-debate -that-changed-the-world-of-politics.

[51]   *Campaign of 1960*, JOHN F. KENNEDY PRESIDENTIAL LIBRARY, www.jfklibrary .org/JFK/JFK-in-History/Campaign-of-1960.aspx.

[52]   *Id.*

[53]   PERLSTEIN, *supra* note 48 at 51–52.

[54]   McGINNISS, *supra* note 6, at 32.

[55]   Olivia Hoffman, "Click with Dick" (1960), https://archive.org/details/calasus _000061.

[56]   *"High Hopes"*, JOHN F. KENNEDY PRESIDENTIAL LIBRARY, www.jfklibrary.org/ learn/about-jfk/life-of-john-f-kennedy/fast-facts-john-f-kennedy/high-hopes (Sung by Frank Sinatra).

[57]   Stephen Fehr, *50-State Strategy May Come Down to 20*, PEW (Sept. 15, 2008), www.pewtrusts.org/en/research-and-analysis/blogs/stateline/2008/09/15/50state -strategy-may-come-down-to-20.

national polling data, the Kennedy team had polls run in separate states.[58] According to Lawrence R. Jacobs and Robert Y. Shapiro, "Interviews and archival records suggest that the Kennedy campaign analyzed the candidate's policy positions and the public's perception of his personal image as interconnected (rather than mutually exclusive) strategic concerns."[59] Kennedy's team realized the change that widespread adoption of TV meant for the campaign, with 88 percent of homes containing a television.[60] In one Kennedy 1960 TV ad, he "projected an image of an anti-establishment candidate."[61] In another ad, African American singer Harry Belafonte sat next to Kennedy and endorsed him for president.[62] One innovation that Kennedy's team brought to political TV ads was the first televised negative campaign ad.[63] In the ad:

> a reporter asks Eisenhower about Nixon's experience: 'I just wonder if you could give us an example of a major idea of his that you had adopted.' Eisenhower responds, to the laughter of others, 'If you give me a week, I might think of one.'[64]

Another innovation was Kennedy's outreach to Hispanic voters through an ad featuring Kennedy's wife Jacqueline speaking in Spanish.[65] All in all, Kennedy's team was running a 1960s campaign in 1960 using TV ads to brand himself as modern, hopeful and inclusive; that's likely why he won.

---

[58] Lawrence R. Jacobs & Robert Y. Shapiro, *Issues, Candidate Image, and Priming: The Use of Private Polls in Kennedy's 1960 Presidential Campaign*, 88 AMERICAN POL. SCI. REV. 527, 528 (1994) ("the Kennedy campaign sought to diminish its uncertainty regarding voters' preferences by ... poll[ing] in separate states and forgo[ing] national surveys and ... avoid[ing] 'separat[ing] our polling from the other problems of strategy.'").

[59] *Id.* at 531.

[60] *Campaign of 1960*, *supra* note 51 ("In 1950, only 11 percent of American homes had television; by 1960, the number had jumped to 88 percent.").

[61] David Plouffe, *JFK's pioneering election campaign and its reverberations through the years*, WASH. POST (May 5, 2017); Joseph A. Palermo, *Here's What RFK Did in California in 1968*, HUFF. POST (May 25, 2011), www.huffingtonpost.com/joseph-a-palermo/heres-what-rfk-did-in-cal_b_80931.html ("Kennedy's primary campaign of 1960 ... relied on organizations outside formal party networks ...").

[62] *1960 Kennedy VS. Nixon*, MUSEUM OF THE MOVING IMAGE (2016), www.livingroomcandidate.org/commercials/1960.

[63] Gonyea, *supra* note 45.

[64] *Id.*

[65] *Id.*

4.   JOHNSON '64

After President Kennedy's assassination in Dallas in 1963, his Vice President Lyndon Johnson became president. One of Johnson's political ads started with the date November 22, 1963 and footage of the day he took office. An announcer's voiceover said that Johnson was determined that "the young president he had served had not lived or died in vain."[66]

Johnson had to face Senator Barry Goldwater in 1964. Goldwater inspired all sorts of concerns, including about his mental fitness to be president. Psychiatrists offered opinions about his mental health. This created a crisis for mental health professionals. Later, professional associations established the "Goldwater rule," which prevented psychiatrists from offering opinions on the mental health of public officials that they had not treated.[67]

Goldwater was defiantly conservative and sought to brand himself in that way. In his acceptance of the Republican nomination, he said, "extremism in the defense of liberty is no vice! And let me remind you also that moderation in the pursuit of justice is no virtue!"[68] At the time, Goldwater's followers were described in *The New York Review of Books* as cult-like.[69] And this same piece warned, "One can only sympathize ... with the Republican moderates in the formidable ... enterprise ... of retaking the party from the cult that now runs it ..."[70]

Goldwater seemed particularly prone to harming his own presidential run. As the *New Yorker* saw it, "Goldwater's inclination to shoot straight did not waver even when he was aiming at his own foot."[71] A Goldwater ad interspersed images of American school children pledging allegiance to the flag with a speech from Nikita Khrushchev saying, "we will bury you" in Russian.

---

[66]   *1964 Johnson VS. Goldwater*, MUSEUM OF THE MOVING IMAGE (2016), www .livingroomcandidate.org/commercials/1964.

[67]   Olivia B. Waxman, *Why the Goldwater Rule Keeps Psychiatrists From Diagnosing at a Distance*, TIME (July 27, 2017), http://time.com/4875093/donald-trump -goldwater-rule-history/ ("the American Psychiatric Association's 1973 'Goldwater Rule,' ... prohibits ... members from making such judgments about individuals they haven't personally evaluated ...").

[68]   Joshua Mound, *What Democrats Still Don't Get About George McGovern*, NEW REPUBLIC (Feb. 29, 2016), https://newrepublic.com/article/130737/democrats -still-dont-get-george-mcgovern.

[69]   Richard Hofstadter, *A Long View: Goldwater in History*, N.Y. REV. OF BOOKS (Oct. 8, 1964).

[70]   *Id.*

[71]   Louis Menand, *He Knew He Was Right*, NEW YORKER (Mar. 26, 2001).

The announcer's tagline was "Vote for Goldwater, in your heart you know he's right."[72]

By 1964, TV ownership reached 92 percent.[73] And Johnson had been in politics for a long time. Since 1937, he had been a congressman, the Senate majority leader and vice president before he ran for re-election for president. In 1964, Johnson's campaign seemed to push the boundaries of politics and propriety with his TV ads.[74] His media team took his personality and translated it into some of the most bizarre political ads that have ever aired.[75] The most infamous of all the Johnson spots was the "Daisy" ad. Here is Robert Mann's description:

> A 3-year-old girl in a simple dress counted as she plucked daisy petals in a sun-dappled field. Her words were supplanted by a mission-control countdown followed by a massive nuclear blast in a classic mushroom shape. The message was clear if only implicit: Presidential candidate Barry Goldwater was a genocidal maniac ... [76]

While the "Daisy" ad was the most notorious, this was just one of many eerie ads that Johnson's team ran. Another ad showed a girl eating ice cream while a voiceover spoke about nuclear radiation entering the food supply.[77] Another four-minute long ad was called "Confessions of a Republican" and in it the actor facing the camera said of Goldwater, "This man scares me."[78] Another ad showed members of the Ku Klux Klan (KKK) in white hoods and a burning cross, and insinuated that the KKK was supporting Goldwater.[79] These ads were meant to brand Goldwater as an "inhumane and trigger-happy extremist ..."[80] Most of the Johnson ads ended with the tagline "Vote for President Johnson on November third, the stakes are too high for you to stay home."[81]

---

[72]   *1964 Johnson VS. Goldwater, supra* note 66.

[73]   ROBERT MANN, DAISY PETALS AND MUSHROOM CLOUDS LBJ, BARRY GOLDWATER, AND THE AD THAT CHANGED AMERICAN POLITICS 126 (2011).

[74]   Robert Mann, *How the 'Daisy' Ad Changed Everything About Political Advertising*, SMITHSONIAN MAG. (Apr. 13, 2016) ("Doyle Dane Bernbach (DDB) ... didn't set out to revolutionize political advertising; what they wanted to do was to break the established rules of political ads ... by injecting creativity and emotion.").

[75]   PAUL K. CONKIN, BIG DADDY FROM THE PEDERNALES 190 (1986).

[76]   Mann, *supra* note 74.

[77]   *Id.*

[78]   *Id.*

[79]   *1964 Johnson VS. Goldwater, supra* note 66.

[80]   Hofstadter, *supra* note 69.

[81]   *1964 Johnson VS. Goldwater, supra* note 66.

All of these ads played on the emotions of voters.[82] And this is why the medium's critics were so outraged by this campaign. As Robert Spero argued, this "is where politics veers far from the ordinary truthful instincts that most people use to govern their lives—and why politicians do such great damage to the people they have been elected to serve."[83] The funding of these ads was made possible because campaign finance laws were still lax. Even Johnson would go on to call them "more loophole than law."[84] Whether it was Goldwater's foot in his mouth or Johnson's over-the-top TV ads, Johnson carried 44 states for a total of 486 electoral votes.

5.   NIXON '68 AND '72

The election in 1968 was a rollercoaster. First, President Johnson decided not to run for re-election, telling the nation, "I shall not seek, and I will not accept the nomination of my party for another term as your president."[85] Then one of the frontrunners, Robert Kennedy, was assassinated. As one author described the event, "Minutes after declaring victory [in the California primary], he was shot in the Ambassador Hotel, in Los Angeles. He died on June 6th, along with the seeds of whatever future America he carried within him."[86] Also that year, Martin Luther King Jr. was assassinated. There was a police riot against political protesters outside of the Democratic National Convention in Chicago.[87] Kathleen Hall Jamieson described the scene: "As the stunned nation watched, the police beat student protestors in the streets of Chicago while inside the convention hall the orchestra played 'Happy Days Are Here Again.' After Chicago, the Democrats were severely fragmented ..."[88]

---

[82]   Mann, *supra* note 74 ("the Daisy ad made emotions a much more potent weapon in our political campaigns, employing techniques that had previously only been applied to selling cars and soap.").

[83]   SPERO, *supra* note 1, at 83.

[84]   Lyndon Johnson, *Letter to the President of the Senate and to the Speaker of the House Transmitting Proposed Election Reform Act of 1966*, AMERICAN PRESIDENCY PROJECT (May 26, 1966), www.presidency.ucsb.edu/documents/letter-the-president -the-senate-and-the-speaker-the-house-transmitting-proposed-election.

[85]   Tom Curry, *In 1968, Democratic split helped Nixon win*, NBC NEWS (Sept. 29, 2008), www.nbcnews.com/id/26840327/ns/politics/t/democratic-split-helped-nixon -win/#.W0NM5LgnaUk.

[86]   Louis Menand, *Lessons From the Election of 1968*, NEW YORKER (Jan. 8, 2018).

[87]   *Hubert Humphrey, 38th Vice President (1965–1969)*, US SENATE, www.senate .gov/artandhistory/history/common/generic/VP_Hubert_Humphrey.htm ("The raucous Chicago convention—with nationally televised images of police beating young antiwar protesters in the parks—further weakened Humphrey's standing in the polls ...").

[88]   Marianne Worthington, *The Campaign Rhetoric of George Wallace in the 1968 Presidential Election*, UCUMBERLANDS, www.ucumberlands.edu/downloads/ academics/history/vol4/MarianneWorthington92.html.

In 1962, after losing the race for governor of California, Nixon declared, "You won't have Nixon to kick around anymore."[89] But he couldn't stay away from politics. The presidential race in 1968 involved two vice presidents: Humphrey for the Democrats and Nixon for the Republicans. The general election turned into a three-way race with Governor George "Segregation forever" Wallace, who ran as an American Independent. "[Wallace's] old campaign slogan 'Stand Up For Alabama' was revised to 'Stand Up For America.'"[90] Wallace's race baiting and extremism made Nixon seem moderate.

Humphrey wasn't ready for primetime. He could have resigned himself to having Robert Kennedy win the race, when he was abruptly killed.[91] Before his death, crowds were looking to Kennedy like he was a messiah. According to Joshua Zeitz, "At frantic rallies and in frenzied motorcade swings through black and Latino neighborhoods, Kennedy transformed into something bordering between Christ-like and celebrity."[92] Joseph A. Palermo paints a similar portrait: "[Kennedy] had unleashed a very tactile street politics. His hands were scabbed and bloodied from the thousands of handshakes over the past weeks; people felt they had to touch this candidate."[93] No one was flocking to touch Humphrey, who "was not groovy. Nor was he at all cool."[94] But the brand Humphrey tried to push on the electorate during the social turmoil was "the politics of joy."[95]

The same ad agency that had worked wonders for Johnson in 1964 was tasked with handling Humphrey's race:

> Arie Kopelman … ran the Humphrey account and knew precisely how he was going to advertise the vice president. 'When I wrote the media plan, we looked at it as if we were marketing a product for Heinz or Procter and Gamble.'[96]

But the ads that were created for Humphrey were a mess, in part because Humphrey had to run against two opponents.

[The ad men's] solution, to combine both enemies within the framework of single commercials, was simply bad advertising in a medium where the cardi-

---

[89]   Nicole Hemmer, *Richard Nixon's Model Campaign*, N.Y. TIMES (May 10, 2012).

[90]   Worthington, *supra* note 88.

[91]   Joshua Zeitz, *The Bobby Kennedy Myth*, POLITICO (June 5, 2018), www.politico .com/magazine/story/2018/06/05/rfk-bobby-kennedy-myth-legend-history-218593 ("Bobby Kennedy has come to embody the Democratic Party's lost dream.").

[92]   *Id.*

[93]   Palermo, *supra* note 61.

[94]   PERLSTEIN, *supra* note 48 at 267.

[95]   *Id.* at 310 ("The happy warrior with the mawkishly inappropriate campaign slogan—'the politics of joy'—spent the week moping.").

[96]   SPERO, *supra* note 1, at 91.

nal rule is 'never build a commercial around more than one idea.' In a typical commercial for Humphrey, ... the off-camera announcer talking pejoratively, first about Nixon on Vietnam, then Wallace on law and order ... Not until the final seconds ... did the viewer learn that the commercial was about Hubert Humphrey. It was murky, directionless advertising.[97]

One unique Humphrey ad just showed the words "Agnew for Vice President?" while a disembodied voice laughed, and then showed the words: "This would be funny if it weren't so serious."[98]

By 1968, Nixon had learned his lesson from losing in 1960 and 1962 that "[w]hat's on the tube is what counts."[99] Nixon also paved the way for his election by making nice with conservative journalists in 1966.[100] Conservative media outlets piled on with endorsements.[101] Behind the scenes, John Ehrlichman saw a ruthless Nixon. "In 1968, Nixon demanded that his staff conduct his campaign as if we were in an all-out war."[102] Nixon was particularly impatient with protestors. Ehrlichman added, "Nixon wanted me to create some kind of flying goon squad of our own to rough up the hecklers, take down their signs and silence them."[103]

While the Democrats were in disarray, Nixon and his media team plowed forward with a deceptively simple media plan: pretend to hold a series of "spontaneous" town hall style events, ten in all,[104] which were really just scripted events filled with Republican volunteers, from the people on stage with Nixon to the people in the audience.[105] These one-hour spectacles were produced by a young Roger Ailes.[106] This tactic was similar to what Eisenhower had done, but it was taken to an absurd new extreme.

The Nixon media team also ran short political ads—often using still images over Nixon speeches without showing him until the very end. After badmouth-

---

[97]   *Id.* at 95.

[98]   *1968 Nixon VS. Humphrey VS. Wallace*, MUSEUM OF THE MOVING IMAGE (2016), www.livingroomcandidate.org/commercials/1968.

[99]   SPERO, *supra* note 1, at 90 (quoting Richard Nixon).

[100]   Hemmer, *supra* note 89 ("Nixon began courting right-wing journalists and writers in August 1966 ...").

[101]   *Id.* ("Once he clenched the nomination, endorsements sprouted up everywhere: the newsweekly *Human Events*, *National Review*, *The Manchester Union-Leader*.").

[102]   JOHN EHRLICHMAN, WITNESS TO POWER: THE NIXON YEARS 49–50 (1982).

[103]   *Id.* at 50.

[104]   MCGINNISS, *supra* note 6, at 62–63.

[105]   *Id.* at 39–40 and 58–59 (Nixon was "[o]n live, but controlled, TV.").

[106]   *Id.* at 63; Rebecca Harrington, *Roger Ailes produced one of the most infamous political ads of all time, and it helped George H.W. Bush win the presidency*, BUSINESS INSIDER (May 18, 2017), www.businessinsider.com/roger-ailes-revolving-door-ad -bush-election-2017-5.

ing Madison Avenue ad agencies, in 1968, Nixon went all in.[107] The Nixon tagline was "This time vote like your whole world depended on it."[108] Then the campaign essentially hid Nixon from any media opportunities that could be risky, hostile or real. As Joe McGinniss put it, Nixon in 1968 "depended on a television studio the way a polio victim relied on an iron lung."[109] As Humphrey imploded, Nixon calmly walked from scripted event to scripted event. In a particularly ballsy move, the campaign ran an ad in the *New York Times* which included this: "We choose Mr. Nixon with the full knowledge that America will not live happily ever after November 5th."[110] By the end of it, Nixon emerged victorious. And once he was in the White House, Nixon brought in ad men to help him there, too.[111]

At the end of 1971, Congress amended the campaign finance laws to require more transparency. The new laws did not take effect until April of 1972. Nixon took advantage of the four-month gap before the new transparency rules took effect to raise millions of what he assumed would be untraceable money. When Nixon stood for re-election in 1972, his campaign was cheating all the way down.[112] The 1972 Nixon campaign was partially funded by illegal money and it did illegal and immoral things to win the White House a second time.[113] The cheating was so rampant that some of the malefactors got caught red handed, including the White House-directed burglars who were nabbed by local D.C. police breaking into the Democratic National Committee headquarters in the Watergate building.[114] The strange thing about the underhanded tactics

---

[107]   James Boyd, *Nixon's Southern Strategy*, N.Y. TIMES (May 17, 1970) ("millions of dollars spent by Madison Avenue lightweights who converted certain victory into near defeat.")

[108]   *1968 Nixon VS. Humphrey VS. Wallace*, *supra* note 98.

[109]   McGINNISS, *supra* note 6, at 138.

[110]   *Id.* at 144.

[111]   SPERO, *supra* note 1, at 107 ("No senior White House staff in history had contained advertising people; Nixon's had them in key positions. It was no accident.").

[112]   Dave Johnson, *What Do You Mean 'Sanders Might Be Another George McGovern'?*, HUFF. POST (Jan. 29, 2016), www.huffingtonpost.com/dave-johnson/what-do-you-mean-sanders_b_9116398.html ("He went up against Nixon and the divisive, race-baiting, media-savvy (Roger Ailes!) Republican politics of big money, corruption, lawbreaking, cynicism and manipulation.").

[113]   Ciara Torres-Spelliscy, *How Much Is an Ambassadorship? And the Tale of How Watergate Led to a Strong Foreign Corrupt Practices Act and a Weak Federal Election Campaign Act*, 16(1) CHAPMAN L. REV. 71 (Spring 2012).

[114]   Carl Bernstein & Bob Woodward, *FBI Finds Nixon Aides Sabotaged Democrats*, WASH. POST (Oct. 10, 1972) ("FBI agents have established that the Watergate bugging incident stemmed from a massive campaign of political spying and sabotage conducted on behalf of President Nixon's re-election and directed by officials of the White House and the Committee for the Re-election of the President ... During their Watergate

by Nixon and his Committee to Re-Elect the President (CREEP) is that they were most likely unnecessary. Nixon's opponent Senator George McGovern was more accomplished than history remembers and his campaign's inability to effectively brand him as such likely cost him the election. As Hendrick Hertzberg noted, "McGovern, who was incapable of boasting, made a different choice. His eloquent acceptance address to the 1972 Democratic convention contains not a single word about his military service ... His stump speeches and campaign advertisements were likewise reticent."[115] Thus, George McGovern was easily branded and caricatured by Hugh Scott, the Senate minority leader, as "the three A's: Acid, Amnesty, and Abortion" candidate.[116] Nixon could have played it straight and still won.

The cheating eventually caught up with Nixon, who had to resign from office in disgrace two years into his ill-gotten second term. Nixon's campaign finance shenanigans inspired Congress to enact the first major overhaul of the campaign finance laws in decades. The new Federal Election Campaign Act of 1974 (a) created the Federal Election Commission, (b) imposed contribution limits, (c) imposed expenditure limits, and (d) created public financing for presidential elections. The Supreme Court upheld all of the Federal Election Campaign Act except the expenditure limits in *Buckley v. Valeo*. This meant the 1976 election was held under new campaign finance rules. From 1976–2004, candidates from the two major political parties (Democrat and Republican) had the exact same amount of money. Thus for 28 years, the difference was really messaging and strategy.

6.   CARTER '76

Gerald Ford was in some ways the luckiest American politician ever. He became vice president after Spiro Agnew had to resign in disgrace over criminal tax issues. Then Ford became president after Nixon resigned over Watergate. One of Ford's ads in 1976 starts with the date August 9, 1974 and includes footage of him saying to the nation, "I'm acutely aware that you have not elected me as your President by your ballots."[117] In Gerald Ford's presidential papers, there are rafts of strategy memos for the '76 campaign, including

---

investigation, federal agents established that hundreds of thousands of dollars in Nixon campaign contributions had been set aside to pay for an extensive undercover campaign aimed at discrediting individual Democratic presidential candidates and disrupting their campaigns.").

[115]   Hendrik Hertzberg, *What McGovern Won*, NEW YORKER (Oct. 22, 2012).

[116]   Mound, *supra* note 68 (quoting Scott).

[117]   *1976 Carter VS. Ford*, MUSEUM OF THE MOVING IMAGE (2016), www .livingroomcandidate.org/commercials/1976.

statements such as: "Administration prima donnas must subvert their personal ambitions to the objective of getting the President elected;"[118] and "We must change the perception of literally millions of voters, and this can only be done through the mass media with the principal emphasis on television."[119] At least on paper, President Ford's team appeared to want to take the high ground, noting, "Our campaign strategy has been developed around the President's actual strengths and aimed at Carter's actual weaknesses."[120] Both Carter and Ford took advantage of the new Presidential Public Financing Program. This meant neither candidate had to raise money during the general election and both had $21.8 million.

Given that President Ford's pardon of Nixon's crimes may have poisoned the well with American voters, it is possible that *any* Democratic opponent could have trounced Ford in 1976. But Jimmy Carter's ace in the hole was the support of the Coca-Cola Company. Governor Carter bragged, "We have our own built-in State Department in the Coca-Cola Company."[121] Governor Carter utilized the company's corporate jets to make a more national name for himself.[122] The book *For God, Country and Coca-Cola* told the story:

> [I]n 1972, Carter revealed that he had ambitions beyond Georgia, asking [Coca-Cola chairman J. Paul] Austin for Coca-Cola's support if he ran for president. Austin laughed and said, 'Sure,' never dreaming that the nationally unknown Carter would actually pull it off.[123] But pull it off he did. As reported in the *New York Times*, "During Jimmy Carter's long march to the White House, he used Coca-Cola money, Coca-Cola jets and Coca-Cola's advertising company."[124] As noted by William Safire, "Austin hosted a luncheon in New York's '21' to raise a major bundle for the Carter Presidential campaign."[125] At the 21 event, "Austin reassured nervous businessmen that his speeches about the 'unholy, self-perpetuating alliances' between money and politics are just talk."[126]

---

[118] *Campaign Strategy Plan for the Ford Campaign*, GERALD R. FORD PRESIDENTIAL LIBRARY, www.fordlibrarymuseum.gov/library/exhibits/campaign/014600004-003.pdf.

[119] *Id.*

[120] *Id.*

[121] TRISTAN DONOVAN, FIZZ: HOW SODA SHOOK UP THE WORLD 146 (2013).

[122] Eben Shapiro, *Cola Coattails Presidential Pop And Circumstance*, N.Y. TIMES (Nov. 1, 1992).

[123] MARK PENDERGRAST, FOR GOD, COUNTRY AND COCA-COLA 292 (2013).

[124] Kurt Eichenwald, *Soda, the Life of the Party*, N.Y. TIMES (July 16, 1985).

[125] William Safire, *Carter, Coke and Castro*, N.Y. TIMES (July 7, 1977).

[126] PENDERGRAST, *supra* note 123, at 292.

Perhaps as useful as the campaign money and rides on Coca-Cola's corporate jets was the assistance that Coke provided Carter with advertising.[127] As Robert Spero noted:

> Coke's advertising, concentrated largely in television had been exceptionally attractive, catchy, clean-cut, rich in color and evocation, and striking for its eminently hummable music. But perhaps its most interesting characteristic is that it is almost never annoying. It has what the industry calls high 'wear rate.' People seem to actually like Coca-Cola commercials. Of all of the accolades heaped on Coke advertising over the years, however, probably the greatest accomplishment is its absolute mastery of image manipulation.[128]

And moreover, "If there was one favor J. Paul Austin's company could do for Jimmy Carter it would be to give him instruction in the art and science of image manipulation— the myth message."[129] Tony Schwartz, Coke's media guru, worked for Carter's '76 campaign.[130] "Schwartz offered further authentication that there is no difference between political and product commercials 'Whether it's Coca-Cola or Jimmy Carter,' he said, 'what we appeal to in the consumer or voter is an attitude.'"[131] The tagline for Carter's ads was "A leader, for a change."[132]

Once in office, President Carter took care of his benefactors at Coke.[133] On a superficial level, Pepsi machines were out and Coke machines were in at the White House.[134] On a more significant basis, Charles Duncan, Coca-Cola's ex-president in the early 1970s, became Carter's Secretary of Energy.[135] Joseph Califano, an outside lawyer for Coke, became Carter's Secretary of Health, Education and Welfare.[136] Griffin Bell, another outside counsel for Coke, was Attorney General.[137] Carter's administration also made J. Paul Austin a member of the National Council for US-China Trade, which was "the perfect battering

---

[127] SPERO, *supra* note 1, at 143–44.

[128] *Id.* at 142–43.

[129] *Id.* at 143.

[130] *Id.* at 144 (1980).

[131] *Id.* at 145 (1980).

[132] *1976 Carter VS. Ford*, *supra* note 117.

[133] SPERO, *supra* note 1, at 141 ("The relationship between Coca-Cola chairman J. Paul Austin (and his chamberlains at Coke, his attorneys at King & Spalding, his bankers at the Trust Company of Georgia, ...) and candidate Carter had been strong and enduring ...").

[134] Joyce Leviton, *J. Paul Austin, First Over the Wall, Prepares to Teach China What Things Go Better*, PEOPLE (Jan. 8, 1979).

[135] Ernest Holsendolph, *Duncan to Resign Today As Coca-Cola President*, N.Y. TIMES (May 7, 1974).

[136] Phil McCombs, *Joe Califano, Still Smokin'*, WASH. POST (Oct. 13, 1992).

[137] *Bitter Sugar for the Coca-Cola Connection?*, WASH. POST (July 28, 1977).

ram for getting Coke into China."[138] Indeed, "[f]or Austin, who has personally supervised the Coca-Colonization of the world from developing Africa to Asia, adding China was the capstone of 30 years with the company."[139]

7.   REAGAN '80 AND '84

By the end of Carter's administration, the "ah-gosh" sincerity of the Georgia peanut farmer had worn thin. The gas shortages and Iranian hostage crisis made Carter look ineffective.[140] The Republicans smelled blood in the water. They nominated a former actor and governor of California, Ronald Reagan, to challenge the sitting president. Reagan had made a name for himself during the 1964 campaign by taping a "closing argument" in favor of Goldwater that was shipped around the country. It was an underground hit.[141] Reagan won the California governorship from 1967–75. As Colleen Shogan explained, "Reagan's 1980 campaign can be described as a repudiation of the nation's direction."[142] Also in 1980, a new television station called CNN was launched offering 24 hours of news to a national audience.

The 1980 election turned into a three-way race between Carter, Reagan and Congressman John Anderson. All three candidates participated in the Presidential Public Financing Program. Carter and Reagan each got $29.4 million, though Anderson got far less in public funds ($4.2 million) because he was running as a third-party candidate. Both major parties were initially worried that Anderson might prove to be a spoiler. And for a while, Anderson had his core following.[143] But Anderson's appeal faded: "'The Anderson Difference' ha[d] not made enough of a difference ... The polls show[ed] his supporters being pulled away like iron filings drawn to a more powerful magnet."[144] Perhaps Anderson was too honest.[145] As Walter Shapiro reported: "[Congressman Anderson] said to his wife, 'I keep hearing the question the

---

[138] DONOVAN, *supra* note 121, at 147.

[139] Leviton, *supra* note 134.

[140] Chris Jackson & Clifford Young, *Brand Risk in the New Age of Populism: Four Key Tactics for Surviving Hyper-Partisan Consumers*, IPSOS 8 (2017) ("in the late 1970s ... confidence in the executive branch plummeted while confidence in major corporations held constant; possibly due to the Iran hostage crisis.").

[141] *1964 Johnson VS. Goldwater*, *supra* note 66.

[142] Colleen Shogan, *Presidential Campaigns and the Congressional Agenda: Reagan, Clinton, and Beyond*, 2 (2004).

[143] Dan Balz, T. R. Reid & Joseph A. O'Brien, *John B. Anderson: 12 Years On the Road to Discovery*, WASH. POST (Mar. 6, 1980).

[144] Peter Behr, *John Anderson*, WASH. POST (Oct. 26, 1980).

[145] Walter Shapiro, *John Anderson: The Nice Guy Syndrome*, ATLANTIC (Feb. 1980) ("[Anderson] is bright, articulate, independent, and thoughtful.").

guy in the restaurant asked: "Why are you running for President? It's such a terrible job." I wish I had a better answer.'"[146] A worse person and better candidate would have just made up a catchy well-branded answer.[147]

In the pro-Reagan ads, the candidate bragged about his accomplishments as governor. "'We can control inflation,' Reagan insists in one of the new commercials. 'We did it in California and we can do it for America.'"[148] In another ad, Reagan claimed that he could "make America great again."[149] Reagan's platform seemed to promise the impossible to voters, as he vowed to "lower taxes, increase military spending, and balance the federal budget."[150] His opponent Anderson said, "Reagan could do all this only 'with mirrors.' [George H.W.] Bush [Reagan's soon to be vice president] derisively called Reagan's fiscal plans 'voodoo economics.'"[151] But little matter; these impossible promises were wrapped in a bow of conservative moralizing and Reagan's brand was selling well.[152]

If Carter in 1976 was compared to Coke, the ad men pushing Reagan in 1980 were back to comparing their candidate to soap and cereal. As Robert G. Kaiser wrote:

> The viewer is told [in pro-Reagan TV ads] that Reagan saved California from bankruptcy, was the greatest tax reformer in the state's history, and improved the quality of life in California so fair-mindedly that even the state director of the AFL-CIO sang his praises. (That same labor official is a staunch Carter supporter this year, but no matter.) Peter Dailey, the California ad man responsible for Reagan's commercials, is unabashedly proud of this one, and will keep showing it intensively until election day on Nov. 4 … Daily … compared [the Reagan ads] to a serious ad campaign for soap or cereal …[153]

Voters bought it. Off to the White House Reagan went.

In 1984, even though he was the oldest man to hold the office, Reagan ran for re-election against Walter Mondale, President Carter's former vice president. Both Mondale and Reagan participated in the Presidential Public Financing

---

[146]   *Id.*

[147]   *Id.*

[148]   Robert G. Kaiser, *Carter and Reagan Media Strategies*, Wash. Post (Oct. 12, 1980).

[149]   *1980 Reagan VS. Carter VS. Anderson*, Museum of the Moving Image (2016), www.livingroomcandidate.org/commercials/1980.

[150]   Lou Cannon, *Ronald Reagan: Campaigns and Elections*, UVA Miller Center, https://millercenter.org/president/reagan/campaigns-and-elections

[151]   *Id.*

[152]   Shogan, *supra* note 142.

[153]   Kaiser, *supra* note 148.

Program, receiving $40.4 million each. In the 1984 election, Americans had to consider if they wanted four more years of what Reagan was offering.[154]

 Reagan brought patriotism back in vogue—at least in certain quarters. Reagan's political ads in 1984 tried to capitalize on patriotic tropes. "The mood was captured by the Reagan campaign theme, expressed radiantly in feel-good television commercials: Morning Again in America."[155] Meanwhile, the Reagan campaign was getting more sophisticated with the behind-the-scenes technology. As the *New York Times* noted, "The Reagan organization's computer program is called PINS, for Political Information Systems."[156] The PINS program was used by the Reagan campaign "to test its campaign strategy on a daily basis by analyzing polls, census data, economic conditions and the assessments of its top political operators."[157]

Critics of Reagan could not believe that the patriotic pap was being lapped up so eagerly by voters and the press alike. William Grieder criticized Reagan, stating that he "avoids the issues and is content to pose with the flag, the Bible and selected heroes from American life, like Olympic jocks and legless war veterans. That is the president's campaign strategy, and the news media spinelessly go along."[158] And according to Grieder:

> the accepted wisdom seems to be that Reagan kept his biggest promise of the 1980 campaign — to reign [sic] in big government and cut it down to size. Lots of Americans believe this because the news media repeat the claim so uncritically and so often. The reality is just the opposite. By any objective measure, Ronald Reagan made big government bigger ...[159]

Some of Reagan's boosters wanted to use the presidency to wag the dog should the re-election campaign go poorly. "Lee Atwater, deputy director of Reagan's re-election campaign, wrote a shocking memorandum entitled 'The Great American Fog Machine' recommending a strategy for the Reagan campaign in case the president bombed in the second debate."[160] According to the *Washington Post*, Atwater's memo "talked about scapegoating the press. It talked about polarizing the country, South against North, East against West. Finally, it talked about Reagan going to Grenada on October 25, the first anni-

---

[154] Cannon, *supra* note 150.

[155] *Id.*

[156] David Burnham, *Reagan's Campaign Adds Strategy Role to Use of Computer*, N.Y. TIMES (Apr. 23, 1984).

[157] *Id.*

[158] William Grieder, *What If Reagan Is Reelected?*, ROLLING STONE (Oct. 11, 1984).

[159] *Id.*

[160] William Schneider, *The 1984 Election: On the Record and Behind the Scenes*, WASH. POST (July 21, 1985).

versary of the intervention."[161] Journalists Jack Germond and Jules Witcover said of the Atwater memo, "today's combat for the American presidency generates ... deceptions that threaten the integrity and effectiveness of the political process itself."[162]

One of Mondale's only memorable zingers in the election was used against Gary Hart in a primary debate when he asked of Hart, "Where's the beef?"—a reference to a Wendy's commercial tagline.[163] Mondale was given contradictory advice from his advisers:

> 'Get tough' with President Reagan, the Democratic elders have told their nominee. Then, in the next breath comes the solemn warning that, of course, Mr. Reagan is so popular that it would be a deadly political mistake for anyone to attack him 'personally.'[164]

Mondale mostly stuck to the issues. In many of his ads, he focused on the nuclear proliferation.[165] Mondale only won his home state of Minnesota and D.C. The rest of the map fell to Reagan in 1984. In the skunkworks of the Reagan campaign was Roger Ailes, who had previously helped Nixon. According to Tim Dickinson, Ailes "papered over Ronald Reagan's budding Alzheimer's in 1984, ... sa[id] former Reagan campaign manager Ed Rollins. '[Ailes] was our Michelangelo.'"[166]

8. BUSH I '88

Vice President George H.W. Bush had been in Reagan's shadow and had to make a case for his own *bona fides* with voters.[167] Running against him was Governor of Massachusetts Michael Dukakis. Both Bush and Dukakis participated in the Presidential Public Financing Program, each receiving $46.1 million.

---

[161] *Id.*

[162] *Id.*

[163] Kenneth T. Walsh, *6 Best 'Zingers' From Past Presidential Debates*, US NEWS (Oct. 1, 2012).

[164] Howell Raines, *Wedding Mondale to a Poor Strategy*, N.Y. TIMES (Sept. 11, 1984).

[165] *1984 Reagan VS. Mondale*, MUSEUM OF THE MOVING IMAGE (2016), www.livingroomcandidate.org/commercials/1984.

[166] Tim Dickinson, *How Roger Ailes Built the Fox News Fear Factory*, ROLLING STONE (May 25, 2011).

[167] Gerald M. Boyd, *Bush Campaign Tactics: Good Guy or Bad Guy?*, N.Y. TIMES (June 22, 1988).

"Dukakis emerged from the Democratic convention in July with ... highly favorable polls and party regulars rushing to his side after a powerful acceptance speech."[168] But he lacked the slogans and packaging that typically go with a successful candidate. "The Dukakis campaign has never had an enduring slogan other than 'Mike Dukakis for President.'"[169] And like Adlai Stevenson before him:

> Dukakis disdained TV imagery. With no direction, his advertising team wrote so many scripts--1,155 by one count--that some propped up office plants. 'He thinks TV commercials are beneath him and silly,' said Ken Swope, a longtime media adviser who quit in frustration.[170]

Bush's goal was to "tear down the positive image Mr. Dukakis has before it grows."[171] Ailes (who had aided Nixon and Reagan before) was happy to lend a hand to George H.W. Bush with negative TV political commercials. In one ad, the Republicans had Dukakis to thank for providing absurd footage of himself riding in a tank: "as the giant tank rumbled across a dusty field, the Democratic nominee for President suddenly popped up with a Snoopy-like helmet with earphones on his head and a nervous smile on his face."[172] Dukakis thought this would make him look tough. But it made him look ridiculous.[173] Soon enough, Ailes had an ad up using the tank imagery mocking Dukakis.[174]

The other Ailes ad which is controversial to this day is known as the "Willie Horton" ad. This ad criticized Dukakis for allowing criminal furloughs from prison:

> William Horton, a convicted murderer serving a life sentence in Massachusetts, was granted a weekend furlough in 1986 but did not return to prison. Nearly a year later, he turned up in Maryland, where he had bound, gagged and stabbed a man in his home, raped his fiancee and then escaped in a car belonging to the man.[175]

---

[168] Bob Drogin, *How Presidential Race Was Won–and Lost: Michael S. Dukakis*, L.A. Times (Nov. 10, 1988).

[169] E. J. Dionne Jr., *Political Memo; Dukakis Remains on Course, Dismissing Polls and Advice*, N.Y. Times (July 11, 1988).

[170] Drogin, *supra* note 168.

[171] Boyd, *supra* note 167.

[172] *Id.*

[173] *Id.* ("When Michael S. Dukakis climbed into an M-1A1 battle tank in mid-September, two aides warned him he would look silly, not tough, on TV ...").

[174] *Id.* ("The tank fiasco—which Republicans gleefully turned into a TV ad—was only a snapshot in Dukakis' 20-month campaign.")

[175] Eugene Scott, *How the Willie Horton ad factors into George H.W. Bush's legacy*, Wash. Post (Dec. 3, 2018).

A third Ailes ad called the "Revolving Door" struck many of the same themes. The ad "shows men [who are actors] walking in and out of prison [through a fake revolving door] as a narrator accuses Democratic presidential candidate and former governor of Massachusetts Michael Dukakis of being soft on crime."[176] Some of the ad copy included: "'While out, many committed other crimes like kidnapping and rape,' the narrator says. 'And many are still at large. Now Michael Dukakis says he wants to do for America what he's done for Massachusetts. America can't afford that risk.'"[177] In a 1988 *CBS News/New York Times* poll, voters picked the "Revolving Door" ad as the one that had the biggest effect on them.[178] Playing on longstanding racial fears, the "Willie Horton" and "Revolving Door" ads made minced meat out of Dukakis' aspiration of being president. At the time, "Atwater and Ailes insisted the ad, and their campaign, wasn't racially charged."[179] Years later, at least Atwater showed remorse: "shortly before his death from cancer, Bush's campaign manager Lee Atwater apologized for saying he would 'make Willie Horton [Dukakis's] running mate.'"[180]

In a lesser-known positive ad, George H.W. Bush's daughter-in-law and some of his grandchildren are with him as she speaks to the camera in Spanish. Bush says, "As President I have reasons to help Hispanics everywhere because I'll be answering to my grandkids, not just to history."[181] Which was the real George H.W. Bush? The one who relied on negative racialized appeals or the one who loved his Hispanic grandchildren? Either way, he became president.

9.   CONCLUSION

The period 1952–88 was the age of the broadcast ad and lowest common denominator appeals. The TV age valued appearances over substance. The period from 1976–88 was also marked by the provision of equal public funding for presidential candidates from the two major parties. Cable channels and viewership were about to explode. "By the end of the decade [1980s], nearly 53 million households subscribed to cable, and cable program networks

---

[176]   Harrington, *supra* note 106.

[177]   *Id.*

[178]   *Candidate Ads: 1988 George Bush "Revolving Door"*, INSIDE POLITICS (1996), www.insidepolitics.org/ps111/candidateads.html.

[179]   Harrington, *supra* note 106.

[180]   Scott, *supra* note 175.

[181]   *1988 Bush VS. Dukakis*, MUSEUM OF THE MOVING IMAGE (2016), www.livingroomcandidate.org/commercials/1988.

had increased from 28 in 1980 to 79 by 1989."[182] And that would change politics too.

---

[182] *History of Cable*, CALIFORNIA CABLE & TELECOMM. ASSOC. (undated), www
.calcable.org/learn/history-of-cable/ (last visited Jan. 2, 2019).

6. Branding candidates online

> "We are governed, our minds are molded, our tastes formed, our ideas suggested, largely by men we have never heard of."[1]

1. INTRODUCTION

In the 1990s, the same computer technology that was revolutionizing the way people worked was also seeping into campaigns. Although it took until 1996 for both nominees for president to have a webpage, once the Internet became ubiquitous, campaigns began to spend more of their resources crafting messages not just for broadcast media, but also for online platforms. The explosion of smartphone use in the United States from 10 percent in 2008 to 80 percent in 2016 meant political advertisers had another way to get inside voters' heads. By 2016, any video could also be played on a smartphone, placed on a social media feed and shared worldwide.

Some tricks used by campaigns at the turn of the millennium were old, like using musical jingles to get candidates' names stuck in the minds of the public. This musical trick was deployed in American politics long before there was television. "Tippecanoe and Tyler Too" was a song to sell the election of William Henry Harrison to voters back in 1840.[2] It worked. Barack Obama's 2008 run was helped by Will.i.am's online viral video for the song "Yes We Can." That worked too.

And some techniques were new, like mastering the use of social media ads. The art of running a modern political campaign is deploying ad dollars wisely. As Amy Gershkoff, Obama's media-planning director, said, "'If you think about the universe of possible places for an advertiser, it's almost infinite ...'"[3] She continued, "'There are tens of millions of opportunities where a campaign

---

[1]   EDWARD BERNAYS, PROPAGANDA 37 (1928).

[2]   Debra Liese, *Political (Dis)chord? Jennifer Lena talks political branding through song*, PRINCETON UNIV. PRESS BLOG (Apr. 11, 2012), http://blog.press.princeton.edu/2012/04/11/political-dischord-jennifer-lena-talks-political-branding-through-song/.

[3]   Sasha Issenberg, *How Obama's Team Used Big Data to Rally Voters*, MIT TECHNOLOGY REVIEW (Dec. 19, 2012), www.technologyreview.com/s/509026/how-obamas-team-used-big-data-to-rally-voters/ (quoting Gershkoff).

can put its next dollar.'"[4] The team that can use big data to market its candidate to voters more effectively is the victor.

At the start of this book, the question asked in reference to Donald Trump was: "How did America elect a brand president?" Maybe the more accurate question is: "When has America *not* elected a brand president?" Political advertising is the way that most politicians brand themselves. As Robert Spero wrote in *Duping of the American Voter*, "political advertising—now the principal means of communication and persuasion between candidate and voter—is without peer as the most deceptive, misleading, unfair, and untruthful of all advertising, especially on television. ..."[5] He notes that, compared to advertisements for commercial products, political advertisements are far more manipulatively false.[6] According to his critique of presidential candidates' television ads: "political commercial[s] did not turn politicians into liars; it only amplified the lie beyond the politicians' fondest dreams and broadcast it simultaneously into every cranny of the nation ..."[7]

If, back in the 1950s, Eugene Burdick thought of presidents as father figures, today psychologist Clotaire Rapaille has a different take. He suggests, "We don't want a father figure. We want a biblical figure [like Moses] ... a rebellious leader of his people with a strong vision and the will to get them out of trouble."[8] According to Dr. Rapaille, "We want someone with a strong reptilian side who can take care of our country ... and lead us into the Promised Land because he knows what is wrong and how to fix it."[9] Thus, he predicts that the more reptilian candidate will win.[10]

Unsurprisingly, the more famous a person is before he gets into politics, the harder it will be for anyone to rebrand him because the public will already hold a set of connotations about that person. For example, Jesse "The Body" Ventura was a professional wrestler before becoming a politician. He was famous for being "strong;" thus, it was difficult, if not impossible, for political opponents to try to frame him as "weak." He was elected as governor of Minnesota. Below are highlights of the campaign media choices made by American presidential candidates between 1992–2016.

---

[4]   *Id.* (quoting Gershkoff).
[5]   ROBERT SPERO, DUPING OF THE AMERICAN VOTER 3 (1980).
[6]   *Id.* at 12 ("Had [politicians] revised their commercials to meet product advertising standards, there would have been very little left of the originals.").
[7]   *Id.* at 186.
[8]   CLOTAIRE RAPAILLE, THE CULTURE CODE: AN INGENIOUS WAY TO UNDERSTAND WHY PEOPLE AROUND THE WORLD LIVE AND BUY AS THEY DO 186 (2007).
[9]   *Id.* at 186.
[10]   *Id.* at 189 ("[Americans] do not want a president who thinks too much. Except under extraordinary circumstances, the more reptilian candidate always wins.").

2.   CLINTON '92 AND '96

In 1992, Democrats had a real shot at the presidency, if only because of one-party-rule fatigue. Another advantage that Governor of Arkansas Bill Clinton had was his campaign manager, James Carville, who wrote on a whiteboard in Clinton campaign headquarters, "Change vs. More of the Same," "The Economy, Stupid" and "Don't forget healthcare."[11] These were the themes that animated the campaign.[12] One of his positive ads was called "Hope." The ad showed Clinton's humble beginnings and emphasized that he had worked his way through law school, without mentioning that it was Yale, a school where George H.W. Bush was also an alum. As Clinton branded himself a "New Democrat,"[13] his campaign adopted the tagline "For people, for a change."[14] One of the great innovations of the Clinton campaign was getting materials to voters online first. As Jeff Eller recalled, "There was no World Wide Web and no websites. But there were Compuserve forums. So we'd post ... [p]osition statements and papers."[15]

Another thing that made Bill Clinton electable was a third-party candidate named Ross Perot, who won 19 percent of the vote and essentially acted as a spoiler. Perot's approach was to buy blocks of TV time for long-form informercials starring himself. During the summer of 1992, Perot quit the presidential race several times. The *Chicago Tribune* noted:

> No one considered Perot a factor. Then, when he returned a month before the election, he was only at 7 percent. That's when his campaign kicked in--a television blitz of infomercials and advertisements combined with credible performances in the debates--that pushed him near 20 percent.[16]

---

[11] Alan McGauley, *Clinton's 1992 War Room was an engine of anti-establishment politics*, CONVERSATION (Oct. 19, 2016), https://theconversation.com/clintons-1992-war-room-was-an-engine-of-anti-establishment-politics-65695.

[12] Stephen Buel, *Clinton strategists describe winning blueprint*, UPI (Nov. 4, 1992),   www.upi.com/Archives/1992/11/04/Clinton-strategists-describe-winning-blueprint/5023339413605/.

[13] Jake Novak, *Is Donald Trump following Bill Clinton's playbook from 1992?*, CNBC (May 10, 2016), www.cnbc.com/2016/05/10/is-donald-trump-following-bill-clintons-playbook-from-1992-commentary.html ("his 1992 campaign ... sent a clear message that the Arkansas governor was a new kind of Democrat.").

[14] *1992 Clinton VS. Bush VS. Perot*, MUSEUM OF THE MOVING IMAGE (2016), www.livingroomcandidate.org/commercials/1992.

[15] Mike Shields, *An Oral History of the First Presidential Campaign Websites in 1996*, WALL ST. J. (Feb. 18, 2016).

[16] Gerald Posner, *Perot's Flawed Campaign Strategy*, CHIC. TRIB. (Sept. 4, 1996).

While Bush and Clinton both used the Presidential Public Financing Program, Perot was a self-financed billionaire. Clinton and Bush each had $55.2 million dollars to work with. Roger Ailes was brought in late in the game to help Bush. But it was too late.[17] After the election, Bush's Vice President Dan Quayle griped about their campaign: "They never had a message …"[18] Thanks to Bush and Perot splitting the vote, Clinton moved into 1600 Pennsylvania Avenue.

For Clinton's re-election campaign in 1996 against Senator Bob Dole, Mark Penn ran multiple polls to try to gauge what was important to voters. "The top six issues on people's minds were crime and violence; balancing the budget fairly; protecting children from smoking ads, TV violence and drugs; strengthening the family; improving education; and protecting the environment. These would become Clinton's focus."[19] Polling had long opened with the question whether the voter thought the country was on the right track or the wrong track:

> 'Almost as many people think the country is on the right track as think it's going in the wrong direction,' [communications director Don Baer] said. The metaphor was staring [the Clinton team] in the face … the slogan [became] 'On the Right Track to the 21st Century,' and Clinton repeated it at every whistle-stop along the way.[20]

Showing the power of persuasion, "each day [President Clinton] said it, the 'right track-wrong track' numbers inched up."[21] If Clinton's camp was overly reliant on polling, over on the Dole side, "[n]o ideas were percolating, no plans being made, no strategy forming."[22]

In 1988, a younger Bill Clinton had introduced Michael Dukakis at the Democratic National Committee in a speech that nearly ruined his career because it was so long.[23] Clinton said of Dukakis that he was "a builder who wants to build a bridge to tomorrow: strong enough to carry our heaviest load; wide enough for all of us to walk across together; long enough to take us into

---

[17]   *The Media and the Message; Bush's '88 Strategist, Ailes, Gets Bigger Role*, N.Y. Times (Aug. 20, 1992).

[18]   Maureen Dowd, *The 1992 Elections: Disappointment – Road To Defeat*, N.Y. Times (Nov. 5, 1992).

[19]   Richard Stengel & Eric Pooley, *Inside the high-tech machine that set Clinton and Dole polls apart*, CNN (Nov. 6, 1996), www.cnn.com/ALLPOLITICS/1996/elections/time.special/pollster/index.shtml.

[20]   *Id.*

[21]   *Id.*

[22]   *Id.*

[23]   Tara Golshan, *Bill Clinton's first major appearance at a convention almost destroyed his career*, Vox (July 26, 2016), www.vox.com/2016/7/26/12285312/bill-clinton-dnc-1988-speaker-late-night.

the 21st century."[24] Whoever won the 1996 race would be president when the millennium started. Clinton seized on the image of the bridge to the twenty-first century; but this time he applied the metaphor to himself. As he was only 50 years old in 1996, running against 73-year-old Dole and 66-year-old Perot, he could make the argument that only a young leader like himself could lead the nation into 2000. At the Democratic National Convention:

> [President Clinton] distilled his first-term accomplishments into a few impressive paragraphs--10.7 million new jobs, 4.5 million new home owners, and on and on in a giddy boast that took flight and soared clear into tomorrow: 'Let us build a bridge together, wide enough and strong enough to carry all of us into the bright future that is America in the 21st century.'[25]

Clinton, Dole and Perot all participated in the Presidential Public Financing Program. Clinton and Dole each received $61.8 million. Perot received less public financing than his competitors ($29 million).

Dole's campaign struggled to craft effective TV ads:

> On Aug. 15, the campaign's long-awaited ... federal funds arrived. ... The first postconvention ad ... was an old-fashioned, positive commercial about Dole: Midwestern childhood, war wound, man of his word ... [Dole] hated it. 'Did you test it?' Dole barked ... Dole was on to something; the ad had not scored well.[26]

By contrast, Clinton's team was meticulous about testing TV ads before they aired. By the end of the 1996 campaign, "Clinton's response ads were tested, refined and retested until they actually left voters feeling better about the President than they had before seeing the original Dole attack."[27] Perot was back in 1996 with his infomercials "at least once a week, all focusing on Perot's core issues such as the deficit, campaign finance reform and the repeal of the North American Free Trade Agreement."[28] Perot only got 8.4 percent of the vote in 1996.

In 1996 Fox News and MSNBC both launched 24-hour news channels. Fox News was the brainchild of Roger Ailes. In 1996, the Internet had become more of a factor in elections, but it still wasn't important enough for Dole to

---

[24] Charles M. Madigan & Frank Jackman, *It's Official: Michael Dukakis*, Chic. Trib. (July 21, 1988).

[25] *Id.*

[26] *Id.*

[27] *Id.*

[28] Posner, *supra* note 16.

hire professionals to run his website. Instead, the Dole campaign hired two students. One, named Rob Kubasko, later told the *Wall St. Journal*:

> if you didn't have a website you were old and antiquated and Bob Dole didn't need to seem any more antiquated than he was. But was there a plan? Nooo! Literally it was, 'we need to have a website, and it needs to be better than Bill Clinton's.'[29]

If the Dole campaign wanted changes done on the webpage, they would fax changes to Kubasko's dorm room. "I had 17 feet of faxes all over my dorm. It was so ridiculous."[30] The digital team (two guys in a dorm room) got slammed when the candidate mentioned the webpage's name in the middle of his first presidential debate without warning.[31]

The Clinton campaign webpage ran into its own difficulties. As one of the web team recalled, "we went to the White House, and the Internet went down. You think about [what it would be like if that were] happening now - but back then, it just wasn't important to anybody at that point."[32] Also, the Clinton-Gore webpage didn't go live until just four months before the 1996 election.[33] For the second Clinton inaugural, the campaign planned to webcast the event, making it the first inaugural to be webcast. But so many people tried to log on that the feed crashed.[34]

3.   BUSH II '00 AND '04

The final few years of Clinton's presidency were chaotic, to put it mildly. He was sued and deposed by Paula Jones, and was caught lying about an affair with a White House intern. He was accused of perjury and impeached by the House. He went through a Senate trial, but was not removed from office. As his Vice President Al Gore ran for office in 2000, Clinton was essentially a millstone around his neck. By 2000, cable TV was also a bigger player in the media ecosystem, as "approximately 7 in 10 television households, more than 65 million, had opted to subscribe to cable."[35] C-SPAN wasn't the only one running the Clinton impeachment wall to wall. Other 24-hour news channels could, and did, run it too.

---

[29]   Shields, *supra* note 15.

[30]   *Id.*

[31]   *Id.* ("Sen. Dole threw his digital team for a loop when, near the close of the first presidential debate ..., he urged voters to visit his [web]site.").

[32]   *Id.*

[33]   *Id.*

[34]   *Id.* ("We planned to do a live broadcast of the inauguration speech on the Internet. There wasn't supposed to be a big audience. ... It crashed ...").

[35]   *History of Cable*, Cal. Cable and Telecommunications Association, www .calcable.org/learn/history-of-cable/.

Vice President Gore ran against Governor of Texas George W. Bush. Bush was the son of the first President Bush and had all of the political connections to match. Pat Buchanan was running on the Reform Party ticket. Buchanan (and Ralph Nader) arguably were spoilers for Gore in Florida. While Bush had opted out of the Presidential Public Financing Program in the primary, Bush, Gore and Buchanan all three used public financing in the general election. Bush and Gore received $67.5 million. Buchanan received $12.6 million. Ralph Nader was also running as a Green Party candidate, but without public financing.

Both Bush and Gore spent a great deal of time pretending to be bipartisan in the 2000 election. For example, "Gore eschewed a partisan appeal. In the three television debates, illustratively, he mentioned his party only four times, twice citing his disagreement with other Democrats on the Gulf War, and twice incidentally."[36] Bush was particularly good at doing the bipartisan head-fake:

> [Bush was] willing to bend the message. On Wednesday in Los Angeles, he praised a group of teachers and said he understood how hard it is to be a teacher. On Thursday in Silicon Valley, he condemned the educational oligopoly -- Republican code for the teachers' unions -- for resisting change.[37]

Meanwhile, Gore could not figure out a way to capitalize on the good U.S. economy,[38] since "he had never found a way to embrace the administration's economic legacy without throwing his arms around Mr. Clinton himself."[39]

Bush branded himself as a "compassionate conservative."[40] Fitting this theme, he was the first presidential candidate to speak Spanish in a TV ad.[41] Another key theme was restoring "dignity to the White House" after years of Clinton's scandals.[42] This was an effective line of attack, as polling showed in July 2000 that "[t]he most common story theme for then-Vice President

---

[36] Gerald M. Pomper, *The 2000 Presidential Election: Why Gore Lost*, 2 POL. SCI. Q. 201 (2001), www.uvm.edu/~dguber/POLS125/articles/pomper.htm.

[37] Dan Balz, *Bush's Campaign Strategy Sets the Pace for 2000*, WASH. POST (July 4, 1999).

[38] Katharine Q. Seelye, *Still Riding Wave, a Confident Gore Heads to Florida for Fall Push*, N.Y. TIMES (Sept. 16, 2000).

[39] Richard L. Berke, *Democrats Remind Gore of the Economy*. N.Y. TIMES (Oct. 30, 2000).

[40] Balz, *supra* note 37 ("The broad themes of his candidacy, embodied in his notion of 'compassionate conservatism,' may be appealing to voters.").

[41] *2000 Bush VS. Gore*, MUSEUM OF THE MOVING IMAGE (2016), www .livingroomcandidate.org/commercials/2000.

[42] Alison Mitchell, *Shifting Tactics, Bush Uses Issues to Confront Gore*, N.Y. TIMES (Sept. 16, 2000) ("the emotional center of the Bush campaign has been a pledge to bring 'dignity and honor' back to the White House after the Clinton years.").

Al Gore's campaign in 2000 dealt with Gore being 'scandal-tainted' and ... a 'liar.'"[43] Also, to distinguish the younger Bush from his father, many referred to him as simply "W." This was a brand in and of itself, which had the advantage of allowing him to avoid negative connotations associated with the Bush name.

Gore, who years later is seen as one of the world's most famous environmentalists, did not make the environment a signature issue, though it was in a single campaign ad.[44] Instead, he spent lots of time questioning Bush's readiness to be president.[45] Gore also pushed healthcare reforms that were difficult to explain because of their complexity.[46] Nothing boiled down to a catchy bumper sticker message. In the end, Gore fought Bush to a near draw. The disputed vote in 2000 in Florida came down to 537 votes in a state where Bush's brother, Jeb, was governor. Gore and Bush litigated the outcome of the Florida vote up to the Supreme Court, where *Bush v. Gore* handed the White House to Bush.

In 2004, Bush ran for re-election against Senator John Kerry. Both Bush and Kerry opted out of the Presidential Public Financing Program in the primary, but both used it in the general election. (Bush didn't have a primary, but Kerry did.) Both campaigns broke new ground by running video ads online.[47]

Bush's team went to work to negatively brand Kerry after they found that the public didn't know him well:[48]

> "'The goal is right now,' said a Bush adviser, 'while he's weak, while they're financially struggling, to strip him of all the good that somehow in my opinion erroneously got attached to him.' ... 'With some candidates there's a hard shell. With [Kerry] there's a soft skin.'"[49]

---

[43]   *Gore Character Themes*, Pew (July 27, 2000), www.journalism.org/numbers/gore-character-themes/.

[44]   *2000 Bush VS. Gore*, Museum of the Moving Image (2016), www.livingroomcandidate.org/commercials/2000.

[45]   Richard L. Berke & Katharine Q. Seelye, *The Vice President; Gore To Embrace Campaign Finance As Central Theme*, N.Y. Times (Mar. 12, 2000).

[46]   Al Gore, *Address Accepting the Presidential Nomination at the Democratic National Convention in Los Angeles* (Aug. 17, 2000), www.presidency.ucsb.edu/documents/address-accepting-the-presidential-nomination-the-democratic-national-convention-los.

[47]   *2004 Bush VS. Kerry*, Museum of the Moving Image (2016), www.livingroomcandidate.org/commercials/2004.

[48]   Jim Rutenberg, *The President; 90-Day Strategy By Bush's Aides To Define Kerry*, N.Y. Times (Mar. 20, 2004).

[49]   *Id.*

The Bush team decided to brand Kerry as a "flip-flopper"—basically, someone who couldn't be trusted to stick to a decision. The Bush campaign spent "about seventy million dollars …, and about two-thirds of that was on negative ads identifying Kerry as a flip-flopper— … every speech that Bush gives, every speech that [Vice President] Dick Cheney gives, they talk about the flip-flops."[50] This was also reinforced by a clever campaign ad of Kerry wind-surfing left and then right and then left again.[51] The voting public absorbed this image of Kerry:

> 'Voters feel comfortable that Kerry is smart and experienced, but when you start going beyond that, the only thing that emerges is that he has a personality that seems distant, and some sense he straddles on issues,' said Democratic pollster Peter Hart.[52]

And the less the public knew about Kerry, the easier it was for the Bush team to paint a distorted picture of him.[53]

Another line of attack against Kerry was his war record in Vietnam, where he had earned a silver star, a bronze star and three Purple Hearts.[54] This could have royally backfired on Bush, who had not served in the military and had led the country into an increasingly unpopular war in Iraq.[55] But it was bizarrely effective. A 527 group called "Swift Boat Veterans for Truth" ran ads questioning Kerry's version of events in his military service in Vietnam.[56] And then TV news covered the ads, thereby magnifying their reach.[57] Kerry's team seemed to be caught flatfooted by the attack.[58] Bush returned to the White House for four more years.

---

[50]   Matt Dellinger, *Coaching Team Kerry*, NEW YORKER (Sept. 20, 2004).

[51]   Ronald Brownstein, *Kerry's Strategy Accents Positive*, L.A. TIMES (July 25, 2004).

[52]   *Id.*

[53]   Rutenberg, *supra* note 48.

[54]   Lauren Johnston, *Kerry Releases Navy Records*, CBS (Apr. 22, 2004), www .cbsnews.com/news/kerry-releases-navy-records/.

[55]   Dellinger, *supra* note 50 ("look at events—more than a thousand soldiers already killed in Iraq, two hundred billion dollars in costs, and counting. There are a lot of events that don't necessarily work to Bush's advantage.").

[56]   *Sources: Democratic leaders urge Kerry campaign changes*, CNN (Sept. 1, 2004), www.cnn.com/2004/ALLPOLITICS/08/31/kerry.campaign/ ("527s are independent, tax-exempt groups that are allowed to accept unlimited donations to fund ads.").

[57]   Dellinger, *supra* note 50 ("even though the Swift Boat Veterans for Truth spent only a few hundred thousand dollars on their ads … The press then repeated them, and suddenly … sixty per cent of the public knew about the Swift-boat ads …").

[58]   *Id.*

Late in Bush's second term, in 2007, *Breitbart News* launched its webpage as an alternative to more liberal webpages like the *Huffington Post*.

4.   OBAMA '08 AND '12

In 2008, the presidential race was wide open after Vice President Dick Cheney decided not to run. On the Republican side, Senator John McCain became the nominee. Senator Barack Obama became the Democrats' choice.

Obama and McCain had a gentlemen's agreement that if both became their parties' nominees, both would opt into the Presidential Public Financing Program, as all major party candidates had done since Carter's race against Ford in 1976. McCain kept his promise. Obama did not. While McCain was funded by a public grant of $84 million, he could not match Obama's higher private fundraising. The extra money gave Obama the ability to pummel his message home in advertising.[59] The result was "McCain couldn't keep up."[60]

Breaking with tradition, during the 2008 campaign Obama used a logo of an O with stripes below it that looked like the American flag. The designer of the Obama logo said that he and his team "did not find any inspiration from looking at political graphics. ... Instead, they approached the design from a ... commercial standpoint. ..."[61] The Obama logo was generally well received:

> Historically, political campaign logos have been rather simple, typically consisting of the candidate's name and some splashy colors. ... The Obama campaign logo represents a break from the conventional notions of political logos and candidate branding. ... The Obama logo works on several levels.[62]

Another *de facto* logo for the Obama campaign was Shepard Fairey's wood-block-style poster of Obama's bust with the word "HOPE" under it. The Obama "O" logo is on the lapel of the candidate in the poster. As the National Portrait Gallery described the piece: "Fairey's Barack Obama 'Hope' poster became the iconic campaign image for the first African American president of the United States. ... The artist's intention that the image be widely reproduced and 'go viral' ... exceeded his greatest expectations."[63] Another web ad for Obama that

---

[59]   Ryan Lizza, *Battle Plans*, NEW YORKER (Nov. 17, 2008).

[60]   *Id.*

[61]   *Obama's Brand Designer Sol Sender (MFA 1999) designed President Obama's iconic logo.*, SAIC (2015), www.saic.edu/150/obama%E2%80%99s-brand-designer.

[62]   Ben Arnon, *Politics Meets Brand Design: The Story of Obama's Campaign Logo*, HUFF. POST (Jan. 18, 2009), www.huffingtonpost.com/ben-arnon/politics-meets -brand-desi_b_151317.html.

[63]   *Now on View: Portrait of Barack Obama by Shepard Fairey*, NATIONAL PORTRAIT GALLERY (2018), https://npg.si.edu/blog/now-on-view-portrait-barack-obama-shepard -fairey.

went viral was a music video by Will.i.am that put one of Obama's speeches to music and repeated the campaign's catchphrase "Yes we can" every few seconds. Images of Obama speaking was interlaced with images of celebrities singing along. The video ended with the word "VOTE."[64]

Obama, like other successful presidential candidates before him, could stay laser focused on the task of campaigning:

> [He earned] the nickname 'No Drama Obama' for the meticulous level of prudence he applied to nearly every campaign speech, strategy decision and personnel appointment. The result was a nearly two-year-long presidential bid most notable for its seeming lack of a damaging gaffe ...[65]

He was also clever about sidestepping controversy: "[Obama] did everything he could to avoid taking dangerously inflammatory stands on hot-button social issues."[66]

Both McCain and Obama were vying for the title of who was the bigger maverick. The Obama campaign painted McCain as a continuation of Bush.[67] Obama offered himself as "change" that America needed.[68] Change was branded all over Obama's campaign:

> Obama almost never delivered a speech from a lectern unless it was festooned with the word 'change.' On Election Day, thirty-four per cent of the voters said that they were looking for change, and nearly ninety per cent of those voters chose Obama.[69]

Not only were there the typical 30-second spots for Obama, on the Wednesday before the election, he also aired a 30-minute advertorial that 33 million viewers saw.[70] The Obama ads were also run in video games like Guitar Hero and Madden NFL 09.[71] After winning the election, "[i]n his acceptance speech

---

[64]   *2008 Obama VS. McCain*, MUSEUM OF THE MOVING IMAGE (2016), www.livingroomcandidate.org/commercials/2008.

[65]   Alexander Mooney, *Obama's vetting could chase away candidates*, CNN (Nov. 22, 2008), www.cnn.com/2008/POLITICS/11/22/obama.vetting/index.html.

[66]   Kevin Drum, *No Drama Obama*, MOTHER JONES (Dec. 26, 2009), www.motherjones.com/kevin-drum/2009/12/no-drama-obama/.

[67]   Lizza, *supra* note 59 ("Axelrod continued, 'So we had a very simple premise ... that these Bush policies had failed, that McCain was essentially carrying the tattered banner of a failed Administration, and that we represented a change from all that.'").

[68]   *Id.* ("The campaign's faith in the strength of such a simple message was constant.").

[69]   *Id.*

[70]   Lizza, *supra* note 59 ("The Obama commercial attracted ... nearly twice the number for the top-rated 'Dancing with the Stars.'").

[71]   *Id.* ("'I mean, dude,' Messina said, 'when you're buying commercials in video games, you truly are being well funded.'").

before a throng of emotional supporters in Chicago's Grant Park, Obama ... [said], 'Change has come to America.'"[72]

McCain distinguished himself at a town hall on August 12, 2008 by responding to a female supporter who said, "I can't trust Obama. I have read about him, and he's not, he's not — he's an Arab." "'No ma'am,' McCain said. 'He's a decent family man, a citizen that I just happen to have disagreements with on fundamental issues. ...'"[73] The reason that this voter had been left with the misimpression that Obama wasn't an American was months of innuendo. Since Obama was the first Black nominee of a major political party, the issue of race was at least in the background.[74] To deal with racial slurs and other smears, the Obama campaign put up a fact-checking webpage.[75] One particularly long-lasting smear was that Obama was not born in America (he was born in Hawaii); another was that he was Muslim (he was Christian).[76]

In a campaign that likely turned on technology, McCain was a bit of a technophobe who didn't use email.[77] Another thing that Obama's pecuniary advantage could buy him was a more robust back office that was humming with data crunchers. "John McCain's campaign had, in most states, run its statistical model just once, assigning each voter to one of its microtargeting segments in the summer."[78] But McCain's camp couldn't revise the model to account for new events. Obama's team could, on a weekly basis.[79]

Obama's team had the luxury of digging deep on polling. "For each battleground state every week, the campaign's call centers conducted 5,000 to 10,000

---

[72]   Jennifer Ludden, *Obama's Winning "Change" Strategy*, NPR (Nov. 5, 2008), www.npr.org/templates/story/story.php?storyId=96810759.

[73]   Lisa Marie Segarra, *Watch John McCain Strongly Defend Barack Obama During the 2008 Campaign*, TIME (Aug. 25, 2018), http://time.com/4866404/john-mccain-barack-obama-arab-cancer/.

[74]   Eliza Gallo, *Campaign Strategy: Why Obama Won and McCain Lost*, U. OF SO. CAL. NEWS (Nov. 7, 2008), https://news.usc.edu/75627/campaign-strategy-why-obama-won-and-mccain-lost/ ("the 2008 race was marked by some really vicious attacks against Barack Obama ... from people on the hard right ... including veiled race-baiting directed at Obama ...").

[75]   Marc Ambinder, *Fight the Smears*, ATLANTIC (June 12, 2008) ("In the past, the campaign refused to talk about the 'smears' because they didn't want to give them credibility. Now they've surrendered to the reality that silence often perpetuates the rumors.").

[76]   Michael Falcone, *Obama Campaign Builds Rumor Debunking Site*, N.Y. TIMES (June 12, 2008) ("A new Web site ... called 'Fight the Smears,' ... already features sections fact-checking rumors that Mr. Obama refuses to say the pledge of allegiance, or has written racially incendiary remarks into his books or that he is a Muslim.").

[77]   Brad Bannon, *How to Rebrand the Republican Party*, US NEWS (Mar. 21, 2013).

[78]   Issenberg, *supra* note 3.

[79]   *Id.*

so-called short-form interviews that quickly gauged a voter's preferences, and 1,000 interviews in a long-form version that was more like a traditional poll."[80] The Obama team also had information flowing to and from volunteers in the field in near-real time, creating a feedback loop of key data about which house could have a persuadable voter.[81]

Obama won the White House, making him the first Black man in history to hold the office. In 2012, President Obama was challenged by Governor Mitt Romney. A big difference between Romney in 2012 and McCain in 2008 is Romney would also forgo public financing. This was the first election since 1976 when neither major party candidate used public financing. This put Obama and Romney in a fight for private funds.[82] Moreover, the campaign finance laws had changed in the interregnum by the Supreme Court. Because of *Citizens United* in 2010, corporations, unions and Super PACs could spend more money in the form of independent expenditures. "The Karl Rove-led American Crossroads and affiliated Crossroads GPS, alone ... raise[d] $300 million ..."[83]

Romney worked for a hedge fund called Bain Capital, so the Obama team branded Romney as an out-of-touch rich guy.[84] Obama was helped by a film of his opponent:

[In] secretly recorded footage of Romney [he spoke] derisively about 'the 47 percent' of Americans who pay no income taxes at a spring fundraiser. 'I'll never convince them they should take personal responsibility and care for their lives,' he told the guests, who paid $50,000-a-plate to attend. [85]

Romney's own words fit into Obama's narrative.[86]

While "Mitt Romney's campaign manager, Stuart Spencer, refused to use Twitter[,]"[87] Romney's team did have some technological innovations. "The Romney campaign ... became the first to launch an advertising campaign with Apple's mobile iAd service on the iPhone ... and the campaign [reached]

---

[80] *Id.*

[81] *Id.*

[82] Scott Wilson & Philip Rucker, *The strategy that paved a winning path*, WASH. POST (Nov. 7, 2012) ("what really worried the Chicago brain trust was money — the hundreds of millions they expected the Romney campaign and outside groups to spend on defeating the president.").

[83] *Id.*

[84] *Id.*

[85] *Id.*

[86] *Id.* ("The video played perfectly into the image, showcased in Obama's Bain ads, of Romney as a candidate whose chief concern was protecting the wealthy.").

[87] Bannon, *supra* note 77.

Android users with mobile online advertising through Google."[88] It claimed to be the first presidential campaign to use Facebook mobile advertising for its ads.[89] The Romney team also used Facebook to spread Romney's message through social networks:[90]

'It's a good way to feed the conversation ...' [Romney's digital team director Zac] Moffatt told *Business Insider*. 'It's just an opportunity for us to share our message to people who are already with Mitt who, in turn, share it with their friends and provide that first-person validation.'[91]

Romney's team also hoped Facebook might be the gateway to reaching disengaged voters,[92] especially since Facebook had just begun allowing advertisers to place ads directly into users' mobile feeds.[93] But if Romney thought Facebook would save him, he had a steep hill to climb. In June of 2012, Obama's Facebook page had 27 million "likes," compared with Romney's 2 million.[94] Also Romney's data team was one-tenth the size of Obama's.

Romney's data team used TargetPoint's National Dialogue Monitor to track around 200 different subjects during the 2012 campaign. They looked at things like how much press coverage a topic received or how much Twitter traffic mentioned it:[95]

Within three or four days of a new entity's entry into the conversation, either through paid ads or through the news cycle, it was possible to make a well-informed hypothesis about whether the topic was likely to win media attention by tracking whether it generated Twitter chatter.[96]

The Romney team saw a basic pattern of how information flowed through the media echo chamber:

> informal conversation[s] among political-class elites typically led to traditional print or broadcast press coverage one to two days later, and that, in turn, might have an impact on the horse race. 'We saw this process over and over again,' says [Alex] Lundry.[97]

---

[88] Brett LoGiurato, *Mitt Romney Has a New Strategy to Dominate the Facebook Campaign Wars*, BUSINESS INSIDER (June 18, 2012), www.businessinsider.com/mitt -romney-campaign-facebook-social-media-zac-moffatt-barack-obama-2012-6.

[89] *Id.*

[90] *Id.*

[91] *Id.*

[92] *Id.* ("Facebook ... [is] another way to reach the so-called 'off the grid' voters ... But any success with Facebook is especially valuable because of users' ability to share stories with hundreds — even thousands — of people with just one click.").

[93] *Id.*

[94] *Id.*

[95] *Id.*

[96] *Id.*

[97] *Id.*

But, understaffed compared to Obama, Romney's team lacked something else more fundamental: a theme to catch America's imagination. As William A. Galston complained, "if Romney has been campaigning since the convention on a theme of bold reform, it has escaped the attention of the press corps and the American people."[98]

In 2012, Obama's data team was back with experience under their belts.[99] Objective number one was to try to get every 2008 Obama voter to be a 2012 Obama voter:

> Obama's campaign began the election year confident it knew the name of every one of the 69,456,897 Americans whose votes had put him in the White House. They may have cast those votes by secret ballot, but Obama's analysts could look at the Democrats' vote totals in each precinct and identify the people most likely to have backed him.[100]

Part of the effort was focused on getting people to vote by mail. Obama's Airwolf program kept track of likely Obama voters who had requested mail in ballots and pestered them with reminders to vote and return their ballots.[101] Another way that the Obama team microtargeted voters was through advertising on particular TV shows. But this was not your grandfather's target marketing:

> Obama's advisors decided that the data made available in the private sector had long led political advertisers to ask the wrong questions ... [Obama's team] wanted '... not to get a better understanding of what 35-plus women watch on TV. It was to find out how many of our persuadable voters were watching those dayparts.'[102]

The Obama team "began negotiating to have research firms repackage their data in a form that would permit the campaign to access the individual [TV viewing] histories without violating the cable providers' privacy standards."[103] Next:

> Under a $350,000 deal ... [with] Rentrak, the campaign provided a list of persuadable voters and their addresses, derived from its microtargeting models, and the company looked for them in the cable providers' billing files. When a record

---

[98]   William A. Galston, *Mitt Romney's Terrible, Horrible, No Good, Very Bad Campaign*, Brookings (Sept. 14, 2012), www.brookings.edu/opinions/mitt-romneys -terrible-horrible-no-good-very-bad-campaign/.

[99]   Wilson & Rucker, *supra* note 82.

[100]   Issenberg, *supra* note 3.

[101]   *Id.*

[102]   *Id.*

[103]   *Id.*

matched, Rentrak would issue it a unique household ID that identified viewing data from a single set-top box but masked any personally identifiable information.

The Obama team had a software platform that they dubbed the Optimizer which split the TV schedules into 15-minute segments across 60 channels so that they could target their media buys at the most persuadable voters watching a particular 15-minute segment of a show.[104] The result was "the Obama campaign advertised heavily on the CBS's sitcom '*2 Broke Girls*,'"[105] but there was intrusive data crunching that led to that decision—a lot of persuadable voters were apparently watching.

If every campaign has tried to get into the mind of the generic American voter, the Obama campaign seemed to want to profile the minds of as many individual voters as possible. One way to achieve this was by placing social scientists in the campaign.[106] As Sasha Issenberg explained, the Obama "campaign didn't just know who you were; it knew exactly how it could turn you into the type of person it wanted you to be."[107]

In the end, Obama's re-election was in part a victory of wise use of data analytics. As Sasha Issenberg summed up:

> Few events in American life other than a presidential election touch 126 million adults, or even a significant fraction that many, on a single day. Certainly no corporation, no civic institution, and very few government agencies ever do. Obama did so by reducing every American to a series of numbers. Yet those numbers somehow captured the individuality of each voter. ... The scores measured the ability of people to change politics—and to be changed by it.[108]

As a result, Obama enjoyed eight years in the White House.

5.   TRUMP '16

After his son Beau died of cancer on May 30, 2015, Obama's Vice President Joe Biden, still reeling from grief, decided against running for president in 2016. This left another free-for-all like 2008, when Vice President Dick Cheney bowed out. There were primaries on both sides of the aisle. On the Democratic side, Bernie Sanders and Hillary Clinton had a long battle to the end. At the beginning of the Republican primary, 17 candidates were vying for the nomination. There were so many that some debates had to be split into

---

[104]   *Id.*
[105]   Wilson & Rucker, *supra* note 82.
[106]   Issenberg, *supra* note 3.
[107]   *Id.*
[108]   *Id.*

two parts. Commentators called the frontrunners the "real" debate, while the candidates with poor polling numbers were relegated to the "kiddie's table" debate. Donald Trump led from nearly the beginning of the primary, buoyed by name ID from his years on television show *The Apprentice* and from free media attention to his outrageous statements and Tweets. As editorial writer Alyssa Katz explained, there was a difference between the real Trump and the image he had built for himself on his TV show:

> Trump on *The Apprentice* was a character he created for TV. But this image of him as a successful businessman really drove voters' response to him. In New York, we knew him before that show as a blowhard developer. New York knew Trump as a huckster of real estate dreams like with Trump University. In New York he was known as the guy who overpaid for the Plaza Hotel and the guy who milked New York City for millions of dollars' worth of tax abatements.[109]

In the end, the race in the general election was between Trump and Clinton. Neither used public financing. Jill Stein, a Green Party candidate, used public financing in the primary, but was ineligible for funds for the general.

Hillary Clinton had been in public life for a long time when she ran for president.[110] She had been first lady of Arkansas, first lady of the United States, U.S. senator from New York and secretary of state. Along the way, she had made many powerful enemies who spent time and money vilifying her. During her time as first lady, she worked on putting together legislation to make health insurance available to more Americans. This effort failed. Enemies of the plan called it "Hillary Care." She seemed to blamed both for trying to help expand healthcare coverage and for failing in the effort. (Even though anyone who was blaming her for trying shouldn't have also have been blaming her for failing. Regardless, the hate she inspired lacked normal logic.) She was also blamed for the deaths of four Americans in Benghazi, Libya in 2012, while she was secretary of state. Republicans in Congress investigated this matter repeatedly. She was also criticized from the left as being too friendly to Wall Street. In 2008, Obama's supporters were frustrated with her sense of entitlement to the nomination.[111] In 2016, Bernie Sanders' supporters leveled similar ire at her.[112] In 2008, a conservative group called Citizens United made a film about her called *Hillary The Movie,* which was 90 minutes of nonstop criticism. All of this is to say that Hillary Clinton had considerable headwinds even before

---

[109] Interview with Alyssa Katz (July 27, 2018).

[110] Philip Rucker & Anne Gearan, *The making of Hillary 5.0: Marketing wizards help re-imagine Clinton brand*, WASH. POST (Feb. 21, 2015).

[111] *Id.*

[112] Molly Ball, *Why Hillary Clinton Lost*, ATLANTIC (Nov. 15, 2016) ("Inevitability didn't work out too well for Clinton in 2008, and it didn't work this year, either.").

Trump's nonstop vomit of hatred and meddling by the Russians were factored into the 2016 election.[113]

In 2016, Clinton had commercial marketers help her with branding. Jimmy Carter was not the only one to have assistance from Coke's advertising wizards; so did Hillary Clinton. "Wendy Clark, who specializes in marketing age-old brands such as Coca-Cola to younger and more diverse customers; and Roy Spence, a decades-long Clinton friend who dreamed up the 'Don't Mess With Texas' anti-littering slogan," helped the Clinton campaign.[114] Clinton's team showed attention to detail on branding, down to her logo.[115] As the *Washington Post* noted, "'She needs to use everything a brand has: dominant color, a logo, a symbol. ... The symbol of McDonald's is the golden arches. What is Clinton's symbol?'"[116] The final Hillary Logo drew derision. *New York Magazine* noted, "Hillary Clinton unveiled her new logo, a blue H with a red arrow through the middle, and everyone on Twitter immediately decided that they hate it."[117]

Emails stolen by the Russians and made public by WikiLeaks showed the struggles within the Clinton campaign to pick a campaign theme. As an editorial writer at the *Tampa Bay Times* wrote:

> The correspondence reveals a campaign that has struggled all year to improve a flawed candidate. As far back as March, aides were keenly aware that she was resistant to the media, perhaps out of touch with regular Americans and unable to convey a clear message to voters. ... 'Do we have any sense from her what she believes or wants her core message to be?' asked Clinton adviser Joel Benenson [in the stolen emails].[118]

Because of the stolen campaign emails, the public had a peek at what it otherwise would not have seen, including the fact that the Clinton campaign considered 84 other slogans before it settled on "Stronger together" and "I'm with her." Among the rejected slogans were "Building a fairer future today," "A fair fight for families," "You've earned a fair shot," "You've earned a fair chance," "No Quit," "Making America work for you," "A promise you can count on," "Climb higher," "Unleash opportunity," "It's about you. It's about time." and

---

[113] Rucker & Gearan, *supra* note 110.

[114] *Id.*

[115] *Id.*

[116] *Id.*

[117] Margaret Hartmann, *Everything That's Wrong With Hillary's New Logo*, N.Y. MAG. (Apr. 13, 2015).

[118] John Hill, *Hacked emails released by Wikileaks show anxiety over Hillary Clinton candidacy*, TAMPA B. TIMES (Oct. 13, 2016).

"Get ahead. Stay ahead."[119] Clinton's inability to narrow down a slogan could have reflected her inability to settle on a central campaign theme.[120] "In an early planning conference call, Clinton shocked her staffers by delegating to them both the slogan and the overarching message. ... No clear answer filled the void."[121]

Pollster Celinda Lake compared the two 2016 candidates thusly: "one of the things that's brilliant about Trump is he understands his brand and he understands his brand's audience." By contrast, Lake said, "Hillary never understood her brand. She would say 'Stronger Together' and then the next sentence would be an attack on Trump. That's an inherent contradiction. You just said 'Stronger Together.' And then you divided us. So that wasn't working."[122]

But even coverage revealed how much she was up against. Take this piece in *Politico*:

> the campaign is all in on the nostalgic memes as it tries to humanize a candidate who has stumbled through a difficult summer, with the controversy over her emails reinforcing the most negative stereotypes of the Clintons as paranoid and secretive, playing by their own set of rules. In polls, a majority of voters think Clinton is untrustworthy, and describe her as 'dishonest.'[123]

The Clinton team made more use of social media in 2016[124] and on Instagram, "Clinton's second-most 'liked' photograph—surpassed only by a selfie with Kim Kardashian—is a picture of a young Hillary and shaggy-haired Bill Clinton, smiling and staring into each other's eyes."[125]

If the presidency of the United States was decided by popular vote, then Clinton would have won the 2016 election by 3 million votes over Donald Trump. But Trump won by 80 000 more votes in three key states—Wisconsin, Pennsylvania and Michigan—and won the Electoral College and election. Postmortems of the election pointed out that Clinton probably should have campaigned in states "such as Wisconsin, where she was narrowly leading in polls but that had the potential to flip to Trump if the election tightened.

---

[119] Simon Dumenco, *84 Rejected Clinton Campaign Slogans, Courtesy of WikiLeaks*, AD AGE (Oct. 19, 2016), https://adage.com/article/campaign-trail/84-rejected-clinton-campaign-slogans-courtesy-wikileaks/306358/.

[120] Jeff Stein, *A new tell-all about the Clinton campaign is a searing indictment of the candidate herself*, VOX (Apr. 24, 2017), www.vox.com/2017/4/24/15369452/clinton-shattered-campaign ("Hillary was at her wit's end when it came to her messaging ...").

[121] *Id.*

[122] Interview with Celinda Lake (Sept. 7, 2018).

[123] Stein, *supra* note 120.

[124] *Id.*

[125] *Id.*

..."[126] In each presidential campaign, there is a law of diminishing returns for money spent on television ads, especially those that are poured into swing states. "Clinton's campaign ... had enormous resources to spend on television advertising, enough that she probably encountered diminishing returns among swing-state voters who had seen as many of her commercials as they could stand."[127]

Just as Obama had painted Romney as a Scrooge-like businessman, Clinton tried the same tactic with Trump. As *Time* reported, "Clinton has presented herself as a cerebral policy-maker and Donald Trump as a heartless business-man. ..."[128] Clinton asked at the Denver stop, "What kind of man does business by hurting other people?"[129]

Sexism was surely a factor in the Trump/Clinton race. Summing up the 2016 race, "'Hope and change, not so much,' said David Plouffe, who managed Mr. Obama's 2008 campaign, referring to the slogan that defined that race. 'More like hate and castrate.'"[130] Outside political spenders "that support Mrs. Clinton prepar[ed] ... ads that would portray Mr. Trump as a misogynist. ..."[131] But the focus on sexism sometimes fell flat. For example, "[t]o the bafflement of Democrats in Wisconsin ... the late Clinton push there did not mirror the economic messaging of the local labor unions. [Instead,] [o]ne played back Trump's worst remarks about women ..."[132]

Meanwhile, the Trump campaign essentially painted a consistent picture of Hillary Clinton as being dishonest.[133] Part of what gave this line of attack legs was that during her time as secretary of state, Clinton had used a private email server for certain government business. Whether this was a violation of the law is debatable. Other government officials, including later Ivanka Trump (Trump's daughter and aide), did the same thing. The use of private emails was investigated by the FBI, which eventually decided not to pursue a criminal case. But the use of the private email was a major political liability, especially in the hands of a blowhard like Trump, who branded her "Crooked Hillary."

---

[126] Nate Silver, *Donald Trump Had A Superior Electoral College Strategy*, FiveThirtyEight (Feb. 6, 2017), https://fivethirtyeight.com/features/donald-trump -had-a-superior-electoral-college-strategy/.

[127] *Id.*

[128] Sam Frizell, *Hillary Clinton's Strategy Against Donald Trump: I'm a Wonk, He's a Scrooge,* Time (Aug. 5, 2016).

[129] *Id.* (quoting Hillary Clinton).

[130] Amy Chozick & Patrick Healy, *Inside the Clinton Team's Plan to Defeat Donald Trump*, N.Y. Times (Feb. 29, 2016).

[131] *Id.*

[132] Abby Phillip, John Wagner & Anne Gearan, *A series of strategic mistakes likely sealed Clinton's fate*, Wash. Post (Nov. 12, 2016).

[133] Frizell, *supra* note 128.

The logo for Crooked Hillary, using handcuffs for the "oo," was created by Cambridge Analytica. Trump repeated the moniker *ad nauseum* during the campaign. "'She's made everybody less safe,' Trump said ... repeating his moniker for her, 'Crooked Hillary.'"[134] Given Trump's own loose relationship with veracity, these accusations against Clinton look like psychological projection. But there was just enough there to keep the taunt going.

At least in terms of money that was reported to the Federal Electoral Commission (FEC), Clinton ($563 756 928) raised and spent much more money than Trump ($333 127 164). That said, serious questions remain about whether any extra funds that were spent during the 2016 election should have been reported by Trump as political contributions or expenditures. For example, American Media Inc., which owns the *National Enquirer*, admitted in a non-prosecution agreement with the Department of Justice that it had illegally provided the Trump campaign with $150 000 by buying the story of a woman named Karen McDougal, who alleged an affair with Trump. And Trump's personal attorney, Michael Cohen, admitted in court that he gave $130 000 to a different woman with the stage name Stormy Daniels to cover up another alleged affair for the benefit of the Trump campaign. If there were other such payments during 2016, then it may well turn out that the Trump campaign and the Clinton campaign had more equivalent financial resources.

The Clinton campaign spent more of its resources on television ads compared to Trump.[135] But from Trump's point of view, he didn't need to pay for TV ads when the media was covering him on a near-continuous basis for free.[136] As *Bloomberg* noted at the time, "Instead of spending a lot on ads, Trump has effectively used the news media to get out his message. During the primaries he frequently called into news programs ... getting free time on air."[137] And from this standpoint, the Trump campaign was a resounding success, as Trump got over $4 billion in free airtime during the campaign.[138]

When Trump first announced his candidacy, there were widespread questions about whether the campaign was just a publicity stunt. Part of what made the announcement suspicious is it did not take place in a location of American historical significance, like Obama's announcement in Lincoln's hometown of Springfield; or in a location of electoral significance, like George W. Bush's announcement in Iowa. Rather, Trump announced his candidacy self-servingly

---

[134] *Id.*

[135] *Clinton and Trump Have Very Different Strategies for the Final Stretch,* BLOOMBERG (Oct. 5, 2016).

[136] *Id.*

[137] *Id.*

[138] Jennifer Saba, *Breakingviews: Trump's $4.6 billion in free media,* REUTERS (Sept. 30, 2016).

in Trump Tower. For a while, the telos of the campaign seemed to be providing an opportunity for product placement of the Trump commercial brand.

At the beginning of the Trump campaign, the question could be fairly asked: was this a hat company or a campaign? The *New York Post* concluded, "Donald Trump moves merch. The Trump campaign reports that 527,845 Make America Great Again caps have been sold through his official site and at events since Aug. 6, 2015."[139] Trump trademarked the phrase "Make America Great Again" in November 2012.[140] In the 2016 primaries, GOP candidates like Cruz and Walker used the phrase "until the Trump operation sent cease-and-desist letters. His trademark allowed him to control his opponents and develop exclusive merchandise, most notably in hat form."[141] The *Washington Post* noticed that as of June 2016, the Trump campaign had spent $2 million on ordering hats.[142] According to calculations on *Quora*, "He sold each hat for $25, made a profit estimated at $8 each. ... So [the Trump Campaign stood to make] about $16 million in profit."[143]

The early trademark on Make America Great Again (MAGA) in 2012 may indicate that Trump was thinking about running for president far earlier than 2016. Another clue is Michael Cohen, Trump's personal lawyer, set up a webpage called "Should Trump Run?" in 2011.[144] Cohen's efforts here generated a complaint to the FEC from a Ron Paul staffer[145] that ShouldTrumpRun should have been registered as a political committee under federal campaign finance law, and that it was violating bans against corporate involvement in a federal campaign.[146] The complaint against ShouldTrumpRun was dismissed by the FEC. Don McGahn, who was a FEC commissioner at the time, put out

---

[139] Dean Balsamini, *Trump campaign has sold more than half a million "MAGA" hats.*, N.Y. Post (Apr. 29, 2017).

[140] Abigail Hess, *Trump caps and "pussy hats": Here's who benefits when your purchase is political*, CNBC (Feb. 7, 2017), www.cnbc.com/2017/02/07/trump-caps-and -pink-hats-who-benefits-when-your-purchase-is-political.html.

[141] *Id.*

[142] Philip Bump, *How many hats has Donald Trump bought, anyway?*, Wash. Post (June 29, 2016).

[143] Dave Haynie, *How much money has Donald Trump made off of his "Make America Great Again" hats?*, Quora (Feb. 6, 2018), www.quora.com/How-much -money-has-Donald-Trump-made-off-of-his-Make-America-Great-Again-hats.

[144] Suzan Clarke, *Should Trump Run? The Story Behind the Website*, ABC News (May 19, 2011), https://abcnews.go.com/m/blogEntry?id=12179218&sid=248&cid=4329156.

[145] Maggie Haberman, *Paul aide files Trump jet complaint*, Politico (Mar. 14, 2011), www.politico.com/story/2011/03/paul-aide-files-trump-jet-complaint-051262.

[146] *First General Counsel's Report re: Trump, et al.*, Federal Election Commission (Jan. 25, 2013), www.fec.gov/files/legal/murs/6462/13044334657.pdf (MUR 6462) (noting the complaint raised against ShouldTrumpRun on Mar. 16, 2011).

a statement in support of Trump's position.[147] McGahn went on to become Trump's election lawyer in 2016 and White House counsel.[148] This whole episode should have put Trump on notice about the campaign finance laws that bar corporations from being involved in campaigns. But it is possible that what he learned from this episode is that campaign finance laws would not be enforced by the FEC.[149]

Trump's son-in-law Jared Kushner apparently used the red MAGA hats to test the microtargeting capacity of Facebook ads. As *Forbes* also reported:

> At first Kushner dabbled, engaging in what amounted to a beta test using Trump merchandise ... The Trump campaign went from selling $8,000 worth of hats and other items a day to $80,000, generating revenue, expanding the number of human billboards--and proving a concept.[150]

And by the way, the phrase "Make America Great Again" is not original to Trump. "Ronald Reagan and George H.W. Bush both said, 'Let's make America great again' in the presidential election of 1980. [And] Bill Clinton used the phrase in his 1991 presidential announcement speech. ..."[151] It's just basic branding. And Trump is always looking ahead: In 2017, he applied for a trademark for the phrase "Keep America Great."[152] In 2019, Trump rolled out the "Keep America Great" slogan as he launched his reelection bid in Orlando.[153]

The overlap between the Trump campaign in 2016 and the Trump Organization was considerable. The Trump campaign paid rent to Trump Towers, held election events on Trump properties, flew from campaign stop to campaign stop on Trump-owned aircraft, dined in Trump restaurants and

---

[147] *Statement of Reasons Vice Chairman Donald F. McGahn & Commissioner Caroline C. Hunter In the Matter of Donald J. Trump MUR 6462*, FEDERAL ELECTION COMMISSION (Sept. 18, 2013), https://eqs.fec.gov/eqsdocsMUR/13044342667.pdf.

[148] Michael S. Schmidt & Maggie Haberman, McGahn, *Soldier for Trump and Witness Against Him, Leaves White House*, N.Y. TIMES (Oct. 17, 2018).

[149] Ciara Torres-Spelliscy, *What Trump Should Have Learned from His Aborted 2012 Presidential Run*, BRENNAN CENTER (Mar. 6, 2019), www.brennancenter.org/blog/what-trump-should-have-learned-his-aborted-2012-presidential-run.

[150] Steven Bertoni, *Exclusive Interview: How Jared Kushner Won Trump The White House*, FORBES (Nov. 22, 2016).

[151] Hess, *supra* note 140.

[152] Alex Weprin, *Trump campaign applies to trademark "Keep America Great!,"* POLITICO (Jan. 24, 2017), www.politico.com/blogs/on-media/2017/01/trump-trademark-keep-america-great-234110.

[153] Lauren Dezenski, *Is KAG the new MAGA?*, CNN (June 19, 2019), https://www.cnn.com/2019/06/19/politics/donald-trump-campaign-slogan-2020/index.html.

had Trump family on the campaign payroll.[154] In a particularly weird campaign event, candidate Donald Trump, like Vanna White, stood near a pile of Trump-brand steaks, Trump-brand wine and Trump-brand water as reporters snapped pictures.[155] Trump even spent one of his last precious days of the campaign, which other candidates would have spent stumping in a swing state, at a grand opening of his D.C. hotel in what many interpreted as free advertisement for the business.[156] In the end, Trump's 2016 campaign paid at least $12.8 million to the Trump Organization and other Trump family members.[157] The Trump 2020 re-election committee is doing the same thing: spending in Trump properties, paying Trump lawyers and buying Trump food.[158]

The Monday night quarterbacking about why Hillary Clinton lost was endless. One theory was that she didn't appeal to enough Black voters and young people.[159] Many of these demographics simply sat out the election.[160] Part of this could have been that she did not inspire them; but another factor highlighted by the Senate Intelligence Committee after its investigation into the 2016 election showed that Russian messaging encouraged voter suppression of Black voters in particular, encouraging them to skip the election. Another behavior among some Black and Latino voters was to vote for a third-party candidate.[161] This too was pushed by Russians. In the end:

> [8 percent of] African American voters under 30 chose a third-party candidate, as did 5 percent of Latinos under 30, according to an analysis of the election results by the Democratic pollster Cornell Belcher. These 'protest votes,' he argued, were enough to seal Clinton's fate ... [162]

---

[154] Ciara Torres-Spelliscy, *The Trump Campaign Is Brought to You by Trump Inc.*, BRENNAN CTR. BLOG (Mar. 15, 2016).

[155] Brett Neely, *Trump Doesn't Own Most of The Products He Pitched Last Night*, NPR (Mar. 9, 2016).

[156] Dave Jamieson, *Donald Trump's Grand Opening For His Hotel Is Greeted With A Boycott*, HUFF. POST (Oct. 26, 2016).

[157] Jim Zarroli, *Trump's Campaign Paid Millions To His Own Properties*, NPR (Feb. 3, 2017).

[158] Ciara Torres-Spelliscy, *Trump Already Profiting From 2020 Campaign*, BRENNAN CTR. BLOG (Aug. 7, 2017); *see also* Soo Rin Kim, Katherine Faulders & Matthew Mosk, *Trump campaign paid legal fees to firm representing Jared Kushner*, ABC NEWS (Feb. 8, 2019), https://abcnews.go.com/Politics/trump-campaign-paid -legal-fees-firm-representing-jared/story?id=60912887.

[159] Ball, *supra* note 112.

[160] Phillip *et al.*, *supra* note 132 ("[Trump] won the state not because he out-performed his predecessor but because Clinton underperformed hers.").

[161] Ball, *supra* note 112.

[162] *Id.*

Another variant of criticism is that Obama voters were just that—*Obama voters*, who owed no allegiance to the Democratic party. When Obama wasn't on the ticket, they defected in 2016, just as they had done in 2010 and 2014.[163] Clinton had the same Obama analytics, but she lacked Obama's charisma.[164]

On top of all the free media that Trump received, he also had social media to get his message directly to voters and to control the media cycle, day after day, by making some outrageous claim online. An entire genre of lazy TV news could be called "Trump Tweeted X." While he was in his 70s, he and his team were able to make good use of social media like Instagram:

> Trump uses his Instagram account, which has more than 650,000 followers, to deliver snarky messages and short videos of him scowling as he delivers pronouncements from his Trump Tower desk. On Twitter, Trump's 5 million followers can keep up with his next appearance ('Will be on @ABC News tonight at 6:30 pm') and new poll numbers.[165]

And when the Trump campaign teamed up with Steve Bannon, they got all of his Cambridge Analytica-tested catchphrases to put into Trump's mouth. Cambridge Analytica's Christopher Wylie said:

> '[Bannon] believes in the whole Andrew Breitbart doctrine that politics is downstream from culture, so to change politics you need to change culture. ... Trump is like a pair of Uggs, or Crocs, basically. So how do you get from people thinking 'Ugh. Totally ugly' to the moment when everyone is wearing them?'[166]

Trump trumpeted Cambridge Analytica catchphrases across the land from political rallies and in tweets, including his famous "drain the swamp." Never mind that this phrase originally came from a Democrat.[167] Again, it was just branding—heavily market-tested branding.

---

[163] Phillip, *et al.*, *supra* note 132.

[164] Ball, *supra* note 112.

[165] Paul Schwartzman & Jenna Johnson, *It's not chaos. It's Trump's campaign strategy*, WASH. POST (Dec. 9, 2015).

[166] Carole Cadwalladr, *"I made Steve Bannon's psychological warfare tool"*, GUARDIAN (Mar. 18, 2018).

[167] Rebecca Harrington, *Here's what Trump means when he says "drain the swamp"*, BUSINESS INSIDER (Nov. 11, 2016), http://www.businessinsider.com/what-does-drain -the-swamp-mean-was-dc-built-on-a-swamp-2016-11.www.businessinsider.com/what -does-drain-the-swamp-mean-was-dc-built-on-a-swamp-2016-11.

Robert Spero may have put it best when he worried:

> A viewer can learn all he or she needs to know about chewing gum in 30 seconds. To think that the credentials and the character of people who seek high office can be examined in the same length of time is absurd.[168]

He predicted: "Someday someone is going to sneak into elective office behind a shield of these hit-and-run commercials who will make Watergate look like child's play."[169] That may be the most accurate assessment of what happened in the 2016 campaign.

6.   CONCLUSION

Looking at the campaigns of Eisenhower through Trump through the lens of branding, it's not just the more reptilian candidate that wins[170]—it's typically the one that is more comfortable being merchandized who wins. Television has been a dominant force from 1952–2016. Candidates who could master the medium (by hook or by crook) typically were those who triumphed.

Or maybe what happened in 2016 is proof that, as Upton Sinclair warned, "all sensible men understand that whichever way the [electoral] contest is decided, business will continue to be business, and money will continue to talk."[171] As CEO of CBS Les Moonves said during the 2016 campaign, "It may not be good for America, but it's damn good for CBS. ... The money's rolling in and this is fun. ... Sorry. It's a terrible thing to say. But, bring it on, Donald. Keep going."[172] Two years later, Moonves would be out at CBS as the tide against sexual harassment, symbolized by the hashtag #Metoo, triggered by Trump, toppled other powerful men.

---

[168]   SPERO, *supra* note 5, at 175.

[169]   *Id.* at 175–76.

[170]   RAPAILLE, *supra* note 8, at 189 ("[Americans] decidedly do not want a president who thinks too much. Except under extraordinary circumstances, the more reptilian candidate always wins.").

[171]   UPTON SINCLAIR, THE BRASS CHECK: A STUDY OF AMERICAN JOURNALISM 222 (1919).

[172]   Paul Bond, *Leslie Moonves on Donald Trump: "It May Not Be Good for America, but It's Damn Good for CBS,"* HOLLYWOOD REPORTER (Feb. 29, 2016).

PART III

When branding gets pernicious

Branding could be used for good to sell useful products to a thriving consumer base. But all too frequently, the techniques of branding are used for pernicious purposes, particularly in politics. For instance, President Trump has deployed the repetitive use of catchphrases to denigrate the free press. By calling legitimate journalists "fake news" and the "enemy of the people," and by sharing bogus news stories as if they are real, he has undermined the status of journalists in the minds of his most ardent followers.

Branding was also used during the 2016 campaign to manipulate voters. Some of this was done by the Trump campaign's partner Cambridge Analytica, which purported to be able to predict voters' psychological proclivities. And a tactic of the Russian Internet Research Agency, which was actively interfering in the 2016 election, was to destroy the credibility of journalism.

Another source of manipulation in the 2016 election was the targeting by Russian intelligence officers of racial minorities for voter suppression efforts. In particular, the Russians created an entire online mirage for Black voters which perpetuated the message that African American voters should not vote at all. This mirage included fake Facebook pages, fake Instagram accounts, fake Twitter personalities and fake webpages. The Russians essentially built an entire echo chamber through clever branding where the core message was to skip the 2016 election if you were Black. Because 90 percent of Blacks are Democrats, this tactic of voter suppression may well have cost Hillary Clinton the 2016 election.

7.   Branding the news

"Men in general are as much affected by what things seem to be as by what they are;
often indeed, they are moved more by appearances than by the reality of things."
Machiavelli

1.   INTRODUCTION

As discussed in "Branding the truth," President Trump has taken lying to a whole new level. As *Washington Post* reporter Philip Rucker put it, "Trump has never been hemmed in by fact, fairness or even logic."[1] Or as economist Jared Bernstein put it, "When facts are on vacation or locked up in a prison somewhere, that makes for troubled times."[2] But one of Trump's categories of lying deserves special attention: the lies about the Fourth Estate—the free press. He makes two basic intertwined attacks on the press: that a particular outlet or story is "fake news" and that the press in general is the "enemy of the people." Both of these are examples of how repetitive branding of a base lie is malevolent.

Law Professor Samuel Issacharoff observed that "norms have broken down under Trump. There is hostility to independent civil society institutions including the press."[3] Why does Trump spend so much time attacking the media? As he has admitted himself, he does it to manipulate the public's perception of news organizations so that the public will discount negative stories about him. Veteran reporter for *60 Minutes* Lesley Stahl revealed an off-camera comment from candidate Trump in the 2016 campaign:

> **Lesley Stahl:** It's just me, my boss, and him—he has a huge office—and [Trump is] attacking the press. There were no cameras, there was nothing going on and I said, 'That is getting tired, why are you doing it? You're doing it over and over and it's

---

[1]   Philip Rucker, '*Full Trumpism': The president's apocalyptic attacks reach a new level of falsity*, WASH. POST (Nov. 4, 2018).

[2]   Interview with Jared Bernstein (Sept. 8, 2018).

[3]   Interview with Samuel Issacharoff (June 25, 2018).

boring. It's time to end that, you've won the nomination. And why do you keep hammering at this?'

Donald Trump: You know why I do it? I do it to discredit you all and demean you all, so when you write negative stories about me, no one will believe you.[4]

In other words, instead of being a blunder, the president's recurring practice of saying "fake news" is part of a strategic attempt to undermine the biggest sources of facts for American citizens — the free press. Calling news that is unflattering to him "fake news" is just branding in its purest evil form.

This chapter will explore why Trump's branding news as "fake" or the press as the "enemy of the people" is so injurious. And this chapter contrasts what he calls "fake news" (real news stories that are critical of him) with "bogus news"—completely made-up stories with no basis in fact that he often retweets or repeats.

2.   DON'T BELIEVE YOUR OWN LYING EYES

George Orwell's *1984* spoke of a dystopian future where there was no objective truth. Rather, truth was what those in power said it was. As Orwell wrote, "The Party told you to reject the evidence of your eyes and ears. It was their final, most essential command."[5] Both as a candidate and as a president, Trump has had message discipline in a few key areas and one is calling mainstream media coverage by professional journalists that is unflattering to him "fake news."[6] As Tamara Keith observed:

> Often when Trump says something is fake, it isn't false. Rather, he just doesn't like it. On May 9th [2018], he posted a tweet that pulled back the curtain on this idea: '91% of the Network News about me is negative (Fake),' he wrote.[7]

---

[4]   Ian Schwartz, *Lesley Stahl: Trump Told Me He Uses Term "Fake News" to Discredit the Media*, REAL CLEAR POLITICS (May 23, 2018), www.realclearpolitics .com/video/2018/05/23/leslie_stahl_trump_told_me_he_uses_term_fake_news_to _discredit_the_media.html.

[5]   GEORGE ORWELL, 1984 29 (1949).

[6]   Haley Britzky, *Everything Trump has called "FAKE NEWS"*, AXIOS (July 9, 2017), www.axios.com/everything-trump-has-called-fake-news-1513303959 -6603329e-46b5-44ea-b6be-70d0b3bdb0ca.html (listing 66 times Trump called something "fake news" in six months in office); *see also* Tamara Keith, *President Trump's Description of What's 'Fake' Is Expanding*, NPR (Sept. 2, 2018), www.npr.org/2018/ 09/02/643761979/president-trumps-description-of-whats-fake-is-expanding ("An NPR analysis found that in the month of August [2018], Trump sent out 46 tweets containing the words 'fake' or 'phony,' far surpassing his previous record.").

[7]   Keith, *supra* note 6.

He also claimed things that happened and were witnessed by an entire nation did not occur. For instance, during the 2016 campaign, a tape of Trump talking with Billy Bush on an *Access Hollywood* outtake tape circulated. In the tape Trump bragged about sexually assaulting women. After the tape was released, candidate Trump offered a rare apology for its contents.[8] But in 2017, President Trump suddenly floated the idea that the *Access Hollywood* tape wasn't real at all.[9] And in mid-2018, Trump was interviewed by British newspaper *The Sun* on tape. When *The Sun* released quotes from him that were critical of U.K. Prime Minister Theresa May, he claimed that *The Sun* was "fake news," even though *The Sun* also released an audio recording of the interview which validated its reporting.[10] As the *Washington Post* noted, "As Trump's critiques of 'fake news' go, this one was particularly ridiculous."[11]

Trump has even told the American public not to believe their own eyes. On July 24, 2018, at a Veterans of Foreign Wars Convention in Kansas City, Missouri, Trump told the audience, "'Just remember, what you are seeing and what you are reading is not what's happening ... Just stick with us, don't believe the crap you see from these people, the fake news.'"[12]

Trump also likes to lie about elections. After the Democrats took control of the House of Representatives in the 2018 election, Trump tweeted, "The Fake News Media only wants to speak of the House, where the Midterm results were better than other sitting Presidents."[13] Statistician Nate Silver noted of the 2018 election, "There shouldn't be much question about whether 2018 was a wave election. Of course it was a wave."[14] Indeed, as Silver stated, "Democratic candidates for the House will receive almost as many votes this year as the 63 million that President Trump received in 2016, when he won the Electoral

---

[8] Jeremy Diamond, *Trump issues defiant apology for lewd remarks—then goes on the attack*, CNN (Oct. 8, 2016), www.cnn.com/2016/10/07/politics/donald-trump-women-vulgar/index.html.

[9] Chris Cillizza, *Trump's latest conspiracy? The 'Access Hollywood' tape was a fake!*, CNN (Nov. 27, 2017), www.cnn.com/2017/11/27/politics/donald-trump-access-hollywood-conspiracy/index.html.

[10] Zachary Basu, *Trump vs. the tape on his explosive Theresa May comments*, AXIOS (July 13, 2018), www.axios.com/donald-trump-sun-interview-theresa-may-brexit-c49a66c6-6fdf-4803-a36f-33ce78850a35.html.

[11] Brian Stelter, *Trump denies he said something that he said on a tape everyone has heard*, WASH. POST (July 13, 2018).

[12] Rob Tornoe, *Trump to veterans: Don't believe what you're reading or seeing*, PHILADELPHIA INQUIRER (July 24, 2018).

[13] Donald J. Trump, TWITTER (Nov. 16, 2018), https://twitter.com/realDonald Trump/status/1063517548258447361.

[14] Nate Silver, *Trump's Base Isn't Enough*, FIVE THIRTY EIGHT (Nov. 20, 2018), https://fivethirtyeight.com/features/trumps-base-isnt-enough/?ex_cid=2018-forecast.

College (but lost the popular vote)."[15] The Democrats picked up 40 seats in the House in 2018. There have only been two presidents since 1980 who had bigger losses in midterms than Trump: President Obama in 2010, when the GOP netted 63 seats, and President Clinton in 1994, when the GOP gained 52 seats.[16]

Another genre of Trump lies are lies about his own election to the presidency in 2016. He is fond of claiming that he won in a landslide.[17] For one, he lost the popular vote, by a deficit of 3 million votes. Rather, he won the Electoral College, and not by a landslide.[18] In 2017, Trump repeatedly lied about there being voter fraud in his own election.[19] Trump set up an entire commission to seek out voter fraud.[20] The Trump Voting Fraud Commission didn't get far before imploding.[21] It found no widespread voting fraud.[22] As election law experts could have told Trump, incidents of in-person voter fraud are rarer than lightning strikes.[23] They do happen, but typically a tiny number occur in a national election with millions of people voting.[24] The fact that the chair of this Voter Fraud Commission was Secretary of State Kris Kobach,

---

[15]   *Id.*

[16]   Dante Chinni & Sally Bronston, *Was it a wave election? Depends on your data set*, NBC NEWS (Nov. 25, 2018), www.nbcnews.com/politics/first-read/was-it-wave -election-depends-your-data-set-n939796.

[17]   Glenn Kessler, *Anatomy of a Trump rally: 70 percent of claims are false, misleading or lacking evidence*, WASH. POST (Sept. 12, 2018) ("False. Trump narrowly won the electoral college, as a swing of less than 50,000 votes would have flipped three states and cost him the election. He is one of the few elected presidents to have lost the popular vote.").

[18]   *Id.*

[19]   Ryan Struyk & Lauren Pearle, *Fact-checking Trump's repeated unsubstantiated claim of widespread voter fraud*, ABC NEWS (May 11, 2017), https://abcnews.go.com/ Politics/fact-checking-trumps-repeated-unsubstantiated-claim-widespread-voter/story ?id=45021067.

[20]   Ali Vitali, Peter Alexander & Kelly O'Donnell, *Trump Establishes Voter Fraud Commission*, NBC NEWS (May 11, 2017), www.nbcnews.com/politics/white-house/ trump-establish-vote-fraud-commission-n757796.

[21]   Alex Johnson, *Trump shuts down voter fraud commission, citing "endless legal battles"*, NBC NEWS (Jan. 4, 2018), www.nbcnews.com/politics/elections/trump -shuts-down-voter-fraud-commission-citing-endless-legal-battles-n834491; Vann R. Newkirk II, *Trump's Voter-Fraud Commission Has Its First Meeting. The Kris Kobach-led effort faces at least seven federal lawsuits and claims of voter suppression as it moves to set its agenda.*, ATLANTIC (July 19, 2017).

[22]   Eli Rosenberg, *"The most bizarre thing I've ever been a part of": Trump panel found no widespread voter fraud, ex-member says*, WASH. POST (Aug. 3, 2018).

[23]   *Debunking the Voter Fraud Myth*, BRENNAN CTR (Jan. 31, 2017), www .brennancenter.org/analysis/debunking-voter-fraud-myth.

[24]   Lorraine C. Minnite, *The Politics of Voter Fraud*, PROJECT VOTE (2007), www .projectvote.org/wp-content/uploads/2007/03/Politics_of_Voter_Fraud_Final.pdf.

who was being sued for violating voters' rights in his home state of Kansas, couldn't have helped its credibility. Not only did Kobach lose that case,[25] but the judge was so dismayed by his performance that she ordered Kobach to take courses in continuing legal education.[26] Voters in Kansas had the last laugh, since Kobach lost a bid to become Kansas's governor in 2018.[27]

In an interview with *ABC News*, Trump claimed the right to lie about the 2016 election if other people believed him:

> Referencing a series of high-profile Republicans who rebuked Trump's bogus claim, *World News Tonight* anchor David Muir asked the obvious question: "Do you think that talking about millions of illegal votes is dangerous to this country, without presenting the evidence?"

Trump's response? "No, not at all, because many people feel the same way that I do." He also said: "Millions of people agree with me when I say that. If you would have looked on one of the other networks, and all of the people that were calling in, they're saying 'We agree with Mr. Trump. We agree.' They're very smart people."[28]

This whole exchange is troubling on a number of levels. For one, it would be nice to have a president who valued telling the truth for its own sake. Moreover, what he is lying about is his own election. He appears to believe erroneously that the 3 million vote difference between himself and Clinton was caused by fraudulent votes. Ironically, one of the few people caught "double-voting" in 2016 was a female Trump supporter in Iowa.[29] All in all,

---

[25] *Fish v. Kobach*, ACLU (June 18, 2018), www.aclu.org/cases/fish-v-kobach ("The court struck down Kansas' documentary proof-of-citizenship law, which disenfranchised thousands of eligible voters. The judge found that the law violates the National Voter Registration Act and the U.S. Constitution.").

[26] Fish v. Kobach, 309 F. Supp. 3d 1048, 1119 (D. Kan. 2018) ("Defendant [Kris Kobach] chose to represent his own office in this matter, and as such, had a duty to familiarize himself with the governing rules of procedure. ... The Court therefore imposes a CLE requirement of 6 hours for the 2018–2019 reporting year in addition to any other CLE education required by his law license.").

[27] Hunter Woodall & Jonathan Shorman, *Democrat Laura Kelly defeats Kris Kobach to become Kansas governor*, KANSAS CITY STAR (Nov. 6, 2018), www .kansascity.com/news/politics-government/election/article221139715.html#storylink= cpy.

[28] Graham Vyse, *Donald Trump says it's okay for him to lie since "people agree with me."*, NEW REPUBLIC (Jan. 25, 2017).

[29] Charly Haley, *Voter fraud suspect arrested in Des Moines*, DES MOINES REGISTER (Oct. 29, 2016), www.desmoinesregister.com/story/news/crime-and-courts/2016/10/28/voter-fraud-suspect-arrested-des-moines/92892042/ ("Terri Lynn Rote, 55, was booked into the Polk County Jail about 3:40 p.m. Thursday on a first-degree election misconduct charge, which is a Class D felony.").

the *Washington Post* could find just four instances of voter fraud in 2016.[30] The other problematic thing about the president's thinking that if other people believe a lie, then it's okay to say it, is that truth then becomes completely unmoored from reality. The truth just becomes something that is subject to popular opinion. And there's a hint of authoritarianism in the idea that the president would get to determine for the rest of the nation what is true.[31] The final trouble with repetition of the idea that "voting fraud is rampant" is it is an utterly bogus conspiracy theory. One would hope that the president would not traffic in conspiracy theories.

Trump as a businessman may have learned something he is deploying in politics—namely, that the first way of getting into people's minds is by getting their attention. This was an insight that was shared by Bill Bernbach, one of the ad men behind the outrageous "Daisy" ad in the Johnson 1964 race. Bernbach observed, "'The truth isn't the truth until people believe you and they can't believe you if they don't know what you're saying; and they can't know what you're saying if they don't listen to you; and they won't listen to you if you're not interesting.'"[32]

3. ACTUALLY BOGUS NEWS

Whether there is a direct causal or correlative effect, amidst all of this White House-generated lying, trust in institutions is falling[33] and trust in news has dropped.[34] In fact, it cratered from 72 percent in 1976 to 32 percent in 2017.[35]

---

[30]   Philip Bump, *There have been just four documented cases of voter fraud in the 2016 election*, WASH. POST (Dec. 1, 2016).

[31]   Keith, *supra* note 6 ("'Donald Trump more and more is calling into question every other source of information besides himself,' said Brendan Nyhan, a professor at the University of Michigan who studies misinformation and trust in the media.").

[32]   Robert Mann, *How the 'Daisy' Ad Changed Everything About Political Advertising*, SMITHSONIAN MAG. (Apr. 13, 2016) (quoting Bernbach).

[33]   *Edelman Trust Barometer: Global Report*, EDELMAN, 11 (2018), www.edelman .com/sites/g/files/aatuss191/files/2018-10/2018_Edelman_Trust_Barometer_Global _Report_FEB.pdf.

[34]   Jennifer Kavanagh & Michael D. Rich, *Truth Decay: An Initial Exploration of the Diminishing Role of Facts and Analysis in American Public Life*, RAND CORPORATION (2018) ("Public opinion data ... show quite clearly that confidence in major institutions, such as government, newspapers, and television news – organizations that used to be primary sources of factual information – has dropped sharply over the past 20 years.").

[35]   Nancy Watzman, *Eleven takeaways from Knight-supported research on restoring trust in news*, MEDIUM (June 6, 2018), https://medium.com/trust-media-and -democracy/nine-takeaways-from-knight-supported-research-on-restoring-trust-in -news-c3d29ae0de3d.

A recent study of individuals in three American cities:

> Kansas City, Fresno, and Macon, Georgia — ... asked ... what was the first word that came to mind when they saw the word 'news.' About 62 percent responded with something negative — 'fake,' 'lies,' 'untrustworthy,' and 'BS' were the sample responses given. ... The remaining 38 percent responded with something positive or neutral (like 'factual').[36]

One of the reasons why the charge that a particular article or story in the news is "fake" is so damning is that bogus, totally made-up nonsense is often reported online as if it were a real news story. Typically, the webpages that traffic in this bogus nonsense are simply set up to generate "clickbait" ad revenue.[37] For example, NPR reporters tracked down a particular bogus story that made the rounds during the 2016 election. The story was entitled, "'FBI Agent Suspected in Hillary Email Leaks Found Dead In Apparent Murder-Suicide.'" "The story is completely false, but it was shared on Facebook over half a million times."[38] The source of the story was a 40-year-old guy in the suburbs who was making money from ad revenue from webpages owned by his company, Disinfomedia, peddling bogus news stories that went viral. According to the source:

> It was just anybody with a blog can get on there and find a big, huge Facebook group of kind of rabid Trump supporters just waiting to eat up this red meat that they're about to get served," [he] says. "It caused an explosion in the number of sites. I mean, my gosh, the number of just fake accounts on Facebook exploded during the Trump election." [He] says his writers have tried to write fake news for liberals — but they just never take the bait.[39]

It's no surprise that Facebook is frequently the highway on which misin-formation travels, since 2.2 billion people worldwide are on the platform.[40]

---

[36] Joshua Benton, *If you hate the media, you're more likely to be fooled by a fake headline.*, NIEMAN LAB (Nov. 19, 2018), www.niemanlab.org/2018/11/if-you-hate-the-media-youre-more-likely-to-be-fooled-by-a-fake-headline/.

[37] Fed. Trade Commn. v. LeadClick Media, LLC, 838 F.3d 158, 163 (2d Cir. 2016) ("Certain affiliates hired by LeadClick used fake news sites to market products. These fake news sites, which were common in the industry at the time, looked like genuine news sites: they had logos styled to look like news sites and included pictures of supposed reporters next to their articles.").

[38] Laura Sydell, *We Tracked Down A Fake-News Creator In The Suburbs. Here's What We Learned*, NPR (Nov. 23, 2016), www.npr.org/sections/alltechconsidered/2016/11/23/503146770/npr-finds-the-head-of-a-covert-fake-news-operation-in-the-suburbs.

[39] *Id.* (quoting Jestin Coler).

[40] Frenkel, *et al., Delay, Deny and Deflect: How Facebook's Leaders Fought Through Crisis*, N.Y. TIMES (Nov. 14, 2018).

A Stanford study concluded that the average American saw at least one fake news story during the 2016 election and that many saw far more.[41] Perhaps even more troubling is that of those respondents who could recall a specific fake news story, about half of them believed it. As former FBI agent Clint Watts testified before the Senate Intelligence Committee, "In the lead up to the 2016 election, fake news stories were consumed at higher rates than true stories."[42]

The *New York Times* found an out-of-work computer scientist in Georgia (the country, not the American state) ginning up fake news during the 2016 American election who claimed, "For me, this is all about income, nothing more. ..."[43] The funding was mostly from Google ads embedded in his fake news webpages.[44] His fake news was nearly all pro-Trump. But fake news also goes in the other ideological direction. A tweet on Twitter claimed falsely that crowds at a Trump rally chanted, "We hate Muslims, we hate blacks, we want our great country back."[45] The only problem is, this never happened. But individuals hostile to Trump were willing to assume the worst of his followers and retweeted the claim until it went viral.[46] Lost in the repeating was the fact that it never happened.

Other bogus news is posted on webpages dedicated to delivering views from one ideological extreme or another; the facts of the stories don't matter, so long as they fit a particular world view. *InfoWars* fits this model and is presently being sued for claiming erroneously that the massacre at Sandy Hook Elementary School on December 14, 2012 never happened.[47] A judge

---

[41]   Hunt Allcott & Matthew Gentzkow, *Social Media and Fake News in the 2016 Election*, 31(2) J. OF ECON. PERSPECTIVES 211–36 (Spring 2017), https://web.stanford.edu/~gentzkow/research/fakenews.pdf.

[42]   Clint Watts, *Statement Prepared for the U.S. Senate Select Committee on Intelligence hearing: "Disinformation: A Primer in Russian Active Measures and Influence Campaigns"* (Mar. 30, 2017), www.intelligence.senate.gov/sites/default/files/documents/os-cwatts-033017.pdf.

[43]   Andrew Higgins, Mike McIntire & Gabriel J.X. Dance, *Inside a Fake News Sausage Factory: 'This Is All About Income'*, N.Y. TIMES (Nov. 25, 2016) (quoting Mr. Latsabidze).

[44]   *Id.*

[45]   *'We Hate Muslims, We Hate Blacks' Chanted at Trump Rally*, SNOPES (Nov. 9, 2016) (finding the claim false.) www.snopes.com/fact-check/trump-rally-chant/.

[46]   Angie Drobnic Holan, *2016 Lie of the Year: Fake news*, POLITIFACT (Dec. 13, 2016), www.politifact.com/truth-o-meter/article/2016/dec/13/2016-lie-year-fake-news/ (noting the increased prevalence of faux news stories in 2016).

[47]   *Sandy Hook families v. Alex Jones: Defamation case explained*, BBC NEWS (Aug. 31, 2018), www.bbc.com/news/world-us-canada-45358890.

allowed discovery to go forward in this suit[48] and is allowing the Sandy Hook families to depose *InfoWars* host Alex Jones.[49] This bogus news, like what is on *InfoWars,* is a descendant of "yellow journalism," which was also full of lies and famously even led to the Spanish-American War.[50]

A majority of adults in the U.S. get news through social media.[51] Readers may not realize that a news story that shows up in a social media feed, for example, is really from a bogus source. In a Twitter feed, news from 10 credible reliable journalists can be mixed in with 10 bogus sources. And given the current structure of Twitter, there is little to alert the reader that a particular source is balderdash all the way down. Getting news aggregated this way blurs the line between opinion and fact for the casual or less careful reader.[52] Moreover, social media feeds can overwhelm readers with more information than they can process.[53] "This volume [on social media feeds] creates a challenge for people seeking to distinguish fact and opinion, effectively overwhelming their cognitive capacity, and creating uncertainty and misperceptions about what is true and what is not."[54]

The public struggles to sort fact from fiction. Troublingly, a November 2016 study:

> found that a group of students was generally unable to distinguish true stories from false ones, to identify advertisements and sponsored content as such, or to consider

---

[48] Glenn Fleishman, *Alex Jones, Infowars Must Hand Over Documents to Sandy Hook Families Suing Conspiracy-Minded Host*, FORTUNE (Jan. 11, 2019), http://fortune .com/2019/01/11/infowars-lawsuit-alex-jones-sandy-hook-judge/.

[49] Owen Daugherty, *Judge rules Sandy Hook families can depose Alex Jones in defamation case*, HILL (Feb. 13, 2919), https://thehill.com/blogs/blog-briefing-room/ 429945-judge-rules-sandy-hook-families-can-depose-alex-jones-in-defamation.

[50] *Crucible of Empire the Spanish American War*, PBS (1999), www.pbs.org/ crucible/frames/_journalism.html ("The Spanish-American War is often referred to as the first 'media war.' During the 1890s, journalism that sensationalized—and sometimes even manufactured—dramatic events was a powerful force that helped propel the United States into war with Spain.").

[51] Kavanagh & Rich, *supra* note 34 ("A 2016 study found that 62% of adults in the United States get their news through social media platforms, such as Facebook, Twitter, and Reddit.").

[52] *Id.* ("Some blurring of the line between opinion and fact also reflects the significant increase in the volume of information available and the relative concentration of opinion (versus fact) disseminated through conventional media sources and social media").

[53] *Id.* ("Studies have suggested that, far from promoting deep knowledge or understanding, the massive increase in the volume of information becomes overwhelming, inhibiting true learning.").

[54] *Id.*

the bias of an information source when determining whether a statement was fact or opinion.[55]

This study, which covered students in middle school through college, concluded: "Overall, young people's ability to reason about the information on the Internet can be summed up in one word: bleak."[56] But before condemning this as a problem merely for the young, consider this study of adults reported by the Neiman Lab at Harvard: "Those who have negative opinions of the news media are less likely to spot a fake headline, less likely to differentiate between news and opinion—but more confident in their ability to find the information they need online."[57]

Examples of bogus news include lies that Democrats in Florida had voted to impose *Sharia* law. When the fact checkers at *Politifact* looked into this claim, they found it to be complete bunk. "It's ridiculous—beyond ridiculous, really—to suggest that Senate Democrats forced on women such elements of Sharia law as burqa-wearing and stoning to death. We rate this claim Pants on Fire."[58] This bogus news problem is particularly pronounced on social media. As a Stanford study found just after the 2016 election:

> Social media platforms such as Facebook have a dramatically different structure than previous media technologies. Content can be relayed among users with no significant third party filtering, fact-checking, or editorial judgment. An individual user with no track record or reputation can in some cases reach as many readers as *Fox News*, *CNN*, or the *New York Times*.[59]

And because more outrageous stories (albeit bogus ones) are likely to attract clicks from Twitter (and other social media), there is an incentive for the underlying webpages that generate bogus news to keep pushing out nonsense. This bogus news might have had a limited effect in the 2016 election, but for the fact that the Trump campaign and sometimes even Trump himself would parrot bogus news stories as if they were truthful.[60] This gave the lies even

---

[55] *Id.*

[56] *Evaluating Information: The Cornerstone of Civic Online Reasoning*, STANFORD HISTORY EDUCATION GROUP 4 (2016), https://stacks.stanford.edu/file/druid: fv751yt5934/SHEG%20Evaluating%20Information%20Online.pdf.

[57] Benton, *supra* note 36.

[58] Amy Sherman, *'Florida Democrats just voted to impose Sharia law on women,'* *bloggers say*, POLITIFACT (May 8, 2014), www.politifact.com/florida/statements/2014/may/08/blog-posting/florida-democrats-just-voted-impose-sharia-law-wom/.

[59] Allcott & Gentzkow, *supra* note 41.

[60] Caitlin Dewey, *Facebook fake-news writer: 'I think Donald Trump is in the White House because of me'*, WASH. POST (Nov. 17, 2016) ("His [Trump's] campaign

wider reach. Indeed, one study found bogus news stories were getting more traction in the 2016 election than *bona fide* news stories.[61]

Social media companies have come under pressure from Congress and consumer groups to curb the problem of bogus news.[62] This has led Google to make certain changes to its algorithm to deprioritize bogus news sources in its results pages and Twitter to purge numerous bogus accounts.[63] Facebook has claimed to be taking the problem seriously.[64] But on further inspection, Facebook has spent more energy on going after its own critics than battling the bogus news plaguing its users.[65]

Partisanship, not surprisingly, influences which sources of news Americans trust.[66] As cognitive scientists have noted, "media are a potentially important

---

manager posted my story about a protester getting paid $3,500 as fact. Like, I made that up. I posted a fake ad on Craigslist.").

[61]   Craig Silverman, *This Analysis Shows How Viral Fake Election News Stories Outperformed Real News On Facebook,* BuzzFeed (Nov. 16, 2016), www.buzzfeed .com/craigsilverman/viral-fake-election-news-outperformed-real-news-on-facebook ?utm_term=.snvv2WJzL#.brjMvgGOn ("In the final three months of the US presidential campaign, the top-performing fake election news stories on Facebook generated more engagement than the top stories from major news outlets such as the *New York Times, Washington Post, Huffington Post, NBC News,* and others, a *BuzzFeed News* analysis has found.").

[62]   Ciara Torres-Spelliscy, *20th Century Law Can't Regulate 21st Century Technology,* Brennan Ctr (Oct. 11, 2017), www.brennancenter.org/blog/20th-century -law-cannot-regulate-21st-century-technology.

[63]   Jennifer Calfas, *Google Is Changing Its Search Algorithm to Combat Fake News,* Fortune (Apr. 25, 2017); Kaya Yurieff, *Justin Bieber and Katy Perry among Twitter users hit hardest by follower purge,* CNN (July 13, 2018), https://money.cnn.com/ 2018/07/13/technology/twitter-purge-biggest-losers/index.html.

[64]   Mike Isaac, *Facebook Considering Ways to Combat Fake News, Mark Zuckerberg Says,* N.Y. Times (Nov. 20, 2016); Nick Wingfield, Mike Isaac and Katie Benner, *Google and Facebook Take Aim at Fake News Sites,* N.Y. Times (Nov. 14, 2016).

[65]   Frenkel, *et al., supra* note 40 ("… as the company's stock price plummeted and it faced a consumer backlash — Facebook went on the attack. While Mr. Zuckerberg has conducted a public apology tour in the last year, Ms. Sandberg has overseen an aggressive lobbying campaign to combat Facebook's critics, shift public anger toward rival companies and ward off damaging regulation."); Mike Murphy, *Facebook admits targeting George Soros after he criticized company,* MarketWatch (Nov. 21, 2018), www.marketwatch.com/story/facebook-admits-targeting-george-soros-after-he -criticized-company-2018-11-21.

[66]   Ken Wheaton, *Political Partisans Agree on One Thing: They Like Amazon,* Ad Age (Oct. 30, 2014), http://adage.com/article/campaign-trail/political-partisans-agree -thing-amazon/295642/ ("YouGov interviewed 600,000 people concerning a portfolio of 1,200 brands … Not surprisingly, *Fox News* (with a –28) came in last with Democrats and *MSNBC* (–31) last with Republicans."); Eli Pariser, The Filter Bubble: How the New Personalized Web Is Changing What We Read and How

source of misperceptions"[67] and "people with the most interest in political news hold the most skewed perceptions about party composition. …"[68] Political news tends to reinforce partisan differences.[69] Americans frequently live in self-reaffirming bubbles where the news comes from sources that reconfirm the viewers' preconceived world views.[70] This is sometimes known as identity-protective cognition.[71] This presents a democratic issue, since "[d]emocracy requires citizens to see things from one another's point of view, but instead we're more and more enclosed in our own bubbles. Democracy requires a reliance on shared facts; instead we're being offered parallel but separate universes."[72] Or as Jennifer Kavanagh and Michael D. Rich note in their report on *Truth Decay*:

> This tendency to hold on to existing beliefs and search for confirming information of these beliefs, also known as motivated reasoning, drives Truth Decay because

---

WE THINK WHAT THE INTERNET IS HIDING FROM YOU 88 (2011) ("[P]artisans of one political stripe tend not to consume the media of another.").

[67] Douglas Ahler & Gaurav Sood, *The Parties in our Heads: Misperceptions About Party Composition and Their Consequences*, 80(3) J. OF POLITICS, 964, 967 (Apr. 27, 2018), http://dx.doi.org/10.1086/697253.

[68] *Id.*

[69] John Fetto, *What Your TV Preferences Say About Your Politics*, EXPERIAN: MARKETING FORWARD BLOG (Nov. 15, 2010), www.experian.com/blogs/marketing -forward/2010/11/15/what-your-tv-preferences-say-about-your-politics/ ("Can the political leaning of a TV show's audience determine the success of the program? The answer is yes. Experian Simmons examined the political party registrations of viewers of over 700 television programs measured in the Spring 2010 … [R]egis-tered Republicans and Democrats, indeed, have different preferences in entertainment programs.").

[70] Evgeny Morozov, *Your Own Facts*, N.Y. TIMES (June 12, 2011), www.ny times.com/2011/06/12/books/review/book-review-the-filter-bubble-by-eli-pariser.html ("But while [Cass] Sunstein worried that citizens would deliberately use technology to over-customize what they read, [Eli] Pariser …, worries that technology companies are already silently doing this for us.").

[71] Dan M. Kahan, *Cultural Cognition as a Conception of the Cultural Theory of Risk*, HANDBOOK OF RISK THEORY, 725–59 (2012) ("Identity-protective cognition refers to the tendency of people to fit their views to those of others with whom they share some important, self-identifying commitments."); Kavanagh & Rich, *supra* note 34 ("Cognitive biases and the ways in which human beings process information and make decisions cause people to look for information, opinion, and analyses that confirm pre-existing beliefs, to weight experience more heavily than data and facts, and to rely on mental shortcuts and the beliefs of those in the same social networks when forming opinions and making decisions").

[72] PARISER, *supra* note 66, at 5; Dan M. Kahan *et al.*, *Culture and Identity-Protective Cognition: Explaining the White-Male Effect in Risk Perception*, 4 J. OF EMPIRICAL LEGAL STUDIES 465–505 (2007) ("Identifying conditions of information dissemination

it means that once a person forms a specific belief – whether it is based on fact, disinformation, or misinformation – that belief is likely to endure.[73]

Some information bubbles are more extreme than others. American film critic at the *New Yorker* "Pauline Kael famously commented, after the 1972 Presidential election, 'I live in a rather special world. I only know one person who voted for Nixon. Where they are I don't know. They're outside my ken.'"[74] In her bubble, Nixon voters did not even exist, so it was startling to her when Nixon won the election. And the scary thing is, conservatives and liberals often perceive the world very differently. Even if conservatives and liberals watch the exact same news stories (and break out of the self-reinforcing bubbles), they are still likely to have discordant interpretations of what they have witnessed.

In 2017, The Harris Poll not only showed that Democrats and Republicans have different views of on-air personalities, but also found:

> the divisive presidential election and the new [Trump] administration's proclaimed 'war on the media' has had an effect on how Democrats and Republicans respond to and view that sector,' said [Wendy] Salomon [vice president at The Harris Poll]. 'The media has become a lightning rod …'[75]

Predictably, *NPR* and *PBS* are liked more by liberals than conservatives.[76] But strangely, Trump's attacks on the media may be tanking one of the only news networks—*Fox News*—that gives him positive coverage. The Harris Poll also showed that "[c]onservatives have become more cautious of the media overall, including *Fox News*."[77]

Russian intelligence was another source of bogus news, injecting misinformation into the 2016 American election for its own nefarious purposes. As

---

that would exploit this effect in the context of real-world policy debates would enable citizens of diverse cultural persuasions to converge on facts that bear on their common welfare.").

[73]   Kavanagh & Rich, *supra* note 34.

[74]   Richard Brody, *My Oscar Picks*, NEW YORKER (2011).

[75]   *CEOs: We Have a Reputation Problem*, HARRIS POLL (Mar. 20, 2017), www .theharrispoll.com/business/CEO-Reputation-Problem.html.

[76]   *Brands of the Year: Trends Impacting the Brands We Love*, HARRIS POLL 23 (Apr. 2017), www.theharrispoll.com/equitrend-information/.

[77]   *Harris Poll Study Shows Political Effect On News Media Brand Equity*, HARRIS POLL (May 2, 2017), www.theharrispoll.com/business/Political-Effect-Media-Brand -Equity.html.

reported to the Senate Intelligence Committee, the Russian Internet Research Agency (IRA):

> ran numerous campaigns that targeted different segments of US Facebook and Instagram users, which were set up by the IRA. ... These personalized messages exposed US users to a wide range of disinformation and junk news linked to on external websites, including content designed to elicit outrage and cynicism.[78]

This campaign reached millions of Americans during the 2016 election. "In total, IRA content was shared by about 31 million users, liked by almost 39 million users, garnered almost 5.4 million emoji reactions, and generated almost 3.5 million comments."[79] And the Russian IRA used a range of tactics to spread misinformation to Americans, including computational propaganda:

> define[d] as the use of automation, algorithms, and big-data analytics to manipulate public life. ... The term [computational propaganda] encompasses issues to do with so-called 'fake news', the spread of misinformation on social media platforms, illegal data harvesting and micro-profiling, the exploitation of social media platforms for foreign influence operations, the amplification of hate speech or harmful content through fake accounts or political bots, and clickbait content for optimized social media consumption.[80]

Again, one of the reasons why the allegation that something is "fake news" is so effective is because completely bogus stories, including lots of conspiracy theories, that are floating out there online are being repackaged as news pieces. This is how a harebrained story about then-candidate Hillary Clinton led to a gunman showing up at a pizzeria in D.C. called Ping Pong Pizza.[81] According to his own take on events, gunman Edgar Maddison Welch was a hero:[82] he thought he was rescuing children from human traffickers.[83] But instead, he had fallen for a nonexistent conspiracy theory that had been ginned up to slander Clinton. Among others pushing this conspiracy was the Russian IRA.[84] This

---

[78]   Philip N. Howard, *et al.*, *The IRA, Social Media and Political Polarization in the United States, 2012–2018* 32 (2018).

[79]   *Id.*

[80]   *Id.* at 39.

[81]   Faiz Siddiqui & Susan Svrluga, *N.C. man told police he went to D.C. pizzeria with gun to investigate conspiracy*, WASH. POST (Dec. 4, 2016).

[82]   Adam Goldman, *The Comet Ping Pong Gunman Answers Our Reporter's Questions*, N.Y. TIMES (Dec. 7, 2016).

[83]   Amanda Robb, *Anatomy of a Fake News Scandal*, ROLLING STONE (Nov. 16, 2017).

[84]   Renee DiResta, *et al.*, *The Tactics & Tropes of the Internet Research Agency* 84 (2018) ("Other retweeted topics included Pizzagate ..."); *Id.* at 84 ("Some IRA Twitter personas promoted conspiratorial rumors by authentic influential accounts such as @

case shows how powerful a conspiracy theory can be if it is repeated though a network of trust. The alleged trafficked children were in a basement, according to the bogus news. In reality, Ping Pong Pizza doesn't have a basement. While Welch shot his gun in the pizzeria, fortunately, no one was hurt in what the press later dubbed derisively "Pizzagate." Welch, the Pizzagate gunman, was sentenced to four years in prison.[85]

So when the president accuses professional journalists of producing "fake news" when they are merely transcribing events as they happened, it is a powerful charge because it reminds readers of clearly bogus news that they have encountered in their newsfeeds on social media. And if the president calls CNN or the *New York Times* or the *Washington Post* "fake news" often enough, he can get at least the thousands of people who attend his political rallies to repeat the charge by breaking into chants of "Fake news! Fake news!"[86] And because he has the bully pulpit, the charge that these sources are "fake news" infects the brains of all who hear the charge, just like a jingle for a product that gets stuck in the mind by dint of brutal repetition. Trump does not just call journalists fake; for years, he has called members of the media "enemies of the people."[87] In an interview with *Axios*, President Trump defended his inflammatory statements.[88] Here's some of that exchange:

> **Axios on HBO:** You are the most powerful man in the world. And if you say that word—'enemy,' 'enemy,' 'enemy'—think about what enemy means.
> **Trump:** I think I'm doing a service [by attacking the press] when people write stories about me that are so wrong …
> **Axios on HBO:** Tens of thousands of people go into a stadium to listen to you, and then people go on social media and they get themselves so jazzed up. There's got

LatestAnonNews, which claimed 'Clinton Underground Child Sex Scandal to break in a couple hours. Happy 5th of November!'").

[85]   Erik Ortiz, *'Pizzagate' Gunman Edgar Maddison Welch Sentenced to Four Years in Prison*, NBC News (June 22, 2017), www.nbcnews.com/news/us-news/pizzagate-gunman-edgar-maddison-welch-sentenced-four-years-prison-n775621.

[86]   Ian Schwartz, *Trump Rally Crowd Chants "CNN Sucks" During Jim Acosta Live Shot*, Real Clear Politics (July 31, 2018), www.realclearpolitics.com/video/2018/07/31/trump_rally_crowd_chants_cnn_sucks_to_jim_acosta_during_live_shot.html.

[87]   Donald J. Trump, Twitter (Feb. 17, 2017 5:48 PM), https://twitter.com/realDonaldTrump/status/832708293516632065 ("The FAKE NEWS media (failing @nytimes, @NBCNews, @ABC, @CBS, @CNN) is not my enemy, it is the enemy of the American People!").

[88]   Marianne Worthington, *The Campaign Rhetoric of George Wallace in the 1968 Presidential Election*, Ucumberlands, www.ucumberlands.edu/downloads/academics/history/vol4/MarianneWorthington92.html ("Another favorite enemy of [George] Wallace were the 'anarchists.' As with the 'law and order' phrase, 'anarchists' was a similar catch-all term that could mean students, liberals, the press, militants, etc., depending on the occasion.").

to be a part of you that's like: 'Dammit, I'm scared that someone is gonna take it too far.'

Trump: It's my only form of fighting back. I wouldn't be here if I didn't do that.[89]

This phrase "enemy of the people" is right out of the dictator's playbook. Dictators like Stalin, Hitler and Mao also said the press was the "enemy of the people."[90] And at least one Trump supporter appeared to take him seriously. A Florida man named Cesar Sayoc stands accused of mailing pipe bombs to CNN, two ex-presidents (Clinton and Obama), and other prominent Democrats on the eve of the 2018 midterm election.[91] None of the bombs exploded. But according to the director of the FBI, Christopher Wray, this was not for lack of trying:

> We [the FBI] can confirm that 13 IEDs [improvised explosive devices] were sent to various individuals across the country. Each device consisted of roughly six inches of PVC pipe, a small clock, a battery, some wiring, and what is known as 'energetic material,' which is essentially potential explosives and material that gives off heat and energy through a reaction to heat, shock, or friction. Though we're still analyzing the devices in our Laboratory, these are not hoax devices.[92]

In other words, these were not fake bombs that were only meant to scare the recipients, who had all been criticized by the president. These were real bombs, albeit poorly made, and all involved were lucky that they didn't explode.

And even more tragically, on the eve of the 2018 midterm election—after the president claimed, without any evidence, that a caravan of migrants heading to the U.S. seeking asylum was funded by Jewish philanthropists—a man named Robert Bowers stepped into a synagogue in Pittsburg and killed 11 people who

---

[89] Jonathan Swan & Jim VandeHei, *Exclusive: Trump says supporters demand his red-hot rhetoric*, AXIOS (Nov. 1, 2018), www.axios.com/trump-axios-hbo-media-enemy-of-the-people-441ae349-3670-4f7d-b5d5-04d339a15f68.html.

[90] Marvin Kalb, *Trump's War on the Press, the New McCarthyism, and the Threat to American Democracy* (Sept. 25, 2018), www.brookings.edu/book/enemy-of-the-people/ ("dictators—notably, Stalin, Hitler, and Mao—had all denounced their critics, especially the press, as 'enemies of the people.'"); Emma Graham-Harrison, *"Enemy of the people": Trump's phrase and its echoes of totalitarianism*, GUARDIAN (Aug. 3, 2018) (quoting Nikita Khrushchev ("[Joseph] Stalin originated the concept 'enemy of the people ...'")

[91] Jason Hanna, *et al.*, *Bomb suspect arrest: What we know about Cesar Sayoc*, CNN (Oct. 26, 2018), www.cnn.com/2018/10/26/politics/suspicious-packages-arrest/index.html.

[92] Press Release, FBI, *FBI Director Christopher Wray's Remarks Regarding Arrest of Cesar Sayoc in Suspicious Package Investigation* (Oct. 26, 2018), www.fbi.gov/news/pressrel/press-releases/fbi-director-christopher-wrays-remarks-regarding-arrest-of-cesar-sayoc-in-suspicious-package-investigation.

were attending a *bris* on a Saturday.[93] The gunman had expressed virulently anti-Semitic views on social media and posted on *Gab* "at 9:49 a.m., just five minutes before police were notified of the shooting ... 'I can't sit by and watch my people get slaughtered,' Bowers wrote. 'Screw your optics, I'm going in.'"[94] The gunman particularly blamed HIAS, a Jewish group that has helped refugees resettle in America for over a century.[95] As Adam Serwer condemned in the pages of *The Atlantic*, "The apparent spark for the worst anti-Semitic massacre in American history was a racist hoax inflamed by a U.S. president seeking to help his party win a midterm election."[96]

4.   CODA: DEEP FAKES

The war over facts and what is real is poised to go into overdrive as the world deals with the technology of "deep fakes," in which videos are cleverly altered so that individuals appear to do and say things that never happened.[97] Right now, this is largely used to place the faces of celebrities into porn movies, which is bad enough for the people involved.[98] But the technology has horrifying potential in the world of politics. Deep fakes have already been made of Trump:

> In May [2018], a video appeared on the internet of Donald Trump offering advice to the people of Belgium on the issue of climate change. 'As you know, I had the

---

[93]   Mark Scolforo & Mark Gillispie, *Pittsburgh synagogue massacre leaves 11 dead, 6 wounded*, AP (Oct. 27, 2018), www.apnews.com/23b04dc5e5af4 129b544ab50cbba3dd6.

[94]   Dakin Andone, Jason Hanna, Joe Sterling & Paul P. Murphy, *Hate crime charges filed in Pittsburgh synagogue shooting that left 11 dead*, CNN (Oct. 29, 2018), www .cnn.com/2018/10/27/us/pittsburgh-synagogue-active-shooter/index.html.

[95]   Masha Gessen, *Why the Tree of Life Shooter Was Fixated on the Hebrew Immigrant Aid Society*, NEW YORKER (Oct. 27, 2018).

[96]   Adam Serwer, *Trump's Caravan Hysteria Led to This. The president and his supporters insisted that several thousand Honduran migrants were a looming menace— and the Pittsburgh gunman took that seriously*, ATLANTIC (Oct. 28, 2018).

[97]   Samantha Cole, *Fake Porn Makers Are Worried About Accidentally Making Child Porn*, MOTHERBOARD (Feb. 27, 2018), https://motherboard.vice.com/en_us/ article/evmkxa/ai-fake-porn-deepfakes-child-pornography-emma-watson-elle-fanning ("This collection of images, or faceset, is used to train a machine learning algorithm to make a deepfake: a fake porn video that swaps Watson's face onto a porn performer's body, to make it look like she's having sex on video.").

[98]   Editorial Board, *A reason to despair about the digital future: Deepfakes*, WASH. POST (Jan. 6, 2019) ("A despairing prediction for the digital future came from an unlikely source recently. Speaking of 'deepfakes,' or media manipulated through artificial intelligence, the actress Scarlett Johansson told *The Post* that 'the Internet is a vast wormhole of darkness that eats itself.'").

balls to withdraw from the Paris climate agreement,' he said, looking directly into the camera, 'and so should you.'[99]

This video outraged many Belgians until it was revealed that the speech "was nothing more than a hi-tech forgery."[100] As Congressman Adam Schiff wrote to Director of National Intelligence Dan Coats:

> Hyper-realistic digital forgeries—popularly referred to as 'deep fakes'—use sophisticated machine learning techniques to produce convincing depictions of individuals doing or saying things they never did, without their consent or knowledge. By blurring the line between fact and fiction, deep fake technology could undermine public trust in recorded images and videos as objective depictions of reality.[101]

And the U.S. military, for one, is taking the threat of deep fakes seriously.[102]

Buzzfeed used video of former President Obama and comic impersonator Jordan Peele to make a public service announcement (PSA) about deep fakes. One of the only tells that the fake Obama in the *Buzzfeed* PSA is a forgery is that Peele says at the end of the video, "Stay woke, bitches"—something the real Barack "No Drama" Obama would not say. The PSA also split-screens Peele and fake Obama so that it is obvious that Peele is voicing the fake. The PSA issues a serious warning, using the fake Obama voiced by Peele, that "these are dangerous times. We have to be more vigilant about what we trust from the internet."[103]

---

[99] Oscar Schwartz, *You thought fake news was bad? Deep fakes are where truth goes to die*, GUARDIAN (Nov. 12, 2018).

[100] *Id.*

[101] Letter from Adam B. Schiff, Stephanie Murphy & Carlos Carbelo, Representatives, to Dan Coats, Director of National Intelligence (Sept. 13, 2018), https://schiff.house .gov/imo/media/doc/2018-09%20ODNI%20Deep%20Fakes%20letter.pdf.

[102] Taylor Hatmaker, *DARPA is funding new tech that can identify manipulated videos and 'deepfakes'*, TECH CRUNCH (Apr. 30, 2018), https://techcrunch.com/ 2018/04/30/deepfakes-fake-videos-darpa-sri-international-media-forensics/ ("SRI International has been awarded three contracts by the Pentagon's Defense Advanced Research Projects Agency (DARPA) to wage war on the newest front in fake news. Specifically, DARPA's Media Forensics program is developing tools capable of identifying when videos and photos have been meaningfully altered from their original state in order to misrepresent their content.").

[103] Ryan Whitwam, *Buzzfeed Created a 'Deepfake' Obama PSA Video*, EXTREME TECH (Apr. 18, 2018), www.extremetech.com/extreme/267771-buzzfeed-created-a -deepfake-obama-psa-video.

5.   CONCLUSION

Does it matter if Trump calls facts fakes and fake news facts? And to be clear, Trump does both things: he spreads false conspiracy theories as if they were facts and slanders truth as "fake." It matters in at least this sense: an authoritarian who insists that others parrot his lies is a very dangerous thing indeed. Because then to be thought loyal, citizens must give up their own sense of what is true to the authoritarian. And without facts as anchors, challenging an authoritarian's grip on power becomes much more difficult.

If Trump is using this branding technique on purpose, then watch out. He likely knows from commercial branding that:

> studies show that repeated exposure to an opinion makes people believe the opinion is more prevalent, even if the source of that opinion is only a single person. So not only do consumers remember a statement that gets repeated, they are more likely to believe it, and think it is the popular opinion.[104]

In other words, not only will more people remember a lie like "fake news" if they hear it enough times, but many will also start to believe it.

---

[104] Jeffry Pilcher, *Say It Again: Messages Are More Effective When Repeated,* FINANCIAL BRAND (Sept. 23, 2014), https://thefinancialbrand.com/42323/advertising -marketing-messages-effective-frequency/.

8. Branding treason

"Patriotism is the last refuge of the scoundrel." Samuel Johnson (1775).

1. INTRODUCTION

One of President Trump's core rhetorical claims, both during his campaign for president and in the early years of his presidency, is that he would put "America First."[1] In his inaugural address, he proclaimed:

> From this moment on, it's going to be *America First*. Every decision on trade, on taxes, on immigration, on foreign affairs, will be made to benefit American workers and American families. ... America will start winning again, winning like never before. ... We will follow two simple rules: Buy American and Hire American.[2]

In a speech to the United Nations, Trump said, "We reject globalism and embrace the doctrine of patriotism."[3] At a campaign rally in Houston, he told a cheering crowd, "I'm a nationalist!"[4] If Trump the businessman was a master at commercial branding, then Trump the politician is trying his hand at political branding. And here he is clearly trying to cement the idea in the minds of the public through brute repetition that he is "patriotic." Previous presidents didn't make this move. The last president to repeat the "America First" slogan *ad nauseum* was Woodrow Wilson and he didn't really mean it.[5]

---

[1] Dan Roberts, *Donald Trump unveils "America first" foreign policy plan*, GUARDIAN (Apr. 27, 2016).

[2] Donald J. Trump, *The Inaugural Address* (Jan. 20, 2017), www.whitehouse.gov/briefings-statements/the-inaugural-address/.

[3] W.J. Hennigan, *"We Reject Globalism." President Trump Took "America First" to the United Nations*, TIME (Sept. 25, 2018), http://time.com/5406130/we-reject-globalism-president-trump-took-america-first-to-the-united-nations/.

[4] Jason Le Miere, *Donald Trump Says "I'm A Nationalist, Use That Word" at Texas Rally For Ted Cruz*, NEWSWEEK (Oct. 22, 2018), www.newsweek.com/donald-trump-nationalist-texas-rally-1182223.

[5] Sean Illing, *How "America First" ruined the "American dream,"* VOX (Oct. 22, 2018), www.vox.com/2018/10/22/17940964/america-first-trump-sarah-churchwell-american-dream (quoting Sarah Churchwell) ("So Wilson was using America First as a way to maneuver his way through a political minefield ...").

While President Trump is branding patriotism, he is simultaneously branding treason. President Trump has outrageously claimed that when the two
papers of record report accurate, but negative stories about him, that they are
guilty of treason. As President Trump said at a campaign rally, "'You look at
the *Washington Post* ... I can never get a good story ... [I]s it subversion? Is it
treason?'"[6] After the *New York Times* published an anonymous op-ed written
by someone in the Trump administration criticizing the president,[7] the president tweeted: "TREASON?"[8]

Trump might want to be more careful in accusing American citizens of
treason. As the Supreme Court noted in *Cramer v. U.S.*, there's an ugly history
of men in power falsely accusing their enemies of treason: "the basic law of
treason in this country was framed by men who ... were taught by experience
and by history to fear abuse of the treason charge almost as much as they
feared treason itself."[9] They built this concern into the U.S. Constitution.
Treason is defined narrowly by Article III, Section 3:

> Treason against the United States, shall consist only in levying War against them,
> or in adhering to their Enemies, giving them Aid and Comfort. No Person shall be
> convicted of Treason unless on the Testimony of two Witnesses to the same overt
> Act, or on Confession in open Court.[10]

Because of this restrictive Constitutional definition, treason is rarely charged
as a crime and essentially has not been used by prosecutors since the middle
of the twentieth century.[11] Some of the rare treason prosecutions include those
of poet Ezra Pound and Tokyo Rose.[12] Any person who could be charged with

---

[6] Glenn Kessler, *Anatomy of a Trump rally*, WASH. POST (Sept. 12, 2018) (quoting
Trump).

[7] Anonymous, *I Am Part of the Resistance Inside the Trump Administration I work
for the president but like-minded colleagues and I have vowed to thwart parts of his
agenda and his worst inclinations.*, N.Y. TIMES (Sept. 5, 2018).

[8] @realdonaldtrump, TWITTER (Sept. 5, 2018), https://twitter.com/
realDonaldTrump/status/1037464177269514240?ref_src=twsrc%5Etfw%7Ctwcamp
%5Etweetembed%7Ctwterm%5E1037464177269514240&ref_url=https%3A%2F
%2Fwww.vox.com%2F2018%2F9%2F5%2F17825062%2Fnew-york-times-trump-op
-ed-treason.

[9] Cramer v. United States, 325 U.S. 1, 21 (1945).

[10] U.S. Constitution, Art. III, Sec. 3; Cramer, 325 U.S. at 29 ("the crime of
treason consists of two elements: adherence to the enemy; and rendering him aid and
comfort.").

[11] Pamela J. Podger, *Few ever charged or convicted of treason in U.S. History*,
SFGATE.COM (Dec. 9, 2001), www.sfgate.com/crime/article/Few-ever-charged-or
-convicted-of-treason-in-U-S-2843242.php ("treason charges have been brought fewer
than 30 times.").

[12] *Id.*

treason has probably been guilty of lesser crimes that are easier to prove. John Walker Lindh—better known as the American Taliban—was charged with material support for terrorism, not treason.[13] And Yaser Hamdi, an American held as an enemy combatant (2001–04) in the War on Terror, was also not charged with treason.[14]

The Supreme Court has made clear that convictions for treason require affirmative acts to aid and abet an enemy. "Thought crimes" are not treason. Merely being critical of the government is protected free speech under the First Amendment.[15] But the lack of actual prosecutions for treason for decades does not take the rhetorical punch out of calling someone a traitor. For example, on May 14, 2018, Trump tweeted angrily that White House leakers were "traitors and cowards … !"[16] He has also called lawmakers who did not stand for him during his State of the Union "un-American:" "Somebody said treasonous … Why not? Can we call that treason?"[17]

Meanwhile, as Trump wraps himself in the flag and accuses people who disagree with him of treason, from 2017–19 multiple investigations have looked at Russian interference in the 2016 presidential election to help elect Donald Trump president. At the sentencing of Trump's former National Security Adviser Michael Flynn, the judge asked the prosecution if they could charge Flynn with treason.[18] This raised eyebrows because the judge had seen redacted filings that the public has not. The question remains: what prompted this judge's query about Flynn's potential treason?

---

[13]   Dan De Luce, Robbie Gramer & Jana Winter, *John Walker Lindh, Detainee #001 in the Global War On Terror, Will Go Free In Two Years.*, FOREIGN POLICY (June 23, 2017) ("Lindh was charged with providing material support for terrorism.").

[14]   Hamdi v. Rumsfeld, 542 U.S. 507, 540 (2004) (Justice Souter Dissenting) ("the Government has not charged him with espionage, treason, or any other crime under domestic law.").

[15]   Cramer, 325 U.S. at 29 ("A citizen … may … harbor sympathies … disloyal to this country's policy …, but so long as he commits no act of aid and comfort to the enemy, there is no treason.").

[16]   @realdonaldtrump, Twitter (May 14, 2018), https://twitter.com/ realDonaldTrump/status/996129630913482755?ref_src=twsrc%5Etfw%7Ctwcamp %5Etweetembed%7Ctwterm%5E996129630913482755&ref_url=https%3A%2F %2Fwww.washingtonpost.com%2Fnews%2Fthe-fix%2Fwp%2F2018%2F05%2F15 %2Ftrump-keeps-lowering-the-bar-for-what-constitutes-treason-which-may-not-be-a -great-idea%2F.

[17]   Aaron Blake, *Trump keeps throwing around the word "treason"*, WASH. POST (May 15, 2018).

[18]   USA v. Flynn, CR 17-232 at 36 (Dec. 18, 2018) (Transcript of Sentencing Proceedings), www.justsecurity.org/wp-content/uploads/2018/12/121818am-USA-v -Michael-Flynn-Sentencing.pdf.

One of the big open questions around the Trump campaign in 2016 is whether anyone was doing anything that a layperson would call "treasonous" or which would fit the Constitutional definition of treason. For a candidate who prided himself on touting "America First," there were a lot of foreigners in and around the Trump campaign.[19] Indeed, Special Counsel Robert Mueller found at least 140 contacts between the Trump campaign and Russians alone, but he did not find sufficient evidence of a criminal conspiracy between the campaign and the Russians to indict members of the campaign.[20]

First, this chapter will look at the vulnerabilities that make American democracy susceptible to foreign manipulation. Then this chapter will look at the actions of Cambridge Analytica, a subsidiary of a British firm retained by the Trump campaign. Finally, this chapter will examine one sliver of the Trump/Russia story that has received less attention: essentially, how did a 29-year-old, red-headed alleged Russian spy and her Russian boss end up at the National Prayer Breakfast attended by President Trump?

2.   AMERICAN DEMOCRACY'S VULNERABILITY TO DISRUPTION

In order to assess what happened in 2016, it is worth thinking about the state of American elections before 2016. Many states ran elections using dated technologies. The last big infusion of federal investment in elections infrastructure had been under the Help America Vote Act in 2002.

"White hat"—that is, benign—hackers have been warning the public about the vulnerabilities in voting technology for years. Fortune smiled on these technological whistleblowers when a storm blew into Dane County, Wisconsin and caused the roof on a building where voting machines were stored to col-

---

[19]   Carole Cadwalladr & Emma Graham-Harrison, *Staff claim Cambridge Analytica ignored US ban on foreigners working on elections*, GUARDIAN (Mar. 17, 2018); Erin Banco, *Rick Gates Tells Mueller About Trump Team's Dealings With Israeli Intelligence Firm*, DAILY BEAST (Jan. 16, 2019), www.thedailybeast.com/rick-gates-tells-mueller -about-trump-teams-dealings-with-israeli-intelligence-firm; Grace Panetta, *Here are all the known contacts between the Trump campaign and Russian government-linked people or entities*, BUSINESS INSIDER (Jan. 22, 2019), www.businessinsider.com/trump -campaign-russia-government-contact-timeline-2018-7.

[20]   Special Counsel Robert S. Mueller, *Report On The Investigation Into Russian Interference In The 2016 Presidential Election*, DEPARTMENT OF JUSTICE (Apr. 18, 2019), www.justice.gov/storage/report.pdf; John Walcott, *"Spot and Assess." The Intelligence Strategy Behind Russia's Political Outreach*, TIME (Apr. 25, 2019), https://time.com/5577630/mueller-report-maria-butina-donald-trump-outreach/ ("The Mueller report describes at least 140 meetings and other contacts between Russians and other individuals with ties to the Kremlin and 18 Trump's associates …").

lapse in 2016.[21] A few of the voting machines that were still in working order ended up on eBay, where they were purchased by the computer scientists who organize DEFCON, a huge computer hacking conference. [22]

Finding the machines on eBay was an important discovery because under normal circumstances, voting machines are protected by a miasma of trade secrets and contractual limitations. Voting machine manufacturers were unlikely to give white hat hackers unfettered access to the equipment and software, since an objective computer scientist might point out flaws in the technology. State elections officials would also be unable to provide open access to white hat hackers because of restrictive covenants in their contracts with the voting technology manufacturers.[23]

Even possession of the voting machines physically didn't mean they had the right to pull them apart to look at the underlying hardware and software. Computer scientists are normally barred from hacking voting machines under the Digital Millennium Copyright Act (DMCA).[24] But as luck would have it, in 2015 the Library of Congress, which has certain powers under the DMCA, issued a three-year exemption for research to investigate the security of voting machines.[25]

The major story out of the 2017 DEFCON25 conference of white hat hackers was a Voting Village in which computer scientists and conference attendees were invited to penetrate more than 25 pieces of election equipment, including voting machines and electronic poll books.[26] The report from DEFCON25 was grim:

> By the end of the conference, every piece of equipment in the Voting Village was effectively breached in some manner. Participants with little prior knowledge and

---

[21] Jeff Glaze, *Flooding causes replacement of Madison's voting machines*, WISC. STATE J. (July 30, 2016), https://madison.com/wsj/news/local/govt-and-politics/ flooding-causes-replacement-of-madison-s-voting-machines-puts-clerk/article _91fcaaa1-5f31-5e52-8853-a1ff1046ed69.html.

[22] *Voting Machine Security*, C-SPAN (Oct. 10, 2017), www.c-span.org/video/ ?435437-1/def-con-hacking-report-warns-voting-machines-vulnerability.

[23] Ciara Torres-Spelliscy, *Why Federalism Keeps Me Up At Night*, BRENNAN CTR (Mar. 28, 2018), www.brennancenter.org/blog/why-federalism-keeps-me-night.

[24] Digital Millennium Copyright Act of 1998, Pub. L. 105-304 (Oct. 28, 1998).

[25] U.S. Copyright Office, Library of Congress, 208 Fed. Reg. 65944 (Oct. 28, 2015) (Exemption to Prohibition on Circumvention of Copyright Protection Systems for Access Control Technologies), www.govinfo.gov/content/pkg/FR-2015-10-28/pdf/ 2015-27212.pdf.

[26] Matt Blaze, *et al.*, *DEFCON 25 Voting Machine Hacking Village Report on Cyber Vulnerabilities in U.S. Election Equipment, Databases, and Infrastructure* (Sept. 2017), www.defcon.org/images/defcon-25/DEF%20CON%2025%20voting %20village%20report.pdf.

only limited tools and resources were quite capable of undermining the confidentiality, integrity, and availability of these systems.[27]

One of the things that troubled the computer scientists at DEFCON is that many of the parts inside voting technologies were foreign manufactured. Accordingly, foreign actors could build backdoors into voting technologies in future American elections.

For years, elections reformers and computer scientists have advocated replacing "paperless" voting machines with those that produce a paper ballot.[28] Unfortunately, 44 million registered voters in states such as Georgia, Pennsylvania and Virginia still relied on paperless machines in 2016. The purpose of having paper ballots is to run risk-limiting audits to check that the computers are counting votes correctly. One silver lining is the 2018 omnibus budget contained $380 million to help secure American elections.[29] Whether that money will be spent strategically to address the paperless machine problem is an open question.[30]

3. BEFORE WE GET TO THE RUSSIANS, LET'S TALK ABOUT THE BRITS AT CAMBRIDGE ANALYTICA

The first set of curious foreigners in the Trump campaign were from a company called Cambridge Analytica. The Cambridge Analytica controversy could not have happened without Facebook's change in policy in 2010:

> In April 2010, Facebook announced the launch of a platform called Open Graph … [which] allowed external developers to reach out to Facebook users and request permission to access a large chunk of their personal data — and, crucially, to access their Facebook friends' personal data too.[31]

---

[27] *Id.*

[28] Lawrence Norden & Ian Vandewalker, *Securing Elections From Foreign Interference*, BRENNAN CTR (June 29, 2017), www.brennancenter.org/publication/securing-elections-foreign-interference.

[29] Dustin Volz, *U.S. spending bill to provide $380 million for election cyber security*, REUTERS (Mar. 21, 2018), https://af.reuters.com/article/worldNews/idAFKBN1GX1Z7.

[30] Ciara Torres-Spelliscy, *You Know Election Systems* Are in *Trouble When It Takes* an *11-Year-Old 10 Minutes* to *Change* the *Results*, BRENNAN CTR (Aug. 14, 2018), www.brennancenter.org/blog/def-con-hackers-illustrate-potential-vulnerabilities-in-election-systems.

[31] Sam Meredith, *Facebook-Cambridge Analytica: A timeline of the data hijacking scandal*, CNBC (Apr. 10, 2018), www.cnbc.com/2018/04/10/facebook-cambridge-analytica-a-timeline-of-the-data-hijacking-scandal.html.

App developers like Aleksandr Kogan used Open Graph to harvest data. Kogan created an app called "thisisyourdigitallife" in 2013. "The app prompted users to answer questions for a psychological profile. Almost 300,000 users were thought to have been paid to take the psychological test. ..."[32] Essentially, if a person used "thisisyourdigitallife," he exposed to Kogan his own data *and* that of any of his Facebook friends with a low privacy setting.

Simultaneously in 2013, Alexander Nix worked at a British company called Strategic Communications Laboratories (SCL).[33] U.K. citizen Nix connected with Canadian Christopher Wylie and they developed what they referred to as psychographic profiling, which paired personality information with traditional microtargeting information to influence people's voting behavior.[34] Nix was introduced to Americans Steve Bannon and billionaire Robert Mercer and pitched them on this idea. Mercer agreed to give Nix seed money to test the concept on the Virginia governor's race.

Even though the Mercer-backed candidate lost in Virginia, apparently Mercer was sufficiently satisfied and invested $15 million with Nix to spin off Cambridge Analytica. Bannon was vice president and secretary of Cambridge Analytica's board.[35] In 2014, Cambridge Analytica teamed up with Kogan. Using his personality quiz, Cambridge Analytica "harvested private information from the Facebook profiles of more than 50 million users without their permission ... making it one of the largest data leaks in the social network's history."[36] Later reporting has placed the breach at impacting 87 million Facebook users. By 2016, Cambridge Analytica claimed to have profiles with several thousand data points for 220 million Americans,[37] including the ability to assign them into "32 distinct personality types."[38]

Many of the political entities that used Cambridge Analytica had also received financial support from the Mercers. According to the *Wall St. Journal*,

---

[32]   *Id.*

[33]   Nicholas Confessore & Danny Hakim, *Data Firm Says "Secret Sauce" Aided Trump*, N.Y. Times (Mar. 6, 2017) ("Cambridge's parent company ... has a long record of trying to understand and influence behavior. Founded in 1993 by a former British adman, the firm has worked for companies and candidates around the world ...").

[34]   Matthew Rosenberg, Nicholas Confessore & Carole Cadwalladr, *How Trump Consultants Exploited the Facebook Data of Millions*, N.Y. Times (Mar. 17, 2018) ("Wylie was interested in using inherent psychological traits to affect voters' behavior and had assembled a team of psychologists and data scientists ...").

[35]   Matea Gold, *The Mercers and Stephen Bannon: How a populist power base was funded and build*, Wash. Post (Mar. 17, 2017).

[36]   Rosenberg, Confessore & Cadwalladr, *supra* note 34.

[37]   Jane Mayer, *The Reclusive Hedge-Fund Tycoon Behind the Trump Presidency*, New Yorker (Mar. 27, 2017).

[38]   Confessore & Hakim, *supra* note 33.

"Most of the 20 organizations that reported having hired Cambridge Analytica ... also received donations from Mr. Mercer."[39] This was true of Super PACs supporting Trump in 2016. As Matea Gold reported, the Mercer-funded Super PAC Make America Number 1 directed "$5.5 million to Cambridge Analytica for consulting, data and ads. Cambridge was also paid at least $6 million for the work it did helping the Trump campaign identify and target voters. ... "[40] In other words, the Mercers would support a political committee and then that same committee would indirectly pay some of the money back by hiring the Mercer's company, Cambridge Analytica. And there were millions flowing through the firm.[41]

Part of what Cambridge Analytica did was test out what messages resonated with voters, including ones that would become central themes in the Trump campaign, like "build a wall," "drain the swamp" and even the "deep state."[42] As Wylie explained:

> [In 2014 Cambridge Analytica was] testing all kinds of messages and all kinds of imagery — that included images of walls, people scaling walls, we tested 'drain the swamp,' testing ideas of the 'deep state.' ... And a lot of these narratives, which at the time would have seemed crazy for a mainstream candidate to run on, those were the things that we were finding that there were pockets of Americans who this really appealed to. And Steve Bannon knew that, because we were doing the research on it. And I was surprised when I saw the Trump campaign and it started ... talking about building walls or draining the swamp.[43]

Ironically, some of the themes that are now thought of as signature Trump catchphrases were concocted years before he was a declared candidate in the bowels of Cambridge Analytica. According to author Joshua Green, political consultants Sam Nunberg and Roger Stone used the phrase "build a wall" as a mnemonic device to remind candidate Trump to talk about immigration.[44] Two years into Trump's presidency, the phrase "build a wall" took on a grim life of its own. Trump closed the government for 35 days in a vain attempt to

---

[39]   Sam Schechner, Jenny Gross & Rebecca Ballhaus, *Cambridge Analytica CEO Promised More Than He Delivered, Clients Say*, WALL ST. J. (Mar. 28, 2018).

[40]   Gold, *supra* note 35.

[41]   Schechner, *et al.*, *supra* note 39.

[42]   Emily Tillett, *Christopher Wylie: Bannon wanted "weapons" to fight a "culture war" at Cambridge Analytica*, CBS NEWS (May 16, 2018).

[43]   *Cambridge Analytica was testing campaign themes in 2014, whistleblower says*, WEEK (Mar. 20, 2018), http://theweek.com/speedreads/761935/cambridge-analytica-testing-trump-campaign-themes-2014-whistleblower-says (quoting Wylie).

[44]   Stuart Anderson, *Where The Idea For Donald Trump's Wall Came From*, FORBES (Jan. 4, 2019), www.forbes.com/sites/stuartanderson/2019/01/04/where-the-idea-for-donald-trumps-wall-came-from/#4d887ada4415.

try to get Congressional funding to build his wall. Then, he declared a national emergency to get funding for the wall by diverting it from other government programs. This declaration prompted multiple lawsuits to stop him.[45]

Cambridge Analytica had worked for Ted Cruz's 2016 presidential campaign. After Cruz flamed out in his run for president in 2016, Brad Parscale, the head of the Trump campaign's data team, hired Cambridge Analytica.[46] When Trump's campaign manager Paul Manafort resigned, the Mercers filled the power vacuum he left.[47] As a result, Bannon, the Mercers' man, became the chief executive of the Trump campaign, while Kellyanne Conway, the Mercers' woman, became the Trump campaign manager.[48] As pollster Celinda Lake (who has co-authored a book with Conway) noted, "remember Kellyanne Conway is an expert pollster."[49] Officially, Bannon wasn't paid by the Trump campaign. Rather, the Mercers' Super PAC paid $5 million to Cambridge Analytica, which shared an address with Bannon Strategic Advisors, Bannon's company.[50] Theresa Hong, who worked with Parscale, told the BBC that Cambridge Analytica helped the Trump campaign target "universes" of voters with nearly $85 million in Facebook ads. She noted that 35 000–40 000 versions of a political ad could be sent out at the same time.[51]

At times, the Trump campaign has downplayed the role of Cambridge Analytica—essentially saying it wasn't relied on heavily. A *Forbes* piece that ran right after the 2016 election stated:

> [Jared] Kushner's crew was able to tap into the Republican National Committee's data machine, and it hired targeting partners like Cambridge Analytica to map voter

---

[45] Damian Paletta, *et al.*, *National emergency: Lawsuits launched in bid to stop Trump building border wall*, INDEPENDENT (Feb. 17, 2019). The Ninth Circuit has so far stopped President Trump's attempt to fund the wall through an emergency declaration. *See* Sierra Club v. Trump, Nos. 19-16102, 19-16299, & 19-16300 (9th Cir. July 3, 2019), http://cdn.ca9.uscourts.gov/datastore/general/2019/07/03/19-16102-order.pdf.

[46] Confessore & Hakim, *supra* note 33 ("Cambridge Analytica, claimed to have … 'psychographic' profiles that could predict the … hidden political leanings of every American adult.").

[47] Mayer, *supra* note 37 ("Manafort was forced to resign, after the press reported his links to Ukrainian oligarchs. In the vacuum, the Mercers soon established control over the Trump campaign.").

[48] Maggie Haberman & Jonathan Martin, *Paul Manafort Quits Donald Trump's Campaign After a Tumultuous Run*, N.Y. TIMES (Aug. 19, 2016).

[49] Interview with Celinda Lake (Sept. 7, 2018).

[50] Mayer, *supra* note 37 ("Although Bannon was running Trump's campaign, … it appears to have paid him nothing.").

[51] *The digital guru who helped Donald Trump to the presidency*, BBC (Aug. 13, 2017), www.bbc.com/news/av/magazine-40852227/the-digital-guru-who-helped-donald-trump-to-the-presidency (quoting Ms. Hong).

universes and identify which parts of the Trump platform mattered most: trade, immigration or change.[52]

A leaked Cambridge Analytica presentation purported to show the impact of Cambridge Analytica on the 2016 election, declaring: "Intensive survey research, data modelling and performance-optimising algorithms were used to target 10,000 different ads to different audiences. ... The ads were viewed billions of times, according to the presentation."[53] Nix bragged about how Cambridge Analytica provided the "secret sauce" that allowed Trump to win. Nix said: "'We did all the research, all the data, all the analytics, all the targeting, we ran all the digital campaign, the television campaign and our data informed all the strategy.'" [54]Cambridge Analytica, which has been called a "propaganda machine," has worked in elections all over the world.[55] While it was working for multiple U.S. presidential campaigns, it also worked on the Leave side of the Brexit vote in the U.K.[56]

Wylie testified to the U.S. Senate that Cambridge Analytica:

> sought to identify mental and emotional vulnerabilities in certain subsets of the American population and worked to exploit those vulnerabilities by targeting information designed to activate some of the worst characteristics in people, such as neuroticism, paranoia and racial biases.[57]

Wylie also testified, "If it suited the client's objective, the firm was eager to capitalise on discontent and to stoke ethnic tensions."[58] Microtargeted political ads are particularly pernicious if the point is to discourage voting.[59] Wylie

---

[52]   Steven Bertoni, *Exclusive Interview: How Jared Kushner Won Trump the White House*, FORBES (Nov. 22, 2016).

[53]   Paul Lewis & Paul Hilder, *Leaked: Cambridge Analytica's blueprint for Trump victory*, GUARDIAN (Mar. 23, 2018).

[54]   *Exposed: Undercover secrets of Trump's data firm*, CHANNEL 4 (Mar. 20, 2018), www.channel4.com/news/exposed-undercover-secrets-of-donald-trump-data-firm-cambridge-analytica.

[55]   Mayer, *supra* note 37.

[56]   *Id.*

[57]   *Id.*

[58]   *Id.*

[59]   Donnie O'Sullivan & Drew Griffin, *Cambridge Analytica ran voter suppression campaigns, whistleblower claims*, CNN (May 17, 2018), www.cnn.com/2018/05/16/politics/cambridge-analytica-congress-wylie/index.html ("Wylie told *CNN* that although he did not take part in voter suppression activities, he alleged that African-Americans were particular targets of Cambridge Analytica's 'voter disengagement tactics ...'").

also told Congress, "under Bannon's leadership at Cambridge Analytica, U.S. clients could request testing voter suppression efforts in their contracts."[60]

In 2018, Wylie said, reflecting back on his time at Cambridge Analytica:

> if you want to fundamentally change society, you first have to break it. It's only when you break it is when you can remold the pieces into your vision of a new society. This [Cambridge Analytica] was the weapon that Steve Bannon wanted to build to fight his culture war.[61]

This is reminiscent of an admonition from PR guru G. Edward Pendray, who once said, "To public-relations men must go the most important social engineering role of them all—the gradual reorganization of human society … structure by structure."[62]

One loose thread is whether any other firms were engaged to do similar work to Cambridge Analytica.[63] One firm under scrutiny is the Israeli firm Psy-Group,[64] whose motto is "Shape reality."[65] It pitched a multimillion dollar disinformation campaign to Donald Trump Jr.[66] at a meeting in Trump Tower along with George Nader, an advisor to the Crown Prince of the United Arab Emirates,[67] and Erik Prince, the brother of soon-to-be Secretary of Education Betsy DeVos.[68] At the time this book was written, Nader was cooperating with the special counsel's investigation.[69] And the redacted copy of the Mueller Report that was released to the public in April 2019 includes references to Nader and Prince, but several words around their names are deleted and hidden

---

[60] Tillett, *supra* note 42.

[61] *Cambridge Analytica whistleblower: 'We spent $1m harvesting millions of Facebook profiles' – video*, GUARDIAN (Mar. 17, 2018), www.theguardian.com/ uk-news/video/2018/mar/17/cambridge-analytica-whistleblower-we-spent-1m -harvesting-millions-of-facebook-profiles-video (quoting Wylie).

[62] VANCE PACKARD, THE HIDDEN PERSUADERS 217 (1969) (quoting G. Edward Pendray).

[63] Jonathan Sapsford, *Trump Tweets Special Counsel Investigation Getting "Ridiculous"*, WALL ST. J. (May 20, 2018).

[64] Simona Weinglass, David Horovitz & Raphael Ahren, *Israeli Firm Under FBI Scrutiny in Trump Probe Allegedly Targeted BDS Activists*, TIMES OF ISRAEL (June 6, 2018), www.timesofisrael.com/israeli-firm-under-fbi-scrutiny-in-trump-probe -allegedly-targeted-bds-activists/.

[65] Byron Tau & Rebecca Ballhaus, *Israeli Intelligence Company Formed Venture with Trump Campaign Firm Cambridge Analytica*, WALL ST. J. (May 23, 2018).

[66] Weinglass, Horovitz & Ahren, *supra* note 64.

[67] Sapsford, *supra* note 63.

[68] Mark Mazzetti, *et al.*, *Trump Inquiry Grows to Include Contacts in Gulf*, N.Y. TIMES (May 20, 2018).

[69] *Adviser to Emirates With Ties to Trump Aides Is Cooperating With Special Counsel*, N.Y. TIMES (Mar. 6, 2018).

under the words "Grand Jury;" thus, it is still unclear whether there is a particular crime at issue here.[70] Meanwhile, Nader was arrested in June of 2019 on unrelated child pornography charges.[71]

Psy-Group allegedly engages in untoward tactics. For instance, "[s]ome of Psy-Group's work involves setting up 'honey traps' …"[72] *The Wall St. Journal* reported that the special counsel has a presentation from Psy-Group that claims fake social media accounts helped Mr. Trump win the presidency.[73] The paper also reported, "The presentation outlines the ways in which social media 'bots' and fake online content were used to help energize voters supportive of Mr. Trump."[74]

Later, as secret tapes of Cambridge Analytica executives spilled into public view, the picture of the firm looked far less benign. The tapes were part of a sting by journalists at the U.K.'s Channel 4, who pretended to be interested in hiring Cambridge Analytica.[75] Nigel Oakes, the CEO of SCL (the parent company of Cambridge Analytica), was caught on tape saying, about the firm's work in the America in 2016:

> It's the things that resonate, sometimes to attack the other group and know that you are going to lose them is going to reinforce and resonate your group. Which is why … Hitler attacked the Jews, because he didn't have a problem with the Jews at all, but the people didn't like the Jews. … So he just leveraged an artificial enemy. Well that's exactly what Trump did. … Trump had the balls, and I mean, really the balls, to say what people wanted to hear.[76]

Nix was caught on tape saying that Cambridge Analytica also used a number of underhanded, if not illegal tactics.[77] According to Channel 4: "In one exchange, when asked about digging up material on political opponents, Mr. Nix said they

---

[70]   Mueller, *supra* note 20, at 151–56.

[71]   Morgan Chalfant & Jacqueline Thomsen, *Key Mueller figure George Nader charged with transporting child porn*, THE HILL (June 3, 2019), https://thehill .com/policy/national-security/446709-key-mueller-figure-george-nader-charged-with -transporting-child-porn.

[72]   Byron Tau & Rebecca Ballhaus, *Israeli Intelligence Firm's Election-Meddling Analysis Comes Under Mueller's Scrutiny*, WALL ST. J. (May 25, 2018).

[73]   *Id.*

[74]   *Id.*

[75]   *Id.*

[76]   Christopher Wylie, *Written Statement to the United States Senate Committee on the Judiciary in the Matter of Cambridge Analytica and Other Related Issues* (May 16, 2018), www.judiciary.senate.gov/imo/media/doc/05-16-18%20Wylie%20Testimony .pdf (quoting Oakes).

[77]   Issie Lapowsky, *Cambridge Analytica Execs Caught Discussing Extortion and Fake News*, WIRED (Mar. 19, 2018), www.wired.com/story/cambridge-analytica-execs -caught-discussing-extortion-and-fake-news/.

could 'send some girls around to the candidate's house,' adding that Ukrainian girls 'are very beautiful, I find that works very well.'"[78] Beyond that, Nix expressed "a willingness to help the purported 'client' disseminate lies. 'These are things that … it sounds a dreadful thing to say, but these are things that don't necessarily need to be true, as long as they're believed,' Nix said."[79]

In the tapes, Mark Turnbull, managing director of Cambridge Analytica, described "how the company created the 'Defeat Crooked Hilary' brand of attack ads [with handcuffs for the "oo"], that were funded by the Make America Number 1 super-PAC and watched more than 30 million times during the campaign."[80] In a separate November 2017 meeting filmed by Channel 4:

> Turnbull appears to admit that the company is in the business of preying on people's fears. 'Our job is to … drop the bucket further down the well than anybody else, to understand what are those really deep-seated underlying fears. … It's no good fighting an election campaign on the facts because actually it's all about emotion …'"[81]

In March 2018, after the Channel 4 tapes surfaced, Mr. Nix was expelled from the company.[82] Cambridge Analytica went out of business in May 2018.[83] But many of the same people have now moved to a firm called Emerdata.[84] Another firm started at the same time by the same people is called Firecrest Technologies Ltd.[85] So Cambridge Analytica (a tainted brand) has turned into new brands Emerdata and Firecrest. According to press reports, Psy-Group has been shut down.[86] Whether it will rebrand is unknown.

---

[78] *Revealed: Trump's election consultants filmed saying they use bribes and sex workers to entrap politicians*, CHANNEL 4 (Mar. 19, 2018), www.channel4.com/news/cambridge-analytica-revealed-trumps-election-consultants-filmed-saying-they-use-bribes-and-sex-workers-to-entrap-politicians-investigation.

[79] Lapowsky, *supra* note 77.

[80] *Exposed: Undercover secrets of Trump's data firm*, *supra* note 54.

[81] Lapowsky, *supra* note 77.

[82] Adam Edelman, *Cambridge Analytica CEO Alexander Nix suspended amid hidden-camera expose*, NBC NEWS (Mar. 20, 2018), www.nbcnews.com/politics/politics-news/cambridge-analytica-ceo-alexander-nix-suspended-amid-hidden-camera-expose-n858406.

[83] Olivia Solon & Oliver Laughland, *Cambridge Analytica closing after Facebook data harvesting scandal*, GUARDIAN (May 2, 2018).

[84] Shaun Nichols, *Cambridge Analytica dismantled for good? Nope: It just changed its name to Emerdata*, REGISTER (May 2, 2018), www.theregister.co.uk/2018/05/02/cambridge_analytica_shutdown/.

[85] Wendy Siegelman, *Cambridge Analytica is dead – but its obscure network is alive and well*, GUARDIAN (July 18, 2018).

[86] Amarelle Wenkert, *Israeli Company Investigated by Robert Mueller's Team Shuts Down*, CALCALIST (May 21, 2018), www.calcalistech.com/ctech/articles/0,7340,L-3738491,00.html.

Cambridge Analytica and the American campaigns it worked on may be investigated for possible violations of the prohibition on foreign nationals being involved in federal elections.[87] As the Federal Election Commission (FEC) explains, participation by foreign nationals in decisions involving election-related activities is not allowed under federal law:

> Commission [FEC] regulations prohibit foreign nationals from … participating in the decision-making process of any person … with regard to any election-related activities. Such activities include, the making of contributions, donations, expenditures, or disbursements in connection with any federal or nonfederal elections in the United States. … Foreign nationals are also prohibited from involvement in the management of a political committee …[88]

Consequently, the use of Cambridge Analytica by the Trump campaign may have run afoul of this foreign national prohibition if significant control or decision-making resided with British subjects like Nix.[89] There is evidence that the Mercers were warned about this legal problem: "Mr. Mercer's daughter, Rebekah, a board member, Mr. Bannon and Mr. Nix received warnings from their lawyer that it was illegal to employ foreigners in political campaigns …"[90] As the *New York Times* reported: "Most SCL employees and contractors were [foreign nationals]." [91]

Also according to the *Times*:

> In a memo to Mr. Bannon, Ms. Mercer and Mr. Nix, the lawyer, then at the firm Bracewell & Giuliani, warned that Mr. Nix would have to recuse himself from 'substantive management' of any clients involved in United States elections. The data firm would also have to find American citizens or green card holders, Mr. Levy wrote, 'to manage the work and decision-making functions, relative to campaign messaging and expenditures.'[92]

In 2018, the nonpartisan nonprofit group Common Cause filed complaints against Cambridge Analytica to the Department of Justice and the Federal

---

[87]   52 U.S.C. § 30121; 11 CFR 110.20; Carole Cadwalladr, *Mueller questions Cambridge Analytica director Brittany Kaiser*, GUARDIAN (Feb. 17, 2019), www .theguardian.com/uk-news/2019/feb/17/brittany-kaiser-trump-russia-robert-mueller -cambridge-analytica.

[88]   Fed. Election Comm'n, *Participation by foreign nationals in decisions involving election-related activities* (June 23, 2017).

[89]   Ciara Torres-Spelliscy, *Mueller Could Have More Than Russia on His Mind*, BRENNAN CTR (Feb. 1, 2019), www.brennancenter.org/blog/mueller-could-have-more -russia-his-mind.

[90]   Rosenberg, *et al.*, *supra* note 34.

[91]   *Id.*

[92]   *Id.*

Election Commission for potentially violating the foreign ban.[93] One thing that is still not clear is whether Cambridge Analytica was just bunk science.[94] Consider that the firm worked for Ted Cruz and he lost.[95] As Jane Mayer noted, Cambridge Analytica "claimed … to use … data to wage both psychological and political warfare."[96] But this could just be bogus marketing, like an alchemist claiming to be able to make gold out of lead. And here's another thought to chew on: the same technology that allowed the Trump campaign to micro-target voters can also be used by foreign powers that wish to disrupt elections. As a report to the Senate Intelligence Committee concluded: "Unfortunately, there is mounting evidence that social media are being used to manipulate and deceive the voting public—and to undermine democracies and degrade public life."[97]

4. THE RUSSIANS INTERFERE IN 2016

Again, foreigners' participating in American elections is illegal.[98] The law banning foreign interference in elections has been around since 1966, when the prohibition became part of the Foreign Agents Registration Act (FARA).[99] The prohibition was later moved to the Federal Election Campaign Act (FECA). The foreign ban was updated in 2002.[100] Even *Citizens United* left the foreign ban intact.[101] In 2012, in *Bluman v. FEC*, the Supreme Court specifically addressed the foreign ban by summarily affirming a lower court that upheld it.[102]

---

[93] Press Release, *DOJ & FEC Complaints Filed Against Cambridge Analytica for Violating Prohibition on Election-Related Activities by Foreign Nationals in Work for Trump, Others,* COMMON CAUSE (Mar. 26, 2018), www.commoncause.org/media/doj-and-fec-complaints-filed-against-cambridge-analytica-for-violating-prohibition-on-election-related-activities-by-foreign-nationals-in-work-for-trump-others/.

[94] Mayer, *supra* note 37 ("David Karpf … calls the firm's claim to have special psychometric powers 'a marketing pitch' that's 'untrue.'").

[95] Schechner, *et al.*, *supra* note 39.

[96] Mayer, *supra* note 37.

[97] Philip N. Howard, *et al.*, *The IRA, Social Media and Political Polarization in the United States, 2012–2018* 39 (2018).

[98] Toni M. Massaro, *Foreign Nationals, Electoral Spending, and the First Amendment,* 34 HARV. J.L. & PUB. POL'Y 663, 665 (2011).

[99] 52 U.S.C. §30121; Ciara Torres-Spelliscy, *Dark Money as a Political Sovereignty Problem,* 28(2) KINGS LAW J. 239–61 (Sept. 15, 2017), https://doi.org/10.1080/09615768.2017.1351659.

[100] McConnell v. Federal Election Commission, 540 U.S. 93 (2003).

[101] Citizens United v. Federal Election Com'n, 558 U.S. 310 (2010).

[102] Bluman v. Federal Election Com'n, 565 U.S. 1104 (2012).

Federal law also bans candidates from soliciting political contributions from foreigners.[103] The Trump campaign in 2016 allegedly violated the foreign donor ban by soliciting money from Members of Parliament in several nations.[104] As the BBC reported at the time:

> Members of parliament in the UK, Iceland, Canada and Australia have reported that they are being inundated on their official government emails accounts with fund-raising pleas from the Trump campaign - some from the candidate himself and others from his sons.[105]

Thus, Mr. Trump, Mr. Trump, and Mr. Trump could all be liable for illegally soliciting foreign money.

According to former Head of the FBI James Comey, in 2016 the Russian government was trying to disrupt America's democracy, and therefore a key question for investigators is whether any American confederates helped it. As he explained to a House Committee:

> The aim of the Russian effort in 2016 was to destabilize, undermine, damage our democracy. ... And understanding whether any Americans were part of that effort is incredibly important because the threat of those Americans by virtue of their alliance with the Russians would pose to our country.[106]

What evidence is there of American confederates? As the *New York Times* reported, "a self-described intermediary for the Russian government [Professor Joseph Mifsud], told a Trump campaign aide, American George Papadopoulos, that the Russians had 'dirt' on Mr. Trump's rival, Hillary Clinton, in the form of 'thousands of emails.'"[107] A drunken Papadopoulos would later brag to an Australian diplomat, Alexander Downer, the former ambassador to the UK, at a London bar that the Russians had dirt on Clinton. Indeed, this is what tipped off the FBI that the Russians were interfering in the American election in 2016, when the diplomat told American intelligence what he had heard. The code

---

[103]   52 U.S.C. § 30121.

[104]   Ciara Torres-Spelliscy, *Trump's Whataboutism on Campaign Finance*, BRENNAN CTR (Jan. 10, 2019), www.brennancenter.org/blog/trumps-whataboutism-campaign -finance.

[105]   Anthony Zurcher, *US election: Trump's emails to British MPs cause uproar*, BBC (June 30, 2016), www.bbc.com/news/world-us-canada-36599724.

[106]   James Comey, *Testimony to House Committee on the Judiciary, Joint with the Committee on Government Reform and Oversight* 85–86 (Dec. 7, 2018).

[107]   Matt Apuzzo, Matthew Rosenberg & Adam Goldman, *Russians Sent "Backdoor" Bid to Meet Trump*, N.Y. TIMES (Nov. 18, 2017).

name for the FBI investigation of the Trump campaign that was ·opened was Crossfire Hurricane.[108]

Meanwhile, as the FBI proceeded with the Crossfire Hurricane investigation, a parallel private investigation was going on at a company called Fusion GPS. This investigation was paid for by Republicans during the primary campaign.[109] Then a Democratic law firm, Perkins Coie, picked up the bill in the general election.[110] The Fusion GPS investigation resulted in what has been known in the press as the Steele Dossier. The "dossier" is a series of memos written by an ex-MI6 British agent named Christopher Steele about Trump and his Russian ties. Steele became so worried about what his investigation was uncovering that he turned his findings over to the FBI and later to the press.[111] As head of Fusion GPS Glenn Simpson explained later: "when [Steele] says we have got to go to the FBI ... he is specifically concerned about ... whether a candidate for President of the United States ... has been kompromatted." [112] After the 2016 election, *BuzzFeed* published the dossier.[113]

An erroneous conservative talking point was that the FBI started investigating the Trump campaign because of the Steele Dossier. This was incorrect. The FBI had already opened an investigation because of loose-lipped Papadopoulos, as Comey explained in testimony before Congress:

Deutch: Mr. Comey, was the FBI's investigation into Russian interference and potential coordination with the Trump campaign started by a fraudulent dossier [from Steele]?
Comey: It was not.
Deutch: Can you explain how you know that?
Comey: Because I know what the basis was for starting the investigation. It was the information we'd received about a conversation that a Trump ... campaign foreign policy adviser had with an individual in London about stolen emails that the

---

[108] Matt Apuzzo, Adam Goldman & Nicholas Fandos, *Code Name Crossfire Hurricane: The Secret Origins of the Trump Investigation*, N.Y. TIMES (May 16, 2018).

[109] Kenneth P. Vogel & Maggie Haberman, *Conservative Website First Funded Anti-Trump Research by Firm That Later Produced Dossier*, N.Y. TIMES (Oct. 27, 2017) ("*The Washington Free Beacon*, a conservative website ... hired the research firm that ... produced ... the salacious dossier ...").

[110] *Id.* ("Clinton's campaign and the Democratic National Committee had begun paying Fusion GPS in April for research that eventually became the basis for the dossier.").

[111] Interview of Glenn Simpson, House Permanent Select Committee on Intelligence, 165 (Nov. 14, 2017), http://docs.house.gov/meetings/IG/IG00/20180118/106796/ HMTG-115-IG00-20180118-SD002.pdf.

[112] *Id.*

[113] Ken Bensinger, Miriam Elder & Mark Schoofs, *These Reports Allege Trump Has Deep Ties To Russia*, BUZZFEED (Jan. 10, 2017), www.buzzfeednews.com/article/ kenbensinger/these-reports-allege-trump-has-deep-ties-to-russia.

Russians had that would be harmful to Hillary Clinton. It was weeks or months later that the so-called Steele dossier came to our attention.[114]

Simpson testified before both Houses of Congress. As Simpson swore: "it was opaque what Donald Trump had been doing on these business trips to Russia ... we gave Chris [Steele] ... [a] pretty open ended [assignment]."[115] Steele investigated and reported back. The memos looked at Trump's "business affairs generally with some of the emphasis on associations with ... Russian organized crime ... "[116] Fusion GPS was not sure what it would uncover, but as Simpson said, "What came back was something ... very different and obviously more alarming, which had to do with ... a political conspiracy ... "[117]

During the 2016 election, Fusion GPS tracked down leads about what the Trumps were doing in Russia. One of the clear ties between Trump and Russia was the 2013 Miss Universe Pageant in Moscow.[118] Another business deal in Russia for Trump was the sale of Trump vodka from 2005–11.[119] And there were Russians who bought condominiums from Trump in the U.S., Canada and Panama,[120] especially after he ran into trouble getting loans from banks in the early 2000s. As Glenn Simpson testified: "by 2003, 2004, Donald Trump was not able to get bank credit ... If you're a real estate developer and you can't get bank loans, ... you've got a problem."[121] A high percentage of these condo sales were all cash.[122] There was also a Russian who bought a home from Trump for $95 million in cash,[123] netting him $50 million.[124]

During the 2016 campaign, Trump lied and told American voters falsely that he had no business dealings in Russia. The way the American public learned about plans for Trump Tower Moscow was through a confession in open court from Michael Cohen, who pleaded guilty to lying to Congress—specifically

---

[114] Comey Testimony, *supra* note 106, at 161.

[115] Senate Judiciary Committee, Interview of Glenn Simpson at 82–83 (Aug. 22, 2017),   www.judiciary.senate.gov/imo/media/doc/Simpson%20Transcript_redacted .pdf.

[116] *Id.* at 142.

[117] *Id.* at 143.

[118] *Id.* at 94.

[119] *Id.* at 95.

[120] *Id.* at 95.

[121] *Id.* at 95.

[122] Thomas Frank, *Secret Money: How Trump Made Millions Selling Condos to Unknown Buyers*, BuzzFeed (Jan. 12, 2018), www.buzzfeednews.com/article/ thomasfrank/secret-money-how-trump-made-millions-selling-condos-to.

[123] Doreen Carvajal, *The Billionaire Who Bought Trump's Mansion Faces Scrutiny in Monaco*, N.Y. Times (Sept. 7, 2018).

[124] *Id.* at 36 ("Dmitry Rybolovlev ... purchased a derelict estate at an extreme markup in Florida.").

about Trump's efforts to ink a deal to build a Trump Tower in Moscow.[125] Cohen said the dealings with Russia about Trump Tower Moscow continued through June 2016 and ended the day that the Russian hack of the Democratic National Committee's (DNC) servers was made public.[126] CNN unearthed a letter of intent signed by candidate Trump on October 28, 2015—the same day as the third Republican primary debate.[127] Trump later admitted he was seeking a deal.[128] The revelations about the Trump Tower Moscow deal included the allegation that the Trump Organization was willing to throw in a $50 million penthouse for free for Russian President Vladimir Putin. Such a deal, if the reporting is true, could well run afoul of the Foreign Corrupt Practices Act.[129]

4.1   Russian Hacking

Russia used multiple vectors to attack the 2016 election in the United States, including hacking political parties and private citizens, stealing Americans' identities, creating a social media disinformation campaign, violating campaign finance laws and breaking into the computer systems of secretaries of state and election technology vendors. In March and April of 2016, the servers at the DNC were hacked and Hillary Clinton's campaign manager John Podesta's email was accessed. The Russians turned the stolen emails over to WikiLeaks and published them on a pop-up webpage called D.C. Leaks. According to the special counsel, this webpage received over 1 million views.[130] On July 27, 2016, then candidate Trump said on live TV, "Russia, if you're listening, I hope you're able to find the 30,000 emails that are missing

---

[125] USA v. Cohen (Criminal Information) (Nov. 29, 2018), http://assets .documentcloud.org/documents/5331441/Cohen-False-Statements-Criminal -Information.pdf.

[126] Josh Kovensky, *What We Now Know About the Trump Tower Moscow Project*, TPM (Nov. 29, 2018), https://talkingpointsmemo.com/muckraker/what-we-now-know -about-the-trump-tower-moscow-project.

[127] *Letter of Intent from Trump Acquisitions LLC* (Oct. 28, 2015), http://cdn.cnn .com/cnn/2018/images/12/18/attachment.1.pdf (re Trump Moscow).

[128] David Smith, *Trump calls Russia deal 'legal and cool' as Mueller inquiry gathers momentum*, GUARDIAN (Nov. 30, 2018).

[129] Aaron Blake, *Is floating a $50 million Trump Tower penthouse for Vladimir Putin illegal?*, WASH. POST (Nov. 30, 2018).

[130] U.S. v. Viktor Borisovich Netyksho, 1:18-cr-215 (D.D.C.) (Indictment July 13, 2018), www.documentcloud.org/documents/5021502-Indictment-as-to-Viktor -Borisovich-Netyksho-Et-Al.html.

[from Clinton's time as secretary of state.]"[131] And according to the special counsel, Russians attempted to hack Hillary Clinton that same day.[132]

4.2   Russian Social Media Noise Storm

According to the special counsel, the Russian Internet Research Agency's budget was "73 million Russian rubles (over 1,250,000 U.S. dollars)" per month. One way this money was used was to pay people to inflame political division in the 2016 election with incendiary social media posts, some of which were amplified by chatbots. The sad thing is, many Americans thought these were legitimate posts from other Americans. Some even got into point-less arguments with Russian chatbots.[133]

Mistaking a chatbot for a human was something predicted by Alan Turing. Turing was a British mathematician who created a computer which broke the Nazi's cryptography during the Second World War. He is also the creator of the "Turing Test," which is a method for determining whether a machine's communications are indistinguishable from those of a human. If the human interacting with the machine can't tell whether he is communicating with a machine or another human, then the machine has passed the Turing Test. In 2014, a Russian-designed chatbot named Eugene that had the persona of a 13-year-old boy passed the Turing Test.[134]

As a report to the Senate Intelligence Committee found:

> the [Russian] IRA [Internet Research Agency] leveraged social media to manu-facture and spread junk news, manipulate public opinion, and subvert democratic processes. Social media platforms are among the most used applications on the Internet. In the US, 85% of the adult population uses the Internet regularly, and 80% of those people are on Facebook ... [135]

And these Russian efforts were to elect Trump—as the same report found, "activity between 2015 and 2016 was designed to benefit President Trump's

---

[131]   David A. Graham, *The Coincidence at the Heart of the Russia Hacking Scandal*, ATLANTIC (July 13, 2018), www.theatlantic.com/politics/archive/2018/07/russia-hacking-trump-mueller/565157/.

[132]   Netyksho Indictment *supra* note 130, at 7–8 ("on or about July 27, 2016, the Conspirators attempted after hours to spearphish for the first time email accounts at a domain hosted by a third-party provider and used by Clinton's personal office.").

[133]   John Markoff, *Automated Pro-Trump Bots Overwhelmed Pro-Clinton Messages, Researchers Say*, N.Y. TIMES (Nov. 17, 2016).

[134]   Alex Hern, *What is the Turing test?*, GUARDIAN (Feb. 21, 2017).

[135]   Howard, *et al.*, *supra* note 97, at 39.

campaign."[136] A separate report to the same Committee found that Russians brought ads to expand the reach of their message. This report noted, "Propagandists need an audience, and paid advertising helped the Internet Research Agency facilitate audience growth."[137] And many of the Russian efforts sought to sow division and even violence. As the report stated:

> The strategy for Right-leaning groups appears to have been to generate extreme anger and suspicion, in hopes that it would motivate people to vote; posts darkly hinted at conspiracy theories, voter fraud, illegal participation in the election, and stated the need for rebellion should Hillary Clinton 'steal' the election.[138]

Another Russian tactic was to hire a small army of Russians to pretend they were Americans and post nonstop nonsense in the hopes of creating dissention among American voters. A report to the Senate Intelligence Committee noted that the Russians created "hundreds of thousands of organic posts …"[139] One of the few outlets to cover this threat in real time was comedian and social critic Samantha Bee. She interviewed Russian hackers in Moscow wearing ski masks who matter-of-factly admitted they were trying to manipulate the American election by trying to reach "simple people" who are "lazy and believe everything they read …"[140] Whether he realized it or not, Donald Trump disseminated electronic propaganda via his Twitter feed to his millions of followers.[141] More disturbingly, ex-FBI agent Clint Watts testified that the Russians, using these fake accounts, continued tweeting at President Trump, hoping to catch his attention and a possible retweet.

---

[136] *Id.* at 19.

[137] Renee DiResta, *et al.*, *The Tactics & Tropes of the Internet Research Agency* 34 (2018).

[138] *Id.* at 83.

[139] *Id.* at 21.

[140] Jen Hayden, *Must watch—Samantha Bee traveled to Moscow, met with hackers trying to influence the U.S. election*, DAILY KOS (Nov. 1, 2016), www.dailykos.com/stories/2016/11/1/1589660/-Must-watch-Samantha-Bee-traveled-to-Moscow-met-with-hackers-trying-to-influence-the-U-S-election.

[141] John McTernan, *Donald Trump is giving a master class in how to use Twitter*, CNN (Dec. 21, 2016), www.cnn.com/2016/12/21/opinions/trump-twitter-mcternan-opinion/.

4.3   Russia's Breaking into State Elections and Vendors

If the DNC hack and social media disinformation campaigns were not trouble-some enough, the Senate Intelligence Committee released a report into Russian interference in the 2016 election that contained this unsettling fact:

> In at least six states, the Russian-affiliated cyber actors went beyond scanning and conducted malicious access attempts on voting-related websites. In a small number of states, Russian-affiliated cyber actors were able to gain access to restricted elements of election infrastructure. In a small number of states, these cyber actors were in a position to, at a minimum, alter or delete voter registration data; however, they did not appear to be in a position to manipulate individual votes or aggregate vote totals.

And this troubling nugget: "It is possible that more states were attacked, but the activity was not detected."[142] According to *Bloomberg*, Russian hackers hit systems in 39 states.[143] The Department of Homeland Security is more modest, telling the Senate Intelligence Committee, "21 states were potentially targeted by Russian government cyber actors."[144] Meanwhile, the FBI has conceded the voter registration databases of Illinois and Arizona were breached, and *ABC News* reported there are at least two other states whose voter registration systems were penetrated.[145] The Mueller Report noted that the Russians were able to gain access to at least one county government in Florida.[146]

---

[142] *Russian Targeting of Election Infrastructure During the 2016 Election: Summary of Initial Findings and Recommendations*, SENATE INTELLIGENCE COMMITTEE (May 8, 2018), www.burr.senate.gov/imo/media/doc/RussRptInstlmt1-%20ElecSec%20Findings,Recs2.pdf.

[143] Michael Riley & Jordan Robertson, *Russian Hacks on U.S. Voting System Wider Than Previously Known*, BLOOMBERG (June 13, 2017), www.bloomberg.com/news/articles/2017-06-13/russian-breach-of-39-states-threatens-future-u-s-elections.

[144] *Testimony of Jeanette Manfra*, SENATE INTELLIGENCE COMMITTEE (June 21, 2017), www.intelligence.senate.gov/sites/default/files/documents/os-jmanfra-062117.PDF.

[145] Mike Levine & Pierre Thomas, *Russian Hackers Targeted Nearly Half of States' Voter Registration Systems*, ABC NEWS (Sept. 29, 2016), https://abcnews.go.com/US/russian-hackers-targeted-half-states-voter-registration-systems/story?id=42435822.

[146] Mueller, *supra* note 20, at 51. ("in November 2016, the GRU sent spearphishing emails to over 120 email accounts used by Florida county officials responsible for administering the 2016 U.S. election. The spearphishing emails contained an attached Word document coded with malicious software (commonly referred to as a Trojan) that permitted the GRU to access the infected computer ... We understand the FBI believes that this operation enabled the GRU to gain access to the network of at least one Florida county government.").

Breaking into a voter registration database is one thing, but controlling the database is something else.[147] But that's exactly the capability the Russians demonstrated, according to a leaked National Security Agency (NSA) document published by *The Intercept*.[148] The NSA found the Russians in 2016 had successfully infiltrated the network of a company believed to be VR Systems, which sells voter registration software. From there, the Russians could have penetrated the computers of VR Systems customers, allowing hackers "to alter or delete voter registration information in such a way as to strategically create delays and chaos at specific polling locations."[149] *The Intercept* report indicated the Russians had also attacked 122 local election officials. Prof. J. Alex Halderman flatly warned, "there is no doubt that Russia has the technical ability to commit wide-scale attacks against our voting system, as do other hostile nations."[150]

But the problem of foreign interference and cybersecurity remained unsolved two years later. In 2018, Sen. Claire McCaskill discovered phishing attacks by Russians aimed at her campaign[151] and the National Republican Congressional Committee was hacked during the 2018 election.[152]

5. THE BUTINA/TORSHIN AFFAIR

Finally, Russians were also in face-to-face contact with the Trump 2016 campaign. There are lots of as-yet unanswered questions for Donald Trump

---

[147] Ciara Torres-Spelliscy, *Can Federalism Cope with Russian Election Meddling?*, Brennan Ctr (July 17, 2017), www.brennancenter.org/blog/can-federalism-cope-russian-election-meddling.

[148] Matthew Cole, Richard Esposito, Sam Biddle and Ryan Grim, *Top-Secret NSA Report Details Russian Hacking Effort Days Before 2016 Election*, Intercept (June 5, 2017),
https://theintercept.com/2017/06/05/top-secret-nsa-report-details-russian-hacking-effort-days-before-2016-election/.

[149] Ben Mathis-Lilley, *Leaked NSA Report Says Russian Hackers Targeted Voter Registration Officials in November 2016*, Slate (June 5, 2017), https://slate.com/news-and-politics/2017/06/russian-hackers-targeted-voter-registration-officials-nsa-report-says.html.

[150] *Russian Interference in U.S. Elections*, C-SPAN (June 21, 2017), www.c-span.org/video/?430128-1/senate-intel-panel-told-21-states-targeted-russia-2016-election.

[151] Zack Beauchamp, *We have the first documented case of Russian hacking in the 2018 election*, Vox (July 26, 2018), www.vox.com/policy-and-politics/2018/7/26/17619818/russia-claire-mccaskill-2018-midterm-hack.

[152] Jessica Taylor, *House GOP Campaign Arm Says It Was Hacked During The 2018 Election Cycle*, NPR (Dec. 4, 2018), www.npr.org/2018/12/04/673287352/house-gop-campaign-arm-says-it-was-hacked-during-the-2018-election-cycle.

Jr. about his meeting with multiple Russians in Trump Tower in June 2016.[153] As the younger Trump tells it, he was lured into conferring with the Russians because he was told he would be furnished with damaging information about Hillary Clinton. What his guests actually wanted to discuss was repeal of an American law that blacklists certain Russians with sanctions. But the approach and the ask seem eerily similar to a request that went through Michael Cohen seeking sanction relief[154] and the offer to George Papadopoulos that the Russians had "dirt" on Clinton.[155]

The Russians who showed up at Trump Tower on June 9, 2016 were not the only ones knocking on the front door of the Trump campaign; Russians were also banging on the back door, rattling the windows and looking for an open side door. For instance, Alexander Torshin was "among a phalanx of Putin proxies" seeking to gain entrance into Trump's inner circle.[156] Torshin's assistant Mariia Butina was also trying to insinuate herself into the mix.

On July 15, 2018, Butina was arrested in Washington, D.C.[157] On December 13, 2018, she pleaded guilty to violating 28 U.S.C. 951—espionage. Before her arrest, she kept making cameos in the Russian investigations. A document from the Senate Judiciary Committee stated:

> The [Senate Judiciary] Committee has obtained a number of documents that suggest the Kremlin used the National Rifle Association as a means of accessing and assisting Mr. Trump and his campaign. Two individuals involved in this effort appear to be Russian nationals Alexander Torshin and Maria Butina.[158]

---

[153] Gregory Krieg, *5 big questions about Donald Trump Jr.'s mystery meeting with a Russian lawyer*, CNN (July 11, 2017), www.cnn.com/2017/07/10/politics/donald -trump-jr-statement-questions/index.html.

[154] Megan Twohey & Scott Shane, *A Back-Channel Plan for Ukraine and Russia, Courtesy of Trump Associates*, N.Y. Times (Feb. 19, 2017).

[155] Andrew Prokop, *Papadopoulos given 14-day sentence as part of the Mueller investigation*, Vox (Sept. 7, 2018), www.vox.com/2018/9/7/17831408/george -papadopoulos-sentencing-jail.

[156] Nicholas Fandos, *Operative Offered Trump Campaign Access to Putin*, N.Y. Times (Dec. 4, 2017).

[157] Debbie Lord, *Who is Maria Butina, the woman charged with acting as a Russian agent in the US?*, Atlanta J. Constitution (July 17, 2018).

[158] *Preliminary Findings About Trump Campaign's Effort to Obtain Incriminating Information on Secretary Clinton from Russia at Trump Tower Meeting*, Senate Judiciary Committee (June 15, 2018), www.feinstein.senate .gov/public/_cache/files/b/3/b3e29bc4-8afd-4145-85d9-618dcad4a133/D0 69EF11DC3784A6D073B097E720572E.2018.05.15-transcript-release-findings-9-am .pdf.

This statement from the Senate Judiciary Committee corroborates the statements of Glenn Simpson in his testimony:

Ms. Speier: What is the interest of Russia with the National Rifle Association?
Mr. Simpson: It appears the Russians ... infiltrated the NRA ... there is a Russian banker-slash-Duma member-slash-Mafia leader named Alexander Torshin who is a life member of the NRA ... Butina, also was a big Trump fan in Russia, and then [she] suddenly showed up here and started hanging around the Trump transition ...[159]

In July 2015, at FreedomFest (a conservative Evangelical event), Butina showed up. Candidate Trump was speaking on stage and took a question from the audience from Butina, who asked, "I'm from Russia ... Do you want to continue the policies of sanctions that are damaging both economies?" In part of Trump's response to Butina, he said, "I know Putin ... I believe I would get along very nicely with Putin, OK? I don't think you'd need the sanctions."[160]

Butina reported to Torshin.[161] But who is he? *Bloomberg* reported Alexander Torshin is "[a] former senator in Vladimir Putin's United Russia party [who] directed dirty-money flows for mobsters in Moscow before he was named a deputy head of the central bank ..."[162] Also according to *Bloomberg*, "Torshin instructed members of the Moscow-based Taganskaya crime syndicate how to launder ill-gotten gains through banks and properties in Spain while he was a deputy speaker of the upper house of parliament ..."[163] Spanish authorities allege Torshin is the equivalent of a mob boss in Russia.[164] Torshin stands accused of many crimes.[165] If the Spanish police are correct, "[t]he formidable and powerful Taganskaya organization['s] ... activities include the appropriation of companies using violent or fraudulent methods, bank scams,

---

[159] House Interview of Glenn Simpson, *supra* note 111, at 142–43.

[160] Josh Meyer & Darren Samuelsohn, *U.S. officials charge NRA-linked Russian with acting as Kremlin agent*, POLITICO (July 16, 2018), https://www.politico.com/story/2018/07/16/russian-agent-conspiracy-guns-724470.

[161] Jose Maria Irujo & John Carlin, *The Spanish connection with Trump's Russia scandal*, EL PAIS (Apr. 3, 2017), https://elpais.com/elpais/2017/03/31/inenglish/1490984556_409827.html.

[162] Esteban Duarte, Henry Meyer & Evgenia Pisennaya, *Mobster or Central Banker?*, BLOOMBERG (Aug. 9, 2016), www.bloomberg.com/news/articles/2016-08-09/mobster-or-central-banker-spanish-cops-allege-this-russian-both.

[163] *Id.*

[164] *Id.* ("Russian politician Alexander Porfirievich Torshin stands above Romanov, who calls him 'godfather' ... Romanov was sentenced to almost four years ...").

[165] Irujo & Carlin, *supra* note 161 ("An investigation carried out between 2012 and 2013 by ... the anti-corruption prosecutors José Grinda and Juan Carrau into Romanov concluded that Torshin was the boss of a Taganskaya criminal operation which laundered money by buying up hotels in Mallorca.").

extortion and the carrying out of contract killings."[166] Spanish officials indicted Torshin based on phone conversations they recorded between him and the now convicted Alexander Romanov.[167] The Spanish police nearly nabbed Torshin in Spain in 2013, but he slipped away.[168]

During the 2016 campaign, Torshin made multiple overtures to meet Trump. In one attempt, Torshin's proposal to meet Trump was:

> in a May 2016 email from Rick Clay, an advocate for conservative Christian causes, to Rick Dearborn, a Trump campaign aide. … The email said that the dinner [Mr. Clay was organizing to honor veterans] would be a chance for Mr. Trump to meet Mr. Torshin.[169]

Before the 2016 election, Torshin built a network of contacts in the United States, including within the upper echelons of the National Rifle Association (NRA).[170] As reported in the *New York Times*, "evidence does appear to show deep ties between Mr. [Paul] Erickson, the N.R.A. and the Russian gun rights community that were formed in the years when many American conservatives … were increasingly looking to Mr. Putin as an example of a strong leader opposing immigration, terrorism and gay rights."[171] One of the ways Torshin attracted NRA officials was by literally creating a bogus Russian gun rights organization called the "Right to Bear Arms."[172] In 2014, Torshin invited members of the NRA to visit the bogus organization in Moscow.[173] In 2015, he repeated the ruse and flew in NRA leaders at the Russians' expense. The public knows about the 2015 trip because one of the officials flown over on this junket was Sheriff David Clarke, who had to file public disclosures about

---

[166] *Id.*

[167] Fandos, *supra* note 156 ("The prosecutors' evidence included 33 audio recordings of phone conversations from mid-2012 to mid-2013 between Torshin and Romanov, who allegedly laundered funds to buy a hotel on the ritzy island of Mallorca.").

[168] Irujo & Carlin, *supra* note 161 ("[Torshin] was on the brink of being arrested in Palma de Mallorca in the summer of 2013 during a meeting with a Mafioso … but he didn't turn up …").

[169] Apuzzo, Rosenberg & Goldman, *supra* note 107.

[170] Michael Isikoff, *White House pulled out of meet and greet with "conservatives favorite Russian" over suspected mob ties*, YAHOO (Apr. 2, 2017), www.yahoo.com/news/white-house-pulled-out-of-meet-and-greet-with-conservatives-favorite-russian-a-suspected-mobster-060026495.html.

[171] Fandos, *supra* note 156.

[172] Wil Donnelly, *The NRA, The Right to Bear Arms and the Trump Campaign – The Russian Connection*, FACTS DO MATTER (July 16, 2017), http://factsdomatter.com/index.php/2017/07/16/nra-right-to-bear-arms-trump-campaign/ ("The Right to Bear Arms appears to have been created as a honey pot to attract right-wing American conservative organizations like the NRA, and it worked.").

[173] Fandos, *supra* note 156.

the trip.[174] Michael Carpenter, former Deputy Assistant Secretary of Defense for Russia, Ukraine and Eurasia, told the press later that "Russians formed this NGO in Moscow called the Right to Bear Arms. *This was what you might call a honey pot NGO* that was designed specifically to lure in conservatives primarily in the United States from the NRA ..."[175]

An email sent on Torshin's behalf by Paul Erickson to the Trump campaign was titled "Kremlin Connection." It sought a meeting between Putin and Trump, and suggested that a Russian would make "first contact" at the NRA's annual convention in Kentucky.[176] Shortly thereafter, in May 2016, Torshin succeeded in dining with Donald Trump Jr. at a restaurant near the NRA convention in Lexington, Kentucky.[177] Donald Trump Jr.'s lawyer has played down the significance of the Torshin encounter as only involving "gun-related small talk."[178] While Donald Trump Jr. may wish to forget the meeting with Torshin ever happened, apparently Torshin kept digital pictures of the event.[179]

Torshin persisted in pestering the campaign to meet the candidate. One email seeking a Torshin/Trump campaign meeting was titled "Russian back-door overture."[180] Public facing reporting, however, indicates that Jared Kushner shut down Torshin's various attempts to get closer during the 2016 campaign.[181] But after Trump won the presidential election in 2016, Butina

---

[174] Alex Altman & Elizabeth Dias, *Moscow Cozies Up to the Right*, TIME (Mar. 10, 2017), http://time.com/4696424/moscow-right-kremlin-republicans/ ("In 2015, a collection of NRA officials flew over to attend Butina's annual gun conference [including] Erickson; former NRA ... chief David Keene; ... NRA first vice president Pete Brownell; and Milwaukee County sheriff David Clarke. ... One of their hosts was Russian Deputy Prime Minister Dmitry Rogozin, who was sanctioned [for] ... Russia's invasion of Ukraine. According to a disclosure filed by Clarke, Butina's group shelled out $6,000 for [his trip.]").

[175] *Transcript 7/14/17 List of Russians*, RACHEL MADDOW SHOW (July 14, 2017) (quoting Carpenter), www.msnbc.com/transcripts/rachel-maddow-show/2017-07-14.

[176] Fandos, *supra* note 156 ("A May 2016 email [from Paul Erickson] to the campaign adviser, Rick Dearborn, bore the subject line 'Kremlin Connection.'").

[177] Isikoff, *supra* note 170 ("While attending ... [a] NRA convention ..., Torshin was introduced to Donald Trump Jr. at a private dinner ...").

[178] Fandos, *supra* note 156 ("'It was all gun-related small talk,' Futerfas told *McClatchy*.").

[179] Duarte, Meyer & Pisennaya, *supra* note 162.

[180] Julia Glum, *Who is Alexander Torshin?*, NEWSWEEK (Nov. 18, 2017), www .newsweek.com/alexander-torshin-donald-trump-jr-meeting-716095 ("Torshin was involved ... in what was described in an email sent to Trump campaign aides as a 'Russian backdoor overture.'").

[181] *Id.* ("Jared Kushner ... denied [Torshin's] request for a meeting with the candidate ...").

showed up during the transition. Butina was at the inaugural, as were several other Russians.[182]

Torshin had hoped to meet newly elected Trump at a special meet and greet before the National Prayer Breakfast in 2017.[183] The meeting was to be at the Washington Hilton,[184] but was called off when someone at the White House finally realized that Torshin was wanted for crimes by the Spanish police.[185] The consolation prize for Torshin was he did get to dine with then-Congressman Dana Rohrabacher.[186]

In January 2018, *McClatchy* reported that the FBI is allegedly investigating whether Torshin may have funneled money into the NRA for the benefit of the candidacy of Trump in 2016.[187] As of December 2018, Torshin had retired from his position as a central banker and Butina remained in prison, but had agreed to cooperate with prosecutors. Butina was sentenced to 18 months in prison and subsequent deportation from the U.S.[188] Mr. Torshin was still at large at the time this book was written.

There's still a lot that the American public doesn't know about the relationship between these Russians and the NRA. There is at least smoke. What we don't know is if there is a smoking gun here too. The same Spanish prosecutor who has been trying to arrest Torshin for money laundering has turned over audio recordings to American prosecutors that apparently mention Donald Trump Jr. All the Spanish prosecutor would say publicly is, "Mr. Trump's son should be concerned."[189]

---

[182] Craig Timberg, Rosalind S. Helderman, Andrew Roth & Carol D. Leonnig, *In the crowd at Trump's inauguration, members of Russia's elite anticipated a thaw between Moscow and Washington*, WASH. POST (Jan. 20, 2018).

[183] Irujo & Carlin, *supra* note 161.

[184] Isikoff, *supra* note 170 ("The event had been planned as a meet and greet with President Trump and Alexander Torshin, ... at the Washington Hilton before the National Prayer Breakfast ...").

[185] *Id.*

[186] Altman & Dias, *supra* note 174.

[187] Peter Stone & Greg Gordon, *FBI investigating whether Russian money went to NRA to help Trump*, McCLATCHY (Jan. 18, 2018), www.mcclatchydc.com/news/nation -world/national/article195231139.html; Ciara Torres-Spelliscy, *An insidious foreign dark money threat: New reports about Russian money going to the NRA could prove watchdogs' fears correct*, DAILY NEWS (Jan. 19, 2018).

[188] Ashraf Khalil & Chad Day, *Russian Maria Butina gets 18 months for being Kremlin agent*, AP (Apr. 26, 2019).

[189] Michael Isikoff, *"Trump's son should be concerned"*, YAHOO (May 25, 2018), www.aol.com/article/news/2018/05/25/trumps-son-should-be-concerned-wiretaps -show-trump-jr-met-with-putin-ally/23443917/ (quoting Jose Grinda).

6.   CONCLUSION

Special Counsel Robert Mueller's investigation into Russian interference in the 2016 election closed on March 22, 2019, when the final report was delivered to the Department of Justice.[190] At the time this book was written, the unredacted report had not been shared with Congress or the American people. Forty percent of the pages in the Mueller Report had at least one redaction and most of the redactions were related to secret but ongoing criminal matters.[191] Consequently, there are still multiple unanswered questions about the relationship between foreigners and the Trump campaign in 2016:

- What happened when the candidate's son met Torshin at the NRA convention?
- Did Psy-Group work for the Trump campaign?
- What were Butina and Torshin trying to accomplish with the NRA and was any of that for Trump's benefit?

Answering these questions will take either further governmental investigations or intrepid digging on the part of the free press.

Trump's repetition of "America First" could just be empty branding lacking the accompanying patriotic sentiment. "America First" may indeed be the legacy of the Trump administration, but perhaps not for the reason that the president thought when he gave his inaugural address with a bunch of Russians in the crowd.[192]

---

[190] *Mueller delivers final Russia report to Justice Department*, PBS NEWS HOUR (Mar 22, 2019), www.pbs.org/newshour/politics/mueller-delivers-final-russia-report -to-justice-department.

[191] Alvin Chang & Javier Zarracina, *The Mueller report redactions, explained in 4 charts We can't see behind the bars. But we can see where they are—and why they're there*, Vox (Apr. 19, 2019), www.vox.com/2019/4/19/18485535/mueller -report-redactions-data-chart.

[192] Timberg, *et al., supra* note 182.

9. Branding racism

"Desperate people do desperate things ... they grab on for anything they can get ahold of, and if it happens to be something nasty, rotten, and false, that doesn't make much difference."[1]

1. INTRODUCTION

Black comic Dave Chappelle asked of Russian interference in the 2016 presidential election: "Is Russia making us racist? Is that who's doing it? Oh OK, oh my God, thank goodness—I thought it was us. If they killed the country that way, then we're the murder weapon," he joked, hitting way too close to home.[2]

In terms of inflaming racial divisions among Americans, as Chappelle intimated, Americans gave Russians a considerable head start. Racial divisions in America have a deep history which cannot be fully canvassed here.[3] But suffice it to say that even though racialized slavery ended with the Thirteenth Amendment (1865), racial equality was guaranteed on paper with the Fourteenth Amendment (1868), and Black men got their voting rights on paper with the Fifteenth Amendment (1870), many of these constitutional rights did not become meaningful until the 1964 Civil Rights Act and the 1965 Voting Rights Act.[4] And even then, decades of litigation and acrimony followed. If the question is why people of color in 2016 didn't trust fellow White Americans, there was a litany of racial harms to point to as causes for

---

[1] Theodore R. Johnson & Leah Wright Rigueur, *Race-Baiting for the Presidency*, ATLANTIC (Nov. 18, 2015) (quoting Warren Rudd).

[2] Azadeh Moshiri, *Dave Chappelle: Russia didn't make us racists*, CNN (Dec. 4, 2018), www.cnn.com/2018/10/30/politics/amanpour-dave-chappelle-jon-stewart -president-trump-russia-racist/index.html.

[3] For more in depth coverage of this topic *see* ERIC FONER, RECONSTRUCTION: AMERICA'S UNFINISHED REVOLUTION, 1863–1877 (1988); CORNEL WEST, RACE MATTERS (1993); WILLIAM JULIUS WILSON, MORE THAN JUST RACE: BEING BLACK AND POOR IN THE INNER CITY (2009).

[4] Karen Grigsby Bates, *Why Did Black Voters Flee The Republican Party in The 1960s?*, NPR (July 14, 2014), www.npr.org/sections/codeswitch/2014/07/14/ 331298996/why-did-black-voters-flee-the-republican-party-in-the-1960s.

distrust. As former presidential speechwriter Michael Waldman said, "Dealing with race has been a democratic conundrum since the 1890s."[5]

But American racial history is complicated, and not all negative. Racial progress has surely been made over the years, some of it through Supreme Court rulings like *Brown v. Board*, *Loving v. Virginia* and *Grutter v. Bollinger*; through Equal Employment Opportunity Commission rulings, Fair Housing Act enforcements and Department of Justice consent decrees; and through millions of everyday people who have committed small acts of kindness across racial lines. Friendships, inter-personal relationships and marriages have all taken place across racial lines. Indeed, "the share of newlyweds married to a spouse of a different race or ethnicity has increased more than five times — from 3 percent in 1967, to 17 percent in 2015 …"[6]

But lest we get too sanguine about race relations, it is worth recalling that "[o]nly in 2015 did the Confederate flag come down from the state capitol in Columbia, [South Carolina] prompted by a young neo-Nazi, Dylann S. Roof, who brandished a handgun and massacred nine people during a Bible study at Emanuel African Methodist Episcopal Church. …"[7] It's an empirical question how many White Americans sympathize with Roof.

It is easy to pretend when Martin Luther King Jr.'s birthday rolls around that racist thinking has been left in the dustbin of history.[8] As Olivia Goldhill explains, "In the 50 years since the death of Martin Luther King, Jr., the memory of the transformative civil rights leader has undergone a 'Disneyfication.' … TV shows often suggest that King's quest for racial and economic equality was ultimately successful."[9] Nonetheless, an undercurrent of racist ideology and racialized beliefs persisted. While racism could exist in isolated enclaves for decades in the pre-Internet world, now racists can find each other online and can reinforce their ideas about racial hierarchy. Just as partisan individuals can encase themselves in a self-reinforcing partisan bubble, so too can racist

---

[5] Interview with Michael Waldman (Apr. 27, 2018).

[6] Hansi Lo Wang, *Steep Rise In Interracial Marriages Among Newlyweds 50 Years After They Became Legal*, NPR (May 18, 2017), www.npr.org/sections/codeswitch/2017/05/18/528939766/five-fold-increase-in-interracial-marriages-50-years-after-they-became-legal.

[7] Ron Stodghill, *In Charleston, Coming to Terms With the Past*, N.Y. TIMES (Nov. 15, 2016).

[8] Olivia Goldhill, *50 years since his death, Martin Luther King Jr.'s philosophical work is all but forgotten*, QUARTZ (Apr. 4, 2018), https://qz.com/1244251/on-the-50th-anniversary-of-martin-luther-kings-death-lets-revisit-his-philosophical-work/. ("In reality, King had deeper theory on how race should be considered in public policy. 'Even in "I have a dream," he's talking about questions of police brutality, reparations. But those are things that people don't highlight,' says [Professor Brandon] Terry.")

[9] *Id.*

individuals encase themselves in a world that only reflects back their distorted world view. Racial bias can cut across partisan divisions.[10]

Calling someone a "racist" is one of the most potent insults a political opponent can raise against another. Yet, there is some indeterminacy in the word "racist." There is conscious hatred of outgroups[11] and then there is implicit unconscious bias against outgroups.[12] As Professor Jennifer Taub articulates:

> Racism is different than bigotry, or bias or animus because racism is a system of oppression where people use race to subordinate a whole class of people. So there is not reverse racism because the minority doesn't have the power to oppress. It's different than bias which a minority person could have.[13]

For some, the pejorative label "racist" only applies to someone whose views line up with the Ku Klux Klan. For others, there is a degree of implicit racial bias in all of us.[14] Like much else in this book, being "racist" is a contested term, which is why it is a likely subject of branding and rebranding.

A key question in American political life has been: which political party gets the racists? One of the ways that the Republican party has tried to appeal to Black voters is to remind them that they are the "Party of Lincoln." And President Abraham Lincoln is a powerful icon to emphasize, since he authored

---

[10] Mark P. Zanna, Leanne S. Son Hing, Greg A. Chung-Yan & Leah K. Hamilton, *A Two-Dimensional Model That Employs Explicit and Implicit Attitudes to Characterize Prejudice*, 94 J. OF PERSONALITY AND SOC. PSYCH. 973 (2008) ("one [might] suspect that prejudice is always found more among those on the political right; however, liberals also demonstrate racial bias.")

[11] *Id.* at 971 ("Historically, prejudice has been assessed as an explicit, consciously held negative evaluation of an outgroup that is retrieved from memory and can be self-reported.")

[12] *Id.* at 971–72. ("researchers have identified indirect means (e.g., response-latency tasks) to assess implicit prejudice, that is, automatically activated negative associations with an outgroup.").

[13] Interview with Jennifer Taub (Aug. 13, 2018).

[14] Jerry Kang & Mahzarin R. Banaji, *Symposium on Behavior Realism: Fair Measures: A Behavioral Realist Revision of "Affirmative Action,"* 94 CALIF. L. REV. 1063, 1083–84 (2006) ("Unconscious stereotypes, rooted in social categorization, are ubiquitous and chronically accessible. They are automatically prompted by the mere presence of a target mapped into a particular social category. Thus when we see a Black (or a White) person, the attitude and stereotypes associated with that racial category auto-matically activate."); Justin D. Levinson, *Forgotten Racial Equity: Implicit Bias, Decisionmaking, and Misremembering*, 57 DUKE. L. J. 345, 351–52 (2007) (noting "[s]ince the 1990's, a number of studies have deconstructed the complicated ways in which the human mind maintains and manifests racially biased implicit attitudes and stereotypes."); *see* Ciara Torres-Spelliscy, Monique Chase & Emma Greenman, *Improving Judicial Diversity*, in WOMEN AND THE LAW (Moriarty, ed., Thompson West Reuters 2009) (discussion of implicit bias passim).

the Emancipation Proclamation and pushed for the Thirteenth Amendment. Many African Americans still gravitate toward the image of the "Great Emancipator."[15] The Radical Republicans in the post-Civil War period changed the U.S. Constitution to provide for racial equality. And the Democratic Party in the South at the same time, and for decades afterwards, embraced a series of awful racist policies, laws and *de facto* practices that essentially made the rights guaranteed by the U.S. Constitution all but meaningless. The answer to who gets the racist voting bloc was very much the Southern Democrats (also known as Dixiecrats). One place the Democratic Party's rank racism of the early twentieth century is preserved forever for all to see is in its (fortunately failing) attempts to get the Supreme Court to recognize that it had the right to be racially discriminatory in the *White Primary Cases*.

When Lyndon B. Johnson signed the Voting Rights Act in 1965, he effectively killed the Democratic Party as it had existed up until that point— a strange coalition of racist Dixiecrats and northern liberals. Over the next few decades, Dixiecrats slowly became Republicans and most Black voters abandoned the GOP.[16] By the turn of the millennium, the parties had a more extreme sort. Democrats were racially diverse, while the Republicans were (with a notable exception of pockets like Cuban exiles) increasingly mono-chromically White.[17] There were prominent Black Republicans, but they could nearly be counted on one hand (like Senator Tim Scott, Lieutenant Governor Michael Steele, Ohio Secretary of State Ken Blackwell and Secretary of Housing and Urban Development Ben Carson). But most GOP governors, senators and presidential candidates were White.

Racial realignment became all the more stark when the Democrats nom-inated a Black man (Obama) as their candidate for the presidency twice, in 2008 and 2012.[18] He won both times. In 2013, the Republicans ordered an

---

[15] Bates, *supra* note 4 ("Republican. Party of Lincoln. Party of the Emancipation. Party that pushed not only black votes but black politicians during that post-bellum period known as Reconstruction.").

[16] Michael Harriot, *How the Republican Party Became the Party of Racism*, THE ROOT (July 23, 2018), www.theroot.com/how-the-republican-party-became-the-party -of-racism-1827779221.

[17] Johnson & Rigueur, *supra* note 1 ("the Republican primary electorate, which, as of 2012, was over 90 percent white.").

[18] Anthony G. Greenwald, Colin Tucker Smith, N. Sriram, Yoav Bar-Anan & Brian A. Nosek, *Implicit Race Attitudes Predicted Vote in the 2008 U.S. Presidential Election*, 9 Analyses of Social Issues and Public Policy 242 (2009) ("In the 2008 United States presidential election, American voters were presented with a choice between a European American, John McCain, and an African American, Barack Obama ... the race difference between the candidates remained an inescapably noticeable feature of the election.").

autopsy to consider what had gone wrong in the 2012 election. The autopsy report suggested that the GOP rebrand itself to attract more millennial voters and to spread the message that the Republican Party was a big tent where all voters, including minorities, were welcome.

The rebranding of the GOP failed, for a number of reasons. First, the messengers were mostly White. And perhaps, there were a number of Republicans who really didn't want the GOP to be a diverse party.[19] Republican elected officials were apt to go off-message and reinforce the narrow-minded old image of Republicans, thus ruining the big tent rebranding effort—whether it was candidate Todd Akin talking about "legitimate rape" in 2014 or Congressman Steve King claiming in 2013 that Hispanics have "calves the size of cantaloupes because they're hauling 75 pounds of marijuana across the desert."[20] An elected official who goes off-brand cannot be fired by an American political party. Thus, GOP leaders who wrote the autopsy lacked command and control of the party's constituent parts to implement the rebranding effort.

Against the backdrop of this failed rebranding effort to make the GOP seem like a big tent (2013–15), the Trump campaign rolled into town. The Trump 2016 campaign was much more akin to the George Wallace campaign in 1968, when racial appeals were explicit. Even Wallace's daughter saw the similarity. "'Trump and my father say out loud what people are thinking but don't have the courage to say,' Peggy Wallace Kennedy told *NPR*. … She believes Trump is exploiting voters' worst instincts, the way her late father once did."[21]

This chapter will look at a few snapshots in time when different political parties embraced racialized voting blocs. First this chapter will explain the *White Primary Cases*, in which the Democrat Party tried to maintain an exclusively White constituency. Then this chapter will look at the third-party campaign of George Wallace. And finally, this chapter will look at the 2016 election of Donald Trump. Trump's Republican campaign used far more racial appeals than any candidate since Wallace. He also did this against a backdrop of Russians pushing racial vitriol into political conversations.

---

[19]   *Id.* ("race attitudes played a role in determining vote, independent of political ideology.").

[20]   Elspeth Reeve, *Steve King Wants to Protect the Border from Cantaloupe-Sized Calves*, ATLANTIC (July 23, 2013).

[21]   Debbie Elliot, *Is Donald Trump A Modern-Day George Wallace?*, NPR (Apr. 22, 2016), www.npr.org/2016/04/22/475172438/donald-trump-and-george-wallace-riding -the-rage.

2. THE *WHITE PRIMARY CASES* AND THE DEMOCRATS

The Supreme Court can't quite seem to decide whether political parties are public or private. In some cases, the Supreme Court finds that the Fourteenth and Fifteenth Amendments apply because the parties have sufficient state action. But in many other cases, the Supreme Court considers political parties mere private groups which are allowed to discriminate, like in *California Democratic Party v. Jones,* where the Court privileged the role of political parties' policing their own boundaries.[22]

Under the state action doctrine, constitutional rights can only be raised against the government or an entity acting under the color of state law. Otherwise, if an individual is being treated unfairly by a purely private group, the Constitution will not provide redress. So if political parties are part of the state, then people who are excluded from a political party can raise Fourteenth Amendment objections against the party. But if political parties are purely private, then people who are excluded cannot raise constitutional objections.[23]

Most brands today try to avoid picking up negative connotations. And today, one of the worst connotations that can attach to a brand is a charge of racism. But this has changed over time, too. For much of American history, the way to insult a political opponent was to call them racially tolerant or pro-miscegenation. Back when being racially tolerant was an anathema, political parties spent a great deal of effort in branding themselves as "all White," "racially pure" and "pro-segregation."

From 1900–60s, many Southern states had devolved into single party states: electing all Democrats (sometimes known as Dixiecrats) all the time. What that meant in practical terms was whomever won the Democratic primary in a Southern state would by default win the general election, because there were few viable Republican candidates. So the question becomes: if the primary is the true election in these states, are primaries "elections" for the purposes of Article I, Section 4 of the Constitution and does the Fourteenth Amendment requirement of equal protection attach to primaries? In a series of cases the Texas Democratic Party attempted a number of aggressive tactics to keep their primaries all-White affairs. The Texas Democrats made the argument that they were private, and just like a private country club can bar particular individuals from its premises, they could ban who they wanted from the Democratic primaries. As Professors Samuel Issacharoff and Richard H. Pildes argue, "the

---

[22] California Democratic Party v. Jones, 530 U.S. 567 (2000).
[23] LAURENCE H. TRIBE, AMERICAN CONSTITUTIONAL LAW 1121 (2d ed. 1988).

white primary was a vehicle through which existing partisan forces leveraged their current political power into a state-imposed lockup ..."[24]

Briefly, here is a review of the *White Primary Cases*, wherein the Supreme Court struggled with the matter of whether political parties and their primaries were public or private and how racially exclusive they could be. In 1927, in *Nixon v. Herndon*, the Supreme Court held a state law disqualifying Blacks from voting in the Democratic primary was a violation of the Fourteenth Amendment's Equal Protection Clause. In response to *Nixon v. Herndon*, Texas repealed that law and gave the power to the party's executive committee to set membership rules. In 1932, in *Nixon v. Condon*, the Court invalidated the Texas Democratic Party's executive committee's resolution which prohibited Blacks from participating in the primary. The Supreme Court said the state had given the executive committee by statute power it never previously had; thus, the executive committee thereby acted as an agent of the state and therefore there was a violation of equal protection.

In response to *Nixon v. Condon,* the Texas Democratic Party had a convention and adopted a resolution restricting party membership to Whites. The key question was: is the Texas Democratic Party like a country club or not? In *Grovey v. Townsend* in 1935, the Court blinked. In a major setback for voting rights for African Americans, the Supreme Court decided that the Texas Democratic Party was a private association which was not subject to constitutional requirements, which meant the party could be racially discriminatory.

In 1944, in *Smith v. Allwright*, there was an additional challenge to the racial exclusions by the Texas Democratic Party. The Supreme Court reversed course once again and ruled that under the Fifteenth Amendment, there is a right to be free from racial discrimination in casting a ballot in a party primary. The Court said that the state's detailed regulation and involvement in the primary process turned the primary into a state function, even if it were conducted by the private Texas Democratic Party. As the Court wrote in *Smith*:

> [w]hen primaries become a part of the machinery for choosing officials, state and national, as they have here, the same tests to determine the character of discrimination or abridgement should be applied to the primary as are applied to the general election. If the state ... endorses, adopts and enforces the discrimination against Negroes, practiced by a party entrusted by Texas law with the determination of the qualifications of participants in the primary. This is state action within the meaning of the Fifteenth Amendment.[25]

---

[24]   Samuel Issacharoff & Richard H. Pildes, *Politics As Markets: Partisan Lockups of the Democratic Process*, 50 STAN. L. REV. 643, 663 (1998).
[25]   Smith v. Allwright, 321 U.S. 649, 664 (1944).

Finally, there was another case arising out of Texas challenging the straw vote conducted by the Jaybird Democratic Association of Fort Bend County, Texas, which was only open to White voters. The winner of the straw vote always won the primary and the primary winner nearly always won the general. In *Terry v. Adams* in 1953, the Supreme Court ruled that even in a Jaybird straw vote, which was like a primary before the primary, Blacks could not be barred from participating. Professor Laurence Tribe argues that the Supreme Court found state action in the *White Primary Cases* because Texas offered preferential ballot access in the general election to the winner of the Democratic primary.[26] The cumulative effect of the Supreme Court's *White Primary Cases* was that political parties could no longer assert a constitutional right to discriminate on the basis of race in their party membership or in primaries. Hence, the effort to brand the Democratic Party as "all White" came to an end constitutionally.

3. GEORGE WALLACE 1968 AND THE INDEPENDENTS

A decade after the Supreme Court had settled the question of whether political parties could be racially exclusionary in the negative, and a few years after the Voting Rights Act became law, the political parties in 1968 were still grappling with where the Dixiecrats would fit in presidential electoral politics. Then, Governor of Alabama George Wallace decided to run as an American Independent Party candidate. He was famous (or perhaps infamous) for saying "'Segregation now. Segregation tomorrow. And segregation forever.'"[27] With the candidacy of Wallace, the American Independents embraced racism. Professor Marianne Worthington argues that the Wallace run was an outlet for "White backlash."[28]

Wallace, the southern demagogue of the 1960s–70s, may not top the charts of politicians to emulate, with this rare exception: he had message discipline. Wallace won five states, which is more than morally upstanding candidates like Walter Mondale or George McGovern could claim. Part of why, to this day, Wallace is thought of as a racist is he proudly branded himself as one. He repeated that he was racist until the idea sank in and the moniker stuck to him like so much tar and feathers. As Worthington described him: "Wallace was known for saying the same things over and over again."[29] Wallace was actually

---

[26] *See* Tribe, *supra* note 23, at 1121.

[27] Elliot, *supra* note 21.

[28] Marianne Worthington, *The Campaign Rhetoric of George Wallace in the 1968 Presidential Election*, UCUMBERLANDS, www.ucumberlands.edu/downloads/academics/history/vol4/MarianneWorthington92.html.

[29] *Id.* (internal quotations omitted).

typical of other effective politicians who stick to a script until the public gets it. Worthington continued:

> a candidate's 'theme song' is ... made up of phrases that the candidate likes and that have demonstrated their ability to spark crowd reaction. ... The repetition is tedious ..., but repetition helps develop a candidate's image in the same way that endless exposure to Anacin or Tylenol commercials fix the names of these products in the minds of television viewers.[30]

Wallace was right when he said during the campaign, "'I want to tell these national parties this—they're going to find out there are a lot of rednecks come Nov. 5th in this country.'"[31] He won 9.9 million votes nationwide out of 73 million: roughly one out of every seven voters pulled the lever for his brand of racial division.

Wallace was somewhat unique in how forthcoming he was in his racist appeals. From Goldwater to George H.W. Bush, most racial appeals were coded more as dog whistles that appealed to racialized White voters without alienating others. Racial codes can range "from Richard Nixon's 'law and order' to Ronald Reagan's 'states' rights' to the euphemistic 'urban' and 'inner-city.'"[32] Goldwater's codes in 1964 included:

> some words that have a more limited and specific meaning for the Southern crowds. Thus, in the Old Confederacy 'Lyndon Baines Johnson' and 'my opponent' means 'integrationist.' 'Hubert Horatio' (it somehow amuses Goldwater to drop the 'Humphrey') means 'super-integrationist.' 'Federal judiciary' means 'integrationist judges.' ... In the code, 'bullies and marauders' means 'Negroes.' 'Criminal defend-ants' means negroes. States rights means 'opposition to civil rights.' 'Women' means 'white women.'[33]

Theodore R. Johnson and Leah Wright Rigueur argue such coded racial appeals do "not mean that those who employ them are racists, but it does show a willingness to exploit societal ills for political gain."[34] But others, like Dave Johnson, make a harsher assessment:

Republicans learned the lesson that dividing the nation along racial, patriotic and cultural lines, ignoring and blatantly violating laws, manipulating and intimidating the media, manipulating the public with media tricks, making

---

[30] *Id.* (quoting John Kessel).
[31] Elliot, *supra* note 21.
[32] Johnson & Rigueur, *supra* note 1.
[33] Richard H. Rovere, *The Campaign: Goldwater*, NEW YORKER (Oct. 3, 1964).
[34] Johnson & Rigueur, *supra* note 1.

corrupt deals to get corporate/billionaire money, smearing and red-baiting opponents, and generally rigging the voting process wins elections.[35]

In the 1960s, there was a huge racial realignment between the two parties. African Americans went from being loyal to the Party of Lincoln to being reliable Democrats.[36] Certainly, contributing factors were Democratic President Johnson's embrace of civil rights laws, as well as White Dixiecrats' simultaneous realignment to the Republican Party. As Larry Sabato argued:

> Democrats owe a debt of gratitude to Goldwater [with his vote against the Civil Rights Act] for creating a near-consensus among African-Americans for their party. Until 1964, presidential nominees from the party of Lincoln would often receive up to a third of the black vote. Goldwater dipped to an estimated 4% among black supporters ...[37]

By 2014, roughly 90 percent of Black voters self-identified as Democrats.[38]

As White racialized voters became identified with the Republican Party, Black voters felt less welcome in the GOP; and as more Black voters identified as Democrats, the more racially isolationist Whites exited the party. As political strategist for Nixon, Kevin Phillips, told the *New York Times*, "'The more Negroes who register as Democrats in the South, the sooner the Negrophobe whites will quit the Democrats and become Republicans.'"[39]

And for a while, politicians who had a "slip of the tongue" and said something overtly racist were often ostracized. Think of Virginia Senator George Allen calling a South Asian young man "Macaca" in 2006.[40] He was rejected by voters and the political establishment. Senator Trent Lott had to apologize after he said the following at Strom Thurman's birthday party in 2002:

---

[35] Dave Johnson, *What Do You Mean 'Sanders Might Be Another George McGovern'?*, Huff. Post (Jan. 29, 2016), www.huffingtonpost.com/dave-johnson/what-do-you-mean-sanders_b_9116398.html.

[36] Bates, *supra* note 4 ("'as late as 1960, only about two-thirds of African-Americans were identified with the Democratic Party,' [Vincent Hutchings] says.").

[37] Larry J. Sabato, *How Goldwater Changed Campaigns Forever*, Politico (Oct. 27, 2014), www.politico.com/magazine/story/2014/10/barry-goldwater-lasting-legacy-112210.

[38] Bates, *supra* note 4 (quoting Vincent Hutchings) ("'today, that number hovers at about 90 percent.'").

[39] James Boyd, *Nixon's Southern Strategy*, N.Y. Times (May 17, 1970), www.nytimes.com/1970/05/17/archives/nixons-southern-strategy-its-all-in-the-charts.html.

[40] Drew Westen, The Political Brain: The Role of Emotion in Deciding the Fate of the Nation 222 (2007) ("a message of this sort [George Allen calling a young man 'Macaca'] activates two networks simultaneously: a conscious one about the ugliness of racism, and an unconscious one associated with negative feelings towards people of color and foreigners.").

I want to say this about my state: When Strom Thurmond ran for president, we voted for him. We're proud of it. And if the rest of the country had followed our lead, we wouldn't have had all these problems over all these years, either.[41]

A few years later, Lott left the Senate. But blatant racism was about to make a political comeback in the United States in 2015.

4. DONALD TRUMP 2016 AND THE REPUBLICANS

With the GOP in 2015 standing at 89 percent White and Democrats coming off of eight years in the White House with America's first Black president, candidate Trump started bulldozing through a field of 17 GOP contenders. What in other election years would have been a liability in a country of immigrants was somehow a strength—Trump was unabashedly anti-immigrant, specifically against those from South of the border. But this was a risky move for a politician who also had a business to run, since one thing that could make the Trump brand toxic is if it is linked to rank racism.[42]

Trump entered the presidential race with a lengthy paper trail. Trump has a long history of making racially charged remarks and has been accused of racial discriminatory practices as a landlord.[43] And in 1989:

> in a controversial case that's been characterized as a modern-day lynching, four black teenagers and one Latino teenager — the 'Central Park Five' — were accused of attacking and raping a jogger in New York City ... [Mr. Trump ran] an ad in local papers demanding, 'BRING BACK THE DEATH PENALTY. BRING BACK OUR POLICE!' The teens' convictions were later vacated after they spent seven to 13 years in prison, and the city paid $41 million in a settlement to the teens. But Trump in October [2016] said he still believes they're guilty, despite the DNA evidence to the contrary.[44]

---

[41] Sheryl Gay Stolberg, *Under Fire, Lott Apologizes for His Comments at Thurmond's Party*, N.Y. TIMES (Dec. 10, 2002).

[42] Nicholas Kristof, *Is Donald Trump a Racist?*, N.Y. TIMES (July 23, 2016) ("Here we have a man who for more than four decades has been repeatedly associated with racial discrimination or bigoted comments about minorities, some of them made on television for all to see. ... I don't see what else to call it but racism.").

[43] German Lopez, Libby Nelson & Andrew Prokop, *Once you know Trump's history, what his campaign has done is unsurprising. That makes him scarier*, VOX (Oct. 11, 2016) ("1973: The US Department of Justice ... sued the Trump Management Corporation for violating the Fair Housing Act. Federal officials found evidence that Trump had refused to rent to black tenants and lied to black applicants about whether apartments were available, among other accusations ... [Trump] signed an agreement in 1975 agreeing not to discriminate to renters of color without admitting to discriminating before.").

[44] *Id.*

Also, for years, Trump argued that the first African American president, Barack Obama, had not been born in the United States.[45] Many interpreted this "birther" claim as racially motivated, as all of Obama's documentation proved he was an American citizen.[46]

During the 2016 presidential campaign, Trump's racial views received a far broader audience, including his hostile comments against Mexicans in the speech launching his campaign. He made many statements hostile to Muslim immigrants throughout the campaign. He also criticized an American-born federal judge based on his Mexican heritage.[47] A prolific user of Twitter, Trump also retweeted White supremacist tweets during the 2016 campaign.[48] As Jennifer Rubin wrote:

> Trump is a man who navigates the world by racial and ethnic stereotyping. He speaks of 'the' blacks and 'the' Hispanics, a classic 'tell' that the speaker considers members of a racial or ethnic group as standing apart from 'us,' an undifferentiated mass in which individual characteristics are subsumed under group identity.[49]

In June 2016, Trump was the presumptive presidential nominee for the Republican Party. He had made a series of racist, sexist and xenophobic comments throughout his campaign.[50] This motivated several advocacy groups to urge companies not to sponsor the Republican National Convention in 2016. This particular campaign had over 360 000 signatories.[51] And it worked. Apple decided to drop its support of the GOP convention,[52] while other companies

---

[45]   Michael Barbaro, *Donald Trump Clung to 'Birther' Lie for Years, and Still Isn't Apologetic*, N.Y. TIMES (Sept. 16, 2016); Lopez, *et al., supra* note 43 ("2011: Trump played a big role in pushing false rumors that Obama — the country's first black president — was not born in the US.").

[46]   Lydia O'Connor & Daniel Marans, *Here Are 13 Examples of Donald Trump Being Racist*, HUFF. POST (Oct. 10, 2016).

[47]   Jennifer Rubin, *Trump's ingrained racism*, WASH. POST (Sept. 28, 2016) ("Trump accused Judge Gonzalo Curiel of not being able to do his job because he is a 'Mexican.' He was actually born in Indiana."); Michael D'Antonio, *Is Donald Trump Racist? Here's What the Record Shows*, FORTUNE (June 7, 2016).

[48]   Kristof, *supra* note 42 (["During his campaign for president,] Trump has also retweeted messages from white supremacists or Nazi sympathizers, including two from an account called @WhiteGenocideTM with a photo of the American Nazi Party's founder ...").

[49]   Rubin, *supra* note 47.

[50]   Jonathan Capehart, *How Trump is "Defining Deviancy Down" In Presidential Politics*, WASH. POST (Nov. 23, 2015); *see also* David Brooks, Opinion, *The Governing Cancer of Our Time*, N.Y. TIMES (Feb. 26, 2016).

[51]   *Id.*

[52]   Tony Romm, *Apple Won't Aid GOP Convention over Trump*, POLITICO (June 18, 2016), www.politico.com/story/2016/06/apple-wont-aid-gop-convention-over-trump -224513.

that dropped sponsorship included Wells Fargo, UPS, Motorola, JPMorgan Chase and Ford.[53]

Trump's 2016 campaign hired Cambridge Analytica to help microtarget voters. Cambridge Analytica had data on the races of voters, as well as their character traits.[54] What's not clear from the public record is whether it used this data to try to suppress the Black vote.[55] According to Christopher Wylie, a one-time employee of Cambridge Analytica turned whistle blower, discussions about suppressing the Black vote were the last straw for him and prompted him to leave the company:

> 'One of the things that provoked me to leave [Cambridge Analytica] was discussions about 'voter disengagement' and the idea of targeting African Americans,' he said, noting he had seen documents referencing this. Facebook posts were targeted at some black voters reminding them of Hillary Clinton's 1990s description of black youths as 'super predators', in the hope it would deter them from voting.[56]

Evidence that the Trump campaign did focus on suppressing the Black vote came from a *BusinessWeek* article published in late October 2016 that was written from inside the Trump campaign. The article stated:

> Instead of expanding the electorate, Bannon and his team are trying to shrink it. 'We have three major voter suppression operations under way,' says a senior official. They're aimed at three groups Clinton needs to win overwhelmingly: idealistic white liberals, young women, and African Americans.[57]

---

[53] Harper Neidig, *Major Companies Decline to Fund 2016 GOP Convention*, Hill (June 16, 2016), http://thehill.com/blogs/ballot-box/presidential-races/283832-major-companies-pull-sponsorship-of-gop-convention.

[54] Ryan Grenoble, *Christopher Wylie Warns Senators: Cambridge Analytica, Steve Bannon Wan 'Culture War,'* Huff. Post (May 16, 2018), www.huffingtonpost.com/entry/christopher-wylie-cambridge-senate-testimony_us_5afc59b0e4b0779345d51218.

[55] Emily Tillett, *Christopher Wylie: Bannon wanted "weapons" to fight a "culture war" at Cambridge Analytica*, CBS News (May 16, 2018), www.cbsnews.com/live-news/senate-cambridge-analytica-whistleblower-christopher-wylie-live-stream-updates-today-2018-05-16/ ("When pressed on how the firm targeted black voters, Wylie said that Cambridge Analytica would target anybody with 'characteristics that would lead them to vote for the Democratic party, particularly African American voters.'").

[56] Olivia Solon, *Cambridge Analytica whistleblower says Bannon wanted to suppress voters*, Guardian (May 16, 2018).

[57] Joshua Green & Sasha Issenberg, *Inside the Trump Bunker*, Bloomberg (Oct. 27, 2016), www.bloomberg.com/news/articles/2016-10-27/inside-the-trump-bunker-with-12-days-to-go.

As *Bloomberg* reported during the 2016 election:

> In San Antonio, a young [Trump] staffer showed off a *South Park*-style animation he'd created of Clinton delivering the 'super predator' line (using audio from her original 1996 sound bite), as cartoon text popped up around her: 'Hillary Thinks African Americans are Super Predators.' The animation will be delivered to certain African American voters through Facebook 'dark posts'—nonpublic posts whose viewership the campaign controls so that, as Parscale puts it, 'only the people we want to see it, see it.' The aim is to depress Clinton's vote total. 'We know because we've modeled this,' says the official. 'It will dramatically affect her ability to turn these people out.'[58]

Another hint at what the Trump team was up to vis-à-vis Black voters came out in a *Bloomberg* exposé in 2018. According to the article, the Trump campaign hired an African American man named Bruce Carter to discourage fellow Blacks from voting in the hopes of helping to elect Trump. One of his efforts was to discourage Black voters from voting early. As reported, "In the final weeks of October, Carter's operation announced a 'Don't Vote Early' campaign designed to convince black voters not to take advantage of early voting, which tended to build up banks of votes for Democrats."[59] Another tactic was to suggest to Black voters that they sit out the election completely. As *Bloomberg* reported: "'If you can't stomach Trump, just don't vote for the other people and don't vote at all,' Carter, 47, recalls telling black voters. It's the message he says the Trump campaign wanted him to deliver."[60] During the election, Carter's efforts on behalf of the Trump campaign were touted by *Breitbart*, which at the time was financially supported by the Mercers (Robert and Rebekah). In *Breitbart*, during the 2016 election Carter was quoted as saying:

> people need to understand how Democrats, and especially congressional black leadership, and Hillary Clinton have used our communities for their personal gain … We're going to go back to these communities in Florida, Ohio, Pennsylvania, Michigan, and across the country to lead people to the facts about the Clintons' and Democrats' failures with our struggling communities.[61]

---

[58] *Id.*

[59] Lauren Etter & Michael Riley, *Inside the Pro-Trump Effort to Keep Black Voters From the Polls*, BLOOMBERG (May 29, 2018), www.bloomberg.com/news/features/2018-05-29/inside-the-pro-trump-effort-to-keep-black-voters-from-the-polls.

[60] *Id.*

[61] Dustin Stockton, *Exclusive: "Black Men for Bernie" Founder to End Democrat "Political Slavery" of Minority Voters … by Campaigning for Trump*, BREITBART (Aug. 26, 2016), www.breitbart.com/politics/2016/08/26/black-men-for-bernie-founder-end-democrat-political-slavery-of-minorities/.

But after the election, Bannon, the Trump campaign and his financial backers all abruptly cut ties with Carter.[62]

And for some minority communities, the impact of the Trump election had a stark impact, as Maria Teresa Kumar reported:

> We at Voto Latino went from providing voter registration before the election to providing 1-800 numbers for suicide prevention after the election. We got an influx of cries for help on our social board. People felt scared and afraid the next day. Their lives had changed.[63]

5.   RACIAL TARGETING BY THE RUSSIAN INTERNET RESEARCH AGENCY

One goal of the Russians during the 2016 election, according to ex-CIA operative Steve Hall, was "they wanted to create as much chaos in our democracy as possible."[64] As the Congress noted in its legislative findings in a 2017 law providing for sanctions against Russia for interference in the 2016 election:

> On January 6, 2017, an assessment of the United States intelligence community entitled, 'Assessing Russian Activities and Intentions in Recent U.S. Elections' stated, *'Russian President Vladimir Putin ordered an influence campaign in 2016 aimed at the United States presidential election.'* ...
>
> It is the sense of Congress that the President— ... should increase efforts to vigorously enforce compliance with sanctions in place as of the date of the enactment of this Act with *respect to the Russian Federation in response ... cyber intrusions and attacks ...*[65]

Dr. Cailin O'Connor explained to Shankar Vedantam on his show *Hidden Brain* that the Russian Internet Research Agency (IRA) microtargeted its propaganda to disrupt the 2016 election: "[The IRA] made Black Lives Matter groups. They made gun rights groups. They made LGBTQ groups. They made an animal lovers group weirdly." Vedantam responded:

> So all over the political spectrum, from left to right - now that seems crazy except that it was based on a psychological insight. If you show someone you are on their side on an issue that is close to their heart, it becomes much easier to nudge them on other issues.

---

[62]   Etter & Riley, *supra* note 59.

[63]   Interview with Maria Teresa Kumar (Sept. 7, 2018).

[64]   Betsy Woodruff, *Kremlin Blessed Russia's NRA Operation, U.S. Intel Report Says*, DAILY BEAST (Jan. 13, 2019), www.thedailybeast.com/kremlin-blessed-russias-nra-operation-us-intel-report-says.

[65]   Public Law 115–44 (Aug. 2, 2017) (emphasis added).

Dr. O'Connor continued:

> It seemed that what [the Russian IRA agents] were doing was trying to use shared beliefs and values to ground trust with people. And then once they grounded that trust, they could use these different pages to try to drive polarization within the United States."[66]

The Senate Intelligence Committee commissioned two in-depth studies of the Russian assault on the U.S. electorate through social media that were delivered to the committee in late 2018. Team one was from Oxford University and included Philip N. Howard, Bharath Ganesh and Dimitra Liosiou, with co-authors John Kelly and Camille François from Graphika. Team two was from New Knowledge and included Renee DiResta, Kris Shaffer, Becky Ruppel, David Sullivan, Robert Matney, Ryan Fox, Jonathan Albright and Ben Johnson. Their findings are some of the only comprehensive public-facing evidence of what the Russians did during the 2016 election.

Coordinated or not, the Russians appeared to have similar goals as the Trump campaign. The range of tactics used by the Russian IRA to create an echo chamber of ideas was broad and intrusive. One tactic was to create "think tank" style webpages, like a group called GI Analytics with a masthead that included Americans.[67] It also used Twitter, Facebook, Instagram, Youtube, Paypal, Vine, Gab, Meetup, VKontakte (Russia's largest social media site), LiveJournal, Reddit, Tumblr, Pinterest and Medium.[68] YouTube was a favorite channel for spreading Russian propaganda via video. As Renee DiResta *et al.* reported:

> Across all [Russian IRA YouTube] channels, 25 videos had election-related keywords in the title (candidate names, 'vote'/'voting', 'election', etc). These videos were all anti-Hillary Clinton. One of the political channels, Paul Jefferson, solicited videos for a #PeeOnHillary video challenge (the hashtag appeared on Twitter and Instagram) and shared submissions that it received.[69]

Meanwhile, on Facebook, the IRA purchased ads to reach certain Americans, as well as generating organic posts from fake personas it had crafted during the 2016 election. The organic posts reached millions of Americans, many of

---

[66] Shankar Vedantam, *Why Did So Many Americans Trust Russian Hackers' Election Propaganda? Transcript*, NPR (Jan. 22, 2019), www.npr.org/2019/01/22/687319805/why-did-so-many-americans-trust-russian-hackers-election-propaganda.

[67] Renee DiResta, *et al.*, *The Tactics & Tropes of the Internet Research Agency* 13 (2018).

[68] *Id.* at 5.

[69] *Id.* at 17.

whom engaged with the posts as they would other legitimate content online. On Facebook:

> 30 [pages] targeted Black audiences and amassed 1,187,810 followers; 25 targeted the Right and amassed 1,446,588 followers, and 7 targeted the Left and amassed 689,045 followers … [On Facebook] there were 76.5 million engagements across 3.3 million Page followers. These included 30.4 million shares, 37.6 million likes, 3.3 million comments, and 5.2 million reactions across the content.[70]

On Twitter, the IRA used popular hashtags to insinuate itself into the conversation including using hashtags that were associated with the Trump campaign, including #MAGA (short for "Make America Great Again").[71] To increase its reach, the IRA also used bots to generate even more content.[72]

The IRA had Russian individuals impersonating American "personas" online who could react with real Americans in real time. DiResta, *et al.* found that:

> While media narratives around the Russian/IRA Twitter activity have often focused on automation and bots, the agency ran human-operated precision personas …The personas were spontaneous and responsive, engaging with real users (famous influencers and media as well as regular people), participating in real-time conversations …[73]

Another way the IRA got its messages out to a broader audience was by having unwitting Americans—especially ones with large social media followings (known as influencers)—share its Russian-produced content.[74] The Russian IRA's "Twitter personas regularly retweeted content by prominent and influential public figures; they were occasionally retweeted by influencers in return."[75] And the more they insinuated themselves into conversations among

---

[70] *Id.* at 21.

[71] Philip N. Howard, *et al.*, *The IRA, Social Media and Political Polarization in the United States, 2012–2018* 27 (2018) ("#MAGA was also used more than 10,000 times in total …").

[72] DiResta, *et al.*, *supra* note 67, at 66 ("The incorporation of local news into their strategy was possibly undertaken because Pew and others have found that Americans have a higher degree of trust in local news.").

[73] *Id.* at 13.

[74] Howard, *et al.*, *supra* note 71, at 7 ("Sharing is particularly important as it exposes even more people to IRA content, including those who do not follow IRA pages. On Facebook, the five most shared and the five most liked posts focused on divisive issues …").

[75] DiResta, *et al.*, *supra* note 67, at 13 ("These [IRA] personas developed relationships with American citizens. They were designed to influence individuals and to shape narratives …").

Americans, the more they could shape the narrative of what was being talked about and the tone of the conversation.[76]

Americans often inhabit self-reinforcing ideological information bubbles.[77] The Russians sought to exploit and exacerbate these bubbles:[78]

> The themes selected by the IRA were deployed to create and reinforce tribalism within each targeted community ... They punctuated cultural-affinity content with political posts, and content demonizing out-groups. Partisan content was presented to targeted groups in on-brand ways, such as a meme featuring Jesus in a Trump campaign hat on an account that targeted Christians.[79]

Facebook's interface made it particularly easy for the Russians to target subsets of Americans.[80] They targeted both left and right.[81] An example of how they exacerbated rifts is that in posts about immigrants to rightwing audiences, the Russians called immigrants "parasites."[82] Each subset of American voters was bombarded with a different message that was likely to appeal to it.[83] As Special Counsel Robert Mueller noted in an indictment against the IRA, "By

---

[76]   *Id.*

[77]   Howard, *et al.*, *supra* note 71, at 18 ("The first [strategy] involved appealing to the narratives common within a specific group, such as supporting veterans and police, or pride in race and heritage, as a clickbait strategy to drive traffic to the Facebook and Instagram pages the IRA set up. Based on an analysis of both ads and posts, we find that the IRA posted content on these pages to which they drove traffic with ads.").

[78]   *Id.* at 27 ("the IRA Twitter data shows a long and successful campaign that resulted in false accounts being effectively woven into the fabric of online US political conversations right up until their suspension. These embedded assets each targeted specific audiences they sought to manipulate and radicalize, with some gaining meaningful influence in online communities ...").

[79]   DiResta, *et al.*, *supra* note 67, at 12.

[80]   Howard, *et al.*, *supra* note 71, at 17–18 ("By selecting interests in Facebook's Ads Manager tool, large audiences (for example African Americans, conservatives and right-wing voters) can be divided into smaller segments: for example, allowing the IRA to target African Americans across mainstream political and cultural issues, but also users with interests in Black Nationalism and identity, or with more specific interests in the prison system ('Incarceration' segment).").

[81]   *Id.* at 18 ("If we look at the amount spent in total, we see that a similar amount was spent on conservatives (a small number of expensive ads) as was spent on targeting African Americans (a large number of cheap ads).").

[82]   *Id.* at 7 ("In some cases, terms such as 'parasites' were used to reference immigrants and others expressed some tolerance of extremist views.").

[83]   *Id.* at 18 ("Messaging to conservative and right-wing voters sought to do three things: repeat patriotic and anti-immigrant slogans; elicit outrage with posts about liberal appeasement of 'others' at the expense of US citizens; and encourage them to vote for Trump. Messaging to this segment of voters focused on divisive, and at times prejudiced and bigoted, statements about minorities, particularly Muslims.").

2016, the size of many [IRA] groups had grown to hundreds of thousands of online followers."[84] The IRA had a budget of over $1 million per month for this operation.[85]

Part of what the IRA was doing was trying to build brands that would appeal to American voters, so that it could persuade them to act and think in a certain way. This is what commercial brands do as well. As commercial branding expert Debbie Millman put it, "Brands create tribes. They allow us to assert moods, tastes, whims and choice. Brands signal our affiliations and can even define our beliefs."[86]

African Americans were particularly targeted by the IRA, especially through paid ads on social media.[87] Black Americans who encountered the Russian propaganda stepped into a hall of mirrors that created a fake world of social media and bogus Russian webpages.[88] One way the IRA built the brands that targeted Blacks (and others) was by creating well-designed logos.[89] Another way that the Russians built appealing brands for their American victims was by trying to piggyback off existing brands.[90] Call it the knock-off brand of propaganda. In America, there is a real group called Black Lives Matter, which started after an unarmed Black teenager named Treyvon Martin was killed by a man named George Zimmerman, who was eventually acquitted of the murder. The Black Lives Matter group expanded in national prominence after an unarmed Black teenager named Michael Brown was killed by police in Ferguson, Missouri. As journalist Ian Millhiser said:

> the reason why Black Lives Matter emerged at the time was a common legitimate grievance held by a large number of Americans who were able to identify 'oh wait.

---

[84]   United States of America v. Internet Research Agency LLC 14 (Indictment Feb. 16, 2018), www.lawfareblog.com/document-special-counsel-indicts-russian-nationals -and-entities.

[85]   U.S. v. Internet Research Agency, *et al.*, 1:18-cr-32 (D.D.C. Feb. 16, 2018).

[86]   DEBBIE MILLMAN, LOOK BOTH WAYS ILLUSTRATED ESSAYS ON THE INTERSECTION OF LIFE AND DESIGN 13–14 (2009).

[87]   Howard, *et al., supra* note 71, at 17 ("… the African American segment was targeted with the most ads. White users were divided into liberal and conservative segments and targeted differently.").

[88]   DiResta, *et al., supra* note 67, at 45 ("A 'media mirage' of interlinked Facebook Pages and Instagram accounts targeting Black Americans.").

[89]   *Id.* at 41 ("The IRA developed their content using digital marketing best practices, even evolving their Facebook Page logos and typography over time.")

[90]   *Id.* at 13 ("the IRA co-opted the names of real groups with existing reputations serving the targeted communities - including United Muslims of America, Cop Block, Black Guns Matter, and L for Life. This was perhaps an attempt to loosely backstop an identity if a curious individual did a Google Search, or to piggyback on an established brand.").

I'm not the only person who thinks this way. All of these other people are talking about this too.' And they were able to organize across geographic barriers because of social media and they were able to elevate this issue that had been neglected for a very long time because they were able to find people that they couldn't in 2006. On the other hand, the Klan can do that too.[91]

The Russians created a fake group called Black Matters and then targeted actual Black people who lived in Ferguson, Missouri and elsewhere in the U.S. with their propaganda.[92] This group had a fake Facebook page, a fake Instagram account and a fake webpage called blackmattersus.com, which expressed its distrust of mainstream media.[93] The IRA would often post similar content across different platforms to reinforce its message to anyone caught in this media mirage,[94] complete with audience-tailored conspiracy theories.[95] "The case study of Black Matters illustrates the extent to which the Internet Research Agency built out one inauthentic media property, creating accounts across the social ecosystem to reinforce its brand and broadly distribute its content."[96] Black Matters increased its following by duping real Black activists in America into thinking it was legitimate. Some of these real Black activists shared the information from Black Matters with their followers.[97] Black Matters' Instagram had nearly 2 million engagements.[98] DiResta *et al.* concluded, "Black Matters content focused on building community – and sowing division – in real life as well as online. Many posts solicited protestors, writers, activists, lawyers, and photographers to attend the property's numerous events."[99]

Russian online propaganda became surreal at points. On occasion, one Russian-created online persona would get into a faux fight with another

---

[91]   Interview with Ian Millhiser (July 19, 2018).

[92]   Howard, *et al.*, *supra* note 71, at 21 ("African Americans in Ferguson, MO were targeted for the 'Black Matters' campaign.").

[93]   DiResta, *et al.*, *supra* note 67 at 43.

[94]   *Id.* at 62 ("The repurposing of the same story across accounts in the media mirage was a deliberate tactic, deployed to reinforce key themes and create the perception that certain messages or opinions were widespread and worthy of attention.").

[95]   *Id.* at 70 ("The Black-targeted groups were presented with distinct historical conspiracies … [like] the idea that Wolfgang Amadeus Mozart was Black, that Shakespeare's plays had been written by a Black woman, and that the Statue of Liberty had originally been made in the likeness of a Black woman …").

[96]   *Id.* at 45.

[97]   DiResta, *et al.*, *supra* note 67, at 43 ("data reveals that influencers with large followings, such as Color of Change, Unapologetically Black, and YourAnonNews, shared Black Matters articles to their own Facebook Pages.").

[98]   *Id.* at 43.

[99]   *Id.* at 44.

Russian-created online persona, presumably in the hopes that real Americans would pick sides in the fight. For example: "[a]t one point, Right-targeted persona @TEN_GOP engaged with Black-targeted persona @Crystal1Johnson: '@Crystal1Johnson Wake up! This will happen if Hillary wins. Stop being slave of Democrat plantation!'"[100]

Many of the tactics of the IRA were deployed purely online and could be dismissed as so much murmuring in the ether. But other Russian government projects had real-world impacts. The IRA was actively trying to recruit human assets to its cause, including by hiring them for various jobs:[101]

> [The IRA] posted job ads for real American writers to create content for blackmattersus.com – a clear example supporting the hypothesis that the IRA engaged in narrative laundering. The goal of working with real Americans is to eliminate the detection and exposure risk of inauthentic personas.[102]

Another part of this recruitment of human assets appeared to be attempts to set up opportunities to blackmail Americans. As reported to the Senate Intelligence Committee:

> Recruiting an asset by exploiting a personal vulnerability – usually a secret that would inspire shame or cause personal or financial harm if exposed – is a timeless espionage practice. So is the tactic of infiltrating protest movements. The IRA attempted both, even going so far as to create help hotlines for people struggling with sexual behavior, creating an opportunity to blackmail or manipulate these individuals in the future.[103]

An additional real-world impact was getting money from unsuspecting marks. One way the IRA raised money was through selling merchandise. "The merchandise strategy ... enabled fundraising, brand building, and the collection of addresses and potentially credit card information. Meetup.com was used to organize Black self-defense classes for the Fit Black/Black Fist IRA accounts."[104]

In another particularly dark effort, the Russian IRA seemed to want to stoke real-world violence among competing American groups. As DiResta *et al.* reported, "At a local level, the IRA promoted riots and rallies to call attention to a myriad of issues and grievances. At the state level, the IRA promoted

---

[100]   *Id*. at 88.
[101]   *Id*. at 39 ("The extent of the human asset recruitment strategy is revealed in the organic data set. It is expansive ...").
[102]   DiResta, *et al*., *supra* note 67, at 44.
[103]   *Id*. at 40.
[104]   *Id*. at 37.

secession (#texit, #calexit) and amplified regional cultural differences."[105] And they found:

> at a national level, the IRA promoted armed insurgency, through exhortations to violence over issues ranging from the Bureau of Land Management to Black Lives Matter, from protesting Confederate monument removal to threatening riots over election legitimacy (if Hillary Clinton were to steal the election). Armed insurrection and the Bundy standoff were talking points on [Russian created fora] Stand for Freedom, Defend the 2nd, Heart of Texas and Being Patriotic – all in favor of it.[106]

These rallies also caught the attention of the special counsel, who noted in his indictment of the IRA:

> Starting in approximately June 2016, [Russian] Defendants and their co-conspirators organized and coordinated political rallies in the United States. To conceal the fact that they were based in Russia, Defendants and their co-conspirators promoted these rallies while pretending to be U.S. grassroots activists who were located in the United States but unable to meet or participate in person.[107]

An additional pernicious real-world impact of the Russian IRA's efforts was the attempted voter suppression, especially those messages that were targeted at suppressing Black voters.[108] As Howard *et al.* found in their analysis, "Messaging to African Americans sought to divert their political energy away from established political institutions by preying on anger with structural inequalities faced by African Americans, including police violence, poverty, and disproportionate levels of incarceration."[109] And even this voter suppression relied on branding techniques. "These campaigns pushed a message that the best way to advance the cause of the African American community was to boycott the election and focus on other issues instead. This often happened through the use of repetitive slogans."[110] One of the repeated themes communicated to Black voters was either that their vote didn't matter or that they should boycott voting. Howard *et al.* found:

> Attacks on Clinton and calls for voter disengagement were particularly clear in [the Russian IRA created persona known as] Blacktivist during September, October, and

---

[105] *Id.* at 72.

[106] *Id.* at 72.

[107] United States of America v. Internet Research Agency LLC, *supra* note 84, at 20.

[108] *Id.* at 8 ("there were three primary variants of specific voter suppression narratives spread on Twitter, Facebook, Instagram, and YouTube.").

[109] Howard, *et al.*, *supra* note 71, at 18.

[110] *Id.* at 18.

November 2016, with statements such as … 'NOT VOTING is a way to exercise our rights' (Blacktivist, 3 November 2016).[111]

These voter suppression messages from Russian avatars were also found by DiResta *et al.*, who noted, "As the election became imminent, … several varieties of voter suppression narratives [were repeated]: don't vote, stay home, this country is not for Black people, these candidates don't care about Black people."[112] These researchers noted that another IRA persona @afrokingdom_ also advocated that Black people not vote: "Black people don't have to vote for Hillary because she is a liar! Black people are smart enough to understand that Hillary doesn't deserve our votes! DON'T VOTE!"[113]

It's hard to know what the impact of Russian voter suppression efforts was among American voters in 2016. What can be measured is the drop in voters. As the *Washington Post* put it, "4.4 million 2012 Obama voters stayed home in 2016—more than a third of them [were] black …"[114] The special counsel noted this destructive behavior in his indictment against the IRA: "In or around the latter half of 2016, Defendants and their co-conspirators, through their personas, began to encourage U.S. minority groups not to vote in the 2016 US. presidential election or to vote for a third-party US. presidential candidate."[115] As Professor Pam Karlan said:

> there was depression in the minority turnout in Michigan where Trump won. There was lack of enthusiasm on one side [for Clinton], and the other side was full of rage [for Trump]. It reminds me of the 'Second Coming' by Yeats who wrote 'The best lack all conviction, while the worst are full of passionate intensity.'[116]

Yet another real-world impact the Russian IRA tried to have was to cast doubt on the legitimacy of the American election. (Recall that Trump was largely forecast to lose the election; thus, casting doubt on the election would have hurt a President-elect Clinton.) There were many Russian posts:

> devoted to creating and amplifying fears of voter fraud; the overwhelming majority of them targeted right-wing audiences. 71 were created in the month leading up to election day, and made claims that certain states were helping Sec. Clinton win, that militia groups were going to polling places to stop fraud (called for volunteers

---

[111] *Id.* at 34.

[112] DiResta, *et al.*, *supra* note 67, at 83.

[113] *Id.* at 88.

[114] Philip Bump, *4.4 million 2012 Obama voters stayed home in 2016—more than a third of them black*, WASH. POST (Mar. 12, 2018).

[115] United States of America v. Internet Research Agency LLC, *supra* note 81, at 18.

[116] Interview with Pam Karlan (May 19, 2018) (quoting Yeats).

to participate), that civil war was preferable to an unfair election or the election of Sec. Clinton …[117]

Finally, the Russian IRA's ultimate hope was to influence the outcome of the 2016 election. The U.S. intelligence community would later assess that the social media disinformation campaign was for Trump's benefit.[118] DiResta *et al.* found, "the goal appears to have been to generate extreme anger and engagement for those most likely to support then-candidate Donald Trump, and to create disillusionment and disengagement on the Left-leaning and Black communities."[119] And "the IRA consistently supported [Trump's] candidacy throughout the primary in Right-leaning groups, keeping their memes and content positive … [A post from] Dec. 18, 2015 … expressed the conviction that Trump was going to have a very sensible Russia policy."[120] As Michael Isikoff and David Corn indicated, the Trump campaign's "work, whether the Trump campaign realized it or not, was aided by the anti-Clinton messages generated by Russian trolls …"[121] Did the Trump campaign welcome the Russians' racist help? This is still an open question, given the current available public-facing evidence. A potential tell that they did welcome it was President-elect Trump thanking Blacks for not voting in a speech in December 2016: "frankly if they [Black voters] had any doubt, they didn't vote, and that was almost as good because a lot of people didn't show up, because they felt good about me."[122]

Russian interference continued after the 2016 election. Some efforts even spiked post-election.[123] And again the Russians tried to create real-world impacts, like protests in the streets. One theme they pushed after the 2016 election was encouraging Americans to participate in "Not my President"

---

[117] DiResta, *et al.*, *supra* note 67, at 77.

[118] Office of the Director of National Intelligence, *Background to "Assessing Russian Activities and Intentions in Recent US Elections": The Analytic Process and Cyber Incident Attribution* (Jan. 6, 2017), https://assets.documentcloud.org/documents/3254237/Russia-Hack-Report.pdf.

[119] DiResta, *et al.*, *supra* note 67, at 84.

[120] *Id.* at 80.

[121] Michael Isikoff & David Corn, Russian Roulette: The Inside Story of Putin's War on America and the Election of Donald Trump 271 (2018).

[122] Benjamin Kentish, *Donald Trump thanks African-Americans for not voting in US presidential election*, Independent (Dec. 11, 2016).

[123] Howard, *et al.*, *supra* note 71, at 34.

protests, as well as "Celebrate Trump" rallies. [124] This was also documented in the special counsel's indictment of the IRA:

> After the election of Donald Trump in or around November 2016, Defendants and their co-conspirators used false U.S. personas to organize and coordinate U.S. political rallies in support of then president-elect Trump, while simultaneously using other false U.S. personas to organize and coordinate U.S. political rallies protesting the results of the 2016 U.S. presidential election.[125]

A super-suspicious and diligent Internet user may have sussed out that some posts from the Russian IRA were coming from foreign IP addresses or Russia telecommunications firms.[126] But as Mueller's February 2018 indictment of the IRA showed, sometimes the Russians took the additional step of stealing real Americans' identities or setting up American IP addresses. So expecting the average American voters to recognize these expert fakes in 2016 could be asking too much. Given that these tactics have been exposed, buyer and voter beware in 2020 and beyond.

6.   CONCLUSION

The theme that links the use of race by American political parties through American history and the actions of the Russian IRA in 2015–16 and beyond is that these groups were counting on American racial division to cement political power. Whether Dixiecrats, the American Independent Party or the Republicans supporting Donald Trump were deep in their heart of hearts racists isn't the point. The point is they all acted in ways to capitalize on the electorate's racial fears to maximize their own electoral fortunes.

What the GOP risks by doing this is alienating minority voters and their allies for generations. As Stanford Professor Pamela Karlan remarked:

> there is a risk of long-term damage to the GOP presented by Trump. Trump is like Prop 187 in California, which alienated Hispanic voters, many of whom are culturally conservative. But because of the California GOP's stance on immigration, these voters turned to the Democratic Party. California was 'purple' until Prop 187, but that turned Hispanics against the GOP. This why Texas could become a 'blue' state

---

[124] DiResta, *et al.*, *supra* note 67, at 92 ("@Crystal1Johnson account immediately called for a #NotMyPresident protest … And … trolls post[ed] pro as well as anti-Trump responses.").

[125] United States of America v. Internet Research Agency LLC *supra* note 84, at 23.

[126] DiResta, *et al.*, *supra* note 67, at 66 ("the metadata associated with the Twitter newsbots reveals that … they were created with obviously Russian device information … and were tweeting from overseas IPs.").

in 10–15 years. If Trump keeps calling Mexicans 'animals' and does nothing to save DACA, he could lose that constituency for the GOP.[127]

And finally, the Russian government's use of racial tropes to interfere in the 2016 election demonstrated vividly that American racial divisions, just like easy-to-hack voting machines, raise a national security issue.

---

[127] Interview with Pam Karlan (May 19, 2018).

PART IV

Rejecting toxic brands

Commercial brands have a minefield to navigate when it comes to modern politics. Consumers are rediscovering old tactics like the political boycott to reject brands that they find morally or politically repugnant. This tactic goes back to the Boston Tea Party, but is as modern as the #grabyourwallet boycott that started in 2016 inspired by candidate Trump.

With a brand as president, the nation has a new set of problems to tackle, including trying to suss out whether President Trump is acting in the interest of his commercial brand or the interest of the nation. This question is being litigated in three lawsuits which raise the issue of whether Trump is receiving unconstitutional emoluments from foreign and domestic governments through his business.

This final part of the book also examinesexamines the complex ways that citizens have tried to fight back against brands that displease them. For example, the last chapter will examine how the survivors of the Parkland massacre in Florida have channeled their rage into a number of tactics to financially cripple the National Rifle Association (NRA). This includes calling for traditional boycotts; but it goes beyond that to try to break the links among commercial brands, the NRA and politicians.

In the epilogue, some policy reforms are summarized to address some of the problems this book has exposed.

10. Branding greed[1]

1.   INTRODUCTION

Just as "corruption" can be branded and rebranded, so too can the concept of "greed." Dante placed the greedy in the Fourth Circle of Hell.[3] Being accused of greed – one of the seven deadly sins – is typically a characteristic that most try to avoid.[4] Perhaps a rare cultural exception to this is Michael Douglas's character in the classic 1980s movie *Wall Street*, Gordon Gekko, who declared defiantly, "Greed is good."[5]

Oddly, in American political discourse, greed is often an accusation foisted upon the poorest Americans, like President Reagan calling women on public assistance "welfare queens."[6] Likewise, even low wage workers who are participating in a struggle for living wages known as "the fight for $15" are often accused of being "greedy."[7] But the wealthy seldom get branded as "greedy."

---

[1]   A version of this chapter was first published in Ciara Torres-Spelliscy, *From a Mint on a Hotel Pillow to an Emolument*, 70 MERCER LAW REVIEW 705 (Spring 2019).

[2]   *Season 8 Quotes, Mountain of Madness/Quotes*, SIMPSONS FANDOM https://simpsons.fandom.com/wiki/Mountain_of_Madness/Quotes.

[3]   DANTE ALIGHIERI, THE DIVINE COMEDY, Canto 7 (1320).

[4]   CLOTAIRE RAPAILLE, THE CULTURE CODE: AN INGENIOUS WAY TO UNDERSTAND WHY PEOPLE AROUND THE WORLD LIVE AND BUY AS THEY DO 121 (2007) ("Americans themselves perceive this preoccupation with money and think it suggests that we are greedy at heart or that we prize material goods over enhancement of the spirit.").

[5]   Jim Zarroli, *Gordon Gekko, Preaching the Gospel of Greed*, NPR (Feb. 17, 2008), www.npr.org/templates/story/story.php?storyId=19105520.

[6]   Theodore R. Johnson & Leah Wright Rigueur, *Race-Baiting for the Presidency*, THE ATLANTIC (Nov. 18, 2015), www.theatlantic.com/politics/archive/2015/11/racial-divisiveness-as-a-campaign-strategy/416412/ ("Reagan still employed a form of racial divisiveness through the coded language of states' rights or welfare queens ...").

[7]   Laura Donovan, *Dunkin Donuts' CEO Just Said Something Insane About the Minimum Wage*, ATTN (July 24, 2015), https://archive.attn.com/stories/2495/dunkin-donuts-ceo-minimum-wage ("Dunkin' Brand CEO Nigel Travis ... said that $15 per hour for fast food workers would be 'absolutely outrageous.'").

Rather, positive attributes are used to brand the wealthy, like "successful," "hardworking," "diligent," "creative," and "job creators."

Rich politicians are often framed by their supporters as "incorruptible" because they already have so much money.[8] And on rare occasions, this turns out to be true. Billionaire Mayor of New York Michael Bloomberg turned out to be a strong leader who did not use his position to grift the city. Patrician politician Franklin Roosevelt was seen as a traitor to his class for his progressive policies that went against his own financial self-interest and favored the poor. But often wealthy politicians are just greedy politicians and cannot resist the temptation to use political office to enrich themselves. This is one of the reasons why campaign finance laws and ethics laws exist: to try to mitigate the baser instincts of men and women who would be tempted to parlay public service into greater personal wealth. Some of these ethical protections are built into the U.S. Constitution, like the two Emoluments Clauses.

During the 2016 election, candidate Trump and his supporters often pointed to Trump's wealth as a reason why he would be a good president. There were a few strains of this argument. One version was that because he was a successful businessman, he could "manage" the country.[9] Another was that his wealth would insulate him from political pressures from wealthy donors.[10] Trump pointed out several times that he was a self-financed candidate. *Politifact* rated this claim "half-true."[11] The reality was Trump was the source of only 20 percent of his campaign's funds in 2016. The other 80 percent came from other people's money.[12] So the image he was building up as a "self-financed" billionaire candidate didn't match up with reality. And as of July 1, 2019, Trump had personally contributed exactly $0 to his 2020 re-election cam-

---

[8]   Jim Zarroli, *When it Comes to Wealthy Leaders, World Abounds with Cautionary Tales*, NPR (Dec. 6, 2016), www.npr.org/sections/parallels/2016/12/06/504553162/ when-it-comes-to-wealthy-leaders-world-abounds-in-cautionary-tales.

[9]   Associated Press, *Donald Trump Says He'll Run America Like His Business*, FORTUNE (Oct. 27, 2016), http://fortune.com/2016/10/27/donald-trump-hillary-clinton -business-management/.

[10]   David A. Graham, *The Lie of Trump's 'Self-Funding' Campaign* (May 13, 2016), www.theatlantic.com/politics/archive/2016/05/trumps-self-funding-lie/48269/.

[11]   Lauren Carroll, *Is Donald Trump self-funding his campaign? Sort of*, POLITIFACT (Feb. 10, 2016), www.politifact.com/truth-o-meter/statements/2016/feb/10/donald -trump/donald-trump-self-funding-his-campaign-sort/ ("Trump said, 'I'm self-funding my own campaign.' … The statement is partially accurate but leaves out important details, so we rate it Half True.").

[12]   *Donald Trump (R) Winner*, CTR FOR RESPONSIVE POLITICS (2016), www .opensecrets.org/pres16/candidate?id=N00023864 (showing the candidate provided 19.77% of the campaign's funds).

paign.[13] Trump's attempt to make himself look selfless didn't fool everyone. As President of the Brennan Center Michael Waldman said, "To the extent Trump had a brand, it was gaudy greed."[14]

This chapter will deal with two civil matters that have arisen during the presidency of Donald Trump: (1) the dissolution of his charity, the Donald J. Trump Foundation; and (2) the three ongoing emoluments suits which allege that Trump is in ongoing violation of at least one of the Constitution's Emoluments Clauses. The thread that links both is the question of whether there is any legal outer limit to his greed. In the Donald J. Trump Foundation case, the attorney general of New York said yes, there is a statutory outer limit to using a charity as a personal piggybank. What remains an open question is whether the other courts in the emoluments cases will also find a constitutional outer limit to his greed.

2. THE TRUMP FOUNDATION

There are so many legal problems swirling around Trump, it is easy to lose track. In his first two years in office, he was sued by a porn star, individuals he had blocked on Twitter, nearly 200 members of Congress and *Apprentice* contestant Summer Zervos, just to name a few. And that doesn't even touch on the criminal liability that could rain down on him, his campaign, his inaugural and his business from ongoing criminal investigations. Trump has also been sued by the attorney general of New York for his misuse of the Donald J. Trump Foundation.

There are strict rules against using a charity for personal gain. At their base, the allegations raised by the New York attorney general against Trump boiled down to whether he could greedily ignore these rules and use his foundation for his own benefit. During the 2016 campaign, there were hints that something dishonest was going on at the foundation. For one, it popped up during his presidential campaign in Iowa, a place one would not expect a foundation to be, because it is illegal for foundations to be involved in electoral politics. On October 3, 2016, the attorney general of New York issued a notice of violation to the Donald J. Trump Foundation.[15] The notice required the foundation to cease and desist from soliciting charitable donations in New York. On June 14, 2018, the attorney general for New York filed a lawsuit in a state court

---

[13] *Donald J. Trump For President, Inc., 2020 Election*, FEC, www.fec.gov/data/candidate/P80001571.

[14] Interview with Michael Waldman (Apr. 27, 2018).

[15] *Notice of Violation*, N.Y. ATTORNEY GENERAL (re: Donald J. Trump Foundation Oct. 30, 2016), https://ag.ny.gov/sites/default/files/trump_foundation_notice_of_violation_9-30-16.pdf.

to dissolve the foundation.[16] This lawsuit was against the Donald J. Trump Foundation and its directors, Donald J. Trump, Donald J. Trump, Jr., Ivanka Trump and Eric Trump. One of the allegations in the suit is that the board, which is made up of the president and his three eldest children, had not bothered to meet in 19 years. This suit sought $2.8 million in restitution.

Part of this case alleges that the Donald J. Trump Foundation served as Trump's personal piggybank for years, including being used to pay for personal items like a portrait of Trump and to pay off the settlement of a lawsuit for his private business. Among the evidence in the case is a handwritten note from Trump on the Donald J. Trump Foundation letterhead approving the use of foundation funds for personal use.[17] The suit also alleges that the foundation was illegally helping the Trump campaign. The State alleges that "the Foundation [was] co-opted by Mr. Trump's presidential campaign, and thereby violated its certificate of incorporation and state and federal law by engaging in political activity and prohibited related party transactions."[18] Non-profits like the Donald J. Trump Foundation are not allowed to get involved in electoral politics under the Internal Revenue Code, because they are 501(c)(3)s. For example, an Internal Revenue Service Tax Guide from 2015 states: "statements of position ... made by or on behalf of [a foundation] in favor of ... any candidate for public office clearly violate the prohibition against political campaign activity ..."[19] The Federal Election Campaign Act (FECA) also bars all corporations, including nonprofit foundations, from giving directly to federal candidates. The judge in the Donald J. Trump Foundation case refused to dismiss the suit, concluding: "Allowing this action to proceed is entirely consistent with the Supreme Court's holding in *Clinton v. Jones* that the President of the United States is 'subject to the laws for his purely private acts.'"[20]

---

[16] Press Release, *Attorney General Underwood Announces Lawsuit Against Donald J. Trump Foundation And Its Board of Directors for Extensive and Persistent Violations of State and Federal Law,* N.Y. ATTORNEY GENERAL (June 14, 2018), https://ag.ny.gov/press-release/attorney-general-underwood-announces-lawsuit-against-donald-j-trump-foundation-and-its.

[17] *Exhibit 33 to* NYS v. Trump, Index No. 451130/2018 (June 14, 2018), https://ag.ny.gov/sites/default/files/ex_33.pdf (stating in Trump's handwriting, "Allen W DJT Foundation $100,000 to Fisher House (settlement of flag issue in Palm Beach) OK D.").

[18] NYS v. Trump, Index No. 451130/2018 at *5 (June 14, 2018), https://ag.ny.gov/sites/default/files/ex_1.pdf (Petition).

[19] *Tax Guide for Churches & Religious Organizations 501(c)(3), Publication 1828,* INTERNAL REVENUE SERVICE (2015), www.irs.gov/pub/irs-pdf/p1828.pdf.

[20] People of the State of New York v. Trump, Index No. 451130/2018 (Oct. 25, 2018), https://ag.ny.gov/sites/default/files/trump_foundation.pdf (decision and order) (internal citations omitted).

On December 18, 2018, the Donald J. Trump Foundation was dissolved.[21] One issue still to be resolved is that the attorney general was also seeking to bar Trump from serving on charitable boards in New York. As the *New York Times* points out, if she wins "it would put him in the unusual position of not being able to serve on the board of his own post-presidential foundation, should it be set up in New York."[22] Thereby, Attorney General Tish James, on behalf of the people of New York, has stopped at least one manifestation of Trump's greed: abusing a charity for his own personal gain. As the Attorney General said, "Make no mistake: No one is above the law, not even the President."[23]

3. THE TRUMP EMOLUMENTS CONTROVERSY

Another limit to Trump's greed could be imposed by the federal courts. The question in the federal emoluments cases at their essence is: "Is President Trump illegally profiting from the presidency?" Answering this question requires constitutional interpretation that breaks new legal ground and could change the rules for all future presidents.[24] The answer may also impact those who wish to deal with the president's businesses. Depending on the outcome of cases invoking the Constitution's two Emoluments Clauses, many commercial interactions with the Trump Organization that are fine today may be ruled unconstitutional tomorrow.

The very first thing Trump did upon assuming the office of the presidency was swear to uphold the Constitution. A key element of upholding the Constitution is abiding by it—including the two Emoluments Clauses. But as former head of the Office of Government Ethics Walter Shaub stated, with Trump there is "an appearance that [his] businesses are profiting from his occupying the presidency …"[25] By contrast to Trump's behavior, President

---

[21] Shane Goldmacher, *Trump Foundation Will Dissolve, Accused of "Shocking Pattern of Illegality"*, N.Y. Times (Dec. 18, 2018), www.nytimes.com/2018/12/18/nyregion/ny-ag-underwood-trump-foundation.html.

[22] *Id.*

[23] Tish James, *Tweet responding to @realdonaldtrump*, Twitter (July 1, 2019 at 2:25 PM), https://twitter.com/NewYorkStateAG/status/1145745174624186368.

[24] Editorial, *Bringing the emoluments clause to bear on Trump's D.C. hotel*, Boston Globe (Aug. 7, 2018), www.bostonglobe.com/opinion/editorials/2018/08/06/bringing-emoluments-clause-bear-trump-hotel/76XhekGBkDfbHuRYfMsNIM/story.html ("the case itself could establish a welcome precedent to constrain any future presidents who might be tempted to hustle some extra cash on the side.").

[25] Ben Popken, *Trump's Presidency Is Bad for Business—His Own*, NBC (Oct. 16, 2017), www.nbcnews.com/business/business-news/trump-s-presidency-bad-business-his-own-n809886 (quoting Walter M. Shaub Jr.).

Jimmy Carter famously put his beloved peanut farm in an independent trust while he was president.[26]

The fact that Trump had a business empire when he was elected immediately set off alarms that he could violate at least one of the U.S. Constitution's two Emoluments Clauses the moment he was sworn in.[27] As Rep. Pocan stated in the *Congressional Record*, "These holdings potentially put President Trump in direct violation of the Emoluments Clause of the Constitution on day one."[28] How far-fetched is a constitutional violation this early? Not far-fetched at all, it turns out. For instance, on August 31, 2018 a man named W. Samuel "Sam" Patten was indicted by the Department of Justice (DOJ) for failure to register as a foreign agent for Ukraine under the Foreign Agent Registration Act (FARA).[29] He was an associate of Paul Manafort, the one-time campaign manager for Trump's 2016 campaign.[30] Patten admitted to the FARA violation, lying to Congress and arranging to make a $50 000 straw purchase for a Ukrainian client of tickets to the Trump inauguration in January 2017.[31] This $50 000 Ukrainian payment was illegal under U.S. campaign finance law

---

[26]   David S. Broder & Susan Morrison, *Ethics Code is Outlined by Carter*, Wash. Post (Jan. 5, 1977), www.washingtonpost.com/archive/politics/1977/01/05/ethics-code-is-outlined-by-carter/e26a96dc-f9f9-40bf-8ce4-1049a961f4e3/?utm_term =.576b9911a345.

[27]   *Introduction of the No Congressional Consent for President Donald J. Trump to Accept Foreign Emoluments of Any Kind Whatsoever,* 163 Cong. Rec. E68 (daily ed. Jan. 13, 2017) (statement of Rep. Kaptur) ("Given the immensity of Mr. Trump's business dealings, grave concerns exist that he will immediately be in violation of this oath ... Any ongoing foreign business relationship threatens to violate the Constitution's Emoluments Clause.").

[28]   *Upholding Our Nation's Values of a Democratic Government*, 163 Cong. Rec. H883-84 (daily ed. Feb. 2, 2017) (statement of Rep. Pocan).

[29]   Katelyn Polantz, *Lobbyist pleads guilty, says he helped steer foreign money to Trump inaugural and lied to Congress*, CNN (Aug. 31, 2018), www.cnn.com/2018/08/31/politics/w-samuel-patten-plea-russia-ukraine/index.html.

[30]   Andrew Prokop, *Robert Mueller got another cooperator Sam Patten, an associate of Paul Manafort and Cambridge Analytica, struck a plea deal.*, Vox (Aug. 31, 2018), www.vox.com/2018/8/31/17805310/sam-patten-mueller-plea-manafort.

[31]   U.S. v. Patten, Case 1:18-cr-00260-ABJ (D.D.C. Aug. 31, 2018) (Statement of the Offense), *available at* http://cdn.cnn.com/cnn/2018/images/08/31/show_temp.pdf; *see also* W. Samuel Patten, Case 1:18-cr-00260-ABJ (Plea Agreement) (D.D.C. Aug. 31, 2018), www.documentcloud.org/documents/4806783-Sam-Patten-plea-agreement .html. This may not have been the only illegal foreign money spent in the 2017 inaugural. A different Ukrainian claimed he spent $200 000 for Trump inaugural tickets. *See* Kenneth P. Vogel, *A Foreigner Paid $200,000 for Tickets to Trump's Inaugural. Now He Says He Was Duped*, N.Y. Times (June 18, 2019), www.nytimes.com/2019/06/18/us/politics/trump-inaugural-lawsuit-pavel-fuks.html.

because the money came from a foreign national.[32] If any of those funds made it to the president, it could also violate the Foreign Emoluments Clause of the U.S. Constitution if they came from a foreign government. The *Washington Post* named the Ukrainian who funneled the $50 000 in question as Serhiy Lovochkin, a member of the Ukrainian Parliament.[33] Normally, inaugural committees don't give money to the president. But the accounting around the Trump inaugural committee's $107 million has been troublingly opaque.[34] Journalists have also found that money from the inaugural went to the Trump Organization, which is ultimately owned by the president.[35] The *Wall Street Journal* reported in December of 2018 that the Trump inauguration is under criminal investigation.[36] This leaves open the possibility that this episode was a violation of the Foreign Emoluments Clause on literally the first day of the Trump Administration.

Shortly into Trump's presidency, three lawsuits were filed, one by nearly 200 members of Congress, one by the State of Maryland joined by the District of Columbia (D.C.) and another by individuals in the hospitality industry, claiming that Trump was in violation of both Emoluments Clauses.[37] A central theme in these lawsuits is that Trump has created an illegal market for his

---

[32]   11 CFR 110.20(j), www.law.cornell.edu/cfr/text/11/110.20 ("A foreign national shall not, directly or indirectly, make a donation to an inaugural committee. ... No person shall knowingly accept from a foreign national any donation to an inaugural committee.").

[33]   Rosalind S. Helderman & Spencer S. Hsu, *American political consultant admits foreign money was funneled to Trump inaugural*, WASH. POST (Sept. 1, 2018), www .washingtonpost.com/local/public-safety/washington-consultant-for-ukraine-party-set -to-plead-guilty-to-violating-lobbyist-disclosure-law/2018/08/31/172cf2c8-ad23-11e8 -a8d7-0f63ab8b1370_story.html?utm_term=.275ff19e633e.

[34]   Chris Riotta, *Nobody Knows Where Trump's Leftover Inauguration Funds Went, Causing Outrage and Change in Washington*, NEWSWEEK (Nov. 17, 2017), www.newsweek.com/donald-trump-inauguration-donations-funds-missing-steve -kerrigan-congress-714118; Fredreka Schouten, *A record $107 million was raised for Trump's inauguration. So where did it all go? No one will say.*, USA TODAY (Jan. 18, 2018), www.usatoday.com/story/news/politics/2018/01/18/one-year-after-trumps -inauguration-no-one-say-how-they-spent-extra-money/1043804001/.

[35]   Itay Hod, *Trump Inauguration Money Went to Trump Organization With Help From Ivanka, Report Says*, THE WRAP (Dec. 14, 2018), www.thewrap.com/trump -inauguration-money-went-to-trump-organization-with-help-from-ivanka-report-says/.

[36]   Rebecca Davis O'Brien, Rebecca Ballhaus & Aruna Viswanath, *Trump Inauguration Spending Under Criminal Investigation by Federal Prosecutors*, WALL ST. J. (Dec. 13, 2018), www.wsj.com/articles/trump-inauguration-spending-under -criminal-investigation-by-federal-prosecutors-11544736455.

[37]   Citizens for Responsibility and Ethics in Washington ("CREW") v. Trump, 276 F.Supp.3d 174, 195 (S.D.N.Y. 2017); D.C. v. Trump, 291 F.Supp.3d 725 (D.Md. 2018); Blumenthal v. Trump, Docket No. 1:17-cv-01154 (D.D.C. filed June 14, 2017).

hotels and real estate businesses that unconstitutionally benefits him while he is president.[38] While there are three emoluments suits, this chapter will primarily focus on *D.C. v. Trump*, because it has progressed the farthest.[39] In an oral argument in January 2018, a lawyer for Maryland named Steven Sullivan argued that "[b]y accepting emoluments, the president creates a constitutionally prohibited market."[40] Judge Messitte's rulings so far indicate that he is open to this argument. Judge Messitte found in *D.C. v. Trump* that Maryland and D.C. had standing to pursue their Emoluments Clauses claims.[41] This court also denied Trump's motion to dismiss the case.[42] As Professor Jennifer Taub explained:

> Judge Messitte has concluded that the word emolument is broad enough to cover market payments for services not just something close to a bribe, which makes sense because *quid pro quo* bribery is separately unlawful. It's not the same thing: emoluments and bribes.[43]

These *D.C. v. Trump* rulings grapple with matters of first impression☐namely, what exactly is an emolument, is the president bound by the clauses and who has standing to sue to enforce the clauses?[44] This chapter will argue that Trump is in violation of both Emoluments Clauses, that the matter is justiciable, and that the plaintiffs who have sued have Article III standing to pursue their respective cases. As the attorney general of Maryland has argued successfully thus far, the meaning of an "emolument" should be broad enough to encompass moneys that pass through a business to the president.

---

[38]   Frank Lesser, *The Trump Taxes March*, SLATE (Jan. 23, 2017, 5:21 PM), www .slate.com/articles/news_and_politics/politics/2017/01/the_trump_taxes_march_on _april_15_let_s_make_it_happen.html ("His administration is already being sued by 'constitutional scholars, Supreme Court litigators, and former White House ethics lawyers' over payments from foreign governments that might violate the Constitution's Emoluments Clause …").

[39]   *Maryland, District of Columbia Sue over Payments to Trump Hotels,* 31 WESTLAW J. WHITE-COLLAR CRIME 1 (2017).

[40]   *Trump Ethics Judge Doesn't Rule But Hints: Emolument Update*, BLOOMBERG (Jan. 26, 2018), www.nreionline.com/finance-investment/trump-ethics-judge-doesnt -rule-hints-emolument-update.

[41]   D.C. v. Trump, 291 F.Supp.3d 725, 752–53 (D.Md. 2018) (order finding the plaintiffs had standing).

[42]   D.C. v. Trump, 315 F.Supp.3d 875 (D.Md. 2018) (denying defendant's motion to dismiss).

[43]   Interview with Jennifer Taub (Aug. 13, 2018).

[44]   Jennifer Rubin, *The emoluments case is the nightmare Trump has long feared*, WASH. POST (July 25, 2018) ("The decision, running over 50 pages, is an impressive, detailed analysis of the Constitution and 18th century language.").

3.1 The Emoluments Clauses' Text

3.1.1 The Foreign Emoluments Clause

As Vice President of Public Citizen Lisa Gilbert said, "'Emoluments' is a word no one knew a couple of years ago, and now it's on everyone's tongue."[45] Unless you were a linguist studying eighteenth century language or perhaps a constitutional law scholar focused on corruption, knowledge of what an "emolument" was likely escaped you.[46] Before delving into what the Emoluments Clauses mean, here is a reminder of what they say. The Foreign Emoluments Clause of the U.S. Constitution states:

> no Person holding any Office of Profit or Trust under them [i.e., the United States], shall, without the Consent of the Congress, accept of any present, Emolument, Office, or Title, of any kind whatever, from any King, Prince, or foreign State.[47]

Simply put, this part of the Constitution bars the president from receiving gifts or other valuables, including potentially payments for business services, from foreign governments unless he has the consent of Congress.

The framers of the Constitution were clearly trying to guard against foreign influences with the Foreign Emoluments Clause.[48] As Delegate Edmund Randolph of Virginia told his constitutional convention delegation, "This restriction [in the Foreign Emoluments Clause] was provided to prevent corruption."[49] It was inserted into the constitutional text at the request of Delegate Charles Pinckney of South Carolina, who "urged the necessity of preserving

---

[45] Interview with Lisa Gilbert (July 19, 2018).

[46] Christal Hayes, *'Emolument' searches skyrocket 9000 percent after Trump loses bid to toss Constitution violation suit*, USA TODAY (July 25, 2018), www.usatoday .com/story/news/politics/onpolitics/2018/07/25/emolument-merriam-webster-trump -constitution/836894002/.

[47] U.S. Constitution, Article I, Section 9, Clause 8.

[48] Toni M. Massaro, *Foreign Nationals, Electoral Spending, and the First Amendment*, 34 HARV. J. OF L. AND PUB. POL'Y 663, 685 (2011) ("One commonly intoned justification for regulation of foreign political expression is that the United States has a legitimate interest in preventing undue foreign influence over elections. A subset of this concern is the government's interest in restricting political propaganda from other nations."); Karl A. Racine, Brian E. Frosh & Norman L. Eisen, *Trump's Emoluments Trap*, N.Y. TIMES (July 26, 2018), www.nytimes.com/2018/07/26/opinion/ trumps-emoluments-trap.html ("[The framers] designed the Emoluments Clauses as a prophylactic measure to prevent actual corruption and the specter of corruption — where a foreign power (or a domestic government) buys favorable policy decisions by engaging with the head of the executive branch commercially, outside the normal avenues of state.").

[49] ZEPHYR TEACHOUT, CORRUPTION IN AMERICA 27 (2014) (quoting Randolph).

foreign Ministers & other officers of the U.S. independent of external influence."[50] In the emoluments suits against Trump, both sides have been trying to claim Pinckney as providing historical support for their side's legal position. While the plaintiffs pointed out that Pinckney introduced the clause, the DOJ argued:

> Historical evidence confirms that the Foreign Emoluments Clause was not designed to reach commercial transactions that a President (or other federal official) may engage in as an ordinary citizen through his business enterprises ... Charles Pinckney, who was credited with proposing the Foreign Emoluments Clause, maintained half a dozen plantations in South Carolina while holding various public offices.[51]

U.S. Supreme Court Justice Joseph Story in the *Commentaries on the Constitution of the United States* observed: "The [Foreign Emoluments] clause, as to the acceptance of any emoluments, title, or office, from foreign governments, is founded in a just jealousy of foreign influence of every sort."[52] As Senior Director of Democracy and Government Reform at the Center for American Progress Liz Kennedy explained:

> The Founders were clear that public power was ripe for corruption and when we formed our own system of government they didn't want foreign powers to hold sway over our new American officials and they wanted the federal government to be neutral among the states as well.[53]

As Professor Zephyr Teachout notes, there is no exception in the Constitution for *de minimis* gifts from foreign governments and the prohibition on foreign emoluments is broader than a ban on bribes, which would require the American official to do something in return for the foreign funds. *All* emoluments from foreign governments—whether reciprocated or not—are treated under the Constitution as disallowed, unless and until Congress blesses them

---

[50]   The Founders' Constitution, *Records of the Federal Convention* (as related to U.S. Constitution Article 1, Section 9, Clause 8) *available at* http://press-pubs.uchicago.edu/founders/documents/a1_9_8s6.html.

[51]   Statement of Points & Authorities in Support of Def's Mot. to Dis., Blumenthal v. Trump, No. 1:17-cv-01154-EGS at 28 (D.D.C. filed Sept. 15, 2017); *see also* Am. Compl, D.C. v. Trump, 2018 WL 1336021 (D.Md. filed Mar. 12, 2018) ("The Foreign Emoluments Clause was ... added without dissent at the request of Charles Pinckney, who 'urged the necessity of preserving foreign Ministers & other officers of the U.S. independent of external influence.'").

[52]   JOSEPH STORY, COMMENTARIES ON THE CONSTITUTION OF THE UNITED STATES, 3 vols. (1833).

[53]   Interview with Liz Kennedy (May 7, 2018).

on a case-by-case basis.[54] Norman L. Eisen, Richard Painter and Laurence H. Tribe note the long history of interpretation of the Foreign Emoluments Clause, including:

> when Simon Bolivar presented President Andrew Jackson with a gold medal, Jackson asked Congress whether he could keep it—and Congress said no. Similarly, Presidents John Tyler and Martin Van Buren both turned to Congress for approval when offered gifts by foreign leaders.[55]

President Lincoln was similarly rebuffed by Congress using the Foreign Emoluments Clause when Lincoln tried to keep unconstitutional gifts from the King of Siam.[56]

Although these parts of the Constitution had never been interpreted by a federal court before 2017, there are Office of Legal Counsel (OLC) memos on the subject of emoluments which give guidance for federal officials, including past presidents, about what is and is not allowed. For example, there was some concern about whether President Obama's receipt of the Nobel Peace Prize was a prohibited foreign emolument, but this did not generate actual litigation.[57] In the end, the OLC decided that this did not constitute a violation: "because the Nobel Committee that awards the Peace Prize is not a 'King, Prince, or foreign State,' the Emoluments Clause does not apply."[58] Another OLC opinion which may be more analogous to the Trump Organization situation is an opinion that federal workers who were lawyers could not draw

---

[54] TEACHOUT *supra* note 49, at 28.

[55] Norman L. Eisen, Richard Painter & Laurence H. Tribe, *The Emoluments Clause: Its Text, Meaning, and Application to Donald J. Trump*, BROOKINGS 9–10 (Dec. 16, 2016), www.brookings.edu/wp-content/uploads/2016/12/gs_121616_emoluments -clause1.pdf. Mr. Eisen and Mr. Painter are Chair and Vice Chair respectively of CREW. Laurence Tribe is a Professor at Harvard Law School and a lawyer in *CREW v. Trump*.

[56] Blumenthal v. Trump, 2018 WL 4681001, at *4 (D.D.C. 2018) (Quoting *Messages and Papers of the Presidents* 1029, 1030 (James D. Richardson ed., 1897) (quoting Joint Resolution No. 20, A Resolution providing for the Custody of the Letter and Gifts from the King of Siam, Res. 20, 37th Cong., 12 Stat. 616 (1862)).

[57] Dep't of Justice, *Applicability of the Emoluments Clause and the Foreign Gifts and Decorations Act to the President's Receipt of the Nobel Peace Prize* (Dec. 7, 2009), www.justice.gov/olc/opinion/applicability-emoluments-clause-and-foreign-gifts-and -decorations-act-presidents-receipt ("The Emoluments Clause of the Constitution does not apply to the President's receipt of the Nobel Peace Prize.").

[58] David J. Barron Acting Assistant Attorney General, *Applicability of the Emoluments Clause and the Foreign Gifts and Decorations Act to the President's Receipt of the Nobel Peace Prize*, OFFICE OF LEGAL COUNSEL (Dec. 7, 2009), www .justice.gov/sites/default/files/olc/opinions/2009/12/31/emoluments-nobel-peace_0 .pdf.

profits from a private law firm because the law firm had foreign governments as clients, even if the lawyer in question did not work directly on the legal matters on behalf of the foreign government clients.[59] This opinion indicates that moneys flowing through a private business (in this case a private law firm) are subject to the Foreign Emoluments Clause.

3.1.2   The Domestic Emoluments Clause
The Domestic Emoluments Clause says:

> The President shall, at stated Times, receive for his Services, a Compensation, which shall neither be increased nor diminished during the Period for which he shall have been elected, and he shall not receive within that Period any other Emolument from the United States, or any of them.[60]

This clause of the Constitution means that the president cannot augment his set salary with money from the 50 states or the federal government.[61]

The Domestic Emoluments Clause also means that Congress cannot, in a fit of rage or pique, dock the president's salary to punish him. In the *Federalist Papers*, Alexander Hamilton explained that this provision provides the president with independence from the legislature. As Hamilton wrote:

> [An] ingredient towards constituting the vigor of the executive authority, is an adequate provision for its support. It is evident that, without proper attention to this article, the separation of the executive from the legislative department would be merely nominal and nugatory. The legislature, with a discretionary power over the salary and emoluments of the Chief Magistrate, could render him as obsequious to their will as they might think proper to make him. They might, in most cases, *either reduce him by famine, or tempt him by largesses, to surrender at discretion his judgment to their inclinations.*[62]

---

[59] *Applicability of the Emoluments Clause to Non-Government Members of ACUS*, 17 Op. O.L.C. 114, 119 (1993), www.justice.gov/file/20456/download (Foreign Emoluments Clause prohibited officers from drawing shares of their law firms' profits because those firms had foreign governmental clients, even where the officers "did not personally represent a foreign government, … had no personal contact with that client of the firm, [and] could not be said to be subject to the foreign government's 'control' in his or her activities on behalf of the partnership").

[60] U.S. Const. art. II, § 1, cl. 7.

[61] Brianne J. Gorod, Brian R. Frazelle & Samuel Houshower, *The Domestic Emoluments Clause: Its Text, Meaning, and Application to Donald J. Trump*, CONSTITUTIONAL ACCOUNTABILITY CTR (July 2017), www.theusconstitution.org/wp-content/uploads/2017/07/20170726_White_Paper_Domestic_Emoluments_Clause.pdf.

[62] Alexander Hamilton, *The Federalist Papers: No. 73* (Mar. 21, 1788), http://avalon.law.yale.edu/18th_century/fed73.asp (emphasis added).

As Hamilton also noted in the text above, the cap on the presidential salary is both a ceiling and floor to prevent the legislature from attempting to control the president by offering him more money. Hamilton continued in his defense of the Domestic Emoluments Clause, stating that the president is also insulated from temptation by the 50 states (or at the time, 13 states), since "[n]either the Union, nor any of its members, will be at liberty to give, nor will he be at liberty to receive, any other emolument ... *He can, of course, have no pecuniary inducement to renounce or desert the independence intended for him by the Constitution.*"[63]

President Ronald Reagan's state pension from his time as the governor of California raised questions of whether it ran afoul of the Domestic Emoluments Clause. The OLC issued an opinion that because Reagan's California pension was fully vested before he became president, it did not violate the clause.[64] This seems like the correct result, since California had no ability to give Reagan a greater or lesser pension to reward or punish his behavior as president.

A vested state pension raises decidedly different issues from Trump's relationship with the 50 states today. Trump can use his influence over federal policy, such as tax policy, to benefit or harm particular states. The 2017 tax bill was particularly onerous on states that had not voted for Trump in 2016 in the Electoral College because the tax law capped the deductibility of local and state taxes, which are particularly high in many "blue" states like New York and California, at $10 000.[65] This tax consequence for "blue" states could be coincidence. It could also be targeted retribution.[66] Other policies, like where offshore oil drilling is permitted, could be used to punish or reward certain states.[67]

---

[63]   *Id.* (emphasis added).

[64]   *Opinions of the Office of Legal Counsel of the United States Department of Justice Consisting of Selected Memorandum Opinions Advising the President of the United States the Attorney General and Other Executive Officers of the Federal Government in Relation to Their Official Duties,* Vol. 5, 187–93 (Ed. Margaret Colgate Love 1985), www.justice.gov/olc/file/626816/download.

[65]   Laura Saunders, *The New Tax Law: State and Local Tax Deductions The tax overhaul caps the deduction for state and local taxes at $10,000 per return,* Wall St. J. (Feb. 13, 2018 12:19 PM), www.wsj.com/articles/the-new-tax-law-state-and-local -tax-deductions-1518542356.

[66]   Carolyn Y. Johnson, Reuben Fischer-Baum & Aaron Williams, *Blue states will be hit hardest by GOP tax plan's limits on deductions,* Wash. Post (Nov. 2, 2017).

[67]   Oliver Milman, *Coastal states to Trump: why is Florida exempt from drilling and not us?,* Guardian (Feb. 14, 2018 12:30 PM), www.theguardian.com/environment/ 2018/jan/10/trump-offshore-drilling-florida-ryan-zinke.

3.2 Examples of Possible Violations of the Emoluments Clauses

The Domestic Emoluments Clause could have been violated when a delegation from the State of Maine including then-Governor LePage paid for 40 hotel rooms in Trump's D.C. hotel, spending $22 000 on Maine taxpayers' dime.[68] Because the Trump Organization's businesses stretch into several corners of the globe at once, there are multiple instances where the Foreign Emoluments Clause could be violated simultaneously.[69] The *Christian Science Monitor* listed actual instances which, depending on how the emoluments suits discussed herein are resolved, could all constitute violations of the Foreign Emoluments Clause, because the foreign sovereign revenues ultimately go to the president of the United States. They include the following:

> In February 2017, the Kuwaiti Embassy held its national day celebration at the hotel ... The Embassy of Bahrain also held a national day celebration there ... The ambassador and permanent representative of Georgia to the United Nations stayed at the hotel during a visit to Washington in April 2017.[70]

The *New York Times* reported, "During the campaign, Mr. Trump's organization continued to file dozens of new trademarks, in China, Canada, Mexico, the European Union and Indonesia ..."[71] On the trademark front, the *Associated Press* found:

> At stake are 49 pending trademark applications—all made during his campaign—and 77 marks already registered under his own name, most of which will come up for renewal during his term ... including Trump toilets, condoms, pacemakers and even a 'Trump International Hotel.'[72]

---

[68]   Scott Thistle & Kevin Miller, *Maine paid for 40 rooms at Trump hotel for LePage, staff*, Press Herald (Feb. 18, 2019), www.pressherald.com/2019/02/17/maine -paid-for-40-rooms-at-trump-hotel-for-lepage-staff/.

[69]   Helaine Olen, *Trump's latest violation of the emoluments clause*, Wash. Post (May 15, 2018) ("reporters asked how, precisely, the involvement of China in the Indonesia resort project didn't violate the emoluments clause of the Constitution, and how it squares with the president's assurances that the Trump Organization wouldn't get involved in 'foreign deals' as long as he remained in the White House.").

[70]   *Id.*

[71]   Danny Hakim & Sui-Lee Wee, *For Trump the Nationalist, a Trail of Global Trademarks*, N.Y. Times (Feb. 21, 2017).

[72]   Associated Press, *Recent Trump win on China trademark raises ethics questions*, Fox News (Feb. 14, 2017), www.foxnews.com/world/2017/02/14/recent-trump-win -on-china-trademark-raises-ethics-questions.html.

Newsweek listed other potential emoluments that could run afoul of the Foreign Emoluments Clause:

> In Indonesia, a local government approved plans to construct a road that would shorten the drive between Trump's new six-star resort ... and the main airport. ... In Panama, the federal government installed sewer and water pipes around the Trump Ocean Club International Hotel and Tower in Panama City to ensure the construction on the sail-shaped skyscraper would be completed after the contractor went bankrupt.[73]

Meanwhile, *Politico* noted, "A lobbying firm working for Saudi Arabia paid for a room at Donald Trump's Washington hotel after Inauguration Day, marking the first publicly known payment on behalf of a foreign government to a Trump property since he became president."[74] Indeed, the *Washington Post* revealed that the Kingdom of Saudi Arabia paid for 500 nights at Trump's D.C. hotel, spending at least $270 000.[75] If a federal court decides that money from foreign governments flowing though the Trump Organization to Trump is a violation of the Foreign Emoluments Clause, then there are multiple examples of violations from right down the street to all around the world. It's also worth noting that Ivanka Trump and her husband Jared Kushner are also subject to the Foreign Emoluments Clause because they work for the federal government and their ongoing international business ties could raise the same constitutional questions as those of the president's businesses.[76]

---

[73] Leah Thomas, *Trump Is Receiving Gifts From Foreign Governments and Violating the Constitution, Ethics Watchdogs Warn*, NEWSWEEK (Jan. 3, 2018), www .newsweek.com/trump-still-doing-business-foreign-governments-769177.

[74] Isaac Arnsdorf, *Saudis foot tab at Trump hotel*, POLITICO (Feb. 9, 2017), www .politico.com/story/2017/02/trump-hotel-saudi-arabia-234878.

[75] David A. Fahrenthold & Jonathan O'Connell, *Saudi-funded lobbyist paid for 500 rooms at Trump's hotel after 2016 election*, WASH. POST (Dec. 5, 2018).

[76] Tucker Higgins, *Ivanka Trump's Chinese trademarks raise questions about potential conflicts of interest*, CNBC (May 29, 2018), www.cnbc.com/2018/05/29/ ivanka-trump-chinese-trademarks-raise-conflict-of-interest-questions.html ("The president's daughter, who was hired as a White House advisor ... continues to receive profits from her brand despite stepping down from her leadership role in the organiza-tion ..."); Benjamin Haas, *Ivanka Trump brand secures China trademarks on day US President met Xi JinPing*, GUARDIAN (Apr. 19, 2017) ("On the day ... Ivanka Trump met the Chinese leader, China granted preliminary approval for three new trademarks for her namesake brand ... Her company, Ivanka Trump Marks LLC, has been granted four additional trademarks since her father's inauguration and has 32 pending ...").

3.3 Emoluments Clause Suits

3.3.1 *CREW v. Trump*

Following Trump's refusal to divest from his global businesses,[77] *CREW v. Trump* was the first emoluments suit to be filed, just days after Trump was inaugurated.[78] The plaintiffs in the case include Citizens for Responsibility and Ethics in Washington (CREW), a nonpartisan nonprofit, and Restaurant Opportunities Centers United, Inc., which represents 30 000 restaurant employees.[79] The other two co-plaintiffs are Eric Goode, who owns hotels, restaurants and bars; and Jill Phaneuf, who books embassy functions in the D.C. market. Collectively, the latter three plaintiffs are known as the "Hospitality Plaintiffs" in the case.

One of the first hurdles that CREW and the Hospitality Plaintiffs faced was the fact that they were the first plaintiffs ever to sue a president for violating the Emoluments Clauses, so there was no guidance for them in existing case law about how to establish standing to sue or what types of injuries would be legally cognizable by the courts under the clauses.[80] *CREW v. Trump* landed in the courtroom of Judge George B. Daniels. He heard arguments from both sides about the meaning of "emolument," justiciability and standing. During oral arguments, a lawyer for CREW stated that Trump's D.C. hotel was "an

---

[77] D.C. v. Trump, 315 F.Supp.3d 875 (D.Md. 2018) ("Donald J. Trump is the President of the United States and the sole or a substantial owner of both the Trump Organization LLC and The Trump Organization, Inc. (collectively, the Trump Organization), umbrella organizations under which many, if not all, of the President's various corporations, limited-liability companies, limited partnerships, and other entities are loosely organized.").

[78] *Citizens For Responsibility and Ethics in Washington v. Trump*, No. 17-458 (S.D.N.Y. Jan. 23, 2017) (Complaint against Donald J. Trump); Stephen F. Rohde, *Is the Emoluments Clause a Threat to Trump's Presidency?*, L.A. Law. 36 (Mar. 2017), www.lacba.org/docs/default-source/lal-back-issues/2017-issues/march-2017 .pdf ("CREW's complaint accuses Trump of violating the emoluments clause as a result of his ongoing business dealings (from which he has refused to divest ownership) with more than 20 governments around the globe.").

[79] Restaurant Opportunities Centers United, Inc., *About Us*, http://rocunited.org/ about-us ("We are over 30,000 people who work in restaurants ...").

[80] Pls.' Mem. in Opp'n to Def.'s Mot. to Dismiss at 15, CREW v. Trump, 2017 WL 3444116 (S.D.N.Y. Aug. 4, 2017).

emoluments magnet."[81] Legal historians in support of CREW's side argued for an expansive definition of "emoluments." They stated:

> the word "emolument" was not a term of art in the eighteenth century ... In particular, "emolument" encompassed profits or advantages arising from private commercial transactions ... DOJ's interpretation of these clauses is inconsistent with the founders' purposes of preventing corruption and conflicts of interest, avoiding dangerous foreign entanglements, and preserving a careful balance of state and federal power.[82]

Alas, Judge Daniels did not get to the merits of the case to address this interpretation of the Clauses. Indeed, Judge Daniels was not persuaded by any of the plaintiffs' arguments in *CREW*. Consequently, he threw every possible obstacle in the way of the *CREW* case proceeding as he dismissed the suit.[83] Judge Daniels ruled on December 21, 2017 that all four plaintiffs in the *CREW* case lacked standing.[84] In essence, the judge ruled that any injury to plaintiffs flowing from Trump's ownership of his businesses was too speculative. The judge also noted that:

> Even before Defendant [Trump] took office, he had amassed wealth and fame and was competing against the Hospitality Plaintiffs in the restaurant and hotel business. It is only natural that interest in his properties has generally increased since he became President. As such, despite any alleged violation on [Trump's] part, the Hospitality Plaintiffs may face a tougher competitive market overall. Aside from [Trump's] public profile, there are a number of reasons why patrons may choose to visit [Trump's] hotels and restaurants including service, quality, location, price and other factors related to individual preference. Therefore, the connection between the Hospitality Plaintiffs' alleged injury and [Trump's] actions is too tenuous to satisfy Article III's causation requirement.[85]

Judge Daniels also claimed that his court could give the plaintiffs no relief under the Foreign Emoluments Clause, because Congress could eventually, at some unknown point in the future, consent to the foreign sovereign money flowing through the Trump Organization to Trump.[86]

---

[81] Sheelah Kolhatkar, *Are the Emoluments Lawsuits Filed Against President Trump Dead?*, New Yorker (Oct. 19, 2017) (quoting CREW's lawyer Deepak Gupta).

[82] CREW v. Trump, 2017 WL 5483629 (S.D.N.Y.) (Legal Scholars Brief).

[83] CREW v. Trump, 276 F.Supp.3d 174, 195 (S.D.N.Y. 2017) ("Accordingly, Plaintiffs' claims and this case are DISMISSED.").

[84] *Id.* at 179 ("Defendant's motion to dismiss for lack of standing under Rule 12(b)(1) is GRANTED.").

[85] *Id.* at 186.

[86] *Id.* at 186–87 ("Congress could still consent and allow Defendant to continue to accept payments from foreign governments in competition with Plaintiffs.").

Then, Judge Daniels went out of his way to slam the courthouse door on CREW and its co-plaintiffs. He noted that the Foreign Emoluments Clause accusations raised non-justiciable political questions.[87] And the judge also asserted this claim was not ripe.[88] On February 16, 2018, the *CREW* plaintiffs appealed the dismissal of the case.[89] Oral argument took place on October 30, 2018 in the Second Circuit.[90] But at least for now, *CREW v. Trump* is not moving forward.

3.3.2   *Blumenthal v. Trump*

On June 14, 2017, nearly 200 members of Congress joined together to sue Trump for violation of the Foreign Emolument Clause.[91] The Blumenthal in the caption of the case refers to Senator Richard Blumenthal from Connecticut. The *Blumenthal* lawsuit alleges, not unlike the other two suits, that "emoluments" include business transactions, and that Trump's turning over management to his sons is not enough to distance himself from these transactions, since he remains the ultimate owner of the Trump Organization.[92] The lawsuit filed by Democratic members of Congress (both House and Senate) alleges that Trump has conflicts of interests in at least 25 countries. The complaint says that Trump needs the consent of Congress before accepting any gifts or emoluments, but no requests for permission from Trump have come to Congress for approval.[93] According to the complaint:

> [Congressional] Plaintiffs seek declaratory relief establishing that Defendant violates the Constitution when he accepts any monetary or nonmonetary benefit—any

---

[87]   *Id.* at 194.

[88]   *Id.* ("Plaintiffs' Foreign Emoluments Clause claims are indeed not ripe for judicial review.").

[89]   CREW v. Trump, Docket No. 1:17-cv-00458 (S.D.N.Y. Feb. 16, 2018) (Notice of Appeal from 103 Order on Motion to Dismiss).

[90]   CREW v. Trump, Docket No. 18-474 (2d Cir.) (Oral Argument on Oct. 30, 2018).

[91]   Blumenthal v. Trump, Docket No. 1:17-cv-01154 at 18, (D.D.C. filed June 14, 2017) (Complaint against Donald J. Trump) ("Plaintiffs, 30 members of the United States Senate and 166 members of the United States House of Representatives, bring this action against President Donald J. Trump to obtain relief from the President's continuing violation of the Foreign Emoluments Clause of the United States Constitution, which was designed to ensure that our nation's leaders would not be corrupted by foreign influence or put their own financial interests over the national interest.").

[92]   Gretchen Frazee, *How the Emoluments Clause is being used to sue Trump*, PBS NEWSHOUR (June 22, 2017), www.pbs.org/newshour/updates/emoluments-clause-used-sue-trump/.

[93]   Compl. at 18-9, Blumenthal v. Trump, No. 17-1154 (D.D.C. filed June 6, 2017) ("Because the Foreign Emoluments Clause requires the President to obtain 'the Consent

'present, Emolument, Office, or Title, of any kind whatever'—from a foreign state without first obtaining 'the Consent of the Congress.'[94]

Judge Emmet Sullivan ruled on September 28, 2018 that *Blumenthal v. Trump* could move forward, finding that members of Congress have standing to sue because the text of the Constitution is clear that Congressional consent to keep foreign emoluments is required.[95] As the Court noted, quoting an OLC opinion "'the language of the Emoluments Clause is both sweeping and unqualified.'"[96] And moreover, because Trump has not bothered to ask Congress for the constitutionally required consent, this has left them with no other recourse besides suing.[97] On June 25, 2019, the judge in *Blumenthal* ordered fact discovery to begin in the case.

3.3.3 *District of Columbia v. Trump*

Along with members of Congress and workers in the hospitality business, states have also been concerned about the potential violation of the Constitution by Trump's ongoing ownership of his business while president.[98] Consequently, D.C. and Maryland sued Trump for violation of the Emoluments Clauses on June 12, 2017, alleging that they have been injured as competitors in the marketplace because Trump has created an unconstitutional market.[99]

---

of the Congress' before accepting otherwise prohibited 'Emolument[s],' Plaintiffs, as members of Congress, must have the opportunity to cast a binding vote that gives or withholds their 'Consent' before the President accepts any such 'Emolument.'"); Brooke Seipel, *Nearly 200 Democrats sue Trump citing Emoluments Clause violation,* THE HILL (June 14, 2017), http://thehill.com/blogs/blog-briefing-room/news/337710 -nearly-200-democrats-file-emoluments-lawsuit-against-trump.

[94] Compl. at 19, *Blumenthal v. Trump*, No. 17-1154 (D.D.C. filed June 6, 2017).

[95] *Blumenthal v. Trump*, 2018 WL 4681001, at *2 (D.D.C. 2018) ("the Court finds that the plaintiffs have standing to sue the President for allegedly violating the Foreign Emoluments Clause.").

[96] *Id.* at *3 (citing 17 Op. O.L.C. 114, 121 (1993)).

[97] *Id.* at *5 ("... although plaintiffs' claims raise separation-of-powers concerns, plaintiffs have no adequate legislative remedy and this dispute is capable of resolution through the judicial process.").

[98] David A. Fahrenthold & Jonathan O'Connell, *What is the 'Emoluments Clause'? Does it apply to President Trump?,* WASH. POST (Jan. 23, 2017) (The Maryland and D.C. Attorneys General believe that ... "A federal officeholder who receives something of value from a foreign power can be imperceptibly induced to compromise what the Constitution insists be his or her exclusive loyalty: the best interest of the United States of America.").

[99] Compl. At ¶ 9, D.C. v. Trump, 2017 WL 2559732 (D.Md. filed June 12, 2017).

Judge Messitte found the plaintiffs factual proffers compelling:

> Plaintiffs['] … allegation is bolstered by explicit statements from certain foreign
> government officials indicating that they are clearly choosing to stay at the
> President's Hotel, because, as one representative of a foreign government has stated,
> they want him to know 'I love your new hotel,' a sentiment the President appears to
> suggest he likes 'very much.'[100]

In *D.C. v. Trump*, the plaintiffs argue Trump has also violated the Domestic
Emoluments Clause by taking money from Governor of Maine Paul LePage,
who stayed in a Trump hotel on a trip to Washington. They also argue he
violated this clause by getting tax breaks for his businesses from D.C. and
Mississippi, which again flow to him—thereby illegally and unconstitutionally
augmenting his base salary as president. The complaint also alleges that the
Domestic Emoluments Clause has also been violated due to the continuation of
the General Services Administration lease for Trump's D.C. hotel.

3.3.3.1 Standing to sue

The plaintiffs in *D.C. v. Trump* argue, in part, that because both D.C. and
Maryland own and run meeting spaces like convention centers that compete
with Trump's D.C. hotel, they are suffering sufficient injuries to be in court.
Judge Messitte ruled on March 28, 2018 that both D.C. and Maryland had
standing.[101] As the judge concluded:

> Plaintiffs have sufficiently alleged that the President is violating the Foreign and
> Domestic Emoluments Clauses of the Constitution by reason of his involvement
> with and receipt of benefits from the Trump International Hotel and its appurte-
> nances in Washington, D.C. as well as the operations of the Trump Organization
> with respect to the same. Plaintiffs have demonstrated their standing to challenge
> those purported violations because they have shown injury-in-fact, fairly traceable
> to the President's acts, and that the injury is likely redressable by the Court.[102]

The judge found it appropriate for D.C. and Maryland to protect the interests
and rights of their citizens who work in the hotel and event space market: "The
Court concludes that Plaintiffs … are, quite plausibly, trying to protect a large
segment of their commercial residents and hospitality industry employees
from economic harm."[103] This result stood in stark contrast to *CREW v. Trump*,
which did not find standing for the Hospitality Plaintiffs, who were actual

---

[100] D.C. v. Trump, 291 F.Supp.3d 725, 749–50 (D.Md. 2018).
[101] *Id.*
[102] *Id.* at 757.
[103] *Id.* at 748 (internal citation omitted).

competitors in the hospitality industry. But in *D.C.,* the States are recognized as having standing to protect their citizens who work in the hospitality industry.

One issue the judge in *D.C. v. Trump* had to confront was if Trump is violating the Emoluments Clauses, he is arguably doing so in multiple locations simultaneously. The judge decided to narrow the issues in the case to the Trump D.C. hotel which was the most direct source of trouble for the plaintiffs in the case.[104] Judge Messitte was careful to note that his decision to limit the instant case to the Trump D.C. hotel should not and would not prevent other plaintiffs in other jurisdictions from suing the president for his other business locations' alleged violations of the Constitution. As he stated:

> This is in no way meant to say that other States or other businesses or individuals immediately affected by the same sort of violations alleged in the case at bar, e.g., a major hotel competitor in Palm Beach (near Mar-a-Lago) or indeed a hotel competitor ... anywhere in the State of Florida, might not have standing to pursue litigation ... [105]

This leaves it to other courts in other jurisdictions to solve potential problems like foreign sovereign money at Mar-a-Lago in Florida, foreign sovereign money in Trump Tower in New York or foreign sovereign money in Trump International Hotel Waikiki.[106]

Judge Messitte recognized the gravity of the problem of a president potentially violating the Constitution through his business dealings. In his ruling, Judge Messitte used the word "illegal" multiple times when referring to Trump's alleged actions.[107] For example, Judge Messitte wrote: "the government official himself [Trump] is the one allegedly receiving illegal benefits ..."[108]

---

[104] *Id.* at 753.

[105] *Id.*

[106] *Id.* at 738 ("during oral argument, Plaintiffs clarified that their alleged competitive injuries—namely, Maryland's claimed injuries to its sovereign interest in taxes, to both parties' proprietary interests, and, to some extent, to both parties' *parens patriae* interests—centered almost exclusively around the District of Columbia-based Trump International Hotel and its appurtenant restaurant, bar, and event space ...").

[107] *Id.* at 736 ("Maryland argues that, like the District of Columbia, it is harmed because these entities compete with the Hotel for the business of both foreign and domestic governments and that the President's violations of the Emoluments Clauses have illegally skewed the hospitality market in his favor."); *id.* at 743–44 ("The Supreme Court has recognized that plaintiffs with an economic interest have standing to sue to prevent a direct competitor from receiving an illegal market benefit leading to an unlawful increase in competition.").

[108] *Id.* at 749.

Perhaps trying to head off claims that Trump is violating the Foreign Emoluments Clause, the Trump Organization said that it would pay the United States Treasury an estimated payment of the profits that it had received from foreign governments.[109] Inquiries from reporters for more details about this payment went unanswered.[110] Interestingly, in *D.C. v. Trump*, Judge Messitte noted:

> According to a recent press report, the President has stated that he has now paid to the U.S. Treasury the profits the Hotel has received from foreign governments. No details with respect to such payments, however, have been provided, viz., how the payments were calculated, who verified the calculations, how much was calculated over what period of time, and which foreign payor(s) were involved.[111]

Presumably, as this case goes forward, Judge Messitte is going to want to see real proof that any money was given to the Treasury by the Trump Organization and in what amount, and the factual basis of the calculations.

3.3.3.2 Motion to dismiss denied

Four months after ruling that plaintiffs had standing to sue, the court turned to Trump's motion to dismiss in *D.C. v. Trump*. A key question in this second opinion was what exactly counts as an "emolument." This is a matter of first impression, as the *CREW v. Trump* case did not reach the merits of the argument (ruling instead that the *CREW* plaintiffs lacked standing to proceed). What's a court to do when it has to decode a part of the Constitution that has somehow escaped judicial interpretation for over 200 years? Like other judges faced with similar quandaries, Judge Messitte started with the text, history and intent of the constitutional provision before him.

Judge Messitte rejected Trump's narrow reading of what counts as an "emolument," which would have led to dismissal of the case.[112] As he wrote:

> the Court finds the President is subject to both Emoluments Clauses of the Constitution and that the term 'emolument' in both Clauses extends to any profit, gain, or advantage, of more than de minimis value, received by him, directly or

---

[109] Lorraine Woellert, *Trump Organization sends $151,470 in foreign profits to Treasury*, POLITICO (Mar. 9, 2018), www.politico.com/story/2018/03/09/trump -organization-treasury-department-foreign-profits-451675.

[110] Tami Abdollah, *Trump company donates foreign profits but won't say how much*, ASSOCIATED PRESS (Feb. 27, 2018), www.bostonglobe.com/news/nation/ 2018/02/26/trump-company-donates-foreign-profits-but-won-say-how-much/ GskDZPfAj1Uj6pwM7EuZmI/story.html.

[111] D.C., 291 F.Supp.3d at 734.

[112] *Bringing the emoluments clause to bear on Trump's D.C. hotel*, BOSTON GLOBE (Aug. 7, 2018) ("The Department of Justice, representing the president, argued that the

indirectly, from foreign, the federal, or domestic governments. This includes profits from private transactions, even those involving services given at fair market value. In the case of the Foreign Emoluments Clause, unless Congress approves, receipt of the emolument is prohibited. In the case of the Domestic Clause, receipt of any emolument is flatly prohibited.[113]

Thus, on July 25, 2018, Judge Messitte denied the president's motion to dismiss *D.C. v. Trump*. This ruling means that D.C. and Maryland can go forward with the suit and can conduct discovery against the president; as a result, the attorneys general of D.C. and Maryland might get their hands on closely guarded internal documents from the Trump Organization. On August 17, 2018, the DOJ asked for special permission from Judge Messitte for the ability to launch an "interlocutory appeal and stay proceedings pending resolution of the interlocutory appeal."[114] Typically, litigants cannot immediately appeal a motion to dismiss, hence why they need Judge Messitte's permission to do so. This seems like a bold effort to stave off discovery. In the meantime, the plaintiffs are pushing forward, asking the judge to approve a discovery schedule.[115] But in December of 2018, the Fourth Circuit Court of Appeals halted discovery and on July 10, 2019 ruled that Maryland and DC lacked standing.[116]

The public does not know how this story will end. But *D.C. v. Trump* demonstrates that federal judges still know that the president is not above the law, including the 231-year-old strictures of the Constitution.[117] As the attorneys general who brought the *D.C. v. Trump* case explained in the *New York Times*, "Judge Messitte's ruling is so important [because] [i]t opens a path to enforcement of the ethics regime that the framers developed as a bulwark against corruption in the highest office in the land."[118]

---

case should be dismissed because ... financial reward from Trump's business would not be covered.").

[113] D.C. v. Trump, 315 F.Supp.3d 875, 904 (D.Md. 2018).

[114] D.C. v. Trump, 2018 WL 3969639 (D.Md.) (request for permission to appeal).

[115] Rept. of Rule 26(f) Meeting, D.C. v. Trump, Docket No. PJM 17-1596 (D.Md. filed Sept. 14, 2018).

[116] Trump, WL 2997909 (4th Cir. July 10, 2019).

[117] BOSTON GLOBE *supra* note 112 ("A federal judge recently cleared the way for a lawsuit related to the [Trump International] hotel that not only might expose the president's deepest financial secrets, but also clarify constitutional guardrails against corruption that the courts have never fully fleshed out—because, for 229 years, no president has been so determined to push the boundaries.").

[118] Karl A. Racine, Brian E. Frosh & Norman L. Eisen, *Trump's Emoluments Trap*, N.Y. TIMES (July 26, 2018), www.nytimes.com/2018/07/26/opinion/trumps-emoluments-trap.html.

4.   CONCLUSION

Author Alyssa Katz noted, "The Founders anticipated a president like Trump—whether it is the Emoluments Clause or other provisions that limit executive power. These are very human impulses to want to aggrandize oneself and they guarded against those impulses."[119] Yet in mid-2018, Trump had a summit with Kim Jong-un and told the leader of North Korea that he had wonderful beaches and "You could have the best hotels in the world right there." [120] This exchange once again raised the prospect that Trump was thinking of his own hotel-building business at that moment, and not the interest of the nation; and that any resulting "Trump Tower North Korea" would violate the Foreign Emoluments Clause.

One question that these cases will eventually resolve is whether the word "emoluments" includes money going through the president's businesses or not. Another way of thinking about this question is to ask whether the Trump Organization can help the president launder money from otherwise constitutionally prohibited sources. A final way of conceptualizing the courts' grappling with this self-enriching behavior is whether federal courts will reach the same conclusion as the New York attorney general and find that there is ultimately a constitutional limit to the president's greed.

In 2017, an artist projected the words "Pay Trump Bribes Here" over the entrance to Trump International D.C. Hotel.[121] That's a somewhat crass way of condensing the argument this chapter has laid out. But the artist is not incorrect. The presidency should not be a get-rich-quick scheme. This question is likely to be resolved by the Supreme Court. As already discussed in this book, the Supreme Court has been busy rebranding corruption; it could also rebrand greed.

---

[119]   Interview with Alyssa Katz (July 27, 2018).

[120]   Pat Ralph, *Trump applauds North Korea's "great beaches," says they would be a perfect location for condos and hotels*, BUSINESS INSIDER (Jun. 12, 2018), www .businessinsider.com/trump-says-north-korea-beaches-great-place-for-hotels-condos -2018-6.

[121]   Nicole Chavez & Emily Smith, *'Pay Trump bribes here' sign projected onto Trump's DC hotel*, CNN (May 16, 2017), www.cnn.com/2017/05/16/politics/trump -hotel-projection/index.html.

11. Branding boycotts

> "The minute we silence that cash register, they can hear everything we say."[1]
>
> E. Randel T. Osburn, Southern Christian Leadership Conference

1. INTRODUCTION

An old joke has two goldfish swimming up to each other. Goldfish 1 says: "The water is great today." Goldfish 2 responds: "What's water?" Commercial branding for most Americans is like the water for Goldfish 2. It is so ubiquitous that it fades into the scenery: the bark of the huckster becomes the normal background noise to everyday existence; the flash of Times Square becomes just another part of the cityscape; the din of banner ads is just one more thing you have to minimize before you can get to the content you seek online.

Where do Americans get the idea that they should always be buying things? The message is hurled at them from all quarters, including occasionally from the mouths of presidents. At a press conference in 1958, President Eisenhower was asked by Robert G. Spivak "what the [American] people should do to make the recession recede." Here is the dialogue that followed:

Eisenhower: "Buy."
Spivak: "Buy what?"
Eisenhower: "Anything."[2]

Similarly days after the terrorist attacks on September 11, 2001, which severely impacted the Pentagon and felled the twin towers of the World Trade Center in New York, President George W. Bush urged Americans to keep shopping[3]

---

[1]   MONROE FRIEDMAN, CONSUMER BOYCOTTS: EFFECTING CHANGE THROUGH THE MARKETPLACE AND THE MEDIA 90 (1999) (Quoting E. Randel T. Osburn).

[2]   *Public Papers of the Presidents of the United States: Dwight D. Eisenhower,* 70 (1958).

[3]   George W. Bush, *"Islam is Peace" Says President* (Sept. 17, 2001), https:// georgewbush-whitehouse.archives.gov/news/releases/2001/09/20010917-11.html ("some don't want to go shopping for their families; some don't want to go about their ordinary daily routines because… they're afraid they'll be intimidated. That should not and that will not stand in America.").

and go to Disney World.[4] Both presidents were tapping into a message that commercial branders have been hitting for years: that to be a true American requires nearly insatiable consumption.[5] As historian V.O. Key Jr. noted, capitalism itself was branded in mid-twentieth century advertisements as the "American Way."[6] As he wrote, many American corporations used their public relations shops to spread this political ideology:

> [C]orporations began to advertise ideology on a large scale. The popular periodicals carried advertisements to point out the merits of the 'American way' ... In this advertising a common ideological theme dominated: a theme of free enterprise, of 'the American way,' of the essential goodness of business. It was made to appear not only impertinent, but unpatriotic to suggest that American business might have its blemishes.[7]

And part of the overarching goal of selling the "American way" to consumers and citizens was to enable *laissez faire* policy outcomes from legislatures:

> The politics of business ... includes aggressive attempts to mold [public] attitudes ... [to] transmute private advantage into the public good ... The assiduous dedication of effort to the capture of public favor lays a foundation of good will on which business groups may build in their attempts to obtain particular legislation or to obstruct undesired governmental action.[8]

Whether they try to put the patriotic gloss of the "American Way" on their commercial branding or not, the norm for producers is to tell the public to "buy, buy, buy," and the basic response of most consumers is not just to buy what they can afford, but also to buy by going into considerable debt. By the end of 2018, consumer debt topped $4 trillion in the U.S.[9] Purchasing con-

---

[4]   George W. Bush, *Remarks by the President to Airline Employees O'Hare International Airport* (Sept. 27, 2001), https://georgewbush-whitehouse.archives.gov/news/releases/2001/09/20010927-1.html ("You stand against terror by [traveling] ... we will not surrender our freedom to travel; ... When they struck, they wanted to create an atmosphere of fear ... Get down to Disney World in Florida.").

[5]   Robert J. Shiller, *Spend, Spend, Spend. It's the American Way*, N.Y. TIMES (Jan. 14, 2012) ("There is even an idea here that it is patriotic to spend, rather than to save.").

[6]   V.O. KEY, JR., POLITICS, PARTIES, & PRESSURE GROUPS 77 (1964 5th ed.) ("business spokesmen expound more or less uniformly a philosophy of laissez faire: free competition, free enterprise, and the 'American way.'").

[7]   *Id.* at 95.

[8]   *Id.* at 91–92.

[9]   Lorie Konish, *Consumer debt is set to reach $4 trillion by the end of 2018*, CNBC (May 21, 2018), www.cnbc.com/2018/05/21/consumer-debt-is-set-to-reach-4-trillion-by-the-end-of-2018.html.

sumer goods on credit is called buying on the "never-never" in the U.K.,[10] and the behavior shows how powerful the lure of buying is—many will go into hock just to get a few more brands, even if their homes are already overflowing with flotsam.[11]

Because the message to buy, buy, buy is droning on every day, from everywhere, there is something particularly disruptive when the message "stop buying" slips through the cracks. "Stop buying" goes against the messages of Eisenhower and Bush; it goes against decades of corporate spin that "to be a consumer is to be patriotic"; it goes against the noise, noise, noise of every advertisement that has tried to grab your attention since birth. "Stop buying" is the scratch on the record when the music stops in a John Hughes movie from the 1980s.

Under most circumstances, consumer complaints against a particular brand are about as impactful as a fly on an elephant's bottom. But every now and then, when thousands or even millions of people lift their voices (and their smartphones) at the same time to say, "Stop buying!" suddenly, the commercial world pauses and listens, and occasionally changes its behavior. [12]

Political protests can come in many forms. For instance, in late 2016 an architect named Jeffrey Roberts was trying to figure out a particular feat: how to obscure a name on the façade of a high-rise in Chicago. His solution was to use giant 30-foot by 15-foot inflatable golden-colored pig-shaped balloons and to fly them at the precise height such that viewers from below would be unable to make out the name.[13] The balloon pigs were a homage to Pink Floyd's "Animals" album cover.[14] The band, of course, owns the intellectual property rights to this image. But when Pink Floyd heard of the plan, they gave their consent for him to go forward with the caper.[15] The name on the building

---

[10]   VANCE PACKARD, THE WASTE MAKERS 147 (1960 reprinted 1971).

[11]   Beth Teitell, *Today's families are prisoners of their own clutter*, BOST. GLOBE (July 9, 201) ("research by UCLA-affiliated social scientists concluding that American families are overwhelmed by clutter, too busy to go in their own backyards, rarely eat dinner together even though they claim family meals as a goal, and can't park their cars in the garage because they're crammed with non-vehicular stuff.").

[12]   Chris Jackson & Clifford Young, *Brand Risk in the New Age of Populism: Four Key Tactics for Surviving Hyper-Partisan Consumers*, IPSOS 9 (2017).

[13]   Priscilla Frank, *Architects Want To Hide Trump Tower Logo With A Bunch Of Flying Gold Pigs.*, HUFF. POST (Dec. 9, 2016).

[14]   *Architect wants to install giant pig balloons to block Trump's name on Chicago high-rise*, CHI. TRIB. (Dec. 7, 2016).

[15]   Karen Brill, *A Series of Flying Pigs Will Block Trump's Chicago Tower*, ARCHITECTURAL DIGEST (May 4, 2017).

that the architect was trying to hide from view was written in platinum-colored letters: TRUMP.[16]

A few months later, on February 24, 2017, activists Ryan Clayton and Jason Charter handed out hundreds of Russian flags in the crowd at the Conservative Political Action Conference (better known as CPAC) as President Trump was about to speak to the group. The Russian flag is red, white and blue. The activists had written the word "Trump" on the Russian flags in gold lettering. Many in the CPAC crowd waved the Russian Trump flags not realizing they were part of a political prank.[17] And on the evening of May 15, 2017, artist Robin Bell used light to project the words "Emoluments Welcome" over the entrance to the Trump International Hotel in D.C.[18]

The impulses of this architect, these prankster activists and this artist were more creative than most, but they were not isolated. Rather, they tapped into an American zeitgeist of ongoing political protests. In 2017 alone, there were multiple marches to protest the Trump administration. Americans live in a time of polarized partisan politics,[19] when business and politics intersect on multiple levels: from companies supporting particular candidates, to companies advertising at political conventions, to political candidates paying their own companies with campaign funds.[20] Most Americans don't have the time to create an epic art project to express their political disenchantment. The protest that is most readily available to the average citizen is to vote with their dollars through boycotts. As consumers, Americans have the ability to make a choice every time they make a purchase. Increasingly, commercial choices take on a political valence.[21] Empirical evidence confirms that customers are willing

---

[16]   Joe Vince, *Flying Pigs Over Chicago's Trump Tower Sign Grounded For Now*, PATCH (July 27, 2017). Thus far, Chicago has not granted the permits for the flying pigs.

[17]   Ali Breland & Taylor Lorenz, *CPAC attendees seen waving Russian flags*, HILL (Feb. 24, 2017).

[18]   Nicole Chavez & Emily Smith, *'Pay Trump bribes here' sign projected onto Trump's DC hotel*, CNN (May 16, 2017); *Emoluments Welcome*, BELL VISUALS (May 15, 2017), http://bellvisuals.com/Emoluments-Welcome.

[19]   *Partisanship and Political Animosity in 2016. Highly negative views of the opposing party – and its members*, PEW (June 22, 2016) (35 percent of Democrats think Republicans are more immoral than other Americans and 47 percent of Republicans think Democrats are more immoral than other Americans).

[20]   Olivia Nuzzi, *Donald Trump Is Paying Himself to Run for President*, DAILY BEAST (Mar. 1, 2016), www.thedailybeast.com/donald-trump-is-paying-himself-to-run-for-president.

[21]   Hillary Greene, *Antitrust Censorship of Economic Protest*, 59 DUKE L.J. 1037, 1041 (2009-2010) ("'as consumers they see that one way they can exercise power is by where they spend their money and where they don't.'").

to end their patronage of businesses over corporate involvement in politics.[22] A poll in 2017 revealed: "Three-quarters (76%) would refuse to purchase a product if they found out a company supported an issue contrary to their beliefs ..."[23] In 2018, YouGov found:

> the clear majority of US adults (67%) support boycotting a brand due to conflicting political views. Furthermore, 59% of Americans concur that they would boycott a brand's products or services if they strongly disagreed with the brand's stance on a particular social issue.[24]

The data above asked a future-oriented question: "Will you boycott?" Other polls have asked a backwards-looking question: "Have you boycotted?" In 2013, the U.S. Census found that most political boycotting was concentrated in Portland and Seattle, where around one-quarter boycotted,[25] compared to the national average of 13 percent.[26] A few years later, the boycotting trend had spread nationwide. In 2017, a poll by Ipsos showed that one-quarter of U.S. consumers claimed that they had in fact boycotted a company for its political stances.[27] Another survey of registered voters in 2017 found half had reported participating in a boycott.[28]

---

[22] *See* Liz Kennedy, *Citizens Actually United: The Bi-Partisan Opposition to Corporate Political Spending and Support for Common Sense Reform*, DEMOS (Oct. 25, 2012).

[23] Press Release, *Americans Willing to Buy Or Boycott Companies Based On Corporate Values, According to New Research by Cone Communications*, CONE (May 17, 2017), www.conecomm.com/news-blog/2017/5/15/americans-willing-to-buy -or-boycott-companies-based-on-corporate-values-according-to-new-research-by-cone -communications.

[24] Yael Bame, *Two-thirds of US adults support boycotting brands over poli-tics*, YOUGOV (Mar. 8, 2017), https://today.yougov.com/topics/politics/articles-reports/ 2017/03/08/two-thirds-US-adults-support-boycotting-brands.

[25] Gene Balk, *Twenty-seven percent of Seattleites are boycotting something*, SEATTLE TIMES (Apr. 2, 2015), www.seattletimes.com/seattle-news/data/seattle-a -champion-city-of-boycotting/.

[26] *2015 Michigan Civic Health Index* 7, MICHIGAN NONPROFIT ASSOCIATION & NATIONAL CONFERENCE ON CITIZENSHIP (2015), www.mnaonline.org/research-publications/michigan-civic-health-index/file (noting the national average for boycotting or buycotting was 13 percent).

[27] Kate Kaye, *Study: 25% of Americans Say Politics Drove Them to Boycott Brands*, AD AGE (June 8, 2017) ("25% of Americans said they had stopped using a brand's goods or services in the previous three months because of protests, boycotts or the brand's perceived political leanings.").

[28] Kyle Endres & Costas Panagopoulos, *Boycotts, Buycotts, and Political Consumerism in America* (Nov. 1, 2017) (Table 1 showing 50 percent of reg-istered voters in 2017 polled reported boycotting), https://doi.org/10.1177/ 2053168017738632https://journals.sagepub.com/na101/home/literatum/publisher/

The word "boycott" was coined in 1880.[29] Today, the word "boycott" can connote everything from a freedom march to unfairly shuttered stores.[30] And both sides of a boycott will try to brand it.[31] The protester will try to claim the moral high ground and so will the merchants. Participating in a boycott can lead participants to other political engagements. Following a boycott in 1973, a spokesperson noted, "It was a consciousness-raising experience ... Consumers now know they can move mountains. And government and industry now know that they know."[32]

There are so many boycotts in American history that others have written entire books about them. Because space is limited, this chapter will explore three big boycotts: (1) the boycotts of tea by American colonists; (2) the Claiborne County, Mississippi boycotts for racial justice; and (3) the boycotts of the Trump brands.

2.   THE REAL BOSTON TEA PARTY

In 2009, a conservative group calling itself the Tea Party emerged to protest against the Obama administration. The Tea Party was sponsored by former Member of Congress Dick Armey's FreedomWorks[33] and partially funded by the Koch Brothers.[34] The name the "Tea Party" was a callback to the Boston Tea Party in 1773. Because the Boston Tea Party is a bit of history that most Americans learn in elementary school, the story gets compressed. Most school children don't learn, and most adults don't realize, that the Boston Tea Party was actually a reaction to a massive corporate bailout.

When it came to the American Revolution, before there were bullets, there were boycotts. The things that got American colonists angry enough to boycott

---

sage/journals/content/rapa/2017/rapa_4_4/2053168017738632/20171031/images/large/10.1177_2053168017738632-table1.jpeg.

[29]   *See* LAWRENCE B. GLICKMAN, BUYING POWER 115 (2009) ("James Redpath ... coined the eponymous phrase to describe the weapon of ostracism used by Irish peasants ... against an exploitative British land agent named Charles Cunningham Boycott.").

[30]   GARY MINDA, BOYCOTT IN AMERICA: HOW IMAGINATION AND IDEOLOGY SHAPE THE LEGAL MIND 6 (1999).

[31]   FRIEDMAN, *supra* note 1, at xvi.

[32]   FRIEDMAN, *supra* note 1, at 79 (quoting May 1973 newsletter of the Virginia Citizens Consumer Council).

[33]   Kate Zernike & Jennifer Steinhauer, *Years Later, Armey Once Again a Power in Congress*, N.Y. TIMES (Nov. 14, 2010).

[34]   Frank Rich, *The Billionaires Bankrolling the Tea Party*, N.Y. TIMES (Aug. 28, 2010) ("David Koch, is ... the founder of the Americans for Prosperity Foundation, which, as [Jane] Mayer writes with some understatement, 'has worked closely with the Tea Party since the movement's inception.'").

were British taxes, especially since they did not have a representative in Parliament. Thus, one of the rallying cries of the rebellion was, "No taxation without representation." After the Seven Years War, the British government imposed taxes on the colonies. The Stamp Act of 1763 required American colonists to print legal documents, diplomas and newspapers on papers that bore an official "stamp" that were taxed. As historian Leora Auslander explains:

> The inclusion of newspapers within the taxable goods was particularly offensive to the colonists, since it was perceived, if not as a form of censorship, at least as a constraint on the diffusion of knowledge. American colonists responded to the Act in 1765–1766 by boycotting the sale of these stamps.[35]

At the center of the battle between the English government and its obstreperous colonists was the East India Company. This company was incorporated by royal charter in 1600.[36] The East India Company in the mid-1700s essentially took over much of the Indian subcontinent through force.[37] As poet William Cowper described the East India Company's takeover of India:

> Build factories with blood, conducting trade
> At the swords point, and dyeing the white robe
> Of innocent commercial justice red.[38]

On the eve of the American Revolution, the company had a surplus of £17 million of unsold tea. With tea rotting in its warehouses, it appealed to the British government for help. The British government came to its rescue. The British monarchy was a major shareholder of the East India Company.[39] The result was the Tea Act—one of the first recorded corporate bailouts.[40] Perhaps the East India Company was the first firm that was "too big to fail."[41]

---

[35] Leora Auslander, Cultural Revolutions Everyday Life and Politics in Britain, North America, and France 84 (2009).

[36] *East India Company*, Encyclopaedia Britannica (Oct. 16, 2018), www.britannica.com/topic/East-India-Company.

[37] *The East India Company: How a trading corporation became an imperial ruler*, BBC History Mag. (Jan. 21, 2017), www.historyextra.com/period/tudor/the-east-india-company-how-a-trading-corporation-became-an-imperial-ruler/.

[38] *Id.*

[39] *The Boston Tea Party*, Mass. Historical Society (2016), www.masshist.org/revolution/teaparty.php.

[40] *The Tea Is Coming*, Mass. Historical Society (undated), www.masshist.org/revolution/doc-viewer.php?item_id=401.

[41] Thom Hartmann, *Boston Tea Party, a chapter from the book* Unequal Protection (2010), www.thomhartmann.com/unequal-protection/excerpt-boston-tea-party.

In protest at the Tea Act, many Americans boycotted tea imported by the East India Company. The black market in black tea thrived. In late 1773, Bostonians calling themselves the "Sons of Liberty" spread broadsides throughout the town declaring, "Countrymen! That worst of Plagues, the detested tea shipped for this port by the East India Company, is now arrived in the Harbor ..."[42] Two of the Massachusetts governor's sons who wished to import British tea warned against colonial boycotts. They called themselves "THE TRUE SONS OF LIBERTY," to contrast with the "Sons of Liberty" who called for boycotts.[43] The battle was on for branding the tea boycott and the sale of tea, and both sides wanted the banner of "liberty."

Whether Parliament had intended to or not, as historian T.H. Been wrote, "Parliament managed to politicize these consumer goods ..."[44] After a contentious town meeting in Boston on December 16, 1773, the crowd descended on three ships that contained East India Company tea. The end result was 342 crates of tea ended up in the sea. One eyewitness account came from Captain James Bruce of the ship the *Eleanor*:

> about one thousand unknown people came down the said wharf and a number of them came on board the said ship some being dressed like Indians and they having violently broke open the hatches hoisted up the said chests of tea upon deck and then and there stove and threw the said chests with their contents overboard into the water ...[45]

Meanwhile, a broadside published right after the Boston Tea Party by someone sympathetic to the Sons of Liberty declared boisterously:

> Bostonian's SONS keep up your Courage good,
> Or Dye, like Martyrs, in fair Free-born Blood.
> How grand the Scene! -- (No Tyrant shall oppose)
> The TEA is sunk in spite of all our foes.

---

[42]   *Boston Tea Party History*, Boston Tea Party Ships & Museum, www
.bostonteapartyship.com/boston-tea-party-history.

[43]   Thomas & Elisha Hutchinson, *Tradesmen's Protest Against the Proceedings of The Merchants Relative to the New Importation of Tea* (Nov. 3, 1773) (Broadside), www.masshist.org/revolution/doc-viewer.php?item_id=398&img_step=1&pid=2& mode=dual#page1.

[44]   Conor Friedersdorf, *The Constitutional Right to Boycott*, Atlantic (Feb. 2, 2018), www.theatlantic.com/politics/archive/2018/02/is-there-a-constitutional-right-to -boycott/552077/ (quoting T.H. Been).

[45]   Tea Leaves: Being a Collection of Letters and Documents Relating to the Shipment of Tea to the American Colonies in the Year 1773 by the East India Company 356–357 (1884 Francis Samuel Drake ed.).

A NOBLE SIGHT -- to see th' accursed TEA
Mingled with MUD -- and ever for to be;
For KING and PRINCE shall know that we are FREE.[46]

When American colonists picked a fight about taxing tea, they were not just picking a fight with the British Empire (on which the sun never set); they were also taking on the East India Company. A few months later, the King intervened by writing to Parliament:

> His Majesty upon information of the unwarrantable practices which have been lately concerted and carried on in ... the Port of Boston, ... with a view to obstructing the Commerce of this Kingdom, and ... hath thought fit to lay the whole matter before his two Houses of Parliament ... to put an immediate stop to the present disorders ...[47]

The Parliament retaliated against the Boston Tea Party by closing the port of Boston until the East India Company was repaid. Lord North argued that Parliament must "punish, control, or yield to [the American colonists]."[48]

Boston wasn't the only place protesting. In the Carolinas, there were also objections to British tea and taxes. On October 25, 1774:

> in Edenton, North Carolina, a group of 51 ladies, in response to the British government's refusal to lift the tax on tea, held what has become known as the "Edenton Tea Party." They drank tea made from a local plant and signed a pledge declaring, ... [continued protest] "until such time that all acts which tend to enslave our Native country shall be repealed."[49]

Lord North seemed taken aback by the colonists' escalating defiance, given how paltry the tea tax was. On January 19, 1775, Lord North declared it was impossible for him "to foretel the Americans would resist at being able to drink their Tea at nine Pence in the pound cheaper."[50] But in the end, the American

---

[46] *Tea, Destroyed By Indians.*, Broadside Boston (1773), www.masshist.org/revolution/doc-viewer.php?item_id=402&img_step=1&pid=2&mode=transcript #page1.

[47] *American Archives, Fourth Series, Containing a Documentary History of the English Colonies in North America from the King's Message to Parliament of March 7, 1774 to the Declaration of Independence of the United States*, at 1, https://play.google .com/books/reader?id=ZU0MAQAAMAAJ&pg=GBS.PR1.

[48] *Id.* at 17.

[49] Janice Shaw Crouse, *Gaining Ground, A Profile of American Women in the Twentieth Century Trends in Selected Indicators of Women's Well-Being* 61 (2001), http://concernedwomen.org/wp-content/uploads/2013/11/gg1-72.pdf.

[50] *American Archives, supra* note 47, at 764.

colonists were outraged that tax incentives had been offered to the world's largest company at their expense and moreover that the law had been enacted without their input. The American Revolution resulted.

3.   THE RIGHT TO BOYCOTT

Civil rights icon Dr. Martin Luther King Jr. advocated boycotting in his final public speech.[51] Typically, this "On the Mountain Top" speech is quoted for its eerily prophetic words: "I've seen the Promised Land. I may not get there with you."[52] King was assassinated the next day.[53] King said, on his last night on earth:

> [T]he American Negro collectively is richer than most nations of the world ... That's power right there, if we know how to pool it. ... We don't need any Molotov cocktails. We just need to go around to these stores, and to these massive industries ... and say, "God sent us by here, to say to you that you're not treating his children right ..." "Now, if you are not prepared to do that, ... [then] our agenda calls for withdrawing economic support from you." And so ... we are asking you tonight ... not to buy Coca-Cola in Memphis ... not to buy Sealtest milk ... not to buy ... Wonder Bread.[54]

One of the things that is remarkable about King's speech is that at the time, there wasn't a clear ruling from the Supreme Court that protected political boycotts. Contemporaneously, Southern states were trying to make political boycotts illegal or at least prohibitively expensive. King's call to action reflected a deeper truth that boycotts are as American as apple pie and are catalysts for social change.[55]

How did Americans get the right to boycott recognized by the Supreme Court? It all started in a small Mississippi county, called Claiborne, in 1966. The Black residents of Claiborne County and Port Gibson, Mississippi, wanted political and social equality with Whites, which was still sorely lacking. Black

---

[51]   Olivia Goldhill, *50 years since his death, Martin Luther King Jr.'s philosophical work is all but forgotten*, QUARTZ (Apr. 4, 2018), https://qz.com/1244251/on-the-50th-anniversary-of-martin-luther-kings-death-lets-revisit-his-philosophical-work/.

[52]   Nikita Stewart, *"I've Been to the Mountaintop," Dr. King's Last Sermon Annotated*, N.Y. TIMES (Apr. 2, 2018).

[53]   FRIEDMAN, *supra* note 1, at 90 ("According to E. Randel T. Osburn of the Southern Christian Leadership Conference, 'The boycott is the most potent economic empowerment weapon that blacks have ...'").

[54]   Stewart, *supra* note 52.

[55]   Goldhill, *supra* note 51.

citizens formed a Human Relations Committee which prepared a petition entitled "Demands for Racial Justice," calling for:

> the desegregation of public schools and public facilities, the hiring of black police officers, public improvements in black residential areas, the selection of blacks for jury duty, the integration of bus stations, and an end to verbal abuse by police."[56]

At the same time, Mississippi Action for Progress (MAP) was organized to develop community programs. The White establishment was unmoved by these efforts. In 1966, in the First Baptist Church, at a local meeting of the National Association for the Advancement of Colored People (NAACP), hundreds of attendees voted unanimously to boycott White-owned businesses. In January of 1967, the boycott was partially ended when the boycotters won concessions like the hiring of 15 Black clerks in local stores and the appointment of a Black policeman and a Black deputy sheriff.[57]

But the boycotts continued against stores that continued to refuse to hire Blacks. This tactic is sometimes referred to as a "Blackout."[58] In 1968, there was another flashpoint between residents when a Black boy was killed by White police officers. This generated more energy for the years-long boycott effort.[59]

The battle for the moral high ground was on. The boycotters branded their cause as an effort to obtain racial justice. The White merchants branded the boycotters as destructive thugs. The multi-year boycott severely impacted the bottom lines of White businesses in the area. In 1969, the *New York Times* summed up the impact of the Blackout:

> Gen. Ulysses S. Grant ... entered this picturesque town [of Port Gibson in Claiborne County, Mississippi] ... and pronounced it 'too beautiful to burn.' ... Now ... many townspeople fear an economic boycott may accomplish what General Grant refused

---

[56] ABRAHAM L. DAVIS & BARBARA LUCK GRAHAM, THE SUPREME COURT, RACE, AND CIVIL RIGHTS: FROM MARSHALL TO REHNQUIST 350 (1995).

[57] *Negroes Are Ending Mississippi Boycott,* N.Y. TIMES 21 (Jan. 27, 1967) ("Negroes will lift a 10-month boycott of white businesses here tomorrow after winning a list of concessions ...").

[58] B. Drummond Ayres Jr., *White Merchants in South Sue Civil Rights Activists in Effort to End Shopping Boycotts by Blacks: Secondary Boycott Charged Chilling Effect,* N.Y. TIMES 23 (Apr. 15, 1974) ("other white mercantile establishments ... have been hit by 'blackouts ...'").

[59] *Boycott Hurting Mississippi Town: Port Gibson Business Feels Pinch of Blacks' Protest,* N.Y. TIMES 36 (Dec. 21, 1969) ("a young Negro named Roosevelt Jackson was shot to death by a white policeman when the officer and a black policeman struggled with him ... 'Now the boycott is stronger than ever ...'").

to try. More than a dozen businesses have failed since blacks began boycotting Port Gibson stores April 1, 1966.[60]

Throughout the Civil Rights movement, one way Black protestors maintained their moral superiority was by remaining non-violent. One of the complicating facts of the Claiborne boycott was the allegation that the boycott was maintained through intimidation. There were assertions that some of the neighbor-to-neighbor "policing" of the boycotts resulted in physical violence among African Americans.[61] There was also violence on the White side, including an incident in 1969 in which "shots were fired at the First Baptist Church, where blacks were meeting."[62]

A Mississippi State representative, who was also a merchant from Claiborne, took his anger at the local boycott to the state capital.[63] He introduced a bill, which the Mississippi legislature eventually enacted, that made particular types of boycotts illegal.[64] In 1969, 23 White businesses, newly empowered by the new Mississippi anti-boycott law, sued over 100 residents of Claiborne, the NAACP and MAP for an illegal boycott. The White plaintiffs sought $3.5 million in damages from the Black defendants.[65] In the trial, each side felt the other posed an existential threat and tried to brand the opposition as such.

In 1976, a Mississippi state trial court decided that the boycott was illegal and held all of the defendants jointly and severally liable for $1.25 million.[66] The ruling stated that the NAACP, MAP and 132 persons had "wrongfully combined and colluded in a civil conspiracy."[67] Moreover, the court held that the defendants had "illegally created a monopoly" for Black businesses and "unlawfully interfered with business relations" between the merchants and

---

[60]   *Id.*

[61]   *Mississippi Supreme Court Finds N.A.A.C.P. Liable Over Boycott*, N.Y. TIMES, Dec. 11, 1980, at 32 ("Witnesses testified that some blacks were beaten for doing business with the white stores …").

[62]   Stuart Taylor Jr., *Port Gibson, Miss., Awaits Ruling on 60's Boycott*, N.Y. TIMES, Dec. 7, 1981, at B16.

[63]   Thomas A. Johnson, *N.A.A.C.P. Seeks Funds for Boycott Case*, N.Y. TIMES, Aug. 13, 1976, at 12 ("this [anti-boycott] legislation was introduced in the Mississippi State Legislature by Robert L. Vaughn …").

[64]   Gary Thatcher, *Boycott ruling in Mississippi shakes NAACP*, CHRISTIAN SCIENCE MONITOR, Sept. 9, 1976, at 4 ("In 1968, the [Mississippi] Legislature passed the anti-trust law, which prohibits 'conspiracies' to restrain trade.").

[65]   *Businessmen Sue In Negro Boycott*, N.Y. TIMES 33 (Nov. 3, 1969).

[66]   Johnson, *supra* note 63 ("A Mississippi court awarded 12 white merchants in the town of Port Gibson a $1,250,599 settlement against the [NAACP] because of the organization's successful boycott of local shops in 1966.").

[67]   Ayres, *supra* note 58 (quoting the court's decision).

customers.[68] The ruling also held that the Mississippi anti-boycott law could be applied retroactively.[69]

Because of the poverty of the Black residents facing this monetary judgment, the liability was really borne by the NAACP. The problem was the NAACP did not have the $1.25 million. Moreover, the NAACP took the position that the Mississippi statute was unconstitutional because boycotts should be protected by the First Amendment.[70] However, in order to appeal the verdict against them and contest their First Amendment rights, the NAACP had to overcome an additional impediment. It needed to put up $1.5 million in bond.[71] There was a real risk that if the NAACP could not raise the money, it could have gone bankrupt.[72] As the NAACP's lawyer Nathaniel R. Jones said, the Claiborne lawsuit "threatens to put us out of business ...'"[73] Charles Evers, one of the organizers of the original 1966 boycott, echoed this view: "'They're trying to break us economically,' ... Evers charged. 'I'm not going to pay them a penny.'"[74] Evers was the younger brother of slain Civil Rights hero Medger Evers.

Because of the threat of joint and several liability, the NAACP lost hundreds of members.[75] The Ford and Rockefeller Foundations had tried to help to raise funds for the litigation, but the Internal Revenue Service stopped this.[76] Into the breach, labor groups, as well as Jewish, Catholic and Protestant groups, came to the NAACP's aid.[77] Collectively, they raised sufficient money to keep

---

[68]   *Id.*

[69]   Peter Kihss, *Reform Jews Meet with Catholics and Protestants to Aid N.A.A.C.P.*, N.Y. Times, Oct. 13, 1976, at 6.

[70]   Ayres *supra* note 58; Thatcher, *supra* note 64 ("NAACP general counsel Nathaniel Jones says the application of the law to consumer boycotts is an unconstitutional abridgment of freedom of speech ...").

[71]   *Mississippi Blacks Picketing Stores in Suit Over Boycott*, N.Y. Times, Sept. 10, 1976, at 18.

[72]   Ayres, *supra* note 58 ("[the NAACP] was in grave financial trouble, barely meeting its payrolls and finding it difficult to meet its increasing legal expenses.").

[73]   Thomas A. Johnson, *N.A.A.C.P. Loses $1.2 Million Lawsuit for 1966 Boycott in Mississippi Town*, N.Y. Times 33 (Aug. 12, 1976).

[74]   *Mississippi Blacks Picketing Stores in Suit Over Boycott*, *supra* note 71, at 18.

[75]   Ayres, *supra* note 58 ("Since the suit was filed, N.A.A.C.P. officials report membership in the association's Port Gibson branch has dropped from a high of more than 1,400 to about 300 persons ... 'Folks are scared they might get hit for damages if we lose this one ...'").

[76]   *Unions Offer Funds for NAACP Bond*, L.A. Times, Oct. 2, 1976, at A6 ("Ford and Rockefeller foundations had been blocked by the Internal Revenue Service from responding to the NAACP's fund-raising efforts.").

[77]   *Id.* ("The AFL-CIO, the United Auto Workers and the AFL-CIO industrial union department have agreed to give the NAACP the [$800,000] it needs to pay a $1.56 million bond growing out of a boycott suit in Mississippi."); Kihss, *supra* note

the litigation alive. As a participating rabbi said: "'If blacks can be thrown into bankruptcy for refusing to patronize merchants they regard as hostile to their interests, the Jews can be similarly victimized for withdrawing their patronage from concerns which discriminate against them ...'"[78]

The Mississippi Supreme Court dismissed the charges that were brought under the Mississippi anti-boycott law because the law was enacted after the boycott had begun, but upheld liability on common law grounds.[79] "The high court ... [wrote] 'Any kind of boycott is unlawful if executed with force or violence or threats,' and ... [concluded that] 'the boycott was illegally oper-ated ...'"[80] The NAACP then appealed the case to the U.S. Supreme Court. Lawyers for the NAACP branded the Mississippi court rulings "a serious threat to American political freedom."[81] Meanwhile, the lawyers for the White merchants branded the Claiborne boycott "a 'reign of terror' against local businesses ..."[82] The stakes were high because the questions in the case raised matters of first impression for the Court, essentially "whether there is a constitutional right to conduct an organized commercial boycott as a weapon of political protest, or whether all participants in such a protest can be held financially liable for violent actions by some."[83]

In *NAACP v. Claiborne Hardware*,[84] the Supreme Court finally recognized that political customer boycotts are protected free speech under the First Amendment. In 1982, the Supreme Court "unambiguously upheld the right of Americans to organize boycotts to achieve social, political, and economic change."[85] As Justice Stevens explained approvingly:

> The boycott was launched at a meeting of a local branch of the NAACP attended by several hundred persons. Its acknowledged purpose was to secure compliance by both civic and business leaders with a lengthy list of demands for equality and racial justice.[86]

---

69 ("a leading Jewish group yesterday brought Jewish, Roman Catholic and Protestant religious organizations together to 'Save N.A.A.C.P.'").

[78]   Kihss, *supra* note 69 (quoting Rabbi Alexander M. Schindler).

[79]   *Mississippi Supreme Court Finds N.A.A.C.P. Liable Over Boycott*, *supra* note 61 ("The Supreme Court of Mississippi ... found the [NAACP] liable for damages stem-ming from a boycott of white-owned businesses ...").

[80]   *Id.*

[81]   Jim Mann, *High Court Will Decide Whether NAACP Can Be Ordered to End Boycott*, L.A. Times, Nov. 10, 1981, at A15.

[82]   *Id.*

[83]   Taylor, *supra* note 62, at B16.

[84]   458 U.S. 886, 911 (1982).

[85]   Glickman, *supra* note 29, at 300.

[86]   *Claiborne Hardware*, 458 U.S. at 907.

The unanimous ruling came as a great relief for the NAACP, which no longer was held financial liable.[87] As the Court ruled, "While the State legitimately may impose damages for the consequences of violent conduct, it may not award compensation for the consequences of nonviolent, protected activity."[88]

4. BOYCOTTING TRUMP

How are the *Claiborne* rights being used today? Many are using them against the Trump brand. As he assumed the presidency, Trump refused to fully divest from his ownership of the Trump Organization.[89] The Trump brand is eponymous; thus, "Trump" refers to both the man (Donald J. Trump) and the brand (associated with the products and services of the Trump Organization).

As Trump's electoral persona evolved during the 2016 presidential campaign, he embraced more xenophobic stances, mostly against Mexican immigrants and Muslim immigrants; more racist stances, mostly against African-Americans and Latinos; more sexist stances, against women.[90] He alienated not just the targets of the attacks, but also White men who find racism and sexism abhorrent. His electorate saw all of these qualities and either were attracted to them or were not repulsed by them. He did not tone down any of these behaviors in the White House. According to *Forbes*, Trump's net worth has dropped substantially during his presidency.[91] Why is this happening? There are many theories, including that his sons are not as talented as their father was at running the business. But another theory is that Trump's presidency is harming his commercial brand.

With Trump, there are far more targets for consumers to boycott than with other presidents. And Trump has continued to do things to outrage his opponents, like pulling out of the Paris Climate Accord, banning transgendered people from the military, backing healthcare bills that would have left 20

---

[87] Robert L. Jackson, *Court Upholds NAACP's Right to Boycott Firms*, L.A. Times, July 3, 1982, at A1 ("The Supreme Court ... upheld the constitutional right of NAACP members to engage in a political and economic boycott without being liable for damages ...").

[88] N.A.A.C.P. v. Claiborne Hardware Co., 458 U.S. 886, 918 (1982).

[89] Chase Peterson-Withorn, *Trump Refuses To Divest Assets, Passes Control To Sons*, Forbes (Jan. 11, 2017).

[90] Paul A. Argenti & Bob Druckenmiller, *Reputation and the Corporate Brand*, 6 Corp. Reputation Rev. 368, 373 (2004) (discussing the risks companies face when an individual "becomes the corporate brand" and that person's reputation is diminished).

[91] Dan Alexander & Chase Peterson-Withorn, *How Trump Is Trying—And Failing—To Get Rich Off His Presidency*, Forbes (Oct. 2, 2018) ("His net worth, by our calculation, has dropped from $4.5 billion in 2015 to $3.1 billion the last two years, knocking the president 138 spots lower on the *Forbes* 400.").

million people uninsured and separating migrant children from their families at the southern border; all of which provide a continual stream of new reasons for his opponents to boycott his company, which is one of the perils of having an eponymous brand.[92]

So what does the Trump commercial brand evoke now that he has become president?[93] Consumer surveys have found contradictory associations with the Trump brand. As reported by NPR's Jim Zarroli in early 2017, "Trump, the brand, is seen as aggressive, selfish and ambitious but also friendly, stylish and elegant …"[94] As criticism of Trump's presidency mounts, there could be transference between the negative criticism generated by the president and the commercial Trump brand.[95] If Trump gets a reputation for being an inept political manager, those negative connotations could transfer to his commercial brand as well.[96] Some of that process may already be underway. As Brand Keys noted in October 2018:

> The Trump brand has changed. Radically. Five years ago the fabulously successful lifestyle brand made a sharp right turn away from the promise of luxury, high living, extravagance, and indulgence and turned into a political brand. Now the Trump brand's values of conservatism, authoritarianism, social dominance, and nationalism resonate.[97]

Brands are notoriously difficult to value and Trump's commercial brand is no different.[98] In 2013, the Trump Organization put the value of the Trump brand

---

[92] Kerry Close, *Is It Worth It to Boycott Donald Trump Products?*, TIME (Oct. 18, 2016).

[93] Hayley Peterson, *The Value of Donald Trump's Brand Is Taking a Beating*, FISCAL TIMES (Oct. 12, 2016) ("That's because the Trump name at the time stood for 'wealth, luxury, and glamour, and for some, wretched excess,' wrote Robert Passikoff …").

[94] Jim Zarroli, *Trump's Role As President May Be Boosting His Brand's Reputation*, NPR (Feb. 8, 2017).

[95] Brian D. Till & Terence A. Shimp, *Endorsers in Advertising: The Case of Negative Celebrity Information*, 27 J. ADVERTISING 67, 80 (1998) ("Also at great risk are brands closely tied to a specific celebrity …").

[96] Darin W. White, Lucretia Goddard & Nick Wilbur, *The Effects of Negative Information Transference in the Celebrity Endorsement Relationship*, 37 INT'L J. RETAIL & DISTRIBUTION MGMT. 322, 331 (2009) ("when consumers are exposed to negative information about a celebrity endorser, a negative transference of the information towards the product may occur.").

[97] Robert Passikoff, *Trump Brand Update*, BRAND KEYS (Oct. 30, 2018), https://brandkeys.com/trump-brand-update/.

[98] Nick Wells, *What's in a name? For Trump, it could be $3.3 billion*, CNBC (July 20, 2016) ("Because brands are intangible assets … there's a lot of disagreement on how to estimate brand valuation.").

at $4 billion.[99] Even *Forbes,* which puts out lists of the world's billionaires, admits there are issues with this valuation.[100] *Fortune* valued the Trump brand at $125 million.[101] *Bloomberg* lowballed the value of the Trump brand at $35 million.[102]

Another way to conceptualize the value of the Trump brand isn't what it would cost to buy it outright, but rather what type of premium customers are willing to pay for a Trump-branded good or service compared with a generic alternative. Using this measure, one analysis of Trump's commercial brand found that it was sinking as he went into the 2016 election, which he was largely anticipated to lose, but that the brand rebounded when he became president in January 2017.[103] However, Brand Keys found a drop in popularity for the Trump commercial brand in late 2018, after two years of a topsy-turvy presidency:

> Three years ago it appeared that more than 20 companies were paying Mr. Trump to distribute or produce Trump-branded products. Now you're hard pressed to find anything beyond MAGA hats, Golf Clubs, and Real Estate that resonates with the Trump brand attached, and even Real Estate has taken a beating.[104]

---

[99] Katherine Clarke, *A Complete Breakdown of Donald Trump's Net Worth,* BUSINESS INSIDER (July 2, 2013) ("the company said it believes the Trump brand is worth some $4 billion."); *but see id.* ("He [Mr. Trump] also has some $451.7 million in debt and other commitments, plus personal cash and marketable securities in the amount of $169.7 million, according to WeiserMazars.").

[100] Catherine Thompson, *Forbes Magazine Puts Trump's Worth at $4.5 Billion: 'We've Settled The Issue',* TALKING POINTS MEMO (Sept. 29, 2015) (Noting that while Trump asserts his brand is worth multiple billions, "*Forbes* talked to 20 brand experts who estimated the worth of the Trump brand anywhere from $125 million to $1.1 billion.").

[101] Erin Carlyle, *Trump Exaggerating His Net Worth (By 100%) in Presidential Bid,* FORBES (June 16, 2015) ("We value his brand at just $125 million …").

[102] Wells, *supra* note 98 (referencing *Bloomberg*).

[103] Will Johnson & Michael D'Antonio, *Trump's Campaign Is Damaging His Brand,* POLITICO (Jan. 11, 2016) ("Among the people Trump's business depends on—the consumer making over $100,000 a year—the value of the Trump name is collapsing.").

[104] Press Release, *Does Trump Have A Brand, Beyond Politics? Survey Finds President Loses Consumer Brand Mojo,* BRAND KEYS (Oct. 22, 2018), http://brandkeys .com/wp-content/uploads/2018/10/Press-Release-Trump-Brand-Beyond-Politics.pdf.

Before election day in 2016, there were widespread reports that Trump hotels were struggling.[105] By one measure, bookings were down 60 percent.[106] Some of this downturn could be attributable to reactions to Trump's campaign. As a meeting planner told *Fortune*:

> There's a pragmatic reason for steering clear of a Trump hotel … The majority of my clients feel that booking one of his hotels would be too polarizing right now, potentially driving away a good portion of their members,' he says. 'There is clear concern about driving away attendees who are or might be against his bigotry, racism, xenophobia, and intolerance.'[107]

On the other hand, Trump's presidency provides him all the press attention that goes with the office. One way that Trump has leveraged public office to the benefit of his commercial brand is by visiting, on nearly a weekly basis, a Trump property. According to *NBC News*, in 892 days in office he spent 266 days at a Trump-owned property.[108] One hypothesis is Trump the president can only help Trump the commercial brand because he can bring positive attention to particular properties and thereby attract more customers at higher prices—especially those properties that generate hefty membership fees. Mar-a-Lago reportedly doubled its membership fee from $100 000 upon Trump's ascendency to the White House to $200 000.[109] Simultaneously, Trump has profited from his status as a landlord, since the Secret Service had to pay rent to be in Trump Tower for several months.[110] Apparently, the Secret Service and the Trump Organization had a dispute over the rent and the Secret Service moved

---

[105] Peterson, *supra* note 93 ("president of the travel company Ovation Vacations … [said] that business was down at least 30% at several of Trump's properties.").

[106] Greg Sterling, *Will brands be forced to take sides in a more polarized marketplace? Being apolitical may no longer be an option for brands in the Trump era.*, MARKETING LAND (Nov. 14, 2016), https://marketingland.com/will-brands-forced-take-sides-polarized-marketplace-198065 ("During the US presidential campaign, bookings at Trump hotel properties saw a whopping 60 percent decline.").

[107] Christopher Elliot, *How Trump's Divisive Campaign Is Hurting His Hotel Business*, FORTUNE (Aug. 1, 2016) (quoting Timothy Aaron).

[108] Sam Petulla, *Tracking President Trump's Visits to Trump Properties*, NBC NEWS (July 1, 2019), www.nbcnews.com/politics/donald-trump/how-much-time-trump-spending-trump-properties-n753366 (updated daily).

[109] Brooke Seipel, *Mar-a-Lago doubles initiation fee to $200,000*, HILL (Jan. 25, 2017); Caleb Melby, *Trump's Net Worth Slips to $2.9 Billion as Towers Underperform*, BLOOMBERG (June 21, 2017) ("Mar-a-Lago … saw a 25 percent jump in sales.").

[110] Julia Glum, *The Government is Paying $2.4 Million to Rent Space in New York City's Trump Tower*, NEWSWEEK (July 19, 2017).

out of Trump Tower in July 2017.[111] A report in August of 2017 showed his D.C. hotel, which had been struggling before the election, was turning a $2 million profit with Trump in the White House.[112] Trump has also profited by having his Trump 2020 campaign pay his businesses.[113]

Another sign of the toxicity of Trump's brand during the 2016 campaign was that nearly no big corporations spent to support his candidacy. During the election, while corporations spent to support congressional candidates and supported other Republicans during the presidential primary, like Jeb Bush and Marco Rubio, most corporate spenders shunned candidate Trump. In fact, the only publicly traded company to support Trump was the GEO Group, a private prison company.[114] Every other publicly traded company avoided supporting him publicly during the campaign.[115] GEO also stood to gain lucrative contracts to detain people on behalf of the new Trump administration[116] and has profited from immigration detentions and family separations.[117] It's also possible that other publicly traded companies were supporting Trump, but hid their support through dark money conduits.[118]

While only a single publicly traded company backed Trump as a candidate, corporations came out of the woodwork to support his inauguration celebrations. As Trump assumed office, corporations including AT&T, Bank of America, Boeing, Dow Jones and Qualcomm each gave at least $1 million to the inaugural committee.[119] Additional corporations on the $1 million list

---

[111] Peter Ryan & Jeremy Venook, *Trump's Interests vs. America's, Secret Service Edition*, ATLANTIC (Aug. 4, 2017).

[112] Jacob Pramuk, *Trump's DC hotel reportedly turns a sizable, unexpected profit*, CNBC (Aug. 11, 2017).

[113] Dan Alexander, *How Donald Trump Shifted $1.1M Of Campaign-Donor Money Into His Business*, FORBES (Dec. 6, 2018) ("his businesses continued to charge the campaign for hotels, food, rent and legal consulting. That means the richest president in American history has turned $1.1 million from donors across the country into revenue for himself.").

[114] Mirren Gidda, *Private Prison Company GEO Group Gave Generously to Trump and Now Has Lucrative Contract*, NEWSWEEK (May 11, 2017).

[115] Ciara Torres-Spelliscy, *Why One Company Backed Donald Trump*, BRENNAN CTR. (Nov. 29, 2016).

[116] Franco Ordoñez, *Did companies' donations buy a Trump change in private prison policy?*, MIAMI HERALD (Mar. 3, 2017).

[117] Marcia Heroux Pounds, *Boca-based GEO Group poised to profit from Trump order for illegal immigrant beds*, SUN SENTINEL (June 25, 2018).

[118] *See generally* Ciara Torres-Spelliscy, *Has the Tide Turned in Favor of Disclosure? Revealing Money in Politics After* Citizens United *and* Doe v. Reed, 27 GA. ST. U. L. REV. 1057 (Summer 2011).

[119] Ashley Balcerzak, *250 donors shelled out $100k or more for Trump's inauguration, providing 91% of funds*, OPEN SECRETS (Apr. 19, 2017).

include Reynolds American, the Madison Square Garden Company, Allied Wallet, Access Industries, Green Plains and MacNeil Automotive Products.[120] As the *New York Times* noted, many of the corporate donors to the Trump inaugural had pending business with the federal government.[121] This corporate embrace of a new president is not unique to Trump. Many of the same corporations, which are repeat players in D.C., gave to Obama's inaugurals as well.[122] So at least with the inaugural, many blue-chip brands were willing to associate themselves with Trump's brand, if only for the day. Though they may wish that they hadn't, since the Trump inaugural is being criminally investigated.[123]

A more curious corporate donor was CITGO, an oil company owned by the Venezuelan government, which gave $500 000 toward Trump's inauguration.[124] This raised eyebrows for a number of reasons. First, Venezuela is destitute and going through severe social upheaval, including riots in the streets.[125] Second, foreigners are not allowed to give money to U.S. candidates.[126] And third, CITGO has financial entanglements with a Russian oil company.[127] This donation to the Trump inaugural committee led to a complaint against CITGO at the Federal Election Commission, questioning its legality.[128]

The assumption that Trump's political ambitions could only help his commercial brand was put to an immediate test as his announcement of his

---

[120] Dave Levinthal, *Donald Trump inauguration bankrolled by corporate giants,* CTR. FOR PUBLIC INTEGRITY (Apr. 19, 2017).

[121] Nicholas Confessore, *Trump Inaugural Drew Big Dollars From Donors With Vested Interests,* N.Y. TIMES (Apr. 19, 2017).

[122] Reuters, *Here's Who Donated to President Trump's Gigantic Inauguration Fund,* FORTUNE (Apr. 20, 2017) (many of these companies also donated to Obama's inauguration).

[123] Andrew Prokop, *The Trump inauguration is now being criminally investigated,* VOX (Dec. 13, 2018), www.vox.com/2018/12/13/18139886/trump-inaugural -committee-inauguration-investigation-sdny.

[124] Julian Borger, *Socialist Venezuela chipped in $500,000 to Trump's inauguration,* GUARDIAN (Apr. 19, 2017).

[125] Ana Campoy, *Venezuela, where people are starving, gave Trump half a million dollars for his inauguration,* QUARTZ (Apr. 19, 2017) ("There are many good uses towards which Venezuela's government could put $500,000. Importing food for its starving citizens and replenishing medical supplies at threadbare hospitals come to mind. Instead, Venezuela chose to donate that amount to [the Trump Inaugural.]").

[126] 52 U.S.C. § 30121.

[127] Vanessa Neumann, *Russia Gave to Citgo, Then Citgo Gave to Trump,* DAILY BEAST (Apr. 27, 2017) ("Many big oil companies funded Trump's inauguration. Only one is deeply in debt to the Kremlin.").

[128] Kat Sieniuc, *FEC Urged To Investigate Citgo's Trump Inauguration Kick-In,* LAW360 (Apr. 26, 2017) ("Free Speech For People ... filed a complaint with the FEC, alleging the committee violated U.S. laws when it accepted the contribution made by Petróleos de Venezuela SA through its U.S. affiliate Citgo Petroleum Corp.").

candidacy included vicious swipes at Mexican immigrants.[129] Most notably, after Trump made these negative comments, Macy's—which had sold his wares for years—ended its relationship with him.[130] As Macy's said, the company "'stands for diversity' and ... 'In light of statements made by Donald Trump, which are inconsistent with Macy's values, we have decided to discontinue our business relationship with Mr. Trump ...'"[131] Many long-term business partners distanced themselves from him. Also in reaction to the anti-Mexican statements, celebrity chef Goeffery Zakarian cancelled plans to open a restaurant in a Trump hotel,[132] as did celebrity chef José Andrés.[133] NBC, which had long supported Trump and his family by airing his show *The Apprentice*, decided not to air his *Miss USA Pageant*.[134] It also kept Trump off of *The Celebrity Apprentice*.[135] Serta also ended its relationship with Trump during the presidential campaign.[136] And NASCAR decided to distance itself from Trump by cancelling an event at Doral—a Trump property.[137] Trump responded to being jilted by his previous business partners by:

> [a]ttacking the companies that have left or plan to leave him ... Trump said 'Macy's, NBC, Serta and NASCAR have all taken the weak and very sad position of being politically correct even though they are wrong in terms of what is good for our country.'[138]

---

[129] *Here's Donald Trump's Presidential Announcement Speech*, TIME (Jun 16, 2015) ("When Mexico sends its people, they're not sending their best. They're not sending you. They're not sending you. They're sending people that have lots of problems, and they're bringing those problems with us. They're bringing drugs. They're bringing crime. They're rapists.").

[130] Leanna Garfield, *The anti-Trump boycott of 70 retailers won't back down – here's how it could affect sales*, BUSINESS INSIDER (Jan. 21, 2017) (quoting Robert Passikoff ("'Brands don't tend to do well when they involve themselves with ideologies.'").

[131] M.J. Lee, *First on CNN: Macy's Dumps Trump*, CNN (July 1, 2015).

[132] Chris Fuhrmeister, *Geoffrey Zakarian on Why He Backed Out of Donald Trump's DC Hotel*, EATER (Nov. 8, 2016).

[133] Ian Simpson, *Trump Hotel, Chef Settle Suit Over Canceled Washington Restaurant*, U.S. NEWS (Apr. 11, 2017).

[134] Neal Hartman, *Are Trump's Insults Harming His Business?*, NEWSWEEK (Jan. 27, 2016).

[135] Stephen Battaglio, *Macy's Cuts Ties with Trump Over Mexican Immigration Comments*, L.A. TIMES (July 1, 2015).

[136] John Santucci, *The Companies That Have Dumped Donald Trump*, ABC NEWS (July 4, 2015) ("Serta ... decided to begin 'unwinding [its] relationship' with Trump ... the company said it 'values diversity and does not agree with nor endorse the recent statements made by Mr. Trump.'").

[137] *Id.* ("On July 3, NASCAR spokesman David Higdon said the ceremony won't be at the Doral this year.").

[138] *Id.*

The process of rejecting the Trump brand included removing his name from street signs in Chicago; they used to say "Trump," but no longer do.[139] Several buildings around the world have also shed the Trump name.[140] For example, after the election, a building in Toronto removed Trump's name from its façade.[141] After Major League sports teams began shunning the property,[142] the Trump Soho Hotel decided to change its name.[143] The Trump name was removed from a hotel in Panama as well.[144] The *Associated Press* found the value of Trump condos in New York was down when the value of most real estate in the city was up.[145] Meanwhile, *Bloomberg* declared Trump Tower the least desirable luxury building in New York.[146] And in early 2019, the Trump Organization shelved plans to expand its hotels into red states including Mississippi.[147]

With a brand in the White House, political objections to the president can be taken out on his commercial brand. For those voters who don't like Trump's performance as president, barring an impeachment, they will have to wait for years before they can vote against him. But boycotts can be done every day for four years. Moreover, organizing a boycott has never been easier, given technological tools like social media and smartphone apps[148] including Buycott,

---

[139] Chicago Tribune Staff, *Chicago removes remaining Donald Trump street signs*, CHI. TRIB. (Dec. 6, 2016).

[140] Press Release, *Does Trump Have A Brand, Beyond Politics? Survey Finds President Loses Consumer Brand Mojo*, *supra* note 103 ("condominium owners ... had the name 'TRUMP PLACE' removed ..."); Peter Wade, *Last Two NYC Buildings Named 'Trump Place' Vote to Remove President's Name And then there were none*, ROLLING STONE (Feb. 23, 2019).

[141] Ian Austen, *Toronto Hotel Is Scrapping the Trump Name*, N.Y. TIMES (June 27, 2017).

[142] Tim Bontemps & David A. Fahrenthold, *Pro sports teams were once reliable patrons of Trump's hotels. Not anymore.*, WASH. POST (Oct. 12, 2017).

[143] Hui-yong Yu & Caleb Melby, *Trump Organization Bought Out of Its Contract for Trump SoHo*, BLOOMBERG (Nov. 22, 2017).

[144] Kim Hjelmgaard, *After 12-day standoff, workers strip Trump name from Panama hotel with crowbar*, USA TODAY (Mar. 6, 2018).

[145] *Trump's businesses take a hit as the brand 'has lost its mojo'*, ASSOCIATED PRESS (Dec. 23, 2018) ("Since Trump has taken office, prices have fallen 9 percent on average and are now down to levels not seen in five years. In that time, Manhattan condos overall have risen 29 percent.").

[146] Shahien Nasiripour, *Trump Tower Is Now One of NYC's Least-Desirable Luxury Buildings*, BLOOMBERG (May 14, 2019).

[147] Grace Dobush, *Trump Organization Halts Its Red State Hotel Expansion Plans*, FORTUNE (Feb. 15, 2019).

[148] Rosa Golijan, *App Makes Boycotting Companies as Easy as Scanning a Barcode*, NBC NEWS (May 16, 2013) ("Boycotting has probably never been simpler.").

Buypartisan and 2nd Vote.[149] There is even an app simply called "Boycott Trump" which enables consumers to avoid Trump products and retailers of Trump products.[150] As of February 2017, the Boycott Trump App had 325 000 users.[151] Boycotters naturally have a variety of motivations, but moral revulsion is a common theme among them.[152] A new app called Goods Unite Us, launched in 2017, promises to "help inform your purchases by exposing who you're supporting when you shop certain brands and companies," running "political background checks on brands and companies so you can put your money where your vote is."[153] The tagline for Goods Unite Us is "Be political by buying political."[154]

The boycotts are not limited to brands associated with Donald Trump; instead, boycotts have metastasized to the brands associated with Ivanka, Eric and Don Jr.[155] One of the things that enable boycotts of the Trump brand is the fact that most products and services the Trump Organization and his children have on offer are not unique. There are alternative hotel rooms, golf courses, ties, clothes and wine for consumers to buy.[156] Or as Erin Keane quipped about Trump's daughter's products, "Ivanka's wearables are economically vulnerable because they are needed by none, and now coveted by few."[157]

---

[149] There are also Ethical Barcode, which allows users to learn more about the ethical ramifications of the products they are about to purchase; Good Guide, which allows customers to access information on a product's social responsibility; and Shop Ethical, which provides information on environmental impacts of goods for the Australian market.

[150] Annalisa Merelli, *An App to Boycott Donald Trump Shows Just How Many Conflicts of Interests He Has*, QUARTZ (Dec. 1, 2016) ("Boycott Trump, an app that lists businesses linked to Trump, was released on Nov. 21 by Democratic Coalition Against Trump.").

[151] Renee Morad, *Want To Boycott Trump-Friendly Companies? These Apps Aim To Assist You*, FORBES (Feb. 14, 2017) ("Boycott Trump app has more than 325,000 users …").

[152] Carmen-Maria Albrecht, Colin Campbell & Daniel Heinrich, *Exploring why consumers engage in boycotts: toward a unified model*, J. OF PUBLIC AFFAIRS 4 (2013) ("Most respondents associated a boycott with the punishing of a company by consumers whose value system was infringed upon through expression of an aversion to objects due to inappropriate behaviors or activities.").

[153] *Home Page*, GOODS UNITE US, www.goodsuniteus.com/#/.

[154] *Alternative products to Goods Unite Us*, PRODUCT HUNT, www.producthunt .com/alternatives/goods-unite-us.

[155] Suzanne Monyak, *Shoppers Boycott Ivanka Trump's Clothing Line to Protest Donald's Misogyny*, SLATE (Oct. 24, 2016).

[156] Close, *supra* note 92.

[157] Erin Kean, *Ivanka goes out of style: More women are refusing to buy what she's selling*.

The three eldest Trump children seem as eager to monetize the presidency as their father. During the campaign and transition period, Ivanka Trump tried to sell her branded items by using the press that followed her father. Ivanka Trump wore an Ivanka Trump™ dress when she introduced her father at the Republican National Convention, and turned around and sold it online for $138. When she appeared with the rest of the Trump family in a 60 Minutes interview, the next day fashion reporters received a picture from her company noting that Ivanka Trump had been wearing "her favorite bangle from the Metropolis Collection," at the hefty price tag of $10 800.

Hostility from women consumers to the Trump brand picked up considerably after an old videotape from *Access Hollywood* aired on October 7, 2016 in which Donald Trump made lewd comments about sexual assault.[158] In response to the *Access Hollywood* tape, two women, Shannon Coulter and Sue Atencio, created the #grabyourwallet boycott.[159] This boycott targets Trump-branded products as well as retailers that sell such products. As the *New York Times* reported about the #grabyourwallet protest, "Thousands of people have contacted the stores Coulter has on her boycott list, including Macy's and Amazon." Even the name "#grabyourwallet" was a bit of branding genius. The original hashtag was #fashionnotfacism. But Coulter, who is a professional marketer, found that too strident and changed it. Coulter told CBS's *Moneywatch,* "College-educated women in particular are well aware of the epic consumer power they wield, and they're flexing that power ..."[160] She also explained, "'The goal came originally from a place of really wanting to shop the stores we loved again with a clear conscience.'"[161]

Measuring the impact of any boycott movement is fraught. But many of the stores that #grabyourwallet targeted in fact stopped selling Trump-branded products months later. Shoes.com was the first to cease selling Trump brands

---

Donald Trump's daughter is learning a hard lesson in politicized American consumerism, SALON (Feb. 11, 2017), www.salon.com/2017/02/11/ivanka-goes-out-of-style -women-dont-want-to-buy-what-shes-selling-anymore/.

[158] *Access Hollywood Archival Footage Reveals Vulgar Trump Comments From 2005,* ACCESS HOLLYWOOD (Oct. 7, 2016).

[159] Christine Rushton, *Shoppers boycott Ivanka Trump's clothes with #GrabYourWallets,* L.A. TIMES (Oct. 25, 2016) ("San Francisco marketing specialist Shannon Coulter launched the #GrabYourWallets campaign after a video surfaced on Oct. 7 of Trump talking about groping women.").

[160] Kerry Close, *The Grab Your Wallet Movement Wants People to Boycott Donald Trump-Affiliated Retailers,* TIME (Nov. 17, 2016).

[161] Rachel Abrams, *The Anti-Trump Activist Taking On Retailers,* N.Y. TIMES (Feb. 25, 2017).

after #grabyourwallet targeted it.[162] Sears followed and stopped selling Trump brands.[163] Both high-end and low-end retailers have since dropped Trump lines. At the top of the market, Nordstrom, Neiman Marcus and Gilt let go of Ivanka Trump's lines.[164] And at the bargain bin, T.J. Maxx, Kmart, Belk and Burlington all backed away from selling Trump products.[165] While none of the stores that dropped the Trump brands would admit that #grabyourwallet or other boycotts were the proximate cause, several stores did point to slumping sales which could be caused by the boycotts.[166] According to the *Wall Street Journal*, Ivanka Trump's sales fell 32 percent in the last fiscal year at Nordstrom.[167] When Nordstrom announced that it was ending its relationship with Trump's daughter, the president took to Twitter to complain: "My daughter Ivanka has been treated so unfairly by Nordstrom ... Terrible!"[168]

Liberal and conservative consumers have had opposite reactions to the Nordstrom/Ivanka feud. According to polling firm Ipsos, after the presidential tweet, "Nordstrom's social media mentions increased a hundredfold overnight, most of which were negative."[169] Ipsos also found: "Those who report boycotting Nordstrom strongly skew Republican ..."[170] The Harris Poll found that "the Ivanka Trump controversy seems to have had an impact. ... Among liberal-leaning consumers, Nordstrom's brand equity rose slightly. ..."[171] The Harris Poll also showed: "The store still managed to be the highest ranked

---

[162] Kate Taylor, *An Anti-Trump Movement Is Calling for the Boycott of These 32 Retailers*, BUSINESS INSIDER (Nov. 15, 2016) ("Shoes.com announced on Twitter that it was removing Ivanka Trump shoes from its inventory ... this was the first time a retailer responded to the Grab Your Wallet movement by actually dropping Trump products."); *see also* Khorri Atkinson, *Canada's largest store chain drops Ivanka Trump's products*, AXIOS (Sept. 18, 2018).

[163] Jeremy Quittner, *Ivanka Trump's Neiman Marcus Products Are No Longer Online*, FORTUNE (Feb. 3, 2017).

[164] Abrams, *supra* note 161.

[165] Chavie Lieber, *Burlington Removes Ivanka Trump's Collection From Its Site*, RACKED (Feb. 12, 2017) ("Ivanka Trump's online presence continues to dwindle ...").

[166] Sarah Halzack, *The woman behind the boycott that is pressuring retailers to dump the Trumps*, WASH. POST (Feb. 13, 2017).

[167] Miriam Gottfried & Suzanne Kapner, *Internal Nordstrom Data Show Sales Decline for Ivanka Trump Brand*, WALL. ST. J. (Feb. 11, 2017).

[168] David A. Fahrenthold & Sarah Halzack, *Nordstrom drops Ivanka Trump-branded clothing and shoes*, WASH. POST (Feb. 2, 2017).

[169] *Brand Risk in the New Age of Populism: Four Key Tactics for Surviving Hyper-Partisan Consumers*, IPSOS 5 (June 7, 2017), www.ipsos.com/sites/default/files/2017-06/IpsosPA_POV_PoliticsAndBrands.pdf.

[170] *Id. at* 6.

[171] Michael Johnson, *Harris Poll: What is in a retail brand? Millennial loyalty*, OWN BRANDS NOW (May 10, 2017), www.ownbrandsnow.com/article/harris-poll-whats-retail-brand-millennial-loyalty.

luxury retail department store in the country."[172] Roughly two months after the Nordstrom dust-up, Ivanka Trump announced that she would join the White House staff in 2017.[173] In mid-2018 Ivanka Trump revealed that she was closing her company.[174] Yet oddly, in late 2018, China granted Ivanka Trump more trademarks, including one for *voting machines*.[175]

5.   CONCLUSION

From the Founding Fathers' and Mothers' boycott of British goods to make a point about political liberty, to the NAACP's boycott of business to further the cause of racial equality, to consumer boycotts to reject the Trump brand, Americans have long used their buying power to make political points. And thanks to *Claiborne Hardware*, the Supreme Court protects the right of customers to boycott for political purposes. In the end, it all boils down to the basic right to protest. As V.O. Key notes, part of what makes a democracy is "freedom for expression of dissent from the actions of authority, with the expectation that protests will be heard and, if not heeded, at least considered and not followed by reprisals."[176]

---

[172] *Brands of the Year: Trends Impacting the Brands We Love*, HARRIS POLL 22 (April 2017), www.theharrispoll.com/equitrend-information/.

[173] Dan Merica, Gloria Borger, Jim Acosta & Betsy Klein, *Ivanka Trump is making her White House job official*, CNN (Mar. 30, 2017).

[174] Kate Taylor & Mary Hanbury, *An anti-Trump movement is calling for the boycott of these retailers*, BUSINESS INSIDER (Jul. 25, 2018), www.businessinsider.com/trump-boycott-retailers-sell-trump-products-2017-1 ("the first daughter announced she would be closing her namesake brand.").

[175] Mary Papenfuss, *Ivanka Trump Set to Gain 16 New Trademarks in China, Including for Voting Machines*, HUFF. POST (Nov. 5, 2018), www.huffingtonpost.com/entry/ivanka-trump-chinese-trademarks-voting-machines_us_5be0d881e4b04367a87fab4f.

[176] KEY, *supra* note 6 at 6.

12. Branding tragedy

"Who Lives, Who Dies, Who Tells Your Story?" Lin-Manuel Miranda[1]

1. INTRODUCTION

Without political protest, there wouldn't an America. But political protests still sharply divide American public opinion. Take now ex-San Francisco 49ers quarterback Colin Kaepernick's decision to peacefully kneel during the national anthem to protest police violence against African Americans.[2] In 2016, over 250 Black people were killed by police in the United States.[3] In late 2016, Kaepernick decided to do something about it—kneel in silent protest of police violence at football games where he was working. For some, this is precisely the type of protest that makes America a vibrant democracy; for others, the protest is disrespectful of the national anthem and, by extension, the nation.[4] Kaepernick paid a steep professional price for his protest. He has been unable to find work in an NFL team, for which he sued the owners of the NFL.[5] In February 2019, he won a settlement against the NFL for an undisclosed amount.[6] The kneeling-during-the-anthem protests have triggered boycotts on both sides of the issue.[7]

---

[1] Original Broadway Cast of *Hamilton, Hamilton* (Sept. 25, 2015).

[2] Josh Levin, *Colin Kaepernick Won In angering the NFL's white billionaire owners*, SLATE (Aug. 18, 2017), https://slate.com/sports/2017/08/colin-kaepernicks -protest-cost-him-his-job-but-started-a-movement.html.

[3] Julia Craven, *More Than 250 Black People Were Killed By Police In 2016*, HUFF. POST (Jan. 1, 2017), www.huffingtonpost.com/entry/black-people-killed-by -police-america_us_577da633e4b0c590f7e7fb17.

[4] Kathryn Casteel, *How Do Americans Feel About The NFL Protests?*, FIVE THIRTY EIGHT (Oct. 9, 2017), https://fivethirtyeight.com/features/how-do-americans -feel-about-the-nfl-protests-it-depends-on-how-you-ask/.

[5] Nate Davis, *Don't ask if Colin Kaepernick is returning to NFL — your team probably already passed on him*, USA TODAY (Nov. 29, 2018).

[6] Langston Wertz Jr., *The NFL reaches a settlement with Colin Kaepernick.*, CHARLOTTE OBSERVER (Feb. 16, 2019).

[7] Jesse Washington, *The NFL is being squeezed by boycotts from both sides over anthem protests*, UNDEFEATED (Sept. 13, 2017), https://theundefeated.com/features/nfl -boycotts-from-both-sides-over-anthem-protests/; Matthew Haag, *Papa John's Chief Executive to Step Down*, N.Y. TIMES (Dec. 21, 2017).

Political protesters like Kaepernick are often told that they are "doing it wrong," "hurting their own cause" or "alienating potential allies and converts."[8] Both sides are typically in a fight to control the narrative and brand themselves favorably. The protesters will explain why they are morally correct. And the protested will often try to vilify the protesters. In this branded world, some companies will even try to make a buck from political protests. Thus, Kaepernick is one of the faces of Nike's 2018 *Just Do It* campaign, despite not playing a single down of professional football in the NFL since the 2016 season.[9] As a skeptic noted:

> [Nike]'s political action committee … give[s] more money to Republicans than to Democrats. 'Believe in something,' the Kaepernick ad demands. Or, if necessary, pretend to believe in something while investing your political money in diametrically opposed beliefs.[10]

The battle for what it means to kneel to protest police violence continues, as one side sees a patriotic struggle for justice and the other sees an insult to patriotism. The fact that the protest is also getting commodified just adds more ways for those on each side to express their position by buying Kap's Nike merch to support him or boycotting Nike to protest him. The question of who won here remains. Was it Kaepernick? The NFL? The anthem? Nike? The Republicans supported by Nike? The answer you give may say more about you than the facts on the ground.

Like many of the other events in this book, there is often a sematic war to control a narrative around tragedies and the responses to tragedies. And with some of the stories, which were literally unfolding as this book was being written, how a particular aspect of the story will end is still unknown. Here are two more stories where the fight to brand the narrative is ongoing. In one story, there is a battle to characterize what happened at a *Unite the Right* rally in Charlottesville in 2017 and President Trump's reaction to it. In the other, there is a battle to brand what happened after a mass shooting in Parkland, Florida in 2018. In both, the question of the real "victim" is a source of the branding

---

[8]   Shannon Van Sant, *NFL Cheerleader Kneels During National Anthem*, NPR (Nov. 2, 2018), www.npr.org/2018/11/02/663594281/nfl-cheerleader-kneels-during-national-anthem.

[9]   Tom Morgan, *Never Mind the Politics, Here's the Brand*, A NEW TYPE OF IMPRINT (Apr. 2018), www.anewtypeofimprint.com/news-2/2018/9/14/never-mind-the-politics-heres-the-brand.

[10]   Francis Wilkinson, *Liberals Can Hold Corporations Accountable Corporate America prefers Republican Voters and Democratic Consumers.*, BLOOMBERG (Dec. 17, 2018), www.bloomberg.com/opinion/articles/2018-12-17/democratic-voters-can-punish-fox-news-party.

battle. Of course, in Charlottesville and Parkland, there are the actual victims who were killed and injured in both tragedies. But the branding battle over narrative in both cases ballooned into a bigger fight. In the mind of the president, the victim after Charlottesville was himself. In the mind of the National Rifle Association (NRA), the victim after Parkland is the NRA. But neither the president nor the NRA gets to make these claims in a vacuum. They are up against a tumultuous scrum of other political actors who are also trying to shape the storyline. And the fact that there are commercial brands in the middle of the fight over these narratives just gives each side swords and shields to deploy in the rhetorical branding brawl.

First, this chapter will explore how some brands find themselves in the middle of political fights around tragedies, including the injuries and deaths in Charlottesville in 2017. It will then look at the aftermath of a massacre at Marjory Stoneman Douglas High School on Valentine's Day 2018. Students who survived the massacre expressed their rage at the prevalence of available assault-style weapons like the one used in the killings at their school. They pointed a finger squarely at the NRA. And then, methodically, they tried to starve the NRA of corporate resources and political power.

2.   REJECTING PRESIDENT TRUMP'S BRAND AFTER CHARLOTTESVILLE

Perhaps because there were so many racialized appeals during the 2016 campaign, Trump's reluctance to condemn racism didn't surprise those who were paying attention. For others less tuned into politics, Trump's comfort with neo-Nazis came as a shock. The question of whether Trump is truly a racist is a subject of debate. For more of a discussion of race, see the chapter "Branding racism." But as Democratic candidate for Governor of Florida Andrew Gillum said of his Republican opponent Ron DeSantis, "I'm not calling Mr. DeSantis a racist. I'm simply saying the racists believe he's a racist."[11] This test could be put to Trump. One of the leaders of the American neo-Nazis, Richard Spencer, certainly seemed drawn to Trump. Spencer once stated, "[Trump] is a nationalist and a he is a racialist. His movement is a white movement. Duh."[12]

Late in the Summer of 2017, there were violent clashes among neo-Nazis, members of the KKK, White supremacists and those opposing them in

---

[11]   Eugene Scott, *'Racists think he's a racist': Gillum on white supremacists' support for DeSantis*, WASH. POST (Oct. 25, 2018).

[12]   MICHAEL WOLFF, FIRE AND FURY INSIDE THE TRUMP WHITE HOUSE 139 (2018) (quoting Richard Spencer).

Charlottesville, Virginia.[13] The events in Charlottesville were organized by neo-Nazi Richard Spencer and were targeted at the planned removal of a statue of Robert E. Lee. The event, called *Unite the Right*, "was explicitly designed to link Trump's politics with white nationalism."[14] As veteran journalist Bob Woodward described the first night of the events:

> Moving across the campus of the University of Virginia in a haunting nighttime torch walk on a steamy August 11 evening, echoing Germany of the 1930s, around 250 white nationalists chanted 'Jews will not replace us' and the Nazi slogan 'Blood and Soil.'[15]

The next day, a White supremacist named James Alex Fields Jr. drove his car into a group of peaceful protestors in Charlottesville, killing a woman named Heather Heyer and injuring 19 others.[16] Trump was at first reluctant to respond to the violent events in Charlottesville. Then he gave an equivocating response that blamed violence on "both sides."[17] Negative reactions to the president's false equivalence between racists and anti-racists at the Charlottesville events spanned the political spectrum. Former Attorney General Eric Holder tweeted: "This is a time to choose sides—simple as that. There is a right side and an immoral one."[18] Senator Orrin Hatch from Utah tweeted: "My brother didn't give his life fighting Hitler for Nazi ideas to go unchallenged here at home."[19] Senator John McCain from Arizona put out a statement which said Charlottesville was "a confrontation between our better angels and our worst demons. White supremacists and neo-Nazis are, by definition opposed to American patriotism and the ideals that define us."[20]

Then Trump issued a more ringing condemnation of the racist gathering in a speech at the White House,[21] where he looked "like a kid called on the carpet.

---

[13]   Sarah Rankin, *3 dead, dozens injured, amid violent white nationalist rally in Virginia*, Associated Press (Aug. 13, 2017).

[14]   Wolff, *supra* note 12, at 292 (2018).

[15]   Bob Woodward, Fear 238 (2018).

[16]   Steve Almasy & Chandrika Narayan, *Heather Heyer died 'fighting for what she believed in*, CNN (Aug. 15, 2017).

[17]   Glenn Thrush & Maggie Haberman, *Trump Is Criticized for Not Calling Out White Supremacists*, N.Y. Times (Aug. 12, 2017).

[18]   Dartunorro Clark, *Democratic, Republican Lawmakers Decry Trump's Latest Charlottesville Remarks*, NBC News (Aug. 16, 2017), www.nbcnews.com/politics/white-house/not-my-president-lawmakers-decry-trump-s-latest-charlottesville-remarks-n793021.

[19]   Woodward, *supra* note 15, at 239 (2018).

[20]   *Id.*

[21]   David Nakamura, *Trump denounces KKK neo-Nazis as 'repugnant' as he seeks to quell criticism of his response to Charlottesville*, Wash. Post (Aug. 14, 2017).

Resentful and petulant, he was clearly reading forced lines."[22] His heart wasn't in it. Before he gave the speech, he told aides, "This doesn't feel right to me."[23] On a flight to New York after he gave this speech:

> [He] kept trying to rationalize why someone would be a member of the KKK—that is, they might not actually believe what the KKK believed, and the KKK probably does not believe what it used to believe, and anyway, who really knows what the KKK believes now?[24]

But then a day later, Trump undercut his own statement "that racism is evil"[25] in a 23-minute press conference where he defended some of those on the White supremacist side as "fine" people.[26] A few days later, on August 17, 2017, Trump lamented that monuments to confederate soldiers were being removed across America.[27] Former KKK leader David Duke tweeted at President Trump: "Thank you President Trump for your honesty & courage to tell the truth about #Charlottesville."[28]

As these events surrounding Charlottesville and Trump's reaction to it unfolded, CEOs who sat on two White House business councils, the Manufacturing Jobs Initiative and the Strategic and Policy Forum, came under increasing pressure from customers and the general public to resign from the councils. For example, on Twitter the hashtag #quitthecouncil was trending.[29] The president's refusal to roundly and forcefully condemn the racist violence in Charlottesville put the CEOs on Trump's business councils to a hard test: did they want their commercial brands to be tainted with Trump's brand, which was getting mired in racist mud?[30] The question in August 2017 was whether other CEOs would follow the lead of Elon Musk of Tesla and Disney CEO Bob Iger, who made early exits from the Manufacturing Jobs Initiative

---

[22]   WOLFF, *supra* note 12, at 295.

[23]   WOODWARD, *supra* note 15, at 242 (quoting Trump).

[24]   WOLFF, *supra* note 12, at 295.

[25]   WOODWARD, *supra* note 15, at 243 (quoting Trump).

[26]   David Jackson, *Trump's assertion left wing protesters just as violent as white supremacists in Charlottesville sets off firestorm*, USA TODAY (Aug. 15, 2017); *The fallout from Trump backtracking on his condemnation of neo-Nazis*, POLITICO (Aug. 16, 2017).

[27]   David Nakamura, *Trump mourns loss of 'beautiful statues and monuments' in wake of Charlottesville rally over Robert E. Lee statue*, WASH. POST (Aug. 17, 2017).

[28]   WOODWARD, *supra* note 15, at 246 (quoting Duke).

[29]   Roger Yu, *Trump disbands economic councils as Charlottesville fallout continues*, USA TODAY (Aug. 16, 2017).

[30]   Rob Tornoe, *As 4th CEO quits Trump council, pressure heats up for Campbell Soup executive*, PHILLY INQ. (Aug. 15, 2017).

to protest Trump's pulling the U.S. out of the Paris Climate Accord.[31] In short, the answer was: they did. First to leave was the CEO of Merck, an African American man named Kenneth Fraizer, who publicly announced that he was leaving the president's manufacturing council in response to the events sur-round the Charlottesville attack.[32] Mr. Fraizer said in a statement, "As CEO of Merck, and as a matter of personal conscience, I feel a responsibility to take a stand against intolerance and extremism."[33] Advocates upset with Trump's seeming inability to condemn violence from White supremacists encouraged other CEOs on the business councils to follow Frazier's lead and leave as well. Over the next two days, several CEOs, including those of Intel, Campbell's Soup, 3M, Under Armour and Ford Motor Company, and the president of the American Federation of Labor and Congress of Industrial Organizations (AFL-CIO) left. Many put out damning press statements condemning racism as they exited, like Campbell's Soup CEO Denise Morrison, who said: "Racism and murder are unequivocally reprehensible and are not morally equivalent to anything else that happened in Charlottesville. I believe the President should have been – and still needs to be – unambiguous on that point …"[34] As the resignations cascaded, the members of the Manufacturing Jobs Initiative decided to disband the group.[35] Trump tried to retake control and put out a tweet claiming that he had disbanded both business councils.[36] But by the time of Trump's tweet, there wasn't much left to disband. Simultaneously, half of Trump's Digital Economy Board of Advisors also left,[37] as did the entire President's Committee on the Arts & the Humanities.[38] Also, in reaction

---

[31]   Dominic Rushe, *Elon Musk and Disney boss quit Trump's business panel over Paris pullout*, GUARDIAN (June 2, 2017).

[32]   Rebecca Savransky, *Merck CEO resigns from presidential council over Trump remarks*, HILL (Aug. 14, 2017).

[33]   *Id.*

[34]   Lydia Ramsey, *'Racism and murder are unequivocally reprehensible': Campbell Soup CEO quits Trump council moments before he disbands it*, BUSINESS INSIDER (Aug. 16, 2017).

[35]   David Gelles, Landon Thomas Jr., Andrew Ross Sorkin & Kate Kelly, *Inside the C.E.O. Rebellion Against Trump's Advisory Councils*, N.Y. TIMES (Aug. 16, 2017).

[36]   Bryan Menegus & Dell Cameron, *Winning: Trump Dissolves Two Advisory Councils After Advisors Flee in Protest*, GIZMODO (Aug. 16, 2017).

[37]   Jessica Guynn & Rachel Sandler, *Trump tech advisory board hit by defections after Charlottesville*, USA TODAY (Aug. 18, 2017) ("A new wave of resignations has hit the Commerce Department's 'digital economy' board as private sector advisers quit in protest of statements President Trump made about the violence in Charlottesville. More than half of the members of the 15-person Digital Economy Board of Advisors have quit, according to *Politico*.").

[38]   Sameea Kamal & Noah Bierman, *All 17 members of White House arts panel resign to protest Trump's response to Charlottesville*, L.A. TIMES (Aug. 18, 2017).

to the Charlottesville White supremacist debacle, several charities cancelled future events at Mar-a-Lago.[39] The whole Charlottesville episode showed how CEOs, artists, charities and others were susceptible to pressure from the public on the issue of racism. And for many of the businessmen and businesswomen involved, associating their brands with the Trump brand was no longer worth the downside.

Roughly 14 months later, in Virginia, some justice was meted out. Heyer's killer James Alex Fields Jr. was sentenced to life plus 419 years and $480 000 in fines.[40] He also received an additional life sentence from federal authorities after pleading guilty to hate crimes once federal prosecutors promised not to pursue the death penalty.[41]

So who has successfully branded the narrative of this tragedy? Members of *Unite the Right* got worldwide coverage of their movement and their objection to the removal of Robert E. Lee's statue. The statue's removal is subject to a lawsuit and still has not happened as of 2019. Did the exiting CEOs win the narrative war? They got to claim the moral high ground on the matter of racism as they distanced themselves from the president and saved their commercial brands from picking up negative connotations of racist appeasement. Who was the victim here? A self-pitying president seemed to think he was the victim of the whole Charlottesville episode. On August 22, 2017, Trump held a political rally in Phoenix and talked about how poorly the press had covered his remarks about Charlottesville. *The New Yorker* described the events thusly: "Trump spoke for seventy-five minutes, giving full voice to the flitting, self-obsessed, self-pitying and openly deceitful qualities that typify his rhetoric."[42] Later, Trump said of his White House speech condemning racism after Charlottesville, "That was the biggest fucking mistake I've made. [Because] [y]ou never make those concessions. You never apologize. I didn't do anything

---

[39]   Drew Harwell & David A. Fahrenthold, *Trump's Mar-a-Lago Club loses its ninth big charity event this week,* WASH. POST (Aug. 19, 2018); revenue is also down at Trump's Doral location. *See* Asher Stockler, *Donald Trump's Flagship Florida Resort Has Seen Its Revenues Sink Amid Tough Times for President's Brand,* NEWSWEEK (May 15, 2019), www.newsweek.com/donald-trump-resort-doral-decline-brand-1426457.

[40]   Madeleine Aggeler, *Man Who Drove Van Through Crowd in Charlottesville Sentenced to Life in Prison,* CUT (Dec. 11, 2018), www.thecut.com/2018/12/james -fields-found-life-sentence-murdering-heather-heyer-unite-the-right-rally.html.

[41]   Denise Lavoie, *Life in prison for Charlottesville car attack,* PBS (June 28, 2019), www.pbs.org/newshour/nation/prosecutors-seek-life-sentence-in-charlottesville -car-attack.

[42]   Amy Davidson Sorkin, *In Phoenix, Trump Lets the Real World Go Away,* NEW YORKER (Aug. 23, 2017).

wrong in the first place. Why look weak? ... That's the worst speech I've ever given."[43]

3.   REJECTING THE NRA'S BRAND AFTER THE PARKLAND MASSACRE

The ultimate example of how commercial brands can get embroiled in American political divisions is exemplified by what happened to brands after a mass shooting in Florida. And here is another battle for branding the narrative of a tragedy. Mass shootings in America are troublingly common. In 2015 *USA Today* published an op-ed that was a template of what typically happens after a mass shooting. The op-ed was entitled, "Why wait for the next mass shooting when you can write the news story now?" The piece stated:

> ANYTOWN, USA – A heavily armed, mentally disturbed young man opened fire yesterday at a school/church/theater/shopping mall, killing ___ people and critically wounding ___. The gunman also died, although it was unclear whether he shot himself or was slain by police responding to the scene.

> The Anytown massacre, the latest in a string of mass shootings across the nation, stunned the normally bucolic community. "I can't believe something like this could happen here," said Anytown Mayor ___ ___. As the sun set over the town, residents gathered to sing Amazing Grace at a candlelight vigil ...

> A spokesman for the NRA said the focus belongs on mental health and, out of respect for the victims, it's too soon to talk about gun control measures. The spokesman noted that the massacre occurred in a supposedly "gun-free" zone and said that if only more people in the school/church/theater/shopping mall had been armed, the gunman could have been stopped sooner ...[44]

What this *USA Today* op-ed hits on is that one of the ways in which gun rights advocates, especially the NRA, have controlled the narrative about gun violence around mass killings is to make the claim immediately after a massacre that it's too soon to talk about gun control, out of respect for the dead and for grieving families. This trope is cynically deployed again and again in mass shooting after mass shooting.[45] What gun sellers and their lobbyists count on is that the rage that is generated by a particular violent event will dissipate before the victims can ask for better gun laws or other fundamental changes that might prevent the next act of gun-related violence. And for years this tactic has worked. Federal gun laws

---

[43]   WOODWARD, *supra* note 15, at 244 (quoting Trump).
[44]   Bill Sternberg, *Flashback—Massacre at Anytown, USA: Opinion*, USA TODAY (Oct. 2, 2015).
[45]   Robyn Urback, *It's always too soon to talk about gun control: Opinion*, CBC (Oct. 4, 2017), www.cbc.ca/news/opinion/gun-control-las-vegas-1.4330409.

were not strengthened after Sandy Hook in 2012, where 20 people, most of them first graders, died.[46] Nor were they changed after 50 young people were killed at the Pulse Nightclub in Orlando in 2016.[47] Nor were they changed after 58 people were killed at an outdoor country music concert in Las Vegas in 2017.[48] The day after Las Vegas, Presidential Spokeswoman Sarah Huckabee Sanders said it was premature to talk about gun policy.[49] Then Parkland happened.

On Valentine's Day 2018, 17 people were killed at Marjory Stoneman Douglas High School in Parkland, Florida.[50] The initial reaction as the news of the shooting spread was typical: individuals started sending "thoughts and prayers" for Parkland. As one commentator said of the repetitive use of the phrase "thoughts and prayers," and its empty sentiment on *CNN*:

> Semantic satiation is the phenomenon in which a word or phrase is repeated so often it loses its meaning. But it also becomes something ridiculous, a jumble of letters that feels alien on the tongue and reads like gibberish on paper. 'Thoughts and prayers' has reached that full semantic satiation."[51]

However, rather than grieve silently or out of public view, many student leaders at the school took hold of their own narrative by rejecting the common platitudes of "thoughts and prayers" that typically flood in after such all-too-common tragedies. After the president tweeted "My prayers and condolences to the families of the victims of the terrible Florida shooting[,]"[52] the

---

[46]   Matt Bennett, *The Promise: The Families of Sandy Hook and the Long Road to Gun Safety*, BROOKINGS (July 15, 2013), http://csweb.brookings.edu/content/research/essays/2013/sandy-hook-promise-gun-safety.html#.

[47]   Barbara Liston, *50 dead, 53 injured after shooting at Orlando nightclub*, REUTERS (June 12, 2016), www.reviewjournal.com/news/nation-and-world/50-dead-53-injured-after-shooting-at-orlando-nightclub/.

[48]   *Las Vegas shooting: 58 dead, hundreds injured in attack on Route 91 Harvest Festival*, ABC (Oct. 2, 2017), www.abc.net.au/news/2017-10-02/las-vegas-shooting-mandalay-bay-hotel-gunman-stephen-paddock/9008372.

[49]   Dan Merica, *Sarah Sanders gets emotional about Las Vegas, dismisses gun control talk*, CNN (Oct. 2, 2017), www.cnn.com/2017/10/02/politics/sarah-sanders-las-vegas/index.html.

[50]   Richard Gonzales & Colin Dwyer, *Sheriff's Office Reports 17 People Dead in South Florida High School Shooting*, NPR (Feb. 14, 2018), www.npr.org/sections/thetwo-way/2018/02/14/585835311/shooter-and-possible-injuries-reported-at-broward-county-fla-high-school.

[51]   AJ Willingham, *How 'thoughts and prayers' went from common condolence to cynical meme*, CNN (May 19, 2018), www.cnn.com/2018/02/20/us/thoughts-and-prayers-florida-school-shooting-trnd/index.html.

[52]   Allie Malloy, *Trump sends condolences to school shooting victims in Florida*, CNN (Feb. 14, 2018), www.cnn.com/2018/02/14/politics/donald-trump-florida-shooting/index.html.

reaction from the ground from students involved was swift and negative. As *The New Yorker* reported about the aftermath of Parkland:

> Douglas High School sophomore named Sarah Chadwick, who informed the President of the United States, via his favorite medium, in words that quickly went viral, "I don't want your condolences you fucking piece of shit, my friends and teachers were shot." In the hours that followed, others joined Chadwick in rejecting the platitudes. On social media, and on live television, the victims were not playing their parts. They were not asking for privacy in their time of grief. They did not think it was 'too soon' to bring up the issue of gun control—in fact, several students would start shouting 'gun control' within the very sanctum of the candlelight vigil [mourning the 17 victims].[53]

This was just the first clue that Parkland would be different. Part of what made Parkland distinct is the victims were talking for themselves (unlike in other tragedies, where surviving parents or family members were the spokespersons). And many of the Parkland survivors reacted against what they saw as the causal links that led to the deaths and grievous injuries of friends, teachers and coaches. These causal links included lax gun laws in Florida, as well as the nation, and the interactions between the NRA, politicians and their corporate supporters who all stood in the way of stronger gun laws. Many of the Parkland students and their supporters spent the year after the tragedy trying to smash the links in the causal chain. This was less like a traditional boycott and more like the siege of Carthage. But instead of a city state as the enemy, the object of their ire was the NRA, which has been around since November 17, 1871.

The Parkland students demanded action from lawmakers in Tallahassee, from the president and from Congress. In Tallahassee, they achieved the previously unthinkable: improvements on gun control in a state where Republicans control both Houses of the Legislature and the governor's mansion.[54] Even the president sat down with some Parkland students, as well as other students and parents who had survived other gun violence. In his hand, the president held a card to remind himself to be empathetic that read: "I hear you."[55] A teenager named Samuel Zeif, who survived Parkland, asked the president through tears and with a voice cracking with anguish, "How did we not stop this after Columbine? After Sandy Hook?"[56]

---

[53]   Emily Witt, *Calling B.S. in Parkland, Florida*, NEW YORKER (Feb. 17, 2018).

[54]   Dan Sweeney, *Gov. Rick Scott signs sweeping gun bill; NRA files suit*, SUN-SENTINEL (Mar. 9, 2018).

[55]   Betsy Klein, *Trump's note card for Parkland shooting discussion: 'I hear you'*, CNN (Feb. 21, 2018), www.cnn.com/2018/02/21/politics/trump-parkland-notecard/index.html.

[56]   Jen Kirby, *Parkland shooting survivor Samuel Zeif to Trump: "How did this not stop after Columbine?"*, Vox (Feb. 21, 2018), www.vox.com/2018/2/21/17038310/parkland-shooting-survivor-samuel-zeif-trump.

Nine days after the Parkland shooting, Trump made mumblings about doing something at the Conservative Political Action Conference (CPAC), stating, "I can speak for all of the senators, congressmen and congresswomen, all of the people in this room that are involved in this decision, that we will act and do something."[57] And then his attention drifted elsewhere. On December 18, 2018, the Bureau of Alcohol, Tobacco, Firearms and Explosives issued a rule banning bump stocks, a tool that had been used in the Las Vegas massacre in 2017.[58] And needless to say, the Republican-controlled House and Senate did nothing to address gun violence after Parkland. In January 2019, the House flipped to the Democrats. Time will tell whether any sensible legislation will emanate from the new Congress, but there are some encouraging signs, at least in the House. On February 8, 2019 the House Judiciary Committee held the first hearing on gun violence in eight years. Many Parkland survivors attended and testified. On February 27, 2019, the House voted in favor of gun control legislation that included universal background checks. So far, the U.S. Senate under the leadership of Mitch McConnell has done *nothing* to address gun violence.

Shortly after the shooting, the Parkland students received financial assistance from celebrities such as Dwane Wade, Gabrielle Union, Carmelo Anthony, George and Amal Clooney, Oprah Winfrey, Steven Spielberg and Kate Capshaw, Jeffrey Katzenberg and Marilyn Siegel, Ellen DeGeneres, Chrissy Teigen and John Legend, among others.[59] They used this financial support to plan the March for Our Lives in D.C. on March 24, 2018. Throughout this event and the weeks running up to it, the students showed that they were digital natives who had a preternatural instinct for branding. For one, the phrase "March for Our Lives" evoked other marches that had been organized since the Trump inauguration like the Women's March, the Tax March, the March for Science and the March for Truth. It also evoked other historical marches like Martin Luther King's March on Washington and the March for Life. The logo for the March for Our Lives was four figures (similar to the figures on men's and women's restrooms) holding hands. This branding was all over D.C. on the day of the march, and showed up on hats and t-shirts for months afterwards.

---

[57] Ali Rogin & Stephanie Ebbs, *President Trump says 'we will act' after Parkland shooting,* ABC News (Feb. 23, 2018), https://abcnews.go.com/Politics/trump-slams -deputy-waited-florida-high-school-shooting/story?id=53303616.

[58] Tim Dickinson, *Why Isn't the NRA Screaming About the Bump Stock Ban?,* Rolling Stone (Dec. 19, 2018).

[59] Sarah Gray, *The March For Our Lives Protest Is This Saturday.,* Time (Mar. 23, 2018), http://time.com/5167102/march-for-our-lives-parkland-school-shooting -protest/.

At the March for Our Lives, many of the Parkland students and other sympathizing youngsters from Florida wore orange price tags that read $1.05. As the March organizers explained, "We've calculated the price of each student in states across the country, based on the millions of dollars politicians have accepted from the NRA."[60] The ad agency McCann made a public service announcement with the $1.05 price tags to help explain the meaning of the gesture.[61] The $1.05 tags were also:

> a jab at Florida Sen. Marco Rubio and the National Rifle Association. Stoneman Douglas freshman Lauren Hogg put it this way as she showed off the tag at the rally in Washington: 'We took the amount of money that Marco Rubio took from the NRA, and we divided it by every single student in the state of Florida,' she said. 'So, this is how much we're worth ...'[62]

In 1920 journalist Walter Lippmann wrote in *Liberty and the News* of the First World War, "Nobody ... saw this war. Neither the men in the trenches nor the commanding general. The men saw their trenches, their billets, sometimes they saw an enemy trench, but nobody, unless it be the aviators, saw a battle." Dark money in our elections leads to similar myopia, where the public can't tell what's really going on as they are asked to do their civic duty and cast their ballots.[63] The NRA had quite the reputation when it came to political spending, long before Parkland. For instance, in 2016 the NRA was the largest dark money spender in the presidential election. The NRA has lots of dark money flowing through it, which is why it's so hard to tell from the outside whether any of the money in the group is from any particular source. The Center for Responsive Politics found in an audit in 2017 that the NRA spent $100 million in 2016.[64] This is much more than the NRA has spent in politics before. The public does know how the NRA spent some of its money. In 2016, the NRA expended $54 million in outside political spending.[65] The NRA spent

---

[60] *Price Tags*, March for Our Lives https://marchforourlives.com/price-tags/.

[61] *March For Our Lives Price on Our Lives* [Ad], McCann (Mar. 2018), www.adsoftheworld.com/media/direct/march_for_our_lives_price_on_our_lives.

[62] Jason Hanna & Dianne Gallagher, *The price tags around these marchers are meant to reflect what they say their lives are worth: $1.05*, CNN (Mar. 24, 2018), www.cnn.com/2018/03/24/us/march-for-our-lives-price-tags-trnd/index.html.

[63] Walter Lippmann, Liberty and the News (1920).

[64] Robert Maguire, *Audit shows NRA spending surged $100 million amidst pro-Trump push in 2016*, Ctr. for Responsive Politics (Nov. 15, 2017), www.opensecrets.org/news/2017/11/audit-shows-nra-spending-surged-100-million-amidst-pro-trump-push-in-2016/.

[65] *National Rifle Assn Profile for 2016 Election Cycle Outside Spending*, Ctr. for Responsive Politics, www.opensecrets.org/orgs/summary.php?id=d000000082&cycle=2016.

$31 million of that money to support Trump's candidacy.[66] As Lisa Gilbert of Public Citizen notes, this is troubling because of what could be hiding among that dark money:

> One of our biggest concerns about our system of money in politics is that it can flow in a very secretive way. And because dark money flows behind the scenes, foreign nations are able to take advantage of the lack of transparency, and influence our politics.[67]

Or, to put a finer point on the matter, the NRA's dark money could be hiding illegal Russian money.

The NRA has also used its political clout to keep dark money dark by opposing legislation like the DISCLOSE Act (2010), which would have, among other provisions, required more transparency of money in politics.[68] The DISCLOSE Act would have also clarified which foreign corporations were banned from spending even after *Citizens United*. The NRA objected to the DISCLOSE Act because it would have required more clarity about money flowing through it and other social welfare organizations organized under Section 501(c)(4) of the Internal Revenue Code.[69] The NRA must have been quite convincing because it managed to wrangle an exemption from the proposed legislation for the NRA alone in the House version.[70] In the end, the DISCLOSE Act was killed by a single vote in the Senate during a filibuster; thus, the NRA carve-out never became law.[71] But the entire episode was a reminder that the NRA can get its way even on policy matters that don't involve the Second Amendment or guns.

---

[66] Nicholas Fandos, *Operative Offered Trump Campaign Access to Putin*, N.Y. TIMES (Dec. 4, 2017) ("the NRA reported spending a record $55 million on the 2016 elections, including $30 million to support Trump …").

[67] Interview with Lisa Gilbert (July 19, 2018).

[68] Matt A. Vega, *The First Amendment Lost in Translation: Preventing Foreign Influence in U.S. Elections After* Citizens United v. FEC, 44 LOY. L.A. L. REV. 951 (2011) ("permitting foreign-owned and foreign-controlled corporations to pour money into U.S. elections has undermined self-governance and threatens our democracy").

[69] *Setting the Record Straight on the "DISCLOSE Act,"* NRA INSTITUTE FOR LEGISLATIVE ACTION (June 18, 2010), www.nraila.org/articles/20100618/setting-the-record-straight-on-the-dis.

[70] Brian Montopoli, *NRA Deal on Campaign Finance Bill Angers Liberals and Conservatives*, CBS NEWS (June 16, 2010), www.cbsnews.com/news/nra-deal-on-campaign-finance-bill-angers-liberals-and-conservatives/.

[71] Ciara Torres-Spelliscy, *Why can 41 senators crush popular will to temper money in politics?*, BRENNAN CTR. (July 28, 2010), www.brennancenter.org/blog/why-can-41-senators-crush-popular-will-temper-money-politics.

The NRA was also center stage in litigation against the last big federal campaign finance law, the Bipartisan Campaign Reform Act (better known as BRCA or McCain-Feingold). In 2002, the NRA and one its PACs, National Rifle Association Political Victory Fund, were plaintiffs challenging the constitutionality of BRCA. This case was consolidated into the case that became *McConnell v. FEC,* which ended up upholding the constitutionality of BRCA, including its campaign finance disclosure requirements. Moreover, in 2001 the NRA was held liable for campaign finance violations from previous federal elections.[72]

Which brings us back to the Parkland students and the moxie they have shown in going after the financial ties between the NRA, corporations and politicians. This truly was a David and Goliath situation; but just as in the parable, this David was not deterred. An early target of the students was a southeastern grocery chain named Publix, which had stepped into this maelstrom when it decided to support Adam Putnam for governor of Florida.[73] Putnam has referred to himself as "an NRA sellout" and bragged about his A+ rating from the NRA.[74] According to the *Tampa Bay Times*, "Publix, the heirs to the company's founder and its current and former leaders have given Putnam $670,000 in the last three years—or enough money to buy 74,527 chicken tender subs."[75] According to www.followthemoney.org, Publix gave $6 651 601 in elections in Alabama, Florida, Georgia, Illinois, Mississippi, New Jersey and South Carolina.[76]

The Parkland students decided to stage "die-ins" at two Publix stores near Marjory Stoneman Douglas High School to protest Publix's support for pro-gun candidate Putnam. The reaction from Publix to this political protest was swift. The corporation announced that it would end all corporate political donations immediately.[77] The Parkland students brought real-time accounta-

---

[72]   Federal Election Comm'n v. National Rifle Association of America, No. 00-5163 (D.C. Cir. 2001).

[73]   Kyle Arnold, *Publix distances itself from NRA after Adam Putnam donation backlash*, ORLANDO SENTINEL (May 16, 2018).

[74]   A.G. Gancarski, *Adam Putnam staff slams Jared Moskowitz for 'untruths' about Parkland reaction*, FLORIDA POLITICS (Mar. 19, 2018), http://floridapolitics.com/archives/259230-jared-moskowitz-ted-deutch-lambaste-gop-gubernatorial-candidates-on-guns-nra-ties.

[75]   Steve Contorno, *Publix is supporting Adam Putnam's run for governor like no politician before*, TAMPA BAY TIMES (May 15, 2018).

[76]   *Publix*, Institute for Money in Politics, www.followthemoney.org/entity-details?eid=2131 ("PUBLIX has given $6,651,601 to 1,278 different filers spanning 24 years.").

[77]   Steve Bousquet, *Publix suspends political contributions amid statewide protests*, TAMPA BAY TIMES (May 25, 2018) ("The supermarket giant acknowledges its support of Adam Putnam has 'led to a divide in our community.'").

bility to brands that got entangled in the NRA-politician nexus. Also, Putnam failed to gain the Republican nomination for governor in 2018.[78]

The Parkland survivors didn't invent consumer activism. This trend was growing before the tragic events unfolded on their campus on February 14, 2018. But with Parkland, consumer activism hit an inflection point. Parkland survivors have gone after the links between commercial brands and the NRA to weaken those sources of financial support. Before the Parkland massacre, the NRA had agreements with many corporate brands to provide discounts to NRA members. Parkland students and their supporters pestered commercial brands to stop these special discounts for NRA members:

> If the #BoycottNRA movement were a land invasion, it would have blitzed across the lightly defended countryside of corporate America in the past three days, pressuring ... [multiple] companies — one after another — to do away with discounts and perks for National Rifle Association members.[79]

Contemporaneously, the *New York Times* reported:

> Unlike hundreds of other boycotts that barely registered with consumers, the current effort has 'taken on significant symbolic purpose' and speed, said Lawrence B. Glickman, a history professor and boycotts expert at Cornell University. 'This wasn't a concerted thing—it just took off and took on a life of its own,' Professor Glickman said ... The #BoycottNRA hashtag, the unofficial unifier of the movement, was trending on Twitter ... and appeared more than 10,000 times in a single four-hour period ...[80]

Using the hashtag #BoycottNRA, Parkland students, with the aid of thousands of engaged strangers, got many businesses to drop discounts for NRA members.[81] As the *New York Times* described, "the protest has pushed a major bank, several car rental companies, two airlines and other businesses to publicly cut

---

[78] Adam C. Smith, *Trump-backed DeSantis wins Republican nomination for Florida governor*, MIAMI HERALD (Aug. 29, 2018).

[79] Avi Selk, *NRA lashes out at boycott movement as United, Delta and other corporations cut ties*, WASH. POST (Feb. 25, 2018).

[80] Tiffany Hsu, *Big and Small, N.R.A. Boycott Efforts Come Together in Gun Debate,* N.Y. TIMES (Feb. 27, 2018).

[81] Jacey Fortin, *A List of the Companies Cutting Ties With the N.R.A.,* N.Y. TIMES (Feb. 24, 2018) ("Eight days after a gunman with an AR-15 rifle killed 17 people at a high school in Parkland, Fla., ... First National Bank of Omaha, was among the first businesses of at least a dozen to scrap special rates ... [for] N.R.A ... members ...").

ties with the N.R.A."[82] The impact on corporate brands was remarkable. As the *Associated Press* noted:

> A portion of corporate America is rethinking its relationship with the National Rifle Assn., taking a closer look at investments, co-branding deals and other ties to the gun industry after the latest school massacre. The NRA has aggressively resisted calls for stricter gun control in the wake of the Feb. 14 shooting at a Florida high school that left 17 dead.[83]

The *Associated Press* listed the following companies as breaking ties with the NRA and no longer offering special discounts to its members: First National Bank of Omaha, Enterprise Holdings Inc. (which also owns Alamo and National), Allied and North American van lines, Avis and Budget car rental, Hertz Corp., TrueCar, MetLife Inc. Symantec Corp. (the software company that makes Norton Antivirus), Simplisafe, Wyndham Hotels, United Airlines, Paramount Rx, Starkey Hearing and Delta Air Lines.[84]

There were also counter-reactions to the Parkland actions. Delta felt the heat from lawmakers in Georgia who were sympathetic to the NRA. As the *Washington Post* noted:

> Lt. Gov. Casey Cagle, who leads the Georgia State Senate, demanded … that … Delta, one of the state's largest employers, make a choice: Reverse its NRA decision, or watch Republican lawmakers strike down a $50 million sales tax exemption on jet fuel, of which Delta would be the primary beneficiary.[85]

This wasn't an idle threat:

> Republican lawmakers in Georgia honored their threat to punish the Atlanta-based airline for ending the NRA's group discounts; those legislators overwhelmingly approved a bill that was stripped of an earlier provision that would have granted a lucrative tax break to Delta.[86]

CEO of Delta, Ed Bastian responded "that his intention had been to 'remain neutral' and 'remove Delta from this [gun control] debate.' Delta, he said, is now planning to end discounts 'for any group of a politically divisive

---

[82]   Hsu, *supra* note 80.

[83]   Associated Press, *These are the companies that have cut ties with the NRA*, L.A. TIMES (Mar. 2, 2018).

[84]   *Id.*

[85]   Marwa Eltagouri, *A Georgia Republican's threat to Delta: Restore NRA benefits, or you won't get your tax break*, WASH. POST (Feb. 27, 2018).

[86]   Freedom du Lac & Marwa Eltagouri, *After NRA boycott backlash, Delta Air Lines will end discounts for 'politically divisive' groups*, WASH. POST (Mar. 2, 2018).

nature.'"[87] Delta's battle with Georgia lawmakers was short lived, as this tax break was later restored to Delta by executive order of the governor of Georgia.[88]

The killer in the Parkland massacre was 19 years old. His age (he was too young to drink) prompted changes in behaviors among some gun sellers:

> L.L. Bean ... says it only sells firearms at its flagship store in Maine and only guns specific to hunting and target shooting, released a statement ... saying that it will no longer sell firearms or ammunition to anyone under 21.[89]

Meanwhile, Edward W. Stack, CEO of Dick's Sporting Goods, wrote in an open letter after Parkland:

> [T]houghts and prayers are not enough. We have tremendous respect and admiration for the students organizing and making their voices heard regarding gun violence in schools and elsewhere in our country. We have heard you. The nation has heard you. We support and respect the Second Amendment, and we recognize and appreciate that the vast majority of gun owners in this country are responsible, law-abiding citizens. But we have to help solve the problem that's in front of us. Gun violence is an epidemic that's taking the lives of too many people, including the brightest hope for the future of America – our kids. Following all of the rules and laws, we sold a shotgun to the Parkland shooter in November of 2017. It was not the gun, nor type of gun, he used in the shooting. But it could have been.[90]

The letter went on to say that Dick's would no longer sell guns to people younger than 21 and would stop selling high-capacity magazines or "assault-style rifles, also referred to as modern sporting rifles. We had already removed them from all DICK'S stores after the Sandy Hook massacre, but we will now remove them from sale at all 35 Field & Stream stores."[91] In subsequent interviews, Stack said, "When you look at those kids and their parents and the grief that everyone's going through [at Parkland], and we don't want to be a part of this story any longer."[92]

---

[87] *Id.*

[88] Ben Nadler, *Georgia Jet Fuel Tax Halted, Months After Delta, NRA Fight*, U.S. NEWS (July 30, 2018), www.usnews.com/news/best-states/georgia/articles/2018-07-30/georgia-jet-fuel-tax-halted-months-after-delta-nra-fight.

[89] Associated Press, *supra* note 83.

[90] *Here's what Dick's Sporting Goods CEO Ed Stack wrote about his company's actions*, ASSOCIATED PRESS (Feb. 28, 2018), www.usatoday.com/story/money/retail/2018/02/28/heres-what-dicks-sporting-goods-ceo-ed-stack-wrote-his-companys-actions/381452002/ (quoting Mr. Stack's letter).

[91] *Id.*

[92] Susan Jones, *Dick's Sporting Goods Bans Certain Gun, Magazine Sales: 'We Don't Want to Be a Part of This Story'*, CNS NEWS (Feb. 28, 2018), www.cnsnews

Dick's generated more attention for its brand as a result of taking this stance. YouGov's BrandIndex examined "the number of people talking positively about Dick's Sporting Goods ... [and found it] spiked to 18% from 2%."[93] Reactions to Dick's actions, however, were largely split along partisan lines. "Adults who identify as Democrat especially drove Dick's increase in perception, while both Republicans and Independents remained steady, the study found."[94] And there are reasons to be skeptical that Dick's is sincere. It had stopped selling assault weapons before, right after the massacre at Sandy Hook elementary. As reported in the *Washington Post*:

> Dick's won the most praise online for ending AR-15 sales. ... But Dick's has previously made—and betrayed—this promise ... it reversed course within eight months when it decided to sell $800 AR-15s at its Field & Stream stores. The CEO had to clarify this past week that the company would now 'permanently' stop selling assault weapons, perhaps to distinguish the new move from the temporary precedent.[95]

In a move that showed its sincerity, Dick's told reporters that instead of returning guns to the manufacturer, "We are in the process of destroying all firearms and accessories that are no longer for sale as a result of our February 28th [2018] policy change ..."[96]

Companies that sold the brands that kept their NRA affiliations also came under pressure from Parkland supporters to stop selling those items. REI decided to break with some brands that stuck by the NRA. The *Denver Post* reported: "REI, a nationwide outdoor retailer and consumer co-op, announced ... that it would, for the time being, no longer be ordering CamelBak, Bell, Giro or any other of the 50 Vista Outdoor brands to sell in its stores."[97]

.com/news/article/susan-jones/dicks-sporting-goods-bans-certain-gun-magazine-sales-we-dont-want-be-part.

[93]   Quentin Fottrell, *Walmart and Dick's Sporting Goods surge in public's esteem after breaking ties with NRA*, MARKETWATCH (Mar. 6, 2018), www.marketwatch.com/story/americans-appear-divided-over-companies-breaking-ties-with-nra-2018-03-01.

[94]   *Id.*

[95]   Heidi N. Moore, *Perspective: Corporations only break with the gun industry when it's cheap and easy*, WASH. POST (Mar. 1, 2018).

[96]   Stephanie Ritenbaugh, *Dick's Sporting Goods will destroy assault-style rifles pulled from shelves*, PITTS. POST-GAZETTE (Apr. 9, 2018).

[97]   Meagan Flynn, *NRA boycott: REI, Mountain Equipment Co-op, stop selling major outdoor brand with NRA ties*, DENVER POST (Mar. 2, 2018), https://www.denverpost.com/2018/03/02/nra-boycott-rei-mountain-equipment/.2, 2018).

If the elimination of NRA member discounts hurt the rank-and-file members of the NRA, the NRA encountered a more existential threat when insurance companies also turned their backs around the same time:

> Chubb Ltd ... announced ... that it is ending participation in the NRA's Carry Guard gun-owner insurance program. ... The program that provided coverage for people involved in gun-related incidents or accidents had been under scrutiny by regulators over marketing issues.[98]

Similarly:

> The insurance company [Lockton Affinity Inc.] announced Monday it no longer will sell NRA-endorsed insurance policies. That includes Carry Guard, promoted to gun owners as a policy to help cover civil and criminal legal costs in cases in which policy holders shoot someone in self-defense.[99]

On May 2, 2018, Lockton and New York State entered into a consent agreement that Lockton would no longer sell Carry Guard because it was illegal to sell in New York State.[100]

What prompted this move by insurance companies? It could well have been the result of a directive from Governor Cuomo to the New York Department of Financial Services (DFS) in April 2018:

> to urge insurance companies, New York State-chartered banks, and other financial services companies licensed in New York to review any relationships they may have with the National Rifle Association and other similar organizations. Upon this review, the companies are encouraged to consider whether such ties harm their corporate reputations and jeopardize public safety.

The directive went on to note:

> DFS is encouraging regulated entities to consider reputational risk and promote corporate responsibility in an effort to encourage strong markets and protect consumers. A number of businesses have ended relationships with the NRA following the Parkland, Florida school shooting in order to realign their company's values.[101]

---

[98] Associated Press, *supra* note 83.

[99] *Id.*

[100] In the Matter of Lockton Affinity LLC (May 2, 2018), www.dfs.ny.gov/about/ea/ea180502.pdf (Consent Order).

[101] Press Release, *Governor Cuomo Directs Department of Financial Services to Urge Companies to Weigh Reputational Risk of Business Ties to the NRA and Similar Organizations* (Apr. 19, 2018), www.governor.ny.gov/news/governor-cuomo-directs-department-financial-services-urge-companies-weigh-reputational-risk.

In April 2018, Cuomo tweeted: "'I urge companies in New York State to revisit any ties they have to the NRA and consider their reputations, and responsibility to the public.'"[102]

According to a subsequent lawsuit filed by the NRA against the State of New York, Governor Cuomo interfered with the NRA's ability to do business with insurance companies after Parkland. Again, according to the NRA and its lawyers, the NYS DFS "complied with an industry memo that cited a public and corporate backlash against the NRA following the Feb. 14 massacre at a high school in Parkland, Florida — essentially telling them to join the backlash."[103] The NRA also complains in the lawsuit that "New York state's campaign to push insurance companies and banks to cut ties with the organization had already cost it 'tens of millions of dollars' this year."[104] Moreover, the NRA claims that it cannot find an insurance company to cover the NRA. "Specifically, the NRA warns that it has lost insurance coverage — endangering day-to-day operations."[105]

The lawsuit also claims that the NRA is teetering on financial ruin. This claim seems to be corroborated by public-facing documents.[106] Open Secrets reported that in 2016 the NRA had a deficit of more than $14.8 million, and "by the end of 2017 … [it] expand[ed] its existing deficit from the previous year to $31.8 million."[107] For his part, the governor of New York is not backing down. In August 2018 he wrote to the NRA, "by the way, I'll see you in court."[108] The American Civil Liberties Union has filed an amicus brief in the case supporting the NRA.[109] On November 6, 2018, a district court dismissed

---

[102] Tim Dickinson, *The NRA Says It's in Deep Financial Trouble, May Be "Unable to Exist"*, ROLLING STONE (Aug. 3, 2018).

[103] Jon Schuppe, *NRA says New York "blacklisting campaign" is driving it out of business*, NBC (Aug. 3, 2018), www.nbcnews.com/news/us-news/nra-says-new-york-blacklisting-campaign-driving-it-out-business-n897521.

[104] *Id.*

[105] Dickinson, *supra* note 102.

[106] Schuppe, *supra* note 103 ("the NRA was struggling financially, reporting a $45 million budget deficit in 2016 tax documents.").

[107] Kaitlin Washburn & Robert Maguire, *Member dues plummet, leaving the NRA in the red for second straight year*, CTR FOR RESPONSIVE POLITICS (Sept. 19, 2018), www.opensecrets.org/news/2018/09/nra-in-the-red-for-2nd-straight-year/.

[108] *Governor Cuomo responds to NRA "…by the way, I'll see you in court."*, ASSOCIATED PRESS (Aug. 8, 2018), https://cbs6albany.com/news/local/governor-cuomo-responds-to-nra-by-the-way-ill-see-you-in-court.

[109] NRA v. Cuomo, 18-cv-0566-TJ-CFH (ACLU brief Aug. 24, 2018), www.aclu.org/legal-document/nra-v-cuomo-aclu-amicus-brief.

many of the claims by the NRA, but allowed its First Amendment objections to Cuomo's actions to proceed.[110]

In April 2019, the NRA's woes continued to mount as New York Attorney General Tish James began investigating whether the NRA has abused its status as a nonprofit organization.[111] (As noted in the chapter "Branding greed," a similar inquiry into the Trump Foundation led to its demise.) She has jurisdiction over the NRA because it is incorporated in New York. Also in 2019, the NRA lost its president and one of its top lobbyists.[112] And in June 2019, the NRA announced that it would shut down its television network, NRATV. Apparently one of the causes of the demise of NRATV was the NRA had failed to pay its advertising agency, which ran NRATV, millions of dollars for previous work. This closure could be further evidence that the NRA is struggling financially.[113]

Parkland changed the landscape for commercial brands, for the NRA and for the gun debate. For example, in October 2018:

> Spike's Tactical, a Florida-based firearms manufacturer, announced ... that representatives from Fifth Third Bank visited the company to inform them of their 'discreet' plans to distance themselves from the firearm industry. ... This announcement falls on the heels of a gunman opening fire at the Fifth Third Center in downtown Cincinnati, killing three and wounding two others before falling in a shootout with police officers.[114]

Then FedEx, which had initially resisted calls to break with the NRA, did so in October of 2018:

> FedEx is ending a partnership with the National Rifle Association that offered discounts to members of the gun-rights group. A spokesman for FedEx said the

---

[110] NRA v. Cuomo, 18-cv-0566-TJ-CFH (Decision & Order Nov. 6, 2018), https://reason.com/assets/db/15416061402473.pdf.

[111] Jason Lemon, *NRA's Finances and Charitable Foundation's Tax Exempt Status Under Investigation by New York Attorney General*, NEWSWEEK (Apr. 28, 2019), www.newsweek.com/nra-charitable-foundation-finances-new-york-attorney-general -1407753.

[112] Alex Isenstadt, *NRA meltdown has Trump campaign sweating*, POLITICO (July 3, 2019), www.politico.com/story/2019/07/03/nra-guns-trump-campaign-1395970.

[113] Minda Smiley, *NRATV Shuts Down, Further Severing Ties Between the NRA and Its Longtime Agency Ackerman McQueen used to operate the now-defunct network*, ADWEEK (June 27, 2019).

[114] *Fifth Third Bank Notifies Customers of Plans to Distance the Company from Firearm Industry*, OUTDOORHUB (Oct. 11, 2018), www.outdoorhub.com/news/2018/ 10/11/fifth-third-bank-notifies-customers-plans-distance-company-firearm-industry/.

decision was not prompted by the mass shooting at a Pittsburgh synagogue that left 11 people dead on Saturday.[115]

Whether Fifth Third Bank and FedEx would had done this before Parkland is unknown. But after Parkland, it took less boldness on the part of these corporations to break ties with Spike's Tactical and the NRA, respectively.

The battle for who controls the narrative of Parkland continues. Parkland students persisted in pushing for changes to gun laws and to encourage civic engagement. But they also have made a point to remember the victims of the shooting. The one-year anniversary of the massacre was a day of service at Marjory Stoneman Douglas High School. But the NRA, as evidenced by its suit against New York, views itself as the real victim here. A few commercial brands caught in the maelstrom demonstrated a real change of heart, as the CEO of Dick's Sporting Goods did by literally destroying certain guns rather than placing them back into circulation in the American market. But whether others will really change their behavior or their relationship to the gun debate is an unfinished story.

4.   CONCLUSION

A tragic death doesn't have to be the way the narrative ends. As Heather Heyer's mother Susan Bro said at her memorial service in Charlottesville, "They tried to kill my child to shut her up. Well, guess what? You just magnified her." She continued, "I want you to pay attention, find what's wrong ... and say to yourself, what can I do to make a difference? And that's how you're going to make my child's death worthwhile."[116] Meanwhile, artist Manuel Oliver, the father of Joaquin "Guac" Oliver, who was killed at Parkland, designed a huge billboard that was put up in Boston with his son's picture and the words "If I had attended high school in Massachusetts instead of Parkland Florida, I would likely be alive today" and "Gun laws save lives."[117] Oliver continues to work for reforms to American gun laws.

The Parkland survivors always had two messages. One was asking for sensible gun control; the other was encouraging greater democratic engagement. One final note on branding and Parkland. Even if you do not like the pressure

---

[115]   Tiffany Hsu, *FedEx Ends Deal for N.R.A. but Says It's Not Because of Pittsburgh Shooting*, N.Y. Times (Oct. 30, 2018).
[116]   Claire Landsbaum, *Heather Heyer's Mother Says White Nationalists "Tried to Kill My Child to Shut Her Up"*, Cut (Aug. 16, 2017), www.thecut.com/2017/08/heather-heyer-mother-susan-bro-memorial-service-death-magnified-her.html.
[117]   Johnny Diaz, *Parkland school shooting victim Joaquin Oliver featured on Boston billboard*, Sun Sentinel (Feb. 11, 2018).

the Parkland students put on retailers and other businesses to punish their relationship with the NRA, here's one thing that they did with which few could find fault: they put an enormous amount of effort into registering young people to vote in a year when there were both midterm elections for Congress and Florida statewide elections.[118] As pollster Celinda Lake said:

> the Parkland kids did a phenomenal job at branding. They did one of the best jobs I've seen of attaching a movement and an issue to traditional politics. They were always very clear. I went to the March for Our Lives in D.C. and they were very clear about 'vote, vote, vote, register to vote.' And that was amazing. Their efforts were phenomenal, brilliant and wildly successful in registering voters.[119]

One of the clever ways they encouraged voter registration was the brainchild of Jammal Lemy, a former Parkland student. Lemy designed a t-shirt that looked like the American flag. But where the stars would normally be, he placed a QR code that directed people to a webpage that linked to the 38 states that allow online voter registration.[120] This, too, was a brilliant bit of branding: it showed patriotism on the part of Parkland supporters wearing the shirts (which at a distance just read as an American flag), while also making it easier for more Americans to register to vote through advanced cryptography.[121] Registration of young people went up in Florida.[122] Who won this round? Youth, resilience and democracy, at least for now.

With a topic as fraught as gun violence, it is easy to despair that nothing can be fixed and nothing can change. But one lesson from the Parkland students is that political pressure can still have an impact and minds can still be changed. Using branding for good—like registering more Americans to vote—is a promising place to start.

---

[118] Brakkton Booker, *Parkland Survivors Launch Tour To Register Young Voters And Get Them Out In November*, NPR (June 16, 2018), www.npr.org/2018/06/16/620486174/parkland-survivors-launch-tour-to-register-young-voters-and-get-them-out-in-nove.

[119] Interview with Celinda Lake (Sept. 7, 2018).

[120] Mekita Rivas, *March for Our Lives Organizers Created a Shirt That Registers Voters*, TEEN VOGUE (Aug. 20, 2018), www.teenvogue.com/story/march-for-our-lives-voter-registration-shirt.

[121] Steve LeVine, *Parkland students blend QR and fashion to register voters*, AXIOS (Aug. 19, 2018) ("We said, 'We are patriotic too'— that Americans have the right to dwell in public spaces peacefully and safely," Lemy tells *Axios*.).

[122] Alex Daugherty, *Analysis: Youth voting registration went up 41 percent in Florida after Parkland shooting*, TAMPA BAY TIMES (July 20, 2018).

Epilogue: needed reforms

After writing this book, I feel like I need a *Silkwood* shower. But there is no time to despair: there are many reforms that Americans need to adopt to ensure a healthier democracy.

Writing a book during 2018–19 was a strange experience as an author. For one, as new events happened—especially in the special counsel's investigation, as well as the prosecution of the president's former attorney, Michael Cohen—I had to continually go back to revise what I had already written.

The heartening thing that I can say is that the rule of law is still alive and well if the former campaign manager of the president, his deputy campaign manager, his national security advisor and his personal attorney can all be charged with serious crimes. (This could all be sullied if undeserved pardons are handed out.)

Another encouraging thing is that voter turnout in the 2018 election was very high for a midterm election. This indicates that U.S. democracy is resilient. But there are a number of deep problems that have been revealed that need addressing. Below are a few suggestions of policies that may help. Some of these reforms have been needed for decades; others have only become a crisis under President Trump.[1]

I urge you, dear reader, to pick one of the reforms below and give it all you've got.

As suggested by the National Task Force on the Rule of Law & Democracy housed at the Brennan Center for Justice at NYU School of Law:

- Congress should require the president and vice president, and candidates for those offices, to publicly disclose their personal and business tax returns.[2]

---

[1] Nota bene, the author is affiliated with the Brennan Center and the Corporate Reform Coalition.

[2] Preet Bharara, Christine Todd Whitman, Mike Castle, Christopher Edley, Jr, Chuck Hagel, David Iglesias, Amy Comstock Rick, & Donald B. Verrilli, Jr., *Proposals for Reform: National Task Force on Rule of Law & Democracy*, Brennan Ctr 2 (Oct. 2, 2018), www.brennancenter.org/sites/default/files/publications/TaskForceReport _2018_09_.pdf.

- Congress should pass a law to enforce the safeguards in the Constitution's Foreign and Domestic Emoluments Clauses, clearly articulating what payments and benefits are and are not prohibited and providing an enforcement scheme for violations.[3]
- Congress should empower agency inspectors general to investigate improper interference in law enforcement matters.[4]
- Congress should pass a resolution expressly and categorically condemning self-pardons.[5]
- Congress should pass legislation providing that special counsel may only be removed "for cause" and establishing judicial review for removals.[6]

As suggested by the Center for American Progress:

- At least nine states already restrict or prohibit lobbyist fundraising; others should follow suit.[7]
- Any state that has not yet enacted automatic voter registration should also be working to make it a reality.[8]
- Election security should be improved. States urgently need to take steps to ensure that in all future elections, votes are properly counted and the final tally reflects the actual votes cast. Such steps include implementing strong cybersecurity protections for election infrastructure such as voter registration systems; requiring voter-verified paper ballots; replacing old voting machines; and conducting fast and effective audits of election results.[9]

As suggested by Public Citizen and Citizens for Ethics in Government (CREW):

- Require the president and vice president to divest assets that pose a risk of conflict of interest within 30 days of the president's inauguration.[10]
- Strengthen the quality of executive branch ethics enforcement by either:

---

[3] *Id.* at 3.
[4] *Id.*
[5] *Id.*
[6] *Id.*
[7] *What States Can Do to Fight Corruption and Empower Voters*, CENTER FOR AMERICAN PROGRESS 1 (Jan. 23, 2019), https://cdn.americanprogress.org/content/uploads/2019/01/22120817/States-Fight-Corruption-factsheet-2.pdf.
[8] *Id.* at 2.
[9] *Id.*
[10] *Trump-Proofing The Presidency: A Plan for Executive Branch Ethics Reform*, PUBLIC CITIZEN & CITIZENS FOR ETHICS IN GOVERNMENT 5 (Oct. 2, 2018), www.citizen.org/sites/default/files/trump_proofing_the_presidency.pdf.

- • creating an overarching inspector general's office to investigate potential ethics violations across the executive branch, including within the White House; or
  - • vesting the Office of Government Ethics with enforcement authority.[11]
- • Improve the specificity of financial disclosure forms to require candidates and officials to disclose the value of their assets, income, transactions and liabilities within reasonably specific ranges and requiring disclosure of key details relating to public officials' privately held businesses, including the identities of any major creditors, investors and customers.[12]
- • Limit contributions to inaugural committees to match the contributions limits and guidelines on contributions to federal candidates for an election cycle, which would limit contributions to about $5000 and require them to come from U.S. natural persons only.[13]
- • Prohibit sitting presidents from collecting money for their future libraries or other legacy building endeavors or, failing that, subjecting such contributions to the rules that cover contributions to federal candidates. At present, there are no limits on the size or source of these contributions.[14]
- • Enhance rules and disclosure requirements for legal defense funds established by executive branch officials.[15]
- • Protect the public from the dangers of nepotism by:
  - • passing legislation clarifying that the current law banning presidents from hiring immediate family members supersedes other laws on White House employment;
  - • restricting the size of federal contracts that family members of a president may receive; and
  - • prohibiting a president's family member from receiving security clearances, except in cases in which the person is independently qualified to receive them.[16]
- • Require disclosure of White House visitor logs to give the public insight into whom White House officials are meeting with.[17]
- • Create policy to govern White House contacts with the DoJ to create bright lines preventing the White House from unduly interfering in DoJ affairs.[18]

---

[11] *Id.*
[12] *Id.*
[13] *Id.*
[14] *Id.*
[15] *Id.*
[16] *Id.*
[17] *Id.* at 6.
[18] *Id.*

- Close loopholes in the Hatch Act to prevent government employees from improperly engaging in political activities.[19]
- Update rules covering special government employees to ensure that people who influence policy are covered by ethics rules.[20]
- Apply ethics and transparency rules to presidential transition teams, and end the practice of post-election transition teams relying on private donations to fund their work.[21]

As suggested by the Corporate Reform Coalition:

- Advocate for a Securities and Exchange Commission rule that would require publicly traded companies to disclose both direct and indirect political spending.[22]
- Ask the president to issue an executive order requiring federal contractors to disclose their political spending.[23]
- Advocate passage of the federal Shareholder Protection Act.[24]

As suggested by the Campaign Legal Center:

- Bring transparency to the digital age: require disclosure for online ads.
- Better yet, upend the campaign finance ecosystem with public funding.[25]
- Ditch the bureaucracy: make voter registration easy.[26]
- Stop letting the foxes guard the hen houses: create an independent congressional redistricting commission.[27]
- Provide accountability with bite: create an ethics enforcement agency for the executive branch.[28]

---

[19] *Id.*

[20] *Id.*

[21] *Id.*

[22] *Understand the Issue*, CORPORATE REFORM COALITION https://corporatereformcoalition.org/policy-solutions.

[23] *Id.*

[24] *Id.*

[25] Four Priorities for H.R. 1, CAMPAIGN LEGAL CENTER (Nov. 21, 2018), https://campaignlegal.org/update/four-priorities-hr-1.

[26] *Id.*

[27] *Id.*

[28] *Id.*

As suggested by the Union of Concerned Scientists:

- Protect public health and safety by investigating the harms caused by anti-science actions and strengthening science-based laws and programs.[29]
- Fight corruption of science-based decision making by investigating inappropriate corporate influence, addressing conflicts of interest and passing reform measures such as legislation to reduce the influence of money in politics.[30]
- Protect science and scientists at federal agencies by passing legislation to strengthen scientific integrity at federal agencies, such as the previously proposed Scientific Integrity Act.[31]

As suggested by Demos:

- Policymakers, grassroots organizations and other community leaders must oppose xenophobic, false populism with concrete policies that are rooted in the realities of people's lives and that genuinely elevate the dignity and economic wellbeing of all working Americans and their families.[32]
- Policymakers, grassroots organizations and community leaders can bring U.S. democracy into balance by:
  - shifting power from wealthy donors to everyday people;
  - modernizing and increasing the inclusivity of voter registration and voting; and
  - expanding the freedom to vote and the principle of "one person, one vote" where it is still being systemically denied, particularly to people of color.[33]
- Directly challenge the deeply rooted racism that pervades American politics and policy. Policymakers, grassroots organizations and other community leaders need to confront racism primarily because it menaces the safety, security, economic opportunity and democratic rights of people of color. Additionally, the relentless racial scapegoating aimed at White Americans makes them cynical about the role of government and fosters resentment

---

[29]   *The State of Science in the Trump Era*, UNION OF CONCERNED SCIENTISTS (2019), www.ucsusa.org/center-science-and-democracy/state-of-science-trump-era?fbclid=IwAR0oYyKxjIWyZL9igg3PQvpkQc4b30LDm06im4OT8iQ58kAjupUpofRuIVI#.XGi2qtF7mi4.

[30]   *Id.*

[31]   *Id.*

[32]   *Everyone's America State Policies for an Equal Say in Our Democracy and an Equal Chance in Our Economy*, DEMOS at I (Summer 2018), www.demos.org/sites/default/files/publications/EveryonesAmerica_July23.pdf.

[33]   *Id.*

about the policies that strengthen democratic participation and advance economic opportunity and security for all working Americans. Our future depends on leaders across the board confronting this strategic use of racism with straightforward talk and action to advance racial equity. Failing to do so demotivates and demobilizes Black, Latino, Asian American and Native American individuals, who seldom see their representatives address the ways that racism constrains their lives. Racist scapegoating and the failure to address it keep us from fulfilling our potential as a nation.[34]

And as suggested by American Promise:

- Organize Americans to win the 28th Amendment to the Constitution to restore American democracy in which We the People—not big money, not corporations, not unions, not special interests—govern ourselves.[35]

Many of the above democratic reforms are embodied in H.R. 1, the For the People Act, comprehensive democracy reform legislation introduced in the House in January 2019.[36] At the time this book was written, this legislation had passed the House and was considered dead on arrival in the Senate.

Finally, let me say: good luck to us all.

Ciara Torres-Spelliscy
Tampa Bay, Florida 2019

---

[34] *Id.* at I-II.
[35] *Our Goal*, AMERICAN PROMISE, www.americanpromise.net/.
[36] H.R.1 - For the People Act of 2019 (116th Congress), www.congress.gov/bill/116th-congress/house-bill/1/text.

Index